Irish America

The Historical Travel Guide
Volume 1

Northern Atlantic States
District of Columbia
Great Lakes Region

Richard Demeter

Cranford Press • Pasadena, California

34015600

Irish America
The Historical Travel Guide
Volume 1

Published by
Cranford Press
500 Cliff Drive
Pasadena, California 91107

Copyright © 1995 by Richard Demeter

First Edition

Library of Congress Catalog Card Number: 95-92465

ISBN 0-9648253-0-9

Printed in the United States of America

Dedication

To my mother

Catherine Mary Coughlin

and

to the memory

of

my grandparents

Leo and Mary (Kelly) Coughlin

and

my great-grandparents

Patrick and Mary (Sullivan) Coughlin,

who emigrated from County Cork, Ireland,

and were married in Philadelphia in 1884

¶ Front Cover Photograph:

The Irish Brigade Monument
Gettysburg battlefield, Pennsylvania

Designed by William O'Donovan, this memorial was dedicated on July 2, 1888, the twenty-fifth anniversary of the Irish Brigade's participation in the battle of Gettysburg, when three Irish companies helped capture Little Round Top. The memorial, in the shape of a Celtic cross, specifically honors the 63rd, 69th, and 88th New York regiments, which initially formed the Irish Brigade. The five medallions on the cross represent the three regiments, New York State, and Ireland. An Irish wolfhound lies at the foot of the cross.

¶ Back Cover Photograph:

Statue of Charles Carroll of Carrollton
Fairmount Park, Philadelphia, Pennsylvania

This statue of Charles Carroll of Carrollton, a member of Maryland's famous Irish Catholic family and a signer of the Declaration of Independence, is one of four surrounding the Catholic Total Abstinence Fountain.

Contents

Acknowledgments / 9

Introduction / 13

Landmarks of Irish America / 17

Works Consulted / 385

Site Index / 405

Subject Index / 419

Acknowledgments

I wish to acknowledge my use of the research facilities at the Huntingon Library in San Marino, California, the Family History Center in Salt Lake City, Utah, and the Presbyterian Historical Society in Philadelphia, Pennsylvnia. I particularly want to thank Frances Rouse and Elsa Sink of the reader services staff at the Huntington Library.

I also wish to acknowledge the following individuals from whom I obtained some of the information and photographs contained in this volume:

- Marcia Anderson, curator, Minnesota Historical Society, St. Paul, Minn.;
- Matt Armentrout, Parks and Recreation Department, Harbor Beach, Mich.;
- Ed Becker, Becker Funeral Home, Mount Olive, Ill.;
- Donna Bjorkquist, St. Paul Public Libary, St. Paul, Minn.;
- Robin Bodo, State Historic Preservation Office, Dover, Del.;
- Anita Bologna, librarian, Westbury Republican-American,, Westbury, Conn.;
- Mary Breister, Fond du Lac County Historical Society, Fond du Lac, Wis.;
- John Brennan, University of Delaware, Newark, Del.;
- Wanda Burch, Johnson Hall State Historic Site, Johnstown, N.Y.;
- Michael Casarella, Charles Dawson Historical Center, Purchase, N.Y.;
- Jennifer Chrisman, Carrollton, Ill.;
- Kathy Christo, Historical Society, Union Township, N.J.;
- Patrick Colman, acquisition librarian, Minnesota Historical Society, St. Paul, Minnesota.
- Joe Cook, National Capital Region Land Records, National Park Service, Washington, D.C.;
- Connie Cooper, Historical Society of Delaware, Wilmington, Del.;
- Father Arthur Coyle, St. Patrick's Catholic Church, Lowell, Mass.;
- Becky Crabb, Lake County Parks and Recreation Department, Lowell, Ind.;
- Bruce David, Kane, Pa;
- Karen Deller, Cullom-Davis Library, Bradley University, Peoria, Ill.;

- Sandy Dively, Derry Presbyterian Church, Hershey, Pa.;
- John Dumville, Division for Historic Preservation, Montpelier, Vt.;
- Carol Durand, Whistler House Museum of Art, Lowell, Mass.;
- Donna Falso, Cranston Print Works, Cranston, R.I.;
- Melissa Frownfelter, Henry Ford Estate-Fair Lane, Dearborn, Mich.;
- John Galvin, Historic Madison, Inc., Madison, Ind.;
- Rodie Ghezzi, Free Public Library, Philadelphia, Pa.;
- Dolores Godlesky, St. Peter's Episcopal Church, Perth Amboy, N.J.;
- Graphic Arts Department, Chicago Police Department, Chicago, Ill.;
- Gay Grant, Gardiner, Maine;
- Susan Henzel, Hagley Museum and Library, Wilmington, Del.;
- Father Joseph Hindelang, Our Lady of Victories Eucharistic Shrine, Boston, Mass.;
- Marilyn Jones, Ronald Reagan Home Preservation Foundation, Dixon, Ill.;
- Mary Karnes, Donegal Presbyterian Church, Mt. Joy, Pa.;
- Mabel Kelly, Sprague Mansion, Cranston, R.I.;
- Bonnie Kersten, Glen View Area Historical Society, Glen View, Ill.;
- Bob Kuhnz, Fond de Lac County Historical Society, Fond du Lac, Wisc.;
- Joseph Landry, Cardinal Spellman Philatelic Museum, Weston, Mass.;
- Michele Lord, Southington Public Library, Southington, Conn.;
- Captain South Lynn, Kennedy Farmhouse, Samples Manor, Md.;
- Mary K. Mannix, Howard County Historical Society, Elliott City, Md.;
- Irene Martin, Toledo/Lucas County Public Library, Toledo, Ohio;
- Kathleen McAuley, Edgar Allan Poe Cottage, New York City;
- Mary McClure, St. Joseph's Catholic Church, Brooklyn, Mich.;
- David McKean, St. Patrick's Catholic Church, Lowell, Mass.;
- Edith McKitrick, Grace Church, New York City;
- Gladys Murray, Centre County Library and Historical Museum, Bellefonte, Pa.;
- Sheila Naticchiona, St. Peter's Catholic Church, Pleasantville, N.J.;
- Betsy Noble, Amherst Public Library, Amherst, N.H.;
- Nancy Noble, Portsmouth Public Library, Portsmouth, N.H.;
- Julie Nolan, Richmondtown Restoration, Staten Island, N.Y.;
- Marie North, State Historical Society, Madison, Wis.;
- Glenor Nowell, Gardiner Public Libray, Gardiner, Maine;
- James O'Donnell, Covington, Ohio;

- Sue Prifogle, Rushville Public Library, Rushville, Ind.;
- Father Gilbert Rahrig, St. Joseph's Catholic Church, Howell, Mich.;
- Catherine Rankin, City Planning and Development Office, Madison, Wis.;
- Reverend James Reisner, First Presbyterian Church, Elizabeth, N.J.;
- Jean Rentmesiter, Galloway House, Fond du Lac, Wis.;
- John Reynolds, Georgetown University, Washington, D.C.;
- Pat Richards, Fair Haven Public Library, Fair Haven, Vt.;
- Ralph Rourke, Hall of Fame for Great Americans, Bronx Community College of the City University of New York, New York City;
- Karen Schwartz, Free Library, Philadelphia, Pa.;
- Kitty Schwarzbach, Public Library, Canonsburg, Pa.;
- Marie Soucy, St. Patrick's Catholic Church, Lowell, Mass.;
- John Stone, Kearny Cottage Historical Society, Perth Amboy, N.J.;
- Cindy Stouffer, Cyclorama Library, Gettysburg, Pa.;
- Monica Sullivan, U.S. Military Academy, West Point, N.Y.;
- Dr. Shawqi Tabia, Catholic University of America, Washington, D.C.;
- Ethel Thieling, Hastings, Minnesota;
- Greg Tucker, National Shrine of the Immaculate Conception, Wasington, D.C.;
- Sandy Wiessinger, Logan County District Library, Zanesfield, Ohio.
- Bonnie Wilson, Minnesota Historical Society, St. Paul, Minn.;
- Jim Winterer, University of St. Thomas, St. Paul, Minnesota.

Grateful acknowledgment is also made to P. J. Kenedy & Sons, in association with R. R. Bowker, for permission to reprint from "Breakfast with Hercules Mulligan" by Shaemus O'Sheel.

Introduction

Interest in Irish-American history has experienced a renaissance in recent years, prompted in part by the sesquicentennial of the Great Famine. Through an unusual outpouring of historical works and dramatic productions, increasing numbers of the 44.3 million Americans of Irish ancestry are learning about the significant influence which their ancestors had in the development of the United States.

These younger Americans are becoming increasingly aware, for instance, that the Irish presence in – and influence upon – the United States began long before the middle of the nineteenth century, when thousands of Irish emigrants fled the famine that ravaged their native land. In fact, from the beginning of British colonization in North America during the seventeenth century, Irish men and women in significant numbers were among the early settlers. Although these earliest arrivals were laborers and indentured servants, during the following century many of these immigrants and their children moved up the social and economic ladder and could be found in all walks of life: as political and religious leaders, as merchants and ship captains, as educators and proprietors, as agriculturalists and militarists.

When Irish immigration reached its peak during the Famine years in the mid 1800s, the émigrés continued to find refuge in America – although their Catholicism and appalling poverty and wretchedness caused many native-born Americans to oppose their admission. (It was at this time that the phrase "Scotch Irish" became common, used to distinguish the descendants of the earlier Presbyterian Irish of Scottish ancestry from the more recent Famine-driven arrivals.)

Quite naturally, many of these newcomers faced a hostility which earlier Irish immigrants had not experienced, and while engaged in the backbreaking business of building America they usually lived and worked under the most oppressive conditions. But most of the newcomers survived the struggle and took their place in the fabric of American society, their many contributions serving as woof to the texture and contours of the larger culture's warp. By the beginning of the twentieth century, these naturalized Americans and their children could – with the Dublin-born musician and composer Victor Herbert – boast:

> I do not wish to brag about the achievements of the Irish
> race, but is it not a fact that on every page of the World's
> history and particularly the history of this country, you
> will find the names of some of the most illustrious sons

13

of Erin, and have we not in generous measure helped to build up this wonderful country since its earliest development?

I undertook the project of writing *Irish America* to fill a void in the treatment of Irish-American history. Although the achievements of Erin's sons – and daughters – and their descendants continue to be popular subjects treated in a variety of publications, the field has traditionally lacked a definitive historical travel guide. *Irish America (Volume 1)* – along with a planned second volume – attempts to satisfy that need in three ways: as a geographical guide to landmarks associated with historical figures of Irish and Irish-American descent, as a source of biographical and anecdotal information about those figures, and as a chronicle of the tribute paid those men and women by later generations (e.g., in the form of statues and monuments).

This first volume includes approximately eight hundred such sites – houses, churches, monuments, statues, memorials, gravesites, birthplaces, museums, libraries, parks, forts, battlefields, and various other public and private buildings – in three areas of the country: the northern Atlantic states, the District of Columbia, and the Great Lakes region. In cases in which I have included landmarks not exclusively associated with Irish-American history, I have presented the history of those sites from an Irish-American perspective.

Although this work naturally includes landmarks associated with Irish and Irish Americans well known to a general audience, its emphasis is on the hundreds of others whose Irish ancestry is not known to most readers or whom the Muse of History has overlooked. In all, this work mentions almost six hundred individuals of Irish birth or descent. Because a significant number of these historical figures are mentioned more than once, the reader should consult the index to find multiple listings. In subsequent references to the name, or when an individual's Irish ancestry might be unclear to the reader, I have placed an asterisk in front of the name. I have also included some historical figures whose Irish heritage is extremely probable but which I was unable to establish conclusively. I have preceded their names with two asterisks.

Whether you claim Irish ancestry or are, as Lyndon Johnson once said about himself, Irish "by osmosis," I hope that you will find in reading *Irish America (Volume 1)* the same appreciation for Irish-American history as I did in writing it.

Richard Demeter
Pasadena, California
August 1995

The Voyage of St. Brendan

Various authorities over the centuries have claimed that the first European to land in North America was the Irish monk St. Brendan ("the Navigator") almost a thousand years before the Vikings. Brendan, who was born in 484 in what is now County Kerry (on the west coast of Ireland), founded four monasteries in that part of his native land and visited Scotland, Wales, England, and Brittany on several occasions. When he made his voyages of exploration into the Atlantic, he was the abbot of the monastery at Clonfert in Galway and was reputedly more than seventy years old.

The most important account of Brendan's sixth-century Atlantic voyages is found in the *Navigatio Sancti Brendani Abbatis*. Internal evidence in the text seems to indicate that Brendan's journeys were no farther west, however, than Iceland, the Hebrides Islands, the Shetland Islands, the Faroe Islands, and the Azores. Because each of these areas is considerably distant from the North American continent, Brendan cannot be considered the "discoverer" of America. Nevertheless, as late as 1580 an English mapmaker tried to substantiate his country's claim to North America by citing Brendan's voyages and those of the fifteenth-century Cabots.

The *Navigatio* is an example of an Irish literary genre known as *imrama*, tales of ocean voyages full of miracles and fantastic events. According to this account, Brendan and his seventeen fellow monks made their explorations in a curragh – a light ribbed vessel covered with oxhides and caulked with tallow – which they had built and equipped. During their seven-year voyage, the crew sighted waterfalls cascading down the side of a rocky island (in Iceland?), landed on what they thought was an island but which was really the back of a whale, and met a winged creature in the Paradise of Birds (probably the Faroe Islands) who said that he and his fellow birds were Lucifer's fallen angels. The monks also sailed into a "coagulated sea" (of ice floes?), saw what the text calls a silver object (an iceberg?) that towered two hundred feet above them, and were attacked by a hirsute creature who threw red-hot lava rocks (from Hecla in Iceland?) at their boat. Brendan and his crew finally arrived in the Land of the Saints, a land of apple trees and continuous daylight which God gave them as an inheritance.

According to other sources, several hundred Irish monks sailed to Iceland in the late seventh and early eighth centuries. There they lived until forced to leave by the arrival of the Vikings. The possibility that some of those monks sailed to the east coast of North America is found in the Norse sagas. The Landnamabok Saga, for instance, tells of an Icelander named Ari who was driven by a storm to Huitramannaland

(White Man's Land), "which some call Irland it Mikla (Ireland the Great), which lies in the western ocean, near to Vinland the Good, west from Ireland." (Historians usually interpret Vinland as New England, and at least one source locates White Man's Land or Ireland the Great in the Carolinas.) Whatever the location of Ireland the Great, it was there that – according to the sagas – Ari was baptized (by the Irish monks?). If, as Samuel Eliot Morison points out, the monks had left Iceland in the ninth century and the Norse sagas record events in the early eleventh, these monks must have lived to an unbelievably advanced age or else abandoned their vow of chastity and married the native women, thereby laying the foundation of an Irish Catholic community that lasted for two hundred years.

The First Irishman in America

An undoubted Irish connection to the discovery of America can be found in Christopher Columbus's first voyage to the New World. The famous explorer's own association with Ireland stemmed from his visit to Galway sometime before making a voyage to Iceland. In the margin of his copy of *Historia Rerum* by Aeneas Sylvius, he wrote, "Men of Cathay which is toward the Orient have come hither. We have seen many remarkable things, especially in Galway of Ireland, a man and a woman of extraordinary appearance in two boats adrift" – a reference most likely to flat-faced Finns or Lapps. On Columbus's later voyage of 1492, one of the men on the roster of his flagship, the *Santa Maria*, was "*Guillermo Ires, natural de Galney, en Irlanda.*" While the Anglicized Christian name of this sailor is undoubtedly "William," various commentators render his surname as "Ayres," "Harris," "Herris," and even "Penrise." Whatever the translation, this native of Galway was one of the forty-three men who, according to Columbus's log for January 2, 1493, were left at the garrison of La Navidad on Española (Hispaniola). The entire contingent was killed by Native Americans, however, before Columbus returned on his second voyage to the New World.

Landmarks of Irish America

Connecticut / 19

Delaware / 26

District of Columbia / 34

Illinois / 70

Indiana / 93

Maine / 105

Maryland / 114

Massachusetts / 137

Michigan / 176

Minnesota / 185

New Hampshire / 201

New Jersey / 209

New York / 225

Ohio / 297

Pennsylvania / 313

Rhode Island / 358

Vermont / 372

Wisconsin / 377

CONNECTICUT

CLINTON

¶ Abraham Pierson Statue, in front of Morgan High School.

This monument by the Irish-born sculptor Launt Thompson honors the first president of Yale, the Reverend Abraham Pierson, who taught the college's first students in his home in Clinton. A replica of the statue stands on the old Yale campus in New Haven, Connecticut.

Thompson was born in Queens County, Ireland, in 1833 and came to America with his widowed mother when he was fourteen. His interest in drawing grew as he studied anatomy in preparation for a career in medicine, but he abandoned such plans in favor of studying with a local sculptor. Nine years later Thompson opened his own studio in New York and proceeded to produce medallion heads and portrait busts that earned him membership in the National Academy of Design. He was noted for his colossal statue of Napoleon I, which was shown at the 1867 Paris Exposition.

In addition to the *Rocky Mountain Trapper* and busts of James Gordon Bennet Sr., Edwin Booth, William Cullen Bryan, and Samuel F. B. Morse, Thompson sculpted statues of General John Sedgwick (West Point, N.Y.), General Ambrose Burnside (Providence, R.I.), and General Winfield Scott (Washington, D.C.). His statue of a bewhiskered Admiral Samuel du Pont long stood in Du Pont Circle in the nation's capital but is now located in Rockford Park in Wilmington, Delaware.

MIDDLEBURY

¶ French and Irish Soldiers Monument, Rochambeau Heights, a park near the juncture of Artillery Road and Break Neck Hill Road.

This memorial was erected to commemorate the encampment here of 6,000 French and Irish troops on their march from Newport, Rhode Island, to Yorktown, Virginia, in 1781. These troops played a decisive role in assuring the American victory against the British at Yorktown that October.

Some of the remarks made during the dedication of the monument in June 1912 pointed out that the French army contained a large number of Irish troops, especially in the Dillon and Walsh regiments of the Irish Brigade. The former regiment was under the immediate command of Count Arthur Dillon, a member of an originally Irish family that had settled in France at the end of the seventeenth century. Earlier in its career Dillon's regiment had taken part in an attack on British-held Savannah (1779) and in the capture of Tobago and St. Eustache (1780). After the war he returned to France, where he was placed in command of a division of the French army and played a prominent role in the battles of Valmy and Verdun. Although he led his troops under the tricolor of the French Republic, he was suspected of being a royalist and was guillotined in April 1794, during the Reign of Terror.

NEW BRITAIN

¶ **New Britain Museum of American Art,** 56 Lexington Street.
Among the museum's 5,000 paintings and sculptures are works by Thomas Hart Benton, Mary Cassatt, *John Singleton Copley, Winslow Homer, Gilbert Stuart, and *James McNeill Whistler. (See Boston and Lowell, Massachusetts.)
§ Open Tuesday-Sunday 1-5. Closed January 1, Easter, July 4, Thanksgiving, and December 25. Phone: 203-229-0257.

NEW HAVEN

¶ **Defenders' Monument,** at the junction of Davenport, Congress, and Columbus avenues.
Designed by James Edward Kelly, this memorial was erected in 1911 in honor of the New Haven citizens and Yale students who helped repulse British invaders in 1779. The monument consists of three bronze statues of representative colonial figures: a student, a farmer, and a merchant.
Kelly was born in New York City in 1855 to Irish parents. His first significant sculpted work was a statuette called *Sheridan's Ride*, which depicted *General Philip Sheridan as he raced astride his steed to rally his men during the battle of Cedar Creek in Virginia in 1864. Kelly also created sketches of other Civil War officers as well as a variety of bas-reliefs and busts. Among the portrait busts were those of Admiral Dewey, Count Rochambeau, *Theodore Roosevelt, and Admiral Sampson. Kelly also designed five panels on the Monmouth battle monument in Freehold, New Jersey.
The Irish-American's other major works are the Soldiers' and Sailors' Monument (Troy, N.Y.), the Sixth New York Cavalry Memorial (Gettysburg, Pa.), the Barbara Fritchie medallion (Frederick, Md.) the *William McKinley Memorial (Wilmington, Del.), and equestrian statues of General William Sherman, *Colonel Theodore Roosevelt, Caesar Rodney, and Fitz-John Porter (the last two in Wilmington, Del.). After designing a monument for the Seneca chief Red Jacket at Buffalo, New York, he was adopted into the tribe with the name *Ga-Nos-Qua* ("Worker in Stone"). He was also known as the "Sculptor of American History."

¶ **Knights of Columbus Grand Council Museum,** 1 Columbus

Plaza.

This museum was built as a tribute to *Father Michael McGivney, the founder of the Knights of Columbus, the international Catholic fraternal order. The museum presents exhibits about the organization's many activities as well as about McGivney and his two brothers, each of whom served as the Knights' national chaplain.

§ Open Monday-Friday 8-4:30, weekends by appointment. Phone: 203-772-2130.

¶ **Samuel Clemens House,** 351 Farmington Avenue.

The turrets and verandas on this orange and black brick mansion resemble the smokestacks and fan decks of a Mississippi steamboat, fitting features for the home of riverboat pilot Samuel Clemens (Mark Twain). The famous author, who was descended through his mother from Irish stock (Caseys and Montgomerys), lived here for seventeen years. In his autobiographical *Life on the Mississippi*, Twain wrote: "Give an Irishman lager for a month, and he's a dead man. An Irishman is lined with copper, and the beer corrodes it. But whiskey polishes the copper and is the saving of him."

§ Open Monday-Saturday 9:30-5, Sunday noon-5. Closed Tuesdays November-May and on major holidays. Admission. Phone: 203-493-6411.

¶ **Soldiers' and Sailors' Monument,** East Rock Park, 1.5 miles northeast of the Green, at the end of Orange Street.

Dedicated in 1887, this 112-foot-high granite memorial is the work of Alexander Doyle and honors the memory of American casualties in the Revolution, the War of 1812, and the Mexican War.

Born in Steubenville, Ohio, in 1857, Doyle became familiar with monument making through his father, who was employed in the quarrying business. The younger man later studied sculpture in Italy, initially while living there with his parents and then when he returned on his own to study at the national academies in Rome, Florence, and Carrara. After establishing himself in New York City, he quickly earned a reputation as a sculptor of monuments. An Indiana newspaper once opined that at the age of thirty-five Doyle had created more public monuments than any other American sculptor and that 20 percent of such monuments in the United States were the product of his hand and chisel. Rather surprisingly for American artists of his time, he was a member of no American art societies and exhibited none of his work at American art shows. Yet he was an honorary member of the Royal Raphael Academy in Urbino, Italy.

Doyle also designed the Francis Scott Key monument (Frederick, Md.) and statues of *Henry Grady (Atlanta, Ga.), *Sergeant William

Jaspar (Savannah, Ga.), *Horace Greeley (New York City), General Philip Schuyler (Saratoga, N.Y.) and General James Garfield (Cleveland, Ohio). Four of his most significant works are in New Orleans: the marble statue Calling the Roll and statues of *Margaret Haughery, General Albert Sidney Johnson, and General Robert E. Lee.

¶ **Yale University,** Old Campus, bounded by Chapel, High, Elm, and College streets.
   • Berkeley College, on the northeast corner of Elm and High streets, is named for George Berkeley, the seventeenth-century Irish missionary and Yale benefactor.
   • Calhoun College, on the northwest corner of Elm and College streets, is named for *John C. Calhoun, an 1804 Yale graduate and a vice president of the United States.
   • The statue of the Reverend Abraham Pierson, on the west side of the old campus, is a replica of the statue by *Launt Thompson in Clinton, Connecticut. Both the replica and the original were donated by Charles Morgan.
   • John Trumbull's famous painting *Surrender of Lord Cornwallis at Yorktown*, in the University Art Gallery, includes Major General Charles O'Hara among the officers. The Irishman's long service in the British army suffered a stain when Cornwallis ordered him to be his stand-in and officially surrender his sword to the victorious Americans.
   • The Eugene O'Neill Collection, Yale University Library, was founded in 1931 by Carlotta Monterey O'Neill, the third wife of playwright *Eugene O'Neill. It includes photographs, notes, and manuscripts of plays.

NEW LONDON

¶ **Eugene O'Neill Memorial Theater Center,** 305 Great Neck Road, west on U.S. 1 in Waterford.
   The center is named for *Eugene O'Neill and recognizes his literary achievements: forty-five plays, four Pulitzer prizes (for *Beyond the Horizon, Anna Christie, Strange Interlude,* and *Long Day's Journey into Night*), and the Nobel Prize for Literature in 1936. The center is open year round for theater study and offers a program of summer performances.
   § Phone: 203-443-5378.

¶ **Monte Cristo Cottage,** 325 Pequod Avenue.
   This boyhood home of Eugene O'Neill was named for his Irish-born father's best known role as the Count of Monte Cristo in the play of the same name. The house has been restored to its appearance as

described in *Ah, Wilderness* and *Long Day's Journey into Night*, both of which are set in the house. Visitors can view O'Neill memorabilia, the research library, and the multimedia presentation.

Much has been made of the biographical and autobiographical nature of *Long Day's Journey into Night*. Although the name of the family in the play is Tyrone, O'Neill's allusion is to Ireland's County Tyrone (*Tir-Eoghan* or *Tir-Owen*), the ancestral home of the O'Neills. The character James Tyrone is unmistakably the author's famous actor-father (James O'Neill), while Edmund, one of the grown sons in the play, is the playwright himself, named for the real-life brother who died in infancy. Mary Tyrone, the mother in the drama, is clearly intended to be the author's own mother, Mary (Quinlan) O'Neill.

The play frequently refers to the small room upstairs in Monte Cristo where she secluded herself and sought relief through morphine. Her flight from the house in a half-crazed state and her attempt to throw herself into the nearby river are immortalized in a scene in the play. This episode captures Eugene's real-life discovery of his mother's addiction, which she blamed on the "cheap quack" whom her husband had hired and who gave her the medicine as a sedative after Eugene's birth. Following these revelations, the young O'Neill finalized his break with Catholicism and religion in general. The next Sunday, as he and his father descended the stairs at Monte Cristo headed for church, the son announced that he never intended to go to mass again.

Monte Cristo Cottage, the boyhood home of Eugene O'Neill.

O'Neill had few favorable comments about New London. His remark that "It wasn't a friendly town" probably understated the disdain which the town's elite showed his family because of his father's shanty-Irish roots and his career as a traveling actor. The author once told a friend that he hoped to return one day to New London in order to shock the bourgeois sentiments of its elite with a "flock of painted whores, hiring a tally-ho of six horses, and having the girls ride up State Street and throw dimes to the crowd." He developed a more favorable view of the town, however, when he learned that traveling salesmen rated its red-light district as the best between New York and Boston.

O'Neill's attitude toward Ireland was equally ambivalent. Although he was proud of his Irish ancestry, he spoke critically of the "Old Sod" in front of his father. The playwright frequently alluded to his O'Neill roots and relished the story of "Red" O'Neill. According to the legend, during a boat race "Red" cut off his hand and threw it in onto the shore in order to be the first to "touch" land and thereby win the large tract of property that was the object of the contest. On one occasion O'Neill the playwright confided that "One thing that explains more than anything about me is the fact that I'm Irish."

§ Open mid April to mid December, Monday-Friday 1-4. Closed holidays. Fee. Phone: 203-433-0051.

SOUTHINGTON

ℐ Rochambeau Monument, French Hill.

Like a similar memorial in Middleton, Connecticut, this nine-foot-high monument commemorates the encampment here of 6,000 French and Irish troops on their way from Rhode Island to Virginia, where they helped force the British to surrender at Yorktown in 1781. Although originally dedicated in 1912, the memorial was rededicated in 1971 as part of celebrations marking the 350th anniversary of Connecticut's founding.

On the front of the monument is a bronze bas-relief of Count Rochambeau, who was the commander-in-chief of the French and Irish troops sent to help the Americans defeat the British during the Revolution. The art work was done by *James Edward Kelly. On the reverse – beneath an Irish harp, a fleur-de-lis, and an American flag – are the names of the officers under the French general's command, one of whom was *Count Arthur Dillon of the Irish Brigade.

WATERBURY

ℐ Father McGivney Statue, Grand and Meadow streets.

This ten-foot-high bronze statue honors Father Michael McGivney, the Waterbury native who founded the Knights of Columbus, the international Catholic fraternal order. The memorial was dedicated in 1957.

One of thirteen children born to Irish immigrants, McGivney worked as a teenager in a Waterbury brass mill before pursuing the priesthood. After attending St. Mary's Seminary in Baltimore, Maryland, he was ordained by *Cardinal James Gibbons in 1877. The new priest's first assignment was at St. Mary's Church in a decidedly anti-Catholic area of New Haven. (Residents there objected to the "aristocratic avenue being blemished by a Roman Catholic edifice.")

While at St. Mary's, McGivney proposed the creation of a mutual aid society of Catholic laymen pledged to the ideals of charity, fraternity, and patriotism. By creating such an organization, he also hoped to counter the influence of the generally anti-Catholic Masons. He and a dozen parishioners founded the fraternal order in 1882. McGivney lived only eight years longer, dying of pneumonia at the age of thirty-eight.

At first the Knights aroused the suspicion of the Catholic hierarchy, chiefly because of its oath and secret rituals, but it soon received official approbation. The Knights later used their influence to help make Columbus Day a national holiday. In 1989 the Knights had 2.5 million members and donated $85 million to charitable causes.

Statue of Father Michael McGivney, the founder of the Knights of Columbus. (Photo courtesy of the Waterbury Republican-American.)

DELAWARE

LEWES

¶ **Fisher-Martin House,** 120 King's Highway at Savannah Road.

Although now the Lewes Chamber of Commerce and Visitor's Bureau, this clapboard structure dates from the 1730s, when it was purchased by the Reverend James Martin, a Presbyterian minister of Scotch-Irish descent and the founder of the Coolspring Presbyterian church.

§ Open summer Monday-Friday 10-3, Saturday 10-2. Phone: 302-645-8073.

¶ **Fisher's Paradise,** 624 Pilottown Road. Private.

This house was built in the early eighteenth century by Major Henry Fisher, an Irish immigrant and probably the first physician of note in Delaware. Because the house was patterned after an English country seat, Fisher's neighbors called it "a paradise."

After coming to this area from Waterford, Ireland, in 1725, Fisher was the only professionally trained physician in Sussex County. His successful practice sometimes took him to Kent County, Maryland, to offer diagnoses in serious cases. He repeatedly turned down offers to transfer his practice to Philadelphia. During the Revolution he informed George Washington that the British fleet had been sighted off Cape Henlopen headed for the Chesapeake. The Continental Congress responded by authorizing Fisher to raise a company of a hundred men, whom he armed at his own expense.

According to tradition, Caesar Rodney, one of Delaware's delegates to the Continental Congress, was a guest at Fisher's house in July 1776 when he received a letter from *Thomas McKean begging him to come to Philadelphia to vote for independence. It was from here that Rodney set out, arriving just in time to vote for the Declaration of Independence. Tradition also tells how the daughter of the Tory postmaster in town had intercepted the letter to Rodney and how a Negro maid in the Tory's household informed Rodney about the note.

ODESSA

¶ **Macdonough House,** 2 miles north on State 13. Private.

This was the birthplace in 1783 of Commodore Thomas Macdonough, the victor of the battle of Plattsburgh in 1814 and the grandson of an immigrant from County Kildare, Ireland.

As a seventeen-year-old midshipman serving under Stephen Decatur against the pirates of Tripoli, Macdonough was seized by a British press gang but later escaped. At the time, he promised himself:

"If I live through this I'll make England remember the day she impressed an American sailor!"

CUBA ROCK

The name of this small town came from Cuba Rock, part of a 250-acre estate which William Penn's daughter sold to Cornelius Hallahan, an Irishman who had come to America in 1730. The first Catholic religious services in Delaware are said to have been held in his house.

NEWARK

¶ **Kells,** 318 South College Avenue.

Now the Y.W.C.A., this stone building with two large square towers was built between 1910 and 1920 by Everett Johnson to house his newspaper, the *Newark Post*. Johnson named the building for the Book of Kells, the famous copy of the Gospels produced in the eighth century at the monastery of Kells in Ireland.

¶ **University of Delaware.**

Some of the buildings on the campus date from the early 1840s, remnants of the original academy on this site. Although that academy was founded in 1743 in New London, Pennsylvania, by the Reverend Francis Alison, it was moved to Newark in 1765. The academy was the predecessor of Delaware College, now the University of Delaware.

A native of Donegal, Ireland, Alison was a Presbyterian minister who had attended the University of Glasgow before coming to America in 1735. While ministering at New London, he bemoaned the fact that, as Ezra Stiles wrote, "there was not a College, nor even a good Grammar School in four provinces, Maryland, Pennsylvania, Jersey, and New York." Once his academy was established, Alison taught not only the classics but also logic, metaphysics, geography, and "other arts and sciences." Hailed by Stiles as "the greatest classical scholar in America, especially in Greek" and by Ben Franklin as "a Person of great Ingenuity and Learning," Alison seems to have possessed only one pedagogical weakness – "proneness to anger." Among the graduates of his academy were Thomas McKean, George Read I, and Charles Thomson, all men of Irish backgrounds who played a major role in the history of their respective colonies.

§ The visitor center is at 196 South College Avenue. Tours Monday-Friday 10, 11:30, and 2; Saturday 10 and 11. Phone: 302-831-8123.

NEW CASTLE

¶ George Read II House and Garden, 42 The Strand.

This Federal-style house was originally built between 1797 and 1804 by George Read II, the son of one of the Irish-American signers of the Declaration of Independence. Following a fire that gutted the house in 1824, his son – George Read III – restored it and hosted the Marquis de Lafayette here when the famous Frenchman made his triumphal tour of the United States.

A native of New Castle, George Read II served for thirty years as U.S. district attorney in Delaware. He also owned a large cotton plantation in Mississippi. He and his father are buried in the graveyard of Immanuel Episcopal Church in New Castle.

§ Open March-December 31, Tuesday-Saturday 10-4, Sunday 12-4; rest of the year, Saturday 10-4, Sunday 12-4. Closed holidays. Fee. Phone: 302-322-8411.

The Federal-style house built by George Read II, the son of one of the Irish-American signers of the Declaration of Independence.

¶ Immanuel Episcopal Church, on the Green at Market and Harmony streets.

The present structure was completed in 1710. Among the famous residents of Delaware buried in the church cemetery are *George Read I and his son, George Read II. The elder Read – the only signer of both the Declaration of Independence and the Constitution – married the widowed daughter of George Ross, the rector of the church.

¶ **Stoneham,** on the northeast corner of 9th and Washington streets. Private.

Now less than an acre, Stoneham (or Stonum) is the only remaining residence associated with George Read I, who purchased it in the 1750s. The original two-story building with an interior chimney was built about 1730.

Read was born in Maryland in 1733 to an Irish father and a Welsh mother. As a youngster he received part of his education at New London, Pennsylvania, from the *Reverend Francis Alison. After studying law in Philadelphia, Read was admitted to the bar at the age of nineteen and established his law office in New Castle at 22 The Strand, a cobblestone street near the river. He served in the colony's legislature for fifteen years and was attorney general and a delegate to the Continental Congress. Although he originally voted against adopting the Declaration of Independence, he signed the document the following August 2.

While serving as the acting president of Delaware immediately following its independence from Britain, he strove relentlessly to raise troops and provisions during the Revolution. He expressed his frustration in a letter to General Washington in 1778: "My situation is rather an unlucky one, in a government very deficient in its laws, and those greatly relaxed in their execution, and a Legislature as yet incomplete, and not disposed to unite and give aid to the executive authority." Read was later a delegate to the Constitutional Convention and was elected to the U.S. Senate. He is depicted in the heroic painting *The Signing of the Declaration* by John Trumbull, now in the Rotunda of the U.S. Capitol.

¶ **William Penn Statue,** 2nd Street.

Following his conversion to the Society of Friends or Quakers, William Penn welcomed his coreligionists to his New World colony, which originally included what is now Delaware. When Penn arrived in New Castle in October 1682, among the 100 passengers aboard his ship was at least one group of Irish Quakers from Enniscorthy in County Wexford – Dennis Rochford, the surviving members of his family, and his two servants. (Rochford's two daughters died en route.)

Rochford had joined the Society of Friends in Ireland in 1662. Seven years later he was arrested for attending Quaker services in Dublin, and the next year he was jailed in Wicklow for the same offense. Beginning in 1675, he and his family lived in England, where he operated a grocer's shop. A year after his arrival in America, the Irishman was elected to represent Chester County in the Pennsylvania Assembly.

WILMINGTON

This bronze relief depicts Caesar Rodney's arrival in Philadelphia to join Thomas McKean (left) in voting for independence.

¶ **Caesar Rodney Monument,** Rodney Square.

The equestrian statue on this monument was sculpted by *James Edward Kelly in tribute to Caesar Rodney, who rode through the night to Philadelphia, arriving just in time to vote for the Declaration of Independence in July 1776. The bas-relief on the pedestal shows Rodney being greeted by Thomas McKean, the man who had urged Rodney to hasten to Philadelphia.

McKean was born in 1734 in New London, Pennsylvania, to parents from County Tyrone, Ireland. He was a member of the Friendly Sons of St. Patrick and the first president of the Hibernian Society for the Relief of Immigrants from Ireland. When, as a delegate to the Continental Congress, his vote for independence was negated by *George Read, his colleague from Delaware, McKean dispatched a messenger to New Castle to urge Caesar Rodney, the third delegate from that colony, to come to Philadelphia to break the tie. Rodney arrived just in time to vote for the resolution in favor of independence on July 2, 1776. (His arrival and reception by McKean are depicted in a bronze relief on the monument.) McKean most likely signed the Declaration sometime after January 18, 1777. Following independence from Britain, he presented one of the drafts from which the Delaware state constitution was written. He later served as president of the state.

¶ **Coffee Run Mission Site,** southeast of Hockessin off State 48.

Just within the entrance to the cemetery is a small chapel marking the site of St. Mary's Church, originally a log structure built in 1772 and the first Catholic church in the state. The church was also the residence of Father Patrick Kenny when he came to this area sometime after 1804. From here he ministered to five other missions in Delaware, Maryland, and Pennsylvania. The Dublin-born priest is buried in the graveyard.

In 1812 Kenny built the two-and-a-half-story stone house on this site. Besides ministering to the spiritual needs of the faithful in and around Wilmington, he supported himself by farming. In a diary entry for January 30, 1823, he reported an explosion at the nearby Du Pont powder mill: "John Kelly, only 2 months from Ireland where he left his wife and 7 children [-] Dead. Also Wm Duffy and Wm Delany – all catholics. 4 Irish Cath wounded." On other occasions he recorded trenchant remarks about his hired hand, Patrick Haw. Seemingly irritated by the latter for some unknown gaffe, the priest described Haw as an "Irish Indian Savage, Drunkard, Egg & cider sucker." An 1827 entry illustrates the depth of the priest's embarrassment about his handyman: "Mr Patrk Haw brought home Drunk in Moses M–'s cart – This Moses M– is as smooth an enemy to Catholics as any violent puritan in America – He was proud of his freight – to the great scandal of my house and place." In another incident, when Haw was bled following a drunken spree, he bragged that his blood was so thick that "it would not come out."

¶ Du Pont Statue, Rockford Park, south of Rockford Tower, at the junction of Tower Road and West 19th Street.

This statue of Admiral Samuel du Pont is the work of *Launt Thompson and stood in Du Pont Circle in Washington, D.C., from 1884 to 1920. During the Civil War, du Pont commanded a squadron of seventy-five vessels at the capture of Port Royal, South Carolina.

¶ Hagley Museum and Library, 3 miles north on State 52 and then 0.5 mile north on State 141.

The museum occupies 230 acres of the original explosives factory established in 1802 by Eleuthère Irénè du Pont, a French immigrant who came to America to manufacture a better and less expensive explosive powder. The property includes a machine shop, a cotton-spinning shop, the ruins of twenty-one powder mills, and Eleutherian Mills (the Georgian mansion built by du Pont in 1803). A restored workers' community includes the Brandywine Manufacturers' Sunday School, built in 1817 with donations from du Pont as a school for his workers and their children and the Gibbons House, where John Gibbons, an Irish foreman at the works, lived with his wife and four children.

Although du Pont's first workers were French, he gradually replaced them almost exclusively with Irish immigrants. Du Pont hired his first Irish workers in 1803, in many cases paying for their passage to America. Yet he had strong reservations about their abilities: Nevertheless, he must have succeeded in training them to his satisfaction because by 1839 only a small number of his employees were of other nationalities.

One of the Irish workers in the du Pont mills that year was John Gibbons, a seventeen year old from Derry, Ireland, who had begun work at the mills for $17.50 a month. During his first few months on the job, he used part of his wages to repay William McCarrow the $43 passage for himself and Mary Anne Gibbons, probably a sister who had accompanied him to America. John at first probably lived in the workmen's dormitories, although by 1841 he was renting a row house opposite the Squirrel Run factory. By 1850 he was earning $24 a month; seven years later he was the foreman at the Hagley Yard.

As foreman he appears to have been entitled to live rent free in what is now called the Gibbons House, although at the time it was referred to as "the 3rd house from the old school house." According to the 1870 Census, Gibbons lived here with his wife, Catherine, and their four children: Charles, Maggie, John, and William. In 1873, to mark his thirty-five-year tenure with the mills, Gibbons was presented with a gold watch by Henry du Pont, the founder's son. Gibbons continued to serve as foreman until his death in 1885, at which time he was earning $55 a month.

Some years later one of Gibbons' sons became involved in an unfortunate incident that would probably have shamed his father. After being laid off from his carpentry job with the company, the twenty-eight-year-old William was part of a group of dissatisfied employees who burned down a number of the du Pont family's barns. Following his arrest, Gibbons was found guilty of arson and received fifteen lashes.

The
Gibbons
House.

Another aspect of the du Ponts' connection with the Irish is found in the story of Eleuthère du Pont's great-grandson Maurice. While visiting Queenstown, Ireland, Maurice fell in love with Margery May Fitz-Gerald, variously described as a barmaid and a housekeeper at a hotel there. Maurice stubbornly insisted that he wouldn't leave Queenstown until she agreed to marry him. Once she consented, however, he returned to America alone, never mentioned the engagement to his family, and only returned to Queenstown for the wedding in Cork in October 1889. The *Wilmington Evening Journal* described the nuptials as "the sensation of two continents," while a Chicago paper claimed that the bride's "beauty and virtue [were] her only dowry."

§ The museum is open March 15-December 31, daily 9:30-4:30; rest of the year, Saturday and Sunday 9:30-4:30. Closed Thanksgiving and December 25 and 31. Fee. Phone: 302-658-2400. The library is open Monday-Friday 8:30-4:30 to serious researchers and students; appointment necessary. Phone: 302-658-2400.

¶ St. Joseph's on the Brandywine Catholic Church, 10 Barley Mill Road.

The original church on this site was built by the du Ponts in 1841 for their Irish employees. Although generally supportive of these Catholic immigrants, the du Ponts were occasionally exasperated by the religious wrangling that marred local Church-State relations. In 1852, for example, St. Joseph's parish priest, *Father John Walsh, attacked the state-supported public school system for its failure to provide financial support to Catholic schools. He once publicly ripped the pages dealing with Martin Luther and Sam Adams from a textbook used in the public schools. Alexis du Pont commented that the local Catholics' opposition to the public schools had taught him to give preference to Protestants when vacancies occurred among his employees. Nevertheless, a later du Pont served as a trustee of St. Joseph's Church – although he was not a Catholic – and publicly declared his opposition to the Know-Nothing movement because of its proposed "proscription of all foreigners and particularly the poor oppressed Irish Catholics."

¶ Wilmington and Brandywine Cemetery, on the north side of Delaware Avenue, between Madison and Adams streets.

Buried here is *Dr. John McKinly, the first president of Delaware after its independence from Britain. A physician of Scotch-Irish Presbyterian background, McKinly was elected president in February 1777 under the state's first constitution. He was later captured by the British, who held him until September 1778, when Congress arranged for his exchange. His remains were reinterred here in 1922 after their removal from the Old First Presbyterian Burial ground.

DISTRICT OF COLUMBIA

In 1791 President George Washington requested Pierre Charles L'Enfant to design plans for the new federal city. One of the commissioners whom Washington appointed to oversee the surveying of the proposed city on the Potomac River was Daniel Carroll of Duddington, a member of the famous Maryland family which traced its roots to the high kings of Ireland.

Before long, L'Enfant committed a serious faux pas involving two of the city's most influential proprietors. As he proceeded to lay out the streets, the Frenchman discovered that two houses obstructed his plan. Dismissive of the fact that one of the structures belonged to Carroll, L'Enfant announced that the houses must be demolished. Carroll's subsequent letter to Washington revealed that the designer had taken matters into his own hands – literally, it seems: "Major L'Enfant has proceeded with his hands to the demolishing of my building, which he has in great measure effected, having entirely destroyed the roof, and thrown down the greater part of the upper story, in fine the building is ruined. This appears to be the most arbitrary act ever heard of." Washington responded by warning L'Enfant in the future "to touch no man's property without his consent, or the previous order of the Commissioners." Nevertheless, L'Enfant continued to run afoul of the commissioners and the president and was dismissed in February 1792.

Following L'Enfant's departure, Andrew Ellicott took his place as surveyor of the District, and James Reed Dermott, a native of Ireland, was later selected as Ellicott's assistant. Almost immediately, though, the two were at loggerheads, Ellicott charging that Dermott had taken L'Enfant's plan of the city, and Dermott confiding that he intended to take Ellicott's job. Although the Irishman claimed that there were inaccuracies in Ellicott's survey of the city, Ellicott feared that his assistant had stolen some documents in order to make it impossible for him to prove the inaccuracies. Ellicott, in turn, feared that the inaccuracies had been Dermott's, a suspicion supported by his other assistants' complaints about having to make so many corrections because of Dermott's "deliberate, nefarious designs," caused apparently by his malicious removal of stakes. One of the assistants revealed that Dermott had "declared that he had put the affairs of the city into such a train, that they should never be set right again."

Events took an even more unpleasant turn when one of Ellicott's brothers placed an advertisement in a Georgetown newspaper seeking Dermott's apprehension for the theft of L'Enfant's plan. Under a headline customarily used to seek a horse thief – "SIX DOLLARS REWARD: STOP THE THIEF" – Ellicott described the alleged thief as "a native of

Ireland, well made, about five feet ten inches high, has a remarkably red face, an impudent brazen look, dark-coloured hair, which he commonly wears tied behind. Whoever shall take up the said thief, and commit him to any jail in the United States, so that he may be brought to condign punishment, shall receive the above reward."

As things turned out, the commissioners expressed to President Washington their confidence in Dermott. They believed that the accusations against him were intended to free Ellicott from blame for a mistake of his own which had thrown the survey off – from a few inches in some places to many feet in others. After Ellicott's departure from the city, the commissioners asked Dermott "to lay off squares into lots, [and] to plot the squares" and then to prepare a plat of the city. From this request came Dermott's so-called "Tin Case Map," the plan of the city that President Adams sent to Congress for approval.

❡ Abraham Lincoln Statue, Judiciary Square, D Street, between 4th and 5th streets, N.W.

This life-size statue of Abraham Lincoln is by Lot Flannery, a native of Limerick, Ireland, and a sculptor who had known the slain president. The monument was dedicated in 1868 on the third anniversary of Lincoln's death.

Although Flannery's permanent address was in Washington, D.C., he studied and traveled in Europe and completed commissions in New York City, New Orleans, and St. Louis. In the 1860s he directed one of Washington's largest stonecutting operations. His other notable works are a statue of Stephen Douglas in St. Louis, the Arsenal Monument in the Congressional Cemetery in Washington, D.C., and busts of Benjamin Franklin and General John Logan.

❡ The Adams Monument, Rock Creek Cemetery, Section E, Rock Creek Church Road and Webster Street, N.W.

Commissioned by Henry Adams for the grave of his suicide wife, this memorial is the most unusual one in the cemetery. The monument consists of a shrouded bronze figure by *Augustus Saint-Gaudens seated upon a boulder and backed by a polished granite block. Saint-Gaudens referred to it as *The Mystery of the Hereafter* and *The Peace of God that Passeth Understanding.*

After *President Theodore Roosevelt referred to the statue as that of a woman, Henry Adams wrote to him: "After March 4, should you allude to my bronze figure, will you try to do St. Gaudens the justice to remark that his expression was a little higher than sex can give. As he meant it, he wanted to exclude sex, and sink it in the idea of humanity. The figure is sexless." Homer Saint-Gaudens said that his father "occasionally explained" the figure "as both sexless and passionless" and that both a man and a woman had posed for it.

¶ **Anderson House,** 2118 Massachusetts Avenue, N.W.

This former private residence is the headquarters, library, and museum of the Society of the Cincinnati, the oldest hereditary military society in North America. Founded in 1783 as the result of a proposal by *Henry Knox, George Washington's chief of artillery, the organization was originally limited to American and French commissioned officers who had served for at least three years during the Revolution. Ten of Washington's generals were Irish natives: Richard Butler, Edward Hand, William Irvine, William Maxwell, Stephen Moylan, John Patton, Griffin Rutherford, John Shee, Walter Stewart, and William Thomson.

The major objectives of the Society of the Cincinnati were to promote the ideals of the Revolution, to maintain the officers' *esprit de corps*, and to offer assistance to officers and family members when needed. The society was named for the Roman general Lucius Quinctius Cincinnatus, the prototypical citizen-soldier who served his country in time of military need but returned to his civilian status immediately afterwards. Membership in the order is hereditary, passing originally only from father to son but now to the oldest male collateral descendant if no direct descendant exists. With a membership of about 2,600 today, the society emphasizes historical research and the endowment of scholarships.

§ Museum open Tuesday-Saturday 1-4; library open by appointment. Closed major holidays. Phone: 202-785-2040.

¶ **Andrew Jackson Equestrian Statue,** Lafayette Square, across Pennsylvania Avenue from the White House.

This statue of *Andrew Jackson, the son of an immigrant from northern Ireland, was the first equestrian statue made in the United States. The bronze was cast in 1853 by Clark Mills from cannon captured by the former president in the War of 1812. Mills at first turned down the request to do such a work, since he had never seen Jackson or an equestrian statue. Nevertheless, he produced a miniature based on a Virginia thoroughbred which he had trained to rear in such a way that its hind feet were under the center of its body. Mills spent two more years creating a plaster model. After erecting his own foundry, he succeeded in casting the body of the horse but only after five attempts. Mills was commissioned to erect an identical statue in New Orleans. It was finally cast in 1856, but only after he had suffered two disasters: the destruction of his studio by a tornado and the loss of his foundry to fire.

In March 1829 an estimated 20,000 people had arrived in Washington to attend Jackson's inauguration. While conservatives compared this event to the "inundation of the northern barbarians into Rome," Jackson's supporters followed their hero as he returned on horseback to the White House from his inauguration at the Capitol. At the White House the "President after having been *literally* nearly pressed to death and almost suffocated and torn to pieces by the people in their eagerness to shake hands with Old Hickory, had retreated through the back way. . . . Cut glass and china to the amount of several thousand dollars had been broken in the struggle to get the refreshments. . . . Ladies fainted, men were seen with bloody noses and such a scene of confusion took place as is impossible to describe – for those who got in could not get out by the door again but had to scramble out of windows. . . . [I]t was the People's day, and the People's President and the People would rule." To draw some of the crowd outside the White House, attendants placed tubs of liquor across the street in Lafayette Square.

¶ **Andrew Mellon Memorial Fountain,** Constitution and Pennsylvania avenues, N.W.

Built at a cost of $300,000, this fountain is a memorial to Andrew Mellon, the industrialist, financier, and secretary of the treasury who created and endowed the National Gallery of Art.

Mellon was of Scotch-Irish stock, his grandfather having come to Pittsburgh, Pennsylvania, from County Tyrone, Ireland. After entering the family banking business in 1873, the younger Mellon soon became known for his ability to identify and finance promising ventures, among them the Aluminum Company of America. He also played an important role in the creation of the Gulf Oil Corporation and the Union Steel Company. At one time he was either a director or an officer of more than sixty corporations. Although by 1920 he was president of the Mellon National Bank, he was little known nationally when President Warren G. Harding chose him as his secretary of the treasury.

In his new position Mellon pursued policies designed to lower taxes and to reduce the national debt. He believed that reduced tax rates would bring prosperity to American business and that the fruits of this prosperity would, in turn, "trickle down" to the working classes. In addition, he rejected the use of the tax code for social engineering: "I have never viewed taxation as a means of rewarding one class of taxpayers or punishing another." In general, Congress lowered federal tax rates, although not to the extent Mellon had sought. Toward the end of the decade he had reduced the national debt by a third (to $16 billion) and the budget by half (to $3.5 billion).

¶ **Basilica of the National Shrine of the Immaculate Conception,** on the campus of Catholic University of America, 4th Street and Michigan Avenue, N.E.

As early as 1848, proposals were made to build in the District of Columbia a Catholic church which would rival any in Europe. Initial steps were not taken, however, until 1913, when *Bishop Thomas Shahan, the rector of Catholic University, sought the support of Catholic women throughout the country. The cornerstone was laid in 1920 by *Cardinal James Gibbons, the archbishop of Baltimore. Although construction of the crypt was finished by 1931, construction of the upper church was postponed because of the Depression and World War II. In 1953, however, the John McShain Company of Philadelphia was awarded the contract to construct the upper church. The basilica was dedicated six years later by *Cardinal Francis Spellman of New York.

Incorporating features of both Byzantine and Romanesque architecture, the basilica is 465 feet long and 238 feet wide at the transept. The dome is 90 feet in diameter and rises 237 feet above the crossing, while the campanile is 329 feet high.

The chief designer for the basilica project was Charles Maginnis, a native of Londonderry, Ireland. He received his early education at Cusack's Academy in Dublin, where he won the Queen's Prize in mathematics. After coming to the United States in 1885, he secured employment in several Boston architectural firms until he became a partner in the firm of Maginnis, Walsh & Sullivan in 1898. He specialized in eccle-

Representation of St. Patrick in the Chapel of Our Lady, Queen of Ireland.

siastical and collegiate architecture and designed structures in those genres in twenty states and in Canada, Cuba, and Mexico. Some of the more famous of the many commissions which his firm accepted were the buildings on the new Boston College campus, sixteen buildings on the University of Notre Dame campus, and the chapel at Trinity College in Washington, D.C. He was honored with a gold medal from numerous associations, including the American Institute of Architects, the American Irish Historical Society, and the Eire Society of Boston.

¶ To the left of the main entrance to the upper level of the basilica is the Chapel of Our Lady, Queen of Ireland. The chapel was dedicated in 1980 as a gift of *John McShain, whose company had constructed the upper church. His family's coat of arms is above the entrance. In the center of the chapel is a statue of the Madonna and Child beneath a Waterford Crystal chandelier. The mosaic on the south wall incorporates the symbols of the four evangelists used in the Book of Kells, while the north wall depicts St. Patrick and ships sailing from Ireland, a representation of the influence of Irish missionaries throughout the world.

¶ Bishop Thomas Shahan, who is buried in the crypt of the National Shrine, was born in Manchester, New Hampshire, to Irish immigrants. Prior to his ordination he attended the Sulpician College in Montreal and the North American College in Rome. He completed graduate work at the University of Berlin and at the Sorbonne and the Institut Catholique in Paris in preparation for a professorship of church history and patrology at Catholic University of America in Washington, D.C. Besides contributing to numerous Catholic periodicals, he was associate editor of the original *Catholic Encyclopedia*, for which he wrote more than 200 articles and rewrote or translated more than a hundred others. He also wrote six books, one entitled *St. Patrick in History*.

¶ **Blaine Mansion,** off DuPont Circle at 2000 Massachusetts Avenue and 20th Street, N.W. Private.

This imposing structure was built in 1881 for James G. Blaine, a prominent political figure of Irish ancestry who served as Speaker of the House of Representatives and secretary of state under President Benjamin Harrison. (See Augusta, Maine.)

¶ **Blair House and Blair-Lee House,** Pennsylvania Avenue, near the White House.

These adjoining townhouses constitute the President's Guest House and are used to accommodate official state visitors. Blair House was the home of President Harry Truman and his family in the summer of 1945 and again during the renovation of the White House during most of Truman's elected term of office.

Built in 1824 by a Washington physician, what is now known as the Blair House was purchased in 1836 by Francis Blair Sr, a journalist from Kentucky and a descendant of an eighteenth-century Scotch-Irish immigrant. Blair, who had come to Washington to establish the *Globe*, the official mouthpiece of the Jackson administration, was still living in the city on the eve of the Civil War. Just before that conflict erupted, he built the adjoining townhouse for his daughter.

¶ **Cardinal Gibbons Statue,** 16th Street and Park Road.

This statue of James Gibbons, the archbishop of Baltimore and the second American cardinal, was erected by the Knights of Columbus and was dedicated in 1932.

Born in Baltimore of Irish immigrants from County Mayo, Gibbons spent five years of his childhood in Ireland before returning to his native city, where he studied for the Catholic priesthood. At the time of his appointment as bishop of North Carolina, he was the youngest of the 1,200 Catholic bishops throughout the world.

Following his consecration as archbishop of Baltimore in 1877, Gibbons banished from the public mind the belief that Catholicism was incompatible with American institutions. Since the nation's capital was at that time within his archdiocese, he made the acquaintance of each president from Jackson to Harding and developed strong friendships with Cleveland, Roosevelt, and Taft. He was also perhaps the first Catholic prelate in America to throw his influence behind observance of Thanksgiving Day by the Catholic community.

Gibbons' subsequent appointment as the nation's second cardinal drew enthusiastic public praise because of his thorough identification with American ideals. He, in turn, attributed the success of the Catholic Church in America to the liberty found in a country "where the civil government holds over us the aegis of its protection, without interfering with us in the legitimate exercise of our sublime mission as ministers of the gospel of Christ." He later drew additional support from the Catholic working classes of America when he intervened to prevent the Vatican from condemning the fledgling Knights of Labor on the erroneous grounds that this early labor union was a secret organization that required it members to take an oath. In 1911, on the twenty-fifth anniversary of his elevation to the cardinalate, he was feted at public ceremonies in Baltimore and eulogized by President Taft and *Theodore Roosevelt, both of whom praised his patriotism and civic virtue.

¶ **Catholic University of America,** 4th Street and Michigan Avenue, N.E.

Following the appointment of *Bishop Thomas Shahan as rector of

Catholic University in 1909, he oversaw an ambitious development program that resulted in the construction of John K. Mullen Memorial Library, Martin Maloney Chemical Laboratory, Cardinal Gibbons Memorial Hall, and McMahon Hall of Philosophy.

¶ McMahon Hall was named for Monsignor James McMahon, a native of Ireland who was educated at the Sulpician seminaries in Paris and Montreal before being ordained in New York City sometime after 1843. Dedicated in 1895, the granite building was named for McMahon because he had donated $400,000 worth of real estate to the university.

¶ A bronze bust of John Boyle O'Reilly, the famous Irish nationalist, editor, and author, is in the university's collection.

In 1896, when the Ancient Order of Hibernians endowed a chair in Celtic languages and literature at the university, some members of the Catholic hierarchy objected. Four years earlier *Bishop Bernard McQuaid of Rochester had reminded Irish Catholics that the bishops of Baltimore, New York City, and Philadelphia had condemned organizations like the Hibernians because of their alleged secrecy and condonation of violence. "That the Molly Maguires of Pennsylvania and the A.O.H. are even one and the same society cannot be denied," McQuaid charged. "This fact was demonstrated beyond gainsay at the trials of the Molly Maguires for brutal murders. This new University Chair ought to be labeled the 'Murderers' Chair.'" McQuaid later changed his opinion about the Hibernians.

¶ **Commodore Barry Statue**, Franklin Park, 14th and K streets, N.W.

This bronze statue depicts John Barry, the "Father of the American Navy," with a great cape around his shoulders and a cocked hat on his head. His right hand grasps the hilt of his sword. On the face of the pedestal is the goddess Victory, standing with sheathed sword on the prow of a vessel, an eagle in her right hand and a laurel in her left.

The statue is the work of John Boyle, who was born in New York in 1851 to parents of Irish descent. After his father's death, the boy supported his mother as a stonecutter and later studied at the Pennsylvania Academy and the Ecole des Beaux-Arts in Paris. At the Columbian Exposition in 1891-92 and in Buffalo ten years later, he received recognition for three statuary groups: *The Savage Age, East and West,* and *Tired Out,* the last an intimate bronze of a mother and her two children.

John Barry was a native of County Wexford, Ireland, where he was born in 1745 and from which he sailed for America at the age of fourteen. Until 1776 he was employed in various capacities in the Philadelphia merchant marine, serving as captain at age twenty-one and eventually becoming an influential shipmaster and shipowner. In 1774 he was the captain of *The Black Prince,* a ship owned by *John Nixon, who two years later was the first to read the Declaration of Independence in public.

Following the start of hostilities with Britain, Barry achieved fame as a naval commander for the aborning nation. In January 1776 he was placed in command of the *Lexington*, the first regular cruiser to put to sea under the authority of the Continental Congress. On April 17 the *Lexington* became the first vessel so commissioned to capture a British warship in actual battle. Barry's was also the first vessel flying the new striped American flag to capture an armed British ship. The Irishman's reputation was further enhanced when he refused a bribe from the British. During the war General Howe had offered Barry up to 20,000 guineas and command of the best British frigate if he abandoned the American cause. Barry replied that he had devoted himself to the cause of his adopted land and that neither wealth nor the promise of command over the whole British fleet would tempt him from continuing to serve her.

In the last year of the war, Barry was appointed commander of the frigate *Alliance*. During a subsequent engagement with two British vessels, he was wounded in the shoulder and was forced below to tend to his injury. After his ship's colors had been shot away, one of his men asked him if he would surrender. "No," the captain replied. "If the ship can't be fought without me, I will be brought on deck." A reenergized crew and a favorable wind allowed the *Alliance* to pound the enemy with a broadside, soon forcing the two British vessels to surrender. In 1794 President Washington named Barry the senior captain of the United States Navy, an appointment which led to Barry's honorific as "Father of the American Navy." That same year he was placed in charge of the *United States*, one of the six frigates recently authorized by Congress, being "of all the naval captains that remained . . . the one who possessed the greatest reputation for experience, conduct, and skill."

In his speech at the dedication of the Barry statue, *President Woodrow Wilson made some pointed remarks, probably to those Americans of Irish descent whose anti-British stance was contrary to his foreign policy. "John Barry was an Irishman," said the president, "but his heart crossed the Atlantic with him. He did not leave it in Ireland. And the test of us all . . . is whether we will assist in enabling America to live her separate and independent life, retaining our ancient affections, but determining everything that we do by the interests that exist on this side of the sea. Some Americans need hyphens in their names, because only part of them have come over. But when the whole man has come over, heart and thought and all, the hyphen drops of its own weight out of his name. This man was not an Irish-American; he was an Irishman who became an American."

¶ **Congressional Cemetery,** G and 18th streets, S.E.
   • Among the many gravesites here is that of *Mathew Brady, the

famous Civil War photographer.

• A marble monument marks the grave of *Governor George Clinton, even though his remains were moved to the graveyard of the Reformed Church in Kingston, New York, in 1911.

• The Arsenal Monument by *Lot Flannery marks the grave of twenty-one women who were killed in the explosion of the Washington Arsenal in 1864.

¶ **Convent of the Visitation,** P and 35th streets, N.W.

In 1797 Alice Lalor, a native of County Kilkenny, Ireland, formed in Philadelphia what later became the first American branch of the Visitation Nuns. When the group's sponsor, *Father Leonard Neale, moved to Georgetown in 1799, the women came with him and eventually established their community in a building of their own on this site.

At first these "Pious Ladies," as they were known, followed a rule similar to that of the Jesuits, but they later adopted the Visitation rule. Lalor (Mother Teresa) led the community for twenty years. The free school for girls which she founded was the genesis of the present school affiliated with the Visitation Convent.

¶ **Corcoran Gallery of Art,** 17th Street and New York Avenue, N.W.

The gallery was established in 1859 by William Corcoran, whose Irish-born father had immigrated to America in 1783, eventually settling in Georgetown and serving as that community's magistrate and postmaster.

Between 1837 and 1840 Corcoran established a reputation in the brokerage and banking industries. So successful was the banking firm of Corcoran & Riggs that in 1847 he completely paid off – with interest – the balance of a $24,000 indebtedness incurred by the bankruptcy of an earlier enterprise. The following year Corcoran & Riggs received 87 percent of a $16 million bond issue by the United States government. When Corcoran successfully placed $5 million of those bonds in London, the resultant rise in the market price of the bonds was so profitable for his firm that his personal fortune was assured.

Following his retirement in 1854, Corcoran devoted his time to art collecting and philanthropy. To house a collection of European paintings which he had begun acquiring on a trip to the Continent in 1849, he commissioned James Renwick Jr. to design a gallery in the Second French Empire style. Construction at the museum's original site – Pennsylvania Avenue and 17th Street – began in 1859. When the museum was completed after the Civil War, Corcoran hosted a gala ball, for which the main picture gallery was lighted by 280 gas jets suspended from the ceiling. Two years later Corcoran created a $900,000 endowment for the museum and donated his own private collection, valued at $100,000. When the museum became too small for its 700 works, a new Corcoran Museum was built at 17th Street and New York Avenue. In 1925 the gallery received a bequest of European paintings, antiquities, and decorative arts from *Senator William Clark of Montana. The old gallery was used by the U. S. Court of Claims until 1964, when it was renamed the Renwick Gallery and was acquired by the Smithsonian Institution.

Among the works in the Corcoran Gallery of Art are a portrait of the museum's founder by Charles Loring Elliott; portraits of the French statesman François Guizot and U.S. presidents *Chester A. Arthur, *James Buchanan, Millard Fillmore, and *Andrew Jackson, all by the Irish-American artist George Healy; and a bust of the Irish poet Thomas Moore by *Jerome Connor.

§ Open Tuesday-Sunday 10-5 (also Thursday 5-9). Closed Thanksgiving and December 25. Fee. Phone: 202-638-3211.

Jerome Connor was born in County Kerry, Ireland, in 1876 and as a young child came to America with his family. Because his parents were so poor, he was forced at age thirteen to earn his own living. After working successively as a sign painter, a machinist, and a stonecutter, he lived and worked in a craftsman colony near Buffalo, New York, where he did metal work, plaster casting, and sculpture. After opening his own studio in Syracuse, he received his first major commission – a marble memorial to Walt Whitman. He later set up a studio in the nation's capital.

Connor was a strong advocate of the Irish independence movement and in 1921 exhibited a portrait bust of Eamon De Valera, the president of the Irish Free State, at the Philadelphia Exhibition of Fine Arts. Four years later he returned to Ireland to work on a memorial County Cork to the victims of the *Lusitania* sinking, which had occurred off Cobh on May 7, 1915. While occupied on this project for fourteen years, he completed a series of relief portraits of the Cabinet members of the Irish Free State government. He died in Dublin in 1943 and was buried in Mount Jerome Cemetery in the Irish capital.

His three other works in the District of Columbia are the *Nuns of the Battlefield Memorial* and statues of *Bishop John Carroll and *Robert Emmet.

§ **Dumbarton Oaks,** 1703 32nd Street, N.W.
Until 1826 this Georgian mansion was occupied by Vice President

John C. Calhoun, the son of an immigrant from County Donegal, Ireland. Considerably altered and enlarged since then, the house is now an art museum and center of medieval studies owned by Harvard University. The mansion is surrounded by fifteen acres of formal gardens.

§ Open Tuesday-Sunday 2-5. Closed holidays. Phone: 202-342-3200.

¶ **Edmund Burke Statue,** Massachusetts Avenue, at 11th and L streets.

This monument honors Edmund Burke, the famous Dublin-born orator who championed the cause of the American Revolution while he was a member of the British Parliament. He was also advocated the independence of Ireland and the extension of civil rights to Catholics.

¶ **Embassy of Indonesia** (formerly the Walsh-McLean House), 2020 Massachusetts Avenue, at 21st Street, N.W.

The embassy was originally built as the private residence of Thomas Walsh, an Irishman from County Tipperary who had made a fortune from gold mining in Colorado during the 1890s. After extracting approximately $23 million worth of gold from his Camp Bird Mine, he sold the concern to a British company for $5.2 million.

Walsh and his wife subsequently moved to Washington, D. C., and took their place among both the *nouveaux* and the *vieux riches*. While traveling in Europe, Walsh met King Leopold II of Belgium, who tried to interest the American in investing in the Congo and promised to visit the him when he attended the St. Louis Exposition in 1903. After returning to America, Walsh purchased this piece of real estate on Massachusetts Avenue and proceeded to spend $835,000 in the construction of the sixty-room mansion and another $2 million on furnishings. One of the Walshes' parties was attended by 325 guests, who consumed 480 quarts of champagne, 288 fifths of scotch, 40 gallons of beer, and 36 bottles of liqueur. Walsh later joined King Leopold in various mining operations in the Congo and died in the nation's capital in 1909.

Before his death, however, Walsh had acquired a reputation for foolish generosity to his daughter, Evalyn. When the young girl complained that having to walk to school in Washington was "trying for my dignity," she asked her father to hire a horse and carriage. Within days the doting father presented her with a blue victoria, a pair of matched sorrels, and a coachman decked out in a silk hat. Some years later he gave his dear Evalyn a $100,000 wedding gift when she married Edward McLean, whose father owned the *Washington Post*. Walsh also succumbed to Evalyn's desire that he purchase the 44.5-carat Hope Diamond for her. As it turned out, though, the curse attached to the $154,000 investment had tragic consequences for Evalyn: her eight-year-old son was killed in a car accident, another son died after a lengthy stay in a sanitarium, her daughter died because of a drug overdose, she herself became addicted to morphine, and her adulterous, alcoholic husband went insane.

¶ **Embassy of Ireland,** 2234 Massachusetts Avenue, N.W.
    § Phone: 202-462-3939.

¶ **Ford's Theater,** 10th Street, between E and F streets, N.W.
    Here on the night of April 14, 1865, President Abraham Lincoln was assassinated by John Wilkes Booth. Only the outer walls remain of the original building. The interior stage, boxes, and sunken floor were rebuilt in the 1960s on the basis of photographs taken by *Mathew Brady a few days after the assassination. Among the historical items in the theater's museum are Lincoln's copy of Parson Weems' *Life of Washington*, the Lincoln family Bible, and several masks of the president.
    § Open daily 9-5. Closed December 25. Phone: 202-426-6924.

¶ **Freer Gallery of Art,** 1200 Jefferson Drive, S.W.
    Modeled after a Florentine palace, this museum exhibits art work from Asia and the Middle East as well as paintings by Winslow Homer, John Singer Sargent, and *James McNeill Whistler. The Whistler collection includes more than a thousand of his oils, watercolors, pastels, and prints. The gallery's Peacock Room, which Whistler decorated with gold and turquoise peacocks, was designed for an English merchant.
    § Open daily 10-5:30. Closed December 25.

¶ **General Grant Memorial,** on the Mall, at 1st Street, S.W.
    A seventeen-foot-high bronze equestrian figure of *Ulysses S. Grant, believed to be the largest such statue in the world, sits atop a central pedestal surrounded by four lions, eleven horses, and eleven Union soldiers. The memorial, which took twenty-two years to complete, was dedicated in 1922, on the centenary of Grant's birth.

¶ **General Meade Memorial,** The Mall, Pennsylvania Avenue and 3rd Street, in front of the U.S. District Court.
    This monument honors George Gordon Meade, the Union commander at the battle of Gettysburg and the great-grandson of an emigrant from County Kerry, Ireland. A gift of the state of Pennsylvania, this eighteen-foot-high monument features Meade at the front of a circle of allegorical figures representing Chivalry, Energy, Fame, Loyalty, Military Courage, Progress, and War.
    At the outbreak of the Mexican War, Meade was engaged in designing and constructing lighthouses in the Delaware Bay with the U.S. Army's Corps of Topographical Engineers. He subsequently saw ser-

vice in the battles of Palo Alto and Resaca de la Palma and participated in the siege of Vera Cruz. After the war he returned to his engineering duties in the Delaware Bay until he was sent to Florida, where he first made surveys and maps of the reefs but later served in the war against the Seminoles.

With the eruption of the Civil War, Meade was appointed brigadier general of volunteers, initially to defend Washington, D.C., from an expected Confederate assault. During the later battle of Glendale, he sustained wounds that caused him medical problems for the rest of his life. As one bullet hit his arm, another pierced his body just above the hip joint, indented his liver, and exited near the spine. Nevertheless, he continued to direct his troops from atop his mount until loss of blood forced him to retire from the engagement. Following service at Second Bull Run, Antietam, and Chancellorsville, he was unwillingly appointed commander of the Army of the Potomac.

¶ **General Rawlins Statue,** Rawlins Park, 18th and E streets, N.W.

This bronze statue commemorates John Rawlins, an officer of Scotch-Irish descent who served as aide-de-camp to *General Ulysses S. Grant during the Civil War.

The two men had met while living in Galena, Illinois, where Rawlins had helped organize the 45th Illinois Infantry soon after the fall of Fort Sumter. During the war he not only was an advisor to Grant but also helped moderate the general's fondness for drink. When the war was over, Rawlins sought the dry climate of the western plains in the hope that it would alleviate his tubercular condition. He accordingly accompanied the chief engineer of the Union Pacific Railroad to Salt Lake City, over the eastern route of the proposed transcontinental railroad. Rawlins' name was later given to a town in Wyoming which had grown up at one of their camp sites.

¶ **General Scott Statue,** U.S. Soldiers' Home, 2nd and Upshur streets, N.W.

This bronze statue of General Winfield Scott, a hero of the War of 1812 and the Mexican War, is the work of *Launt Thompson. The ten-foot-high statue depicts "Old Fuss and Feathers" impeccably attired in his dress uniform, holding his right hand in the breast of his coat and leaning on his sword hilt with his left.

¶ **Georgetown University,** 37th and O streets, N.W., Georgetown.

Georgetown, the first Roman Catholic college in the country, was founded in 1789 by John Carroll, the first bishop of the United States and a member of the distinguished Irish Catholic family of Maryland. A bronze seated statue of the bishop by *Jerome Connor is located in

*Statue of John Carroll
in front of Healy Hall.*

front of Healy Hall. (The sculptor added a stack of books under the bishop's chair when undergraduates took delight in placing chamberpots under the statue.)

¶ Healy Hall is named after Father Patrick Healy, the first African-American Jesuit in the United States and the first African American to become the president of a Catholic university. The son of an Irish immigrant and a mulatto slave in Georgia, Healy was graduated from Holy Cross College in Worcester, Massachusetts, in 1850. After entering the Jesuit Order, he taught at Holy Cross for six years before going to Europe to continue his education, first in Rome and then in Louvain and Liège, Belgium, where he completed a doctorate in philosophy. (He was the first African American to earn a doctoral degree.)

Following his ordination, Healy returned to Georgetown University to serve in a variety of capacities, finally being named its president in 1874. Besides updating its curriculum and better integrating the main campus with the institution's medical and law schools, he expanded the university's facilities. He planned and supervised the construction of a major new building – today's Healy Hall – in Belgian Gothic. The four-story structure – 312 feet long and 95 feet wide at the pavilions – was completed in 1879. The massive building's spire is the highest point in the District of Columbia. Healy is buried near the hall.

¶ The Lauinger Library houses the Americana collection of Dr. John Dawson Shea, editor, historian, and cofounder of the U.S. Catholic Historical Society. Born in New York City in 1824, Shea was the son of an Irish-born schoolmaster who taught at Columbia College in New York City, while his mother traced her descent to a settler who had arrived in Massachusetts with Governor John Winthrop in 1630. The young Shea learned Spanish while working in a Spanish merchant's countinghouse and at age fourteen published a biography of Cardinal Alvarez Carrillo de Arbornóz. Shea went on to study law and was admitted to the New York bar in 1846, but two years later he joined the Society of Jesus (when he took the religious name Gilmary). After completing his studies in canon law in Montreal, he was fluent in French.

In 1852, however, Shea left the Jesuits and began a career as the author or editor of more than 250 works. He first attracted the attention of contemporary scholars with his *Discovery and Exploration of the Mississippi Valley*. The rest of his books usually dealt with American history or the history of the Catholic Church in America. His most famous works were the *History of the Catholic Missions among the Indian Tribes of the U.S. 1529-1854, Early Voyages up and down the Mississippi, The Operations of the French Fleet under Count de Grasse, The Life of Pius IX, The Catholic Church in Colonial Days*, and the four-volume *History of the Catholic Church in the U.S.* He also translated a life of Father Isaac Jogues and edited the *Library of American Linguistics* (including fifteen Native-American grammars and dictionaries) and twenty-six volumes describing the Jesuit explorations in North America.

¶ The Georgetown Astronomical Observatory on the campus was created by Father James Curley, a pioneer astronomer and the observatory's first director. A native of County Roscommon, Ireland, Curley had arrived in the United States in 1817. After working for the next ten years as either a bookkeeper or a mathematics instructor, he joined the Society of Jesus and was ordained in 1833. He taught mathematics and astronomy at Georgetown for forty-eight years.

During that time Curley also planned and supervised the building and furnishing of the observatory, which was completed in 1844. The structure's three-story main building is sixty feet long and thirty feet wide and is surmounted by a rotary dome. Its transit instrument is seven feet long and has a 4.5-inch object glass, while the equatorial telescope in the dome has a 4.8-inch object glass with magnification powers of from 25 to 400. One of Curley's first undertakings following completion of the observatory was to determine the meridian of Washington D.C. (His computation was later found to be more accurate than the government's.) In 1852 he wrote the *Annals of the Astronomical Observatory of Georgetown College*, describing the facility and its instruments.

¶ James Buchanan Statue, Meridien Hill Park, 16th Street and Florida Avenue, N.W.

The funds for this monument to *President James Buchanan were provided by his niece, Harriet Lane, who served as the bachelor's hostess during his years in the White House.

¶ James Hoban Burial Site, Mt. Olivet Cemetery, opposite the National Arboretum.

In May 1863 the body of James Hoban, the Irish-born architect of the White House, was exhumed from the graveyard of St. Peter's Catholic Church and reinterred here. For many years it was customary for the Washington Chapter of the American Institute of Architects to lay a wreath on their earlier colleague's grave.

¶ John F. Kennedy Center for the Performing Arts, Rock Creek Parkway, at the end of New Hampshire Avenue.

This sprawling arts center is the only official memorial in honor of President John F. Kennedy in the nation's capital. The complex includes the Grand Foyer the Eisenhower Theater, the Opera House, the Concert Hall, the Terrace Theater, the Theater Lab, the American Film Institute Theater, three restaurants, and a library. A seven-foot-high bronze bust of Kennedy is located in the Grand Foyer, while the center's river façade is carved with many of the slain president's quotations.

§ Free tours daily. Phone: 202-416-8341.

¶ John F. Kennedy Houses, Georgetown.

During his fourteen years in the U.S. Congress, John F. Kennedy lived in four rented Georgetown houses, all now privately owned. (Two of those addresses are 1528 31st Street, N.W., and 1400 43rd Street, N.W.) The first house in which he and his new bride, *Jacqueline Bouvier, lived was a two-story, white brick house at 3271 P Street, N.W. The couple's last residence before the White House was an eighteenth-century red brick townhouse at 3307 N Street, N.W.

¶ Library of Congress, off Independence Avenue, across from the Capitol.

The bronze statues of Plato and Sir Francis Bacon in the library are the work of *John Boyle.

§ Open Monday-Saturday 8:30-5, Sunday 1-5. Phone: 202-707-5458.

¶ Mathew Brady Photo Studio, 627 Pennsylvania Avenue, N.W. Private.

Beginning in 1859, this was the second studio of the famous photographer Mathew Brady, who described himself as the son of an Irishman. Some of the 3,500 photographs which he and his assistants took during the Civil War are now in the National Archives.

Brady opened his first studio in New York City in 1842, while he was only nineteen. For four consecutive years he won a silver medal for his daguerreotype entries at the annual American Institute exhibit, and in 1849 he was awarded the first gold medal ever presented for that genre. He subsequently earned recognition at the New York and London world fairs. About 1855, however, he abandoned the daguerreotype for the wet-plate process known as photography.

At the commencement of the Civil War, Brady persuaded President Lincoln and the head of the Secret Service to let him and his assistants accompany Union troops into battle. Invariably seen wearing a linen duster and a broad-brimmed flat hat, Brady frequently risked his life to remain close to his "What-is-it" Wagon, which he used as a dark room. In the general panic at the first battle of Bull Run, the wagon was overturned, although Brady was able to retrieve some of his wet plates. A writer for *Humphrey's Journal* acknowledged Brady's ability to capture and convey the horrors of the battlefield: "His are the only reliable records at Bull's Run. . . . His pictures, though perhaps not as lasting as the battle pieces on the pyramids, will nonetheless immortalize those introduced in them. Brady has shown more pluck than many of the officers and soldiers who were in the fight. He went – not exactly like the [Irish] 'Sixty-Ninth,' stripped to the pants – but with his sleeves tucked up and his big camera directed upon every point of interest on the field. . . . [I]t is certain that [those who took flight] did not get away from Brady as easily as they did from the enemy. He has fixed the cowards beyond the possibility of a doubt." Impoverished by the panic of 1873, Brady found temporary financial relief when the U.S. Government purchased 2,000 of his photographs for $25,000. He continued as a photographer in Washington until he was struck by a vehicle and died the next year.

Some of Brady's photographic assistants were fellow Irish Americans. One of them, T. C. Roche, went on to develop bromide photographic papers, while another, Stephen Horgan, invented a procedure that allowed photographs to be printed on paper from copper and zinc plates. Some of the other men – D. F. Barry, Alexander Gardner, T. J. Hines, V. T. McGillycuddy, John Moran, and Timothy O'Sullivan – served as photographic chroniclers of America's westward expansion by participating in various military and scientific expeditions.

¶ **National Archives,** Constitution Avenue, between 7th and 8th streets, N.W.

Exhibition Hall in the archives building displays the three founding documents of the American Republic: the Declaration of Independence, the Constitution, and the Bill of Rights.

Of the fifty-five delegates to the Constitutional Convention in 1787, eight who signed the Constitution were of Irish birth or Irish descent. Their respective positions or proposals at the convention are summarized below:

• Pierce Butler of South Carolina was a champion of a strong central government, although he defended the rights of the South with regard to slavery and was the author of the fugitive slave clause in the Constitution. He opposed taking too many powers from the states, granting the National Legislature the power to veto state laws, and granting citizenship to foreigners without a long residence in the country. He also favored vesting the power to make war in the Executive, preferred the election of the Executive by electors chosen by the state legislatures, and insisted that black slaves should be included equally with whites in determining a state's representation "in a Government which was instituted principally for the protection of property."

• Daniel Carroll of Maryland seconded a motion that the presidential electors be chosen by lot from the National Legislature but later moved that the president be elected "by the people." He also argued that the senators should not be paid by their states because the Senate was "to represent and manage the affairs of the whole" nation.

• Thomas FitzSimons of Pennsylvania was an advocate of a strong national government and opposed giving the National Legislature the power to tax exports but favored granting such a power "when a proper time may call for it."

• James McHenry of Maryland proposed that the National Legislature be forbidden from passing bills of attainder and ex post facto laws

• William Paterson of New Jersey proposed a national government giving equal representation for each state and a federal judiciary consisting of a supreme court appointed by the Executive. He also insisted that black slaves should not be represented in the general government since slaves were not represented in the states in which they resided.

• George Read I of Delaware proposed that the existing state boundaries be abolished and redrawn into thirteen regions of approximately the same population and geographical area. He argued in favor of a national government which would eventually subsume the individual states and reduce them "to the mere office of electing the National Senate." He also expressed his hope that "the objects of the Genl. Govt. would be much more numerous than seemed to be expected by some gentlemen, and that [those objects] would become more & more so."

• John Rutledge of South Carolina opposed using population as the basis of a state's representation in the House but instead believed that such representation be proportionate to the taxes paid by the inhabitants of each state. He also expressed his opinion that the National Legislature would not sit more than six or eight weeks per year and favored a single Executive elected by the Senate, although he opposed giving him "the power of war and peace." He moreover proposed the "supremacy clause" – the constitutional provision that acts of Congress and treaties made under its authority "be the supreme law of the respective States."

• Richard Dobbs Spaight of North Carolina proposed that the House of Representatives be chosen by the state legislatures and that the tenure of the National Executive and members of the House be seven years.

§ Open April-Labor Day, daily 10-9; rest of the year, daily 10-5:30. Closed December 25. Phone: 202-501-5000.

¶ **National Gallery of Art,** Constitution Avenue, between 3rd and 7th streets, N.W.

The gallery was created by Congress in response to the donation by *Andrew Mellon of his personal art collection. When the museum opened in 1941, its holdings consisted of 126 paintings and 26 pieces of sculpture from the Mellon Collection, valued at $35 million. Following the Russian Revolution, Mellon purchased twenty-one masterpieces from the Hermitage collection of Catherine the Great for $10 million. He later paid $1.166 million for Raphael's *Alba Madonna*, reputedly the highest price ever paid for a piece of art prior to that time.

In addition to the gift of his art collection, Mellon provided the nation with securities sufficient to construct a $15 million building and to establish a $15 million endowment for the gallery. Since its creation, the museum has acquired several other private collections, including the 375 paintings and 18 sculptures of the Kress Collection.

§ Open Monday-Saturday 10-5, Sunday 11-6. Closed January 1 and December 25. Phone: 202-737-4215.

¶ **National Portrait Gallery,** F and 8th streets, N.W.

The Hall of Presidents – at the west end of the second floor – contains portraits of all the U.S. presidents through Ronald Reagan, including the fourteen with Irish or Scotch-Irish backgrounds: Andrew Jackson, James K. Polk, James Buchanan, Andrew Johnson, Ulysses S. Grant, Chester A. Arthur, Grover Cleveland, Benjamin Harrison, William McKinley, Theodore Roosevelt, Woodrow Wilson, John F. Kennedy, Richard Nixon, and Ronald Reagan. The portraits of James Buchanan, Abraham Lincoln, Franklin Pierce, and John Tyler were done by *George Healy, the nation's most prolific portrait painter.

The Gallery also contains Healy's paintings of Orestes Brownson,

Henry Clay, *William Corcoran, John Crittenden, Abraham Lincoln, *Cardinal John McCloskey, Albert Myer, George Peabody, William T. Sherman, and Daniel Webster, as well as a self-portrait.

The Meserve Gallery (#212) displays modern prints of famous nineteenth-century Americans made from the original negatives of *Mathew Brady. The Meserve collection contains more than 5,000 glass-plate negatives, most of them made by Brady. Probably the most unusual is the "cracked plate" photograph of Abraham Lincoln – the result of a negative which broke during printing.

§ Open daily 10-5:30. Closed December 25. Phone: 202-357-2700.

¶ National Presbyterian Church, 4101 Nebraska Avenue, N.W.

One of the windows in the Chapel of the Presidents depicts the Reverend Francis Makemie, the Irish-born founder of Presbyterianism in America.

¶ Navy Museum, in Building 76 at the Washington Navy Yard, 9th and M streets, S.E.

The museum surveys the history of the U.S. Navy from Revolutionary times. Among the exhibits are a gun deck section and a foremast fighting top from the U.S.S. *Constitution*; a statue of *Commodore John Barry, the "Father of the American Navy"; and the decommissioned destroyer U.S.S. *Barry*.

§ Open Memorial Day-Labor Day, Monday-Friday 9-5, Saturday, Sunday, and holidays 10-5; rest of the year, Monday-Friday 9-4, Saturday, Sunday, and holidays 10-5. Closed January 1, Thanksgiving, and December 25. Phone: 202-433-2651.

¶ New York Avenue Presbyterian Church, 1313 New York Avenue, N.W.

This church was founded by a group of Scotch-Irish dissenters. A window in the sanctuary depicts *Francis Makemie, *William Tennent, the Neshaminy Log College, and Princeton College – all associated with the history of Presbyterianism in America

¶ Nuns of the Battlefield Memorial, on a triangular plot between M Street and Rhode Island Avenue.

This memorial was dedicated in 1924 by the Ancient Order of Hibernians in honor of the Catholic nuns – many of them Irish – who served as military nurses during the Civil War. The central bronze panel relief depicts nuns in various types of religious garb, while an inscription above describes their heroic work: "They comforted the dying, nursed the wounded, carried hope to the imprisoned, gave in His name a drink to the thirsty." The dedicatory inscription below reads: "To the memory and in honor of the various orders of sisters who gave their services as nurses on battlefields and in hospitals during the Civil War." The memorial was designed by *Jerome Connor.

When the *Nuns of the Battlefield Memorial* was dedicated, fewer than a score of Civil War nuns were still alive. Irish-born Sister Mary Madeleine O'Donnell of the Sisters of Mercy was the only Civil War nun to make the journey to the nation's capital to witness the unveiling. She represented the twenty religious communities that had provided volunteers during the national conflict.

Prior to 1860, American nuns had established twenty-eight hospitals throughout the country. At the outbreak of hostilities, these nuns were the only organized group of women experienced in both nursing and hospital management. As a result, they were sought out by military officials as hospital volunteers. At least 20 percent of all military nurses were religious sisters – nearly 600 volunteers from more than a dozen religious congregations. A large number of the volunteers from many of these religious orders were Irish born or of Irish descent.

One of the most famous of the Irish-born volunteers was Eliza Maria Gillespie, known in religious life as Mother Mary of St. Angela or simply Mother Angela. Although she was born in Pennsylvania, her mother was from County Donegal, Ireland, and had come to America around 1777. During an almost thirty-year tenure as superior of the Sisters of the Holy Cross in the United States, Mother Angela was a pioneer in Catholic education and medical nursing. Besides establishing several academies, providing teachers for parish schools, and editing a series of Catholic textbooks, she founded a number of hospitals. During the Civil War this "Angel of Mercy" supervised the work of her congregation in military hospitals at Cairo, Louisville, Memphis, Mound City, Paducah, and Washington, D.C.

Of more than eighty volunteer nurses from the Sisters of the Holy Cross, fifty-one were Irish born. One of them, Sister de Sales O'Neill of County Cork, left a telling portrait of Mother Angela in an account recalling the day after the battle of Fort Donelson in February 1863: "Mother Angela was assisting the chief surgeon on the lower floor. It was a deliberate and difficult operation and the life of the soldier depended largely upon the accuracy of the surgeon, whose head and that of Mother Angela, on opposite sides, were bent over the poor lad who had fought under the Stars and Bars. Suddenly from above heavy liquid drops fell upon the white coif of Mother Angela who, true to her Celtic strain, did not quiver. Another, and still another, drop after drop, came faster and faster. At last, the final stitch had been taken and the two heads, that of the surgeon, and of the Sister, rose simultaneously, and not til then did the doctor know that a stain of blood, trickling through the open chinks of the upper floor, had fallen steadily upon the devoted head of Mother Angela, who stood before the surgeon with head, and face, and shoulders, and back bathed in the blood of some unknown soldier."

Mary Livermore of the Sanitary Commission provided eloquent testimony about the work done by Mother Angela's nuns. Livermore found that the surgeons at the military hospital in Cairo were so impressed by the quality of Catholic nursing that they were prejudiced against nurses of any other faith. She went on to write that "The world has known no nobler and more heroic women than those found in the ranks of the Catholic Sisterhoods." Yet she sympathized with the sick soldiers who disliked the nuns' "great headgear" – which she described as "a cross between a white sunbonnet and a broken-down umbrella."

While Mother Angela personified the good works of the Sisters of the Holy Cross, the Sisters of Charity had their own "Florence Nightingale." Born in Limerick, Ireland, and educated at the Ursuline Academy in Charlestown, Massachusetts, Sister Anthony (née Mary O'Connell) had entered the Sisters of Charity in 1835. Like other members of her community, she served as a nurse on Civil War battlefields or in hospital camps. She and her fellow nuns – thirty of the thirty-seven were Irish born – transported boat loads of wounded soldiers up the Ohio River and accompanied others on flat cars from Cumberland to the District of Columbia. About their work Sister Anthony wrote: "At Shiloh we ministered to the men on board what were properly known as floating hospitals. We were often obliged to more further up the river, being unable to bear the terrific stench from the bodies of the dead on the battlefield. This was bad enough, but what we endured on the field of battle while gathering up the wounded is beyond description. At one time there were 700 of the poor soldiers crowded in one boat." A glowing tribute to Sister Anthony is preserved in a soldier's diary: "Amid this sea of blood she performed the most revolting duties for those poor soldiers. She seemed like a ministering angel, and many a young soldier owes his life to her care and charity. Happy was the soldier who, wounded and bleeding, had her near him to whisper words of consolation and courage. She was reverenced by Blue and Gray, Protestant and Catholic, alike; and we conferred on her the title of the 'Florence Nightingale of America.' Her name became a household word in every section of the North and South."

¶ **Oak Hill Cemetery,** Georgetown, 30th and R streets, N.W.

This sloping cemetery was established in 1848 on land purchased by *William Corcoran, the founder of the Corcoran Gallery of Art in the District of Columbia. Besides Corcoran, *Peggy O'Neale Eaton and *James G. Blaine are buried here. Blaine's grave is surmounted by a Celtic cross.

Two memorable monuments in the cemetery are the work of *Alexander Doyle: the statue and pedestal over the grave of Bishop William Pinkney and the portrait bust and pedestal that mark the grave of John Howard Payne, the author of "Home, Sweet Home!"

Payne was originally buried in Tunis, where he had died in 1852 while serving as U.S. consul there. Thirty-one years later, however, his body was reinterred in Oak Hill Cemetery, thanks to Corcoran's efforts. In making the bust of Payne for his tomb, Doyle worked from a photograph taken by *Mathew Brady, which showed that the famous song composer had a beard. After the bust was completed, an official at the cemetery was erroneously informed that Payne had never had a beard, whereupon he ordered his stonemason to remove the beard.

¶ Octagon House National Historic Landmark, 1799 New York Avenue.

While the Executive Mansion was being rebuilt following its burning by the British in 1814, this Federal-style house (which is actually hexagonal in shape) served as the presidential residence.

Here *Dolley Madison lived with her "darling little husband," five-foot-four-inch President James Madison, and continued her tradition of beginning each year with an open house. One observer at the festivities of January 1, 1815, wrote that the First Lady wore "a robe of rose-colored satin, trimmed with ermine, with gold chains and clasps around her waist and arms, and a white satin turban upon her head, whence sprang a tiara of white ostrich plumes."

§ Open Tuesday-Friday 10-4, Saturday and Sunday 1-4. Phone: 202-638-3105.

¶ Robert Emmet Statue, Massachusetts Avenue and 24th Street, N.W.

Designed by *Jerome Connor soon after the 1917 Easter Uprising in Dublin, this statue was located elsewhere in the city until it was erected here in 1966. The seven-foot-high bronze statue honors the famous Irish Protestant patriot who led an unsuccessful insurrection of United Irishmen in his native land in 1803. Emmet's body is turned toward the Irish Embassy two blocks away.

The pedestal displays the coat of arms of the United Irishmen and is inscribed with extracts from Emmet's final speech before his execution: "I wished to procure for my country the guarantee which Washington procured for America . . . . I have parted from everything that was dear to me in this life for my country's cause. . . . When my country takes her place among the nations of the earth, *then*, and not until then, let my epitaph be written . . . ."

• Duplicates of this statue stand in Golden Gate Park in San Francisco, St. Stephen's Green in Dublin, and Emmetsburg, Iowa.

¶ **Robert Kennedy Memorial,** Department of Justice courtyard, 10th Street.

Robert Kennedy, who served as U.S. attorney general for his brother, President John F. Kennedy, is remembered by a portrait bust atop a slender pedestal. The chipped left corner of the pedestal symbolizes a life cut short by his assassination in 1968.

¶ **St. Matthew's Cathedral,** 1725 Rhode Island Avenue, N.W.

The initial money to build this church came from the sale of property donated by *Father William Matthews, a priest at St. Patrick's Church in the city and the first native-born American to be ordained a Catholic priest in the United States. The cathedral was the site of funeral services for John F. Kennedy in November 1963.

¶ **St. Patrick's Church,** between 10th and F streets, N.W.

Completed in 1884, the present church is located near the site of an earlier St. Patrick's, the first Catholic church in the country to be named for the Irish saint. That earlier church had been built on land purchased in 1794 by Father Anthony Caffrey, a native of Ireland. The original congregation was formed three years later and at first worshipped in a nearby house. Caffrey remained pastor of St. Patrick's until 1804, when he deeded the property to *Bishop John Carroll before returning to Ireland.

¶ **Settlers of the District of Columbia Memorial,** the Ellipse, 15th Street, between E Street and Constitution Avenue.

This unpretentious shaft honors the eighteen landowners or "original patentees" from whose land grants much of the District of Columbia was created.

One of these patentees was Daniel Carroll of Duddington, a member of the prominent Irish family which could trace its roots in America to 1680. His original property had been part of a land grant made by the second Lord Baltimore in 1663 and included what is now Capitol Hill. The original grant had passed to Ann Rozier, the wife of Daniel Carroll of Annapolis, the grandfather of the Duddington Daniel.

By the time the new federal city was being planned, Daniel Carroll of Duddington was one of the last private owners of his family's vast estate on Capitol Hill. On March 30, 1791, he joined the other proprietors of the land on which the new city was to be built in signing the agreement that established the District of Columbia. In 1800 a chronicler recalled: "There appeared to be but two really comfortable habitations, in all respects, within the bounds of the city, one of which belonged to Daniel Carroll [of Duddington], Esquire, and the other to Notley Young, who were the former proprietors of a large proportion of the land appropriated to the city, but who reserved for their own accommodation ground sufficient for gardens and other useful appurtenances."

Like the other proprietors of land in the area of the new capital, Daniel Carroll had originally believed that their proximity to the seat of power would make them rich. In 1837 he described the ironic results: "After nearly half a century the result is now fully known: the unfortunate proprietors are generally brought to ruin and some with scarcely enough to buy daily food for their families."

¶ Sheridan Circle, Massachusetts Avenue and 23rd Street, N.W.

This circle is named for General Philip Sheridan, a Union cavalry officer during the Civil War and the son of emigrants from County Cavan, Ireland. He is depicted here astride his galloping horse, Rienzi, which carried him through eighty-five battles and skirmishes. According to some accounts, when Sheridan's widow and their three daughters lived in a house across from the circle, they called out to the statue each morning with the greeting "Hello, Papa!"

Sheridan is generally regarded as the third most important Civil War Union general (after *Ulysses S. Grant and William T. Sherman). Although he attended the U.S. Military Academy, he was suspended for a year for lunging at a cadet-officer with a bayonetted rifle. During the Civil War he practically saved the army of General William Rosecrans by holding off a Confederate advance. Later, while in command of the 20th Corps of the Army of the Cumberland, he contributed to *General Grant's victory at Chattanooga. As a result, the Union commander placed him in charge of the 10,000-man cavalry corps of the Army of the Potomac.

In the last year of the war, Sheridan carried out a series of raids that prepared the way for major Union victories. In an attempt to break the Confederate communications line around Richmond, his men destroyed ten miles of railroad track, cut off telegraph communication to the city, and captured many supply trains. After promotion to command of the Army of the Shenandoah, Sheridan laid waste to the Shenandoah Valley, which had long sustained successful guerrilla campaigns against Union lines. In the spring of 1865, he led one final raid, destroying Confederate supply depots and leaving General Robert E. Lee with only one railroad line of communication with the South. Sheridan's final strategic action during the war forced Lee's evacuation of Petersburg and his retreat to Appomattox.

¶ Supreme Court Building, facing the Capitol, between Maryland

Avenue and East Capitol Street, N.E.

Since its creation, the Supreme Court has had sixteen members of Irish ancestry:

• John Rutledge was appointed to the first U.S. Supreme Court in 1790 but resigned the next year because of the long distances associated with circuit riding. Although President Washington returned him to the court as a recess appointment in 1795, the Senate rejected the appointment. Despondent at this rebuff, Rutledge tried to drown himself by jumping into a river in Charleston but was rescued by two slaves.

• William Paterson (1793-1806) wrote the 1795 opinion which invalidated a Pennsylvania statute because it conflicted with the federal and state constitutional protection of property. This decision was the precedent used by Chief Justice John Marshall in the *Marbury v. Madison* case, which established the right of the U.S. Supreme Court to review the constitutionality of legislative acts.

• John McLean (1830-61) traced his Scotch-Irish ancestry to the twelfth century. In 1857 he dissented from the Supreme Court's Dred Scott decision, insisting instead that Congress had the authority to exclude slavery from the territories and to free slaves voluntarily brought into free states.

• Roger Taney (1836-64) was the first Roman Catholic to sit on the court. In the Dred Scott case he ruled that the U.S. Constitution did not recognize slaves as citizens and that the Missouri Compromise of 1820 was unconstitutional because it violated the right of slave owners to take their property in slaves into the territories. During the Civil War he defied Lincoln's suspension of habeas corpus in the border states, ruling that only Congress had the power to suspend this right.

• Descended from Scotch-Irish grandparents, Samuel Nelson (1845-72) sided with the Dred Scott decision, arguing that "the law of the State is supreme over the subject of slavery within its jurisdiction." In addition, in an 1863 dissent he wrote that Lincoln had no authority to blockade Southern ports during the time between the outbreak of hostilities and the declaration of war by Congress three months later.

• John Campbell (1853-61), also of Scotch-Irish descent, voted with the majority in the Dred Scott case, although he had freed his own slaves three years before. He believed that the Union should not be jeopardized by slavery, which he said was "a transitory institution and would necessarily be modified or abrogated in the process of time."

• Edward Douglass White (1894-1921) was descended from Irish Catholic grandparents who had immigrated to America in the 1730s. While on the court, he generally opposed intrusions by the federal government on the power of the states to regulate their own economies.

• Joseph McKenna (1898-1925) was the son of an Irish-born immigrant who operated a small bakery in an Irish neighborhood of Philadelphia. He generally concurred in opinions that supported the growth of federal power, voting, for instance, to uphold the Mann Act (extending federal power over interstate prostitution).

• Charles Evans Hughes (1910-41), whose mother was descended from northern Irish ancestors, is famous for his claim in 1926 that "The Constitution is what the Supreme Court says it is." He usually voted with conservatives on the Supreme Court to strike down much New Deal legislation, although he later reversed his voting pattern.

• James Clark McReynolds (1914-41) was the son of a wealthy surgeon and plantation owner of Scotch-Irish ancestry. McReynolds consistently opposed New Deal legislation on constitutional grounds. In a 1935 case he accompanied his dissent with the comment that "The Constitution as many of us have understood it . . . is gone." (Between 1937 and 1941 he dissented 119 times, bringing to 310 the number of dissents which he delivered during his twenty-six-year term.) Upon retirement, he said that he had tried to protect the nation but that "any country that elects Roosevelt three times deserves no protection."

• Pierce Butler (1923-39) was one of eight children of Patrick and Mary (Gaffney) Butler, who had come to America from County Wicklow after the Irish potato famine. One of the "Four Horsemen," Butler dissented when the court upheld legislation which taxed employers and employees to create old age and unemployment pensions: "The Constitution grants to the United States no power to pay unemployed persons or to require the states to enact laws . . . for that purpose."

• Owen Roberts (1930-45), the son of a Scotch-Irish mother, wrote the majority opinion which struck down the Agricultural Adjustment Act on the grounds that the Constitution did not delegate to Congress authority to regulate agricultural production.

• James Byrnes (1941-42), the grandson of Irish Catholic immigrants, generally believed in "judicial restraint," although he wrote the majority opinion using the commerce clause to strike down a California law to prevent the transportation of indigents into the state.

• Frank Murphy (1940-49) was the grandson of immigrants who had left Ireland in the late 1840s. As an ardent defender of civil liberties, he criticized the internment of Japanese during World War II and used the Fourteenth Amendment to protect racial minorities against discrimination.

• William Brennan (1956-90) was descended from Irish immigrant parents who had come to America just before the turn of the century. Of his more than 1,250 published opinions, 400 were dissents. He helped develop the use of the Fourteenth Amendment to restrict state and municipal authority. He was with the majority when they ruled that voting districts must be approximately equal in population so as to guarantee the principle of "one man one vote."

• Anthony Kennedy's tenure on the court since 1988 has been marked by conservative rulings in the areas of privacy, civil rights, and criminal law enforcement. In a speech prior to his appointment to the court, he remarked that "An essential purpose of the criminal justice system is to provide a catharsis by which a community expresses its collective outrage at the transgressions of the criminal."

§ Open Monday-Friday 9-4:30. Closed holidays. Phone: 202-479-3000.

¶ Theodore Roosevelt Memorial, Roosevelt Island, Potomac River.

Located on an eighty-eight-acre wilderness island in the Potomac, this memorial to *Theodore Roosevelt includes a seventeen-foot-high bronze statue of the president and four huge granite slabs bearing comments he made on nature, youth, manhood, and the state. One of the slabs records Roosevelt's remark that "The nation behaves well if it treats the Natural Resources as assets which it must turn over to the next generation increased and not impaired in value." The site's location amid woodland trails and a wide variety of trees and wildflowers highlights Roosevelt's successful conservation efforts.

§ Accessible by pedestrian bridge from the northbound lane of the George Washington Memorial Parkway. Open daily 7-dusk. Phone: 203-285-2598.

¶ Trinity College, 125 Michigan Avenue, N.E.

Located near Catholic University, Trinity College is the crowning achievement of Sister Julia McGroarty, who conceived the idea of the nation's first Catholic college for women and determinedly saw it through to completion in 1899-1900.

A native of County Donegal, Ireland, Susan McGroarty had immigrated with her parents and nine siblings to Cincinnati, Ohio. Although at age eleven she was still unable to read, the nuns of Notre Dame de Namur in Cincinnati provided her with sufficient education to enter that teaching order, taking the religious name "Julia." During the next thirty-four years, she was primarily engaged in teaching at Notre Dame schools in Massachusetts and Philadelphia. Her free school for African Americans in the latter city attracted the attention and support of Katherine Drexel, the famous heiress-turned-nun who made the education of African Americans her life's work. Later, as superior of her order, Sister Julia founded fourteen convents and took steps to improve the educational standards and curriculum at the order's thirteen academies. In the last years of her life, she received the support of *Cardinal James Gibbons and the rector of Catholic University of America in the creation of Trinity College.

§ **U.S. Capitol Building,** at the east end of the Mall.

From the beginning, Irishmen played a role in both the design and the construction of the Capitol. Although the Frenchman Pierre L'Enfant had been expected to design the Capitol as well as the President's House, when no plans were forthcoming the commissioners resorted to sponsoring a competition. One of the unsuccessful entrants was James Diamond, an Irishman whose design for the Capitol incorporated arcades, loggia, and a dome like that atop the cathedral in Florence, Italy. (Diamond was ridiculed for the outlandish rooster that adorned the dome.) Once construction got under way, several Irishmen were involved in the actual building of the Capitol. In April 1795 the commissioners contracted with John Delahunty and the two brothers Cornelius and Patrick McDermot Roe to do the brick and stone work on the Capitol. Five years later the Irish Catholic John Kearney was granted the commission "for the completion of the plastering and Stucco Work at the Capitol."

§ Two of the heroic-size paintings in the Rotunda include patriots of Irish descent in famous episodes of the Revolution: *The Signing of the Declaration of Independence* (Thomas Lynch Jr., Charles Carroll, Robert Treat Paine, John Hancock, Charles Thomson, George Read I, Edward Rutledge); and *The Surrender of Cornwallis at Yorktown* (Major General Charles O'Hara, Thomas Nelson Jr., Major General James Clinton, General Anthony Wayne, General Edward Hand, and Major General Henry Knox).

§ During the 1860s additional ornamentation on the Capitol was designed by Thomas Crawford, a sculptor of Scotch-Irish descent. For the House and Senate wings, he designed two bronze doors with panels illustrating scenes from the Revolutionary War and the military career of George Washington. He also designed *The Progress of Civilization* on the front pediment of the Senate, a bas-relief of a female "America" flanked by a panorama of figures representing the Indian, the pioneer, the hunter, the soldier, the merchant, the mechanic, the student, and the teacher. Crawford also designed the nineteen-foot-high female figure *Freedom* on top of the Capitol dome. He had originally intended to call this bronze figure "Armed Liberty" and place on its head a liberty cap like the type worn by freed Roman slaves. However, when Secretary of War Jefferson Davis, a Southerner, objected to the statue's allusion to freed slaves, the artist replaced the cap with a helmet adorned with feathers and an eagle head. Crawford's plaster cast of the statue, which he modeled in Rome, was almost lost in a storm during the transatlantic voyage in 1858. After finally being cast in bronze, *Freedom* was hoisted into place in 1863.

§ In 1864 Congress invited each state to send the statues of two of its most notable citizens to what is now known as the National Statuary Hall

A portion of Thomas Crawford's The Progress of Civilization *on the front pediment of the Senate.*

Collection, housed in Statuary Hall and elsewhere throughout the Capitol. The sixteen persons of Irish descent whose statues are in the collection are:

• Francis Blair Jr. (Missouri), Unionist and member of Congress who was influential in preventing Missouri from seceding;

• William Jennings Bryan (Nebraska), secretary of state under Woodrow Wilson and three-time presidential candidate;

• John C. Calhoun (South Carolina), U.S. representative and senator and secretary of war under presidents Monroe and Tyler;

• Charles Carroll of Carrollton (Maryland), member of the Continental Congress, the Maryland Senate, and the U.S. Senate, and last surviving signer of the Declaration of Independence;

• George Clinton (New York), first governor of New York, and vice president under Jefferson and Madison;

• Jefferson Davis (Mississippi), U. S. senator, secretary of war, and president of the Confederacy;

• Robert Fulton (Pennsylvania), developer of the first commercially viable steamboat;

• Sam Houston (Texas), leader in the Texas Revolution against Mexico, first president of the Texas Republic, U.S. senator, and governor of Texas;

• Andrew Jackson (Tennessee), U.S. representative and senator, state supreme court justice, victor at the battle of New Orleans, and president of the United States;

• Philip Kearny (New Jersey), Mexican War officer and Civil War commander who earned the nickname "Perfect Soldier";

• John Kenna (West Virginia), U.S. representative and senator who worked to improve navigation along the Kanawha River in his state so as to tap the area's resources;

• Patrick McCarran (Nevada), state supreme court justice, U.S. senator, and chief sponsor of the Civil Aeronautics Act, the Internal Security Act of 1950, and the McCarran-Walter Immigration Act;

• Ephraim McDowell (Kentucky), pioneer physician who performed the first successful ovariotomy in 1809;

• John McLaughlin (Oregon), medical doctor who became the "ruler" of the Hudson Bay Company's vast territories west of the Rockies and who welcomed the first colonists to the Oregon Territory;

• Will Rogers (Oklahoma), famous humorist who called himself an Irish-American-Indian; and

• James Shields (Illinois), officer in the Mexican War and the Civil War and the only American to represent three states in the U.S. Senate.

❡ The statues of U.S. senators Thomas Hart Benton, *Francis Blair, and *John Kenna are the work of *Alexander Doyle, while the marble statue of Civil War general Lew Wallace was sculpted by Andrew O'Connor.

Born in Worcester, Massachusetts, in 1874, Andrew O'Connor learned the art of sculpture from his father, a cemetery stonecutter. During his formative years he worked successively under the tutelage of William Ordway Partridge in Chicago, Daniel Chester French in New York, and John Singer Sargent in London. Among O'Connor's most notable works are monuments to General Thomas Thomas (Purchase, N.Y.), *Theodore Roosevelt (Glen View, Ill.), and General John Johnson (St. Paul, Minn.) and statues of General Henry Lawton (Indianapolis, Ind.), Abraham Lincoln (Springfield, Ill., and Providence, R.I.), and Lafayette (Baltimore, Md.). He also produced the statue of Lincoln at the Royal Exchange in London and that of Daniel O'Connell in Dublin.

§ Open Memorial Day weekend-Labor Day, daily 9-8; rest of the year, 9-4:30.

❡ **Washington National Cathedral,** Mount St. Alban, at Massachusetts and Wisconsin Avenues, N.W.

• The Lee-Jackson Memorial Windows, a gift of the United Daughters of the Confederacy, commemorate episodes in the lives of *Thomas "Stonewall" Jackson and Robert E. Lee.

• Among the famous Americans buried here are *Woodrow Wilson, **Helen Keller, and *Annie Sullivan, Keller's teacher and almost constant companion. President Wilson's sarcophagus is decorated with a Crusader's cross, which his widow believed best symbolized his personality and political career. Wilson is the only American president interred in the capital.

§ Open Memorial Day weekend-Labor Day, Monday-Friday 10-9, Saturday 10-4:30, Sunday 12:30-4:30; rest of the year, Monday-Saturday 10-3:15, Sunday 12:30-2:45. Phone: 202-537-6200.

¶ **White House,** 1600 Pennsylvania Avenue.

The winner of the contest to design the President's House was the Irishman James Hoban, who, when it came time to collect his "premium," chose the promised $500 medal rather than the cash of equal value. He was also paid 300 guineas to supervise construction of the building.

A native of County Kilkenny, James Hoban had attended the Royal Dublin Society's drawing school as a pupil of the architect Thomas Ivory. There, it seems, Hoban adopted his mentor's preference for the Palladian neoclassical style and most likely worked on the construction of various buildings in Dublin. After coming to the United States in 1785, Hoban worked first as an architect in Philadelphia and then as a "house carpenter" in Charleston, South Carolina. It is possible that he designed Charleston's old statehouse at Broad and Meeting streets as well as other buildings in the city that reflect a distinctly Irish Georgian style. He is known to have designed South Carolina's new capitol building in Columbia. (That structure was completed in 1791 but was destroyed by fire in 1865.)

Although the President's House shows some internal modifications, it seems to have been modeled after Leinster House, a Palladian structure built on the outskirts of Dublin in 1745. Both houses contain eleven bays, a façade of three sections, four engaged columns, and windows with triangular and segmental pediments. Although the American house is only two stories in height, Hoban's original plan had envisioned three stories (including the ground-level basement), as is the case with Leinster House. Today Leinster House is the seat of the Irish Dáil or Parliament.

When the cornerstone of the President's House was laid in 1792, James Hoban assisted in his capacity as master of the Federal Masonic Lodge. During the ceremony a polished brass plate with the following inscription was placed beneath the cornerstone: "The first stone of the President's House was laid the 13th day of October 1792, and in the seventeenth year of the independence of the United States of America. George Washington, President. Thomas Johnson, Doctor Stewart, Daniel Carroll, Commissioners. James Hoban, Architect. Collen Williamson, Master Mason."

¶ The distinction of being the first First Lady of Irish background to inhabit the new executive mansion belonged to Dolley Payne Todd Madison. When the President's Mansion was torched by the British during the War of 1812, Mrs. Madison was led to safety by *Charles Carroll, who brought her to Bellevue (now Dumbarton House), one of the first houses on the heights above the river in Georgetown. The fugitive First Lady recorded that night's events: "Our kind friend, Mr. Carroll has come to hasten my departure, and is in a very bad humor with me because I insist on waiting until the large picture of General Washington is secured, and it requires to be unscrewed from the wall. This process was found too tedious for these perilous moments; I have ordered the frame to be broken, and the canvass taken out. . . ."

¶ After the war the task of rebuilding the soon-to-be-renamed "White House" was entrusted to James Hoban. By 1815 Hoban was regarded as the foremost builder in the District of Columbia, having constructed the original Executive Mansion, of course, as well as the Great Hotel and the Little Hotel. To the position of foreman of the Irish laborers on the job of rebuilding the executive mansion, he assigned an old friend, Nicholas Callan, an Irishman who had worked on the original structure. Hoban supervised the project until it was completed in 1829. During this postwar period he also designed and rebuilt the offices occupied by the State and War departments, additional casualties of the British invasion of the District.

Besides enjoying a reputation as a highly respected builder, Hoban was also viewed as a civic leader. Following the District's incorporation in 1802, Hoban was elected to the city council and served as a councilman until his death. In addition, he was instrumental in establishing St. Patrick's Catholic Church, he was a founding member of the Federal Masonic Lodge, and he was the captain of the local volunteer militia. He and his wife and their ten children and nine slaves lived in a large brick row house near the President's Park (now the White House lawn). At his death in 1831, Hoban left an estate worth $60,000, much of it in the form of real estate. He was buried in the graveyard of St. Peter's Catholic Church in Washington, D.C., but in 1863 his body was reinterred in Mount Olivet Cemetery (opposite the National Arboretum).

His reputation seems not to have suffered from an episode involving *Betsy Donahue, who rented a residence owned by Hoban in the

President's Park. Although the authorities usually overlooked the gambling and drinking indulged in by the workers constructing the executive mansion, those officials objected when Donahue opened a "riotous and disorderly house" in her rented building and began pulling men in off the street. Despite Hoban's testimony on her behalf, the woman was fined and the house was moved from the park.

¶ In 1857 Congress commissioned *George Healy to paint a series of presidential portraits, each for $1,000. In all, he painted the portraits of thirteen U.S. presidents: John Adams, John Quincy Adams, *Chester A. Arthur, *James Buchanan, Millard Fillmore, *Ulysses S. Grant, Rutherford B. Hayes, Abraham Lincoln, James Madison, Franklin Pierce, *James K. Polk, John Tyler, and Martin Van Buren. Except for the portraits of Arthur, Buchanan, and Grant, the paintings are currently in the White House, as is his canvas entitled *The Peacemakers*. This large historical piece depicts a strategy meeting of President Lincoln with *General Ulysses S. Grant, General William T. Sherman, and Admiral David Porter aboard the *River Queen* at City Point, Virginia.

George Healy was born in Boston in 1813, the son of a Merchant Marine captain of Irish descent. Encouraged to develop his artistic talent by the popular Boston painter Thomas Sully, the eighteen-year-old Healy opened his own studio in the Massachusetts capital and was soon exhibiting his own works. His studio was so financially successful that he was able to spend a year studying and painting in Paris. After opening a studio in the City of Lights, he saw his reputation soar as he secured the patronage of King Louis-Philippe and other famous French political leaders. In 1855 he was recognized at the Universal Exhibition for his memorable historical canvas *Franklin Urging the Claims of the American Colonies before Louis XVI*. That same year he returned to America and established a studio in Chicago, where – regrettably – the painting of Franklin was destroyed in the Great Fire of 1871.

While in the United States, George Healy completed commissions given him by King Louis-Philippe to paint the portraits of famous American statesmen. Among those he captured on canvas for his royal patron were John Quincy Adams, Henry Clay, *Andrew Jackson, John Tyler, and Daniel Webster. He also made a copy of one of Gilbert Stuart's many portraits of George Washington. While Healy was working on the portrait of President-elect Lincoln (still *sans barbe*), the politician erupted in laughter as he read a letter from a young girl. Lincoln then remarked to Healy: "She complains of my ugliness. . . . She wishes me to put on false whiskers to hide my horrible lantern jaws. Will you paint me with false whiskers? No?" As all the world knows, Lincoln grew a beard before arriving at the White House. Healy's portrait of him was the last in which the president was clean-shaven.

During his career Healy painted more than 700 portraits, more than the number painted by any other American artist. Among the Americans whose portraits he rendered were John James Audubon, Pierre Beauregard, *James G. Blaine, Orestes Brownson, Lewis Cass, Salmon P. Chase, Henry Clay, *William Corcoran, John Crittenden, Ralph Waldo Emerson, Nathaniel Hawthorne, Robert E. Lee, Abraham Lincoln, Henry Wadsworth Longfellow, *Cardinal John McCloskey, George McClellan, Albert J. Myer, George Peabody, David Porter, William H. Seward, William T. Sherman, Joseph Story, and Daniel Webster. Healy's most famous extant historical composition is the painting *Webster Replying to Hayne*, now in Faneuil Hall, Boston.

Approximately ten years after coming to Chicago, Healy retraced his steps to Europe and assumed a highly profitable peripatetic career. During that time he painted Pope Pius IX and Franz Liszt in Rome, King Charles I in Rumania, Louisa May Alcott in Switzerland, and Charles Goodyear in Paris. He also executed portraits of Swedish singer Jenny Lind, several members of the English nobility, and the European statesmen Otto von Bismark, François Guizot, and Louis Adolphe Thiers. While in Italy, he became the first American ever requested to contribute a self-portrait to the Uffizi Gallery in Florence.

Other works by Healy can be found in the Corcoran Art Gallery, the National Gallery of Art, the National Portrait Gallery, the Smithsonian Institution, the U.S. Capitol, the Metropolitan Museum of Art, the New York Historical Society, the Newberry Library, and the Virginia Museum of Fine Arts.

§ Free tours of the White House Tuesday-Saturday 10-noon. Tickets are required Memorial Day weekend to Labor Day and can be obtained on tour days on the Ellipse at Constitution Avenue and 16th Street. Phone: 202-456-7041.

¶ Wilson House National Historic Landmark, 2340 S Street, N.W.

With the money he received from winning the Nobel Peace Prize, *President Woodrow Wilson purchased this house in 1921 for his second wife. Wilson never recovered from the stroke he suffered in the last year of his presidency and lived as an invalid in this twenty-three-room mansion until his death in 1924.

The house contains original furnishings and Wilson memorabilia, carefully assembled and saved by his widow until her own death in 1961. One of the items on display is a miniature reproduction of the Robert Emmet statue located near the house.

§ Open Tuesday-Sunday 10-4. Closed major holidays. Fee. Phone: 202-387-4062.

ILLINOIS

CAIRO

¶ Magnolia Manor, 2700 Washington Avenue.

This brick Italianate house was built in 1869 for Charles Galigher, a local milling merchant, at a cost of $75,000. In 1880 the house was the scene of a reception for *President Ulysses S. Grant and his wife after their return from a world tour.

The son of a merchant hatter of Scotch-Irish descent, Galigher – while still a teenager – began a ten-year career as the master of a steamboat in which he was part owner. He suffered a major reversal, however, after the failure of a milling venture into which he had invested his accumulated fortune of $20,000. Attempting to make a fresh start, he moved to Cairo, Illinois, and became part owner of a small flour mill, an enterprise which was immediately successful. In 1866 Galigher purchased his partners' share of the business, which within a few years was producing 50,000 barrels of flour annually. Before his mills were destroyed by fire in 1889, he had amassed a fortune of almost $500,000.

§ Open April-December 31, Monday-Saturday 9-5, Sunday 1-5; rest of the year, Wednesday-Saturday 9-5, Sunday 1-5. Closed January 1 and December 24-25. Fee. Phone: 618-734-0201.

CARBONDALE

¶ General Logan Statue, Michigan Avenue and 9th Street.

This equestrian statue of John Logan, the famous Civil War general and U.S. senator, is the work of *Augustus Saint-Gaudens.

Logan, whose Scottish father emigrated from northern Ireland, commanded the 31st Illinois Volunteers during the conflict between the North and the South. After the war he orchestrated the first effort to remember the Civil War dead by decorating their graves in Woodlawn Cemetery in Carbondale in April 1867. A year later, as commander of the Grand Army of the Republic, he designated May 30 "for the purpose of strewing flowers or otherwise decorating the graves of comrades who died in defense of their country during the late rebellion, and whose bodies now lie in every city, village and hamlet churchyard in the land."

CARROLLTON

¶ Rainey Memorial Park, State 267 and 6th Street.

This park honors Henry Rainey, the Speaker of the House of Representatives from March 1933 until his death in August 1934. A bronze statue of Rainey depicts him holding a gavel.

Of Scotch-Irish ancestry, Rainey was elected to Congress in 1906, the first of fifteen terms in the House of Representatives. During that tenure he voted with the liberal branch of the Democratic Party, especially on issues of free silver and tariff reform. While on the Ways and Means Committee, he helped draft the Underwood Tariff Bill. Although he resigned his seat when Congress declared war in April 1917 so he could join the war effort, he withdrew his resignation at the request of *President Woodrow Wilson and subsequently helped prepare and pass the various war revenue bills. He enthusiastically supported the idea of a deep waterway linking the Great Lakes with the Gulf of Mexico, and he worked to convene an international conference on tariff reduction during the first two years of the Great Depression. When the election of Franklin Roosevelt brought a Democratic majority to the House, Rainey was elected Speaker, from which position he advanced the passage of the New Deal's legislation.

¶ **Thomas Carlin Monument,** Greene County Courthouse, 519 North Main Street.

This memorial outside the courthouse was erected in memory of Thomas Carlin, the founder of Carrollton and the seventh governor of Illinois. Born in Kentucky in 1789 to a father of Irish descent, Carlin was the county's first sheriff, served in the state legislature, and commanded a battalion during the Black Hawk War. While governor from 1838 to 1842, he vigorously promoted a program of internal improvements, among them the Illinois and Michigan Canal.

¶ **Walnut Hall,** 1 mile west on State 108. Private.

This three-story brick house fronted by Greek columns was the focal point of a 485-acre farm owned by *Henry Rainey, Speaker of the House of Representatives. During his days here the farm was open to the public as a show place and park. The house is currently being restored by its owners.

CHICAGO

¶ **Art Institute of Chicago,** Michigan Avenue and Adams Street.

Among the institute's many collections is a reconstruction of the Trading Room of the Chicago Stock Exchange Building. The walls and ceilings of the room are covered with intricate stencil patterns by Louis J. Millet and *Louis Sullivan. The Exchange Building, which formerly stood at 30 North LaSalle Street, was designed by Sullivan and was erected in 1894. The exchange entryway – a stone and terra-cotta arch – stands today in the nearby reflecting pool in Grant Park.

Sullivan was born in Boston, the son of an Irishman who had promoted himself from a wandering minstrel to the owner of a dancing academy in London and who had prospered in the same line of work after arriving in Boston in 1847. Determined upon a career as an architect, the younger Sullivan entered the Massachusetts Institute of Technology, but his study of architecture produced in him a distaste for the classical and a preference for the Romanesque revival in vogue in Boston at the time. After leaving M.I.T., he worked briefly in architectural firms in Philadelphia and Chicago before sailing for Paris with hopes of matriculating at the Ecole des Beaux-Arts. For six weeks he studied eighteen hours a day in preparation for the entrance test. After less than a year at the Beaux-Arts, however, he returned to Chicago, still without having discovered the underlying architectural law which he sought.

In 1881 he became the second half of Adler and Sullivan, a new architectural firm which soon became the second most sought after practice in Chicago. As his clientele grew, Sullivan became increasingly absorbed with answering the major question facing designers of large buildings: how to provide increased light for such structures and how to raise them to greater heights. Sullivan found his answer in what was called the Chicago School of Architecture, a movement which pioneered the use of iron and steel skeleton frames. Particularly through the Wainwright Building in St. Louis and the Gage Building in Chicago, he illustrated his discovery of the architectural principle which he had so long sought: "Form follows function." Convinced that such a modern form as the skyscraper required a new method of expression, he pointed out the incongruity of clothing such a structure in the classical accoutrements of the past. More than any other man he helped make the skyscraper America's most significant architectural contribution.

§ Open Monday-Friday 10:30-4:30, Tuesday until 8, Saturday 10-5, Sunday and holidays 12-5. Closed December 25. Phone: 312-443-3500.

¶ **Auditorium Building and Theater,** 430 South Michigan Avenue.
Built in 1889 from a design by Dankmar Adler and *Louis Sullivan, this structure originally had 136 offices, 400 hotel rooms, and a 4,200-seat auditorium. At the time of its completion, it was the city's greatest monument. Although its exterior was in the fashionable Romanesque style, its interior marked Sullivan's sharp rejection of the past. The theater's highly foliated interior decoration was an early example of Art Nouveau and of the innovative bent which earned for him the nickname "the Whitman of American architecture."

In 1946 the Auditorium Building was purchased and renovated by Roosevelt University, which maintains a collection of Sullivan memorabilia in the lobby. The theater in the complex has also been restored and was reopened in 1968.

¶ "Big Jim" O'Leary's Saloon, 4183-85 South Halsted Street.

This famous landmark was built in 1906 and was named for "Big Jim" O'Leary, a Chicago gambling king and the son of the famous *Kate O'Leary, whose cow reputedly started the Great Fire of 1871. ("Big Jim" insisted that the fire had been started by some tramps smoking near his parents' barn.) O'Leary's own watering hole was located next door, at 4187 South Halsted. With its maze of secret rooms, it was thought to have been the largest gambling house in Chicago.

¶ Carson, Pirie, Scott & Company Building, State and Madison streets.

Originally built for the Schlesinger & Meyer retail store between 1899 and 1904, this structure was designed by *Louis Sullivan and is one of Chicago's fine clothing stores. The building's rounded entrance and long, horizontal windows reflect Sullivan's penchant for innovation, as does his trademark cast-iron grillwork on the exterior of the first two floors.

§ Open Monday and Thursday 9:45-7:30, and Tuesday, Wednesday, Friday, and Saturday 9:45-5:45.

¶ Chicago Fire Academy, 558 West DeKoven Street, between South Jefferson and West Taylor streets.

The academy's modern brick structure stands on the site of a house and a barn owned by *Patrick O'Leary and Kate O'Leary, whose cow allegedly knocked over the lantern which started the disastrous 1871 fire. In front of the academy is the *Pillar of Fire*, a huge art work of intertwined bronze flames commemorating the blaze.

The fire, which began about 9 o'clock Sunday evening, October 8, ravaged the city until the following Tuesday. In all, a 200-acre swath – covering what is now the Loop, the North Side, Sandburg Village, Old Town, and the Gold Coast – was destroyed. The conflagration left an estimated 200 to 300 people dead, 94,000 more homeless, and almost 16,000 buildings in ruins. Damage from the fire ranged from $175 million to $300 million. More people died in the conditions after the fire than from the flames.

After the conflagration Mrs. O'Leary testified that she and her husband and five children were in bed the night of the fire when they were awakened by *Daniel Sullivan, a neighbor who had spent about an hour at the O'Learys' house earlier that evening. Despite his wooden leg, Sullivan entered the burning barn and untied two of the cows before the intensity of the flames forced him to leave, but not before he caught his wooden leg between two boards. After righting himself, he rescued a calf whose back hair was on fire. By then the fire had spread to the O'Leary house, forty feet from the barn.

When Mrs. O'Leary's husband saw the fire, he led the children into the street and proceeded to throw water on the burning house until one o'clock in the morning. Although he feared that he might be blamed for starting the fire, he said that he wouldn't fault any man in America for hanging him if he had been responsible. His wife was described as "almost crazy on account of losing all her property – a barn, wagons, harness, six cows and a horse . . . ."

§ Open Monday-Friday 4-9 Phone: 312-747-7239.

ℐ Chicago Historical Society, 1601 North Clark Street.

A statue of Abraham Lincoln by *Augustus Saint-Gaudens stands on the lawn. The society's museum contains artifacts and exhibits pertaining to the Great Fire of 1871.

§ Open Monday-Saturday 9:30-4:30, Sunday noon-5. Fee. Phone: 312-642-4600.

ℐ Comiskey Park, 324 West 35th Street.

The nation's oldest major league ballpark was named for *Charles Comiskey, the founder of the American League and the Chicago White Sox.

In 1908 Comiskey paid $15,000 for the park site's original fifteen acres between 34th and 35th Streets and Shields and Wentworth Streets. The White Sox played their first game in Comiskey Park on April 15, 1910.

ℐ Corpus Christi Catholic Church, 49th Street and Dr. Martin Luther King Jr. Drive (formerly Grand Boulevard).

This South Side parish was founded in 1901 to serve the "Gold Coast" Irish who had built mansions along the boulevard. It was here that author James Farrell, the son and grandson of Irish Catholic working-class laborers, was born and raised and went to elementary school. This predominantly Irish neighborhood of Washington Park became the setting for Farrell's short stories and four mammoth fictional cycles that portray the Irish-American experience in Chicago between 1900 and 1930. Farrell's most famous works are the Studs Lonigan trilogy and the O'Neill-O'Flaherty pentalogy (*A World I Never Made, No Star Is Lost, Father and Son, My Days of Anger,* and *The Face of Time*).

ℐ Garfield Park

The park contains two works by the sculptor *Charles Mulligan:
• a statue of Abraham Lincoln as a youthful railsplitter and

• a statue of John Finerty, the Chicago journalist, congressman, and president of the United Irish League of America.

Born in Galway, Ireland, in 1846, John Finerty came to the United States eighteen years later and almost immediately volunteered for the Union army. During a career as a newspaper reporter, he worked for three Chicago journals – the *Republican*, the *Tribune*, and the *Times*. While on the staff of the last publication, he reported the Indian wars, including Custer's campaign against Sitting Bull in 1876. He later served one term in the House of Representatives and was among the Irish who uncharacteristically supported *James G. Blaine, the Republican presidential nominee in 1884. Long active in Irish and Irish-American affairs, he served numerous times as president of the United Irish League of America and the United Irish Societies of Chicago. He was the editor of the *Chicago Citizen* and the author of *Warpath and Bivouac* and *People's History of Ireland*.

Charles Mulligan, meanwhile, left his native County Tyrone, Ireland, at age seventeen to become a stonecutter near Chicago, where he came under the tutelage of the sculptor Lorado Taft. The latter made the young Irishman his assistant in the sculpture department at the Art Institute of Chicago, where his enthusiasm infected the night students there. Even after succeeding Taft as chair of the department, Mulligan continued to carve his own designs rather than give his plaster models to someone else to be rendered in stone. Among his other works are the Illinois Monument (Vicksburg, Miss.); *Home* (Chicago); and statues of George Rogers Clark (Quincy, Ill.), *William McKinley (Chicago), and Abraham Lincoln (Chicago and Pana, Ill.).

¶ **General Sheridan Statue,** Sheridan Road and Belmont Avenue.

In this 1923 equestrian work by Gutzon Borglum, *General Philip Sheridan is depicted on his horse, Rienzi, after leaving Winchester, Virginia, to lead his men against a Confederate force. After the Chicago fire of 1871, Sheridan was placed in charge of keeping order in the city.

¶ **Graceland Cemetery,** North Clark Street and West Irving Park Road.

Among the illustrious Chicagoans who lie buried beneath the cemetery's impressive statues and memorials is *Louis Sullivan, the famed architect and designer of many of the city's buildings. He designed the cemetery's bronze gates as well as the 1890 Getty Tomb, which Frank Lloyd Wright called "a symphony in stone." Sullivan's grave is marked by a monolith erected by the architects and builders of Chicago. The monument is inscribed with the following words: "By his buildings great in influence and power; his drawings unsurpassed in originality and beauty; his writings rich in poetry and prophecy; his teachings persuasive and eloquent; his philosophy where, in 'Form Follows Function,' he summed up all truth in Art, Sullivan has earned his place as one of the greatest architectural forces in America."

¶ **Grant Park,** along Lake Michigan, between Randolph Street and Roosevelt Road.

This sprawling park was named for *Ulysses S. Grant and contains several pieces of art work associated with other Irish Americans:

• the arched entryway of the 1894 Chicago Stock Exchange, built from a design by *Louis Sullivan and standing in the park's reflecting pool,

• a seated statue of Abraham Lincoln by *Augustus Saint-Gaudens, and

• an equestrian statue of John Logan, the famous Illinois lawmaker and Civil War soldier, also by *Saint-Gaudens.

¶ **Haymarket Square,** Desplaines and Randolph streets.

This was the scene of the country's most bloody labor confrontation, coming within the context of widespread agitation for an eight-hour workday.

On May 4, 1886, 2,000 people were in the square listening to labor leaders denounce alleged police brutality. At about 10:30 p.m., a large force of police led by two captains entered the square and ordered the crowd to disperse. When a bomb thrown into the ranks of the police exploded, the officers fired into the crowd, some of whom returned the gunshot. A thirty-four-year-old policeman named *Mathias Degan died almost immediately from loss of blood when a main artery was severed by a bomb fragment. Five other policemen died later of injuries, and fifty to sixty others were injured. During the battle at least two workers died and a dozen more sustained injuries. Besides Degan, four of the slain policemen had Irish names: John Barrett, Timothy Flavin, Thomas Reddin, and Michael Sheehan. Two years later a sixth Irish officer – Timothy Sullivan – died of complications caused by wounds suffered from the Haymarket incident.

¶ **Holy Trinity Orthodox Cathedral,** Leavitt Street and Haddon Avenue.

This Russian Orthodox church was designed by *Louis Sullivan, who decorated the interior with stenciled polychrome patterns and the exterior with geometric trim around the doors, windows, and roof lines.

¶ *Home*, Humboldt Park, Augusta Boulevard and Sacramento Avenue.

This pyramidal sculpture of a miner and his child, at the east end of the park, is the work of *Charles Mulligan.

¶ **International Harvester Company,** in the Equitable Life Assurance Society Building, North Michigan Avenue.

The site on which the Equitable Building stands was where *Cyrus McCormick manufactured the reapers which he had developed from an earlier invention by his father. In 1847 the younger McCormick came to Chicago to establish his enterprise because he believed that Illinois would be both the best market and the best transport center for his invention. In 1902 his son merged the original McCormick Company with several other firms to form the International Harvester Company.

¶ **Irish Castle,** on the northeast corner of 103rd Street and Longwood Avenue.

Constructed in 1886 in imitation of the proverbial Irish turreted castle, this mansion was originally constructed to attract home buyers into the neighborhood. Today the building is the Beverly Unitarian Church.

¶ **Lincoln Park,** along Lake Shore Drive, from North Avenue to Hollywood Avenue.

Two renowned statues of famous Civil War figures are located in this sprawling park:

• *Lincoln Standing Before the Chair of State* at the Dearborn Parkway entrance. This larger than life statue by *Augustus Saint-Gaudens was unveiled in 1887. In sculpting the model for this work, Saint-Gaudens used a life mask of Lincoln created by sculptor Leonard Volk before Lincoln went to Washington. As a boy, Saint-Gaudens had seen Lincoln and had later viewed him in death.

• The *General Grant Statue* on Lake Shore Drive. This equestrian bronze of *Ulysses S. Grant stands on a massive stone arch and was dedicated in 1891.

The bronze statuary group *An Indian Family* by *John Boyle shows a male Indian surrounded by a squaw, a papoose, and their dog. Before he started work on this piece, Boyle lived with Indians for two months in order to learn about their way of life.

¶ *Lincoln, the Orator,* Oak Woods Cemetery, 1035 East 67th Street.

This statue of Lincoln by *Charles Mulligan seems out of place among the 6,000 Confederate soldiers buried here.

¶ **McCormick Place Convention Complex,** East 23rd Street and South Lake Shore Drive.

This massive convention and exposition center was completed in 1970 on the site of an earlier such structure destroyed by fire. Both buildings were named for *Robert McCormick (1880-1955), the editor and publisher of the *Chicago Tribune*.

A grandnephew of the famous inventor *Cyrus McCormick, Robert R. McCormick was a spokesman for Midwestern conservatism during the 1940s, a strong opponent of Franklin Roosevelt, and a leader in the isolationist movement prior to World War II. Under his management the *Tribune* led the nation in nontabloid circulation and the world in advertising revenues.

¶ **McCormick Theological Seminary,** 800 West Belden Avenue.

Founded by inventor *Cyrus McCormick, a devout Presbyterian and church leader, this theological institution is directed by the General Assembly of the United Presbyterian Church, U.S.A. Despite its Presbyterian affiliation, the seminary prepares students for the Christian ministry without regard to denomination.

¶ **McKinley Statue,** McKinley Park.

Dedicated in 1905, this statue of *President William McKinley was sculpted by *Charles Mulligan and was cast from a bronze statue of Columbus that once stood in Lincoln Park.

¶ **Newberry Library,** Clark, Walton, and Dearborn streets.

The library owns thirty-four portraits of famous Americans by *George Healy, among them paintings of Pierre Beauregard, *Ulysses S. Grant, Abraham Lincoln, *Philip Sheridan, and William Sherman.

¶ **O'Hare International Airport,** 17 miles northwest of the Loop, at Mannheim Road and Kennedy Expressway.

One of the world's busiest airports was named for *Edward "Butch" O'Hare. In 1942 this graduate of the U.S. Naval Academy was a naval aviator aboard the *Lexington* when the carrier was attacked by Japanese bombers. Single-handedly he shot down five of the nine incoming planes and damaged three others. For his bravery he was promoted to lieutenant commander and awarded the Medal of Honor. By the time he was listed as missing in action at the end of 1943, he had downed a total of twelve Japanese bombers.

Although O'Hare's father – *"Artful Eddie" O'Hare – ran Al Capone's dog track in Cicero, Illinois, he was responsible for helping bring the Chicago gangster to justice. After Capone tried to bribe the jurors in his income tax evasion trial, O'Hare informed the federal court. O'Hare was gunned down many years later, not long after Capone's release from prison.

¶ **Police Training Academy,** 1300 West Jackson.

Inside the atrium of the academy stands the Haymarket Monument,

The Haymarket Monument.
(Photo courtesy of the
Chicago Police Department.)

a statue modeled after an Irish policeman and dedicated to the eight
police officers – six of them Irish – who died as the result of violence
which erupted in Haymarket Square on May 4, 1886.

The bronze statue depicts a police officer with his right hand raised,
a stance like that of Captain William Ward when, just before the bomb
blast, he called out to the crowd, "In the name of the people in the State
of Illinois, I command this meeting immediately and peaceably to disperse." The pedestal is inscribed with the words "The Law is Common
Sense," taken from the remarks of Judge Joseph Gary when he sentenced eight alleged anarchists for the deaths of those killed in the
Haymarket Riot. The statue was originally unveiled in 1889 in Union
Park, where it stood for more than fifty years. After being twice damaged by bombs in the 1960s, the statue was placed in storage until it
was reinstalled here in 1976 in the presence of *Mayor Richard Daley.

§ Phone: 312-746-8310.

¶ Richard J. Daley Center and Plaza, Randolph and Clark streets.

Named in honor of Chicago's last machine boss, this 31-story, 648-
foot building houses city and county offices and civil courts. An eternal flame in Hiz Honor's memory burns in the neighboring plaza.

Richard Daley was born in 1902 in the predominantly Irish area of

Bridgeport on Chicago's South Side. Although he began working for the local Democratic political organization when he was only twelve, he won his first elective office as a write-in Republican. After switching parties, he continued his climb up the political ladder as state senator, chairman of the Cook County Democratic Central Committee, and finally mayor of Chicago from 1955 until his death in 1976. His power seemed almost complete when, in the last year of his tenure, the city council gave him virtual control over 40,000 government jobs when it voted to abolish the city's civil service commission.

Although Daley's administration was known for revitalizing the city, it suffered some serious embarrassments. In response to charges of political corruption, the mayor alluded to Christ's betrayal by one of his disciples: "If our Lord couldn't have perfection, how are we going to have it in city government?" During the rioting which rocked the city following the assassination of Martin Luther King Jr. in 1968, Daley created additional controversy by his shoot-to-kill order against arsonists. Later that year he drew national attention when his police force was involved in what was later called "a police riot" against demonstrators during the Democratic National Convention. Daley emphatically defended his officers, calling the demonstrators a "lawless, violent group of terrorists." To later charges that he abused his authority while in office, Daley replied: "I don't think I am a powerful man. I'm just an ordinary mayor of an ordinary city. I'm trying to do an ordinary job."

¶ **St. Patrick's Church,** 700 West Adams Street.

The original St. Patrick's church on this site was erected in 1846. The present Romanesque revival structure was completed in 1856 by working-class Irish in the neighborhood. The pastor at the time was Father Dennis Dunne, a native of County Laois and the uncle of Irish-American humorist Finley Peter Dunne. Although the area surrounding the church was destroyed in the Great Fire of 1871, St. Patrick's was spared.

The church's two towers – one Byzantine and the other Gothic – represent the different ethnic groups in the parish community. The stained-glass windows in the nave depict the most important Irish saints and are the work of *Thomas O'Shaughnessy. The church also contains his stained-glass work of 150,000 pieces honoring Terence MacSwiney, the mayor of Cork, who died in 1920 while on a hunger strike.

The church is located in what was once the predominantly Irish neighborhood of Bridgetown, where Finley Peter Dunne was born to Irish immigrants. In 1884 the sixteen-year-old Dunne began a newspaper career that saw him work for six of the city's newspapers, first as a police and sports reporter, then as a features and editorial writer, and finally as managing editor of the *Post*. In 1890 he created the first of three Irish characters whom he used as vehicles for satire or political commentary in his columns: Colonel Thomas Jefferson Dolan; Colonel Malachi McNeery, based on the pensive real-life saloon keeper James McGarry; and Martin Dooley, the more famous derivative of the previous character.

In more than 300 weekly columns, Finley Peter Dunne used Mr. Dooley to recreate what Charles Fanning called "the first fully realized Irish ethnic neighborhood in American literature." Although on many occasions Dooley waxes nostalgic about the Great Famine and the hardships of immigration and assimilation, he also dispenses insight into the Irish character and the human condition. After opining, for example, that "f'r an impetchoos an' darin' people th' Irish is th' mos' cowardly whin it comes to mathrimony that iver I heerd tell iv," Dooley cites "Dacey th' plumber, who'd niver 'v married if he hadn't got into th' wrong buildin' whin he wint to take out a license f'r his dog, an' got a marriage license instid." Other Dooley pieces illustrate the gap between the immigrants and their more Americanized children: After scandalizing the neighborhood by wearing bloomers while riding a bicycle, Molly Donahue is sent off to confession, where she receives "a pinance th' like iv which ain't been knowed in Bridgeport since Cassidy said Charles Stewart Parnell was a bigger man thin th' pope." Dunne received national attention with the publication of *Mr. Dooley in Peace and War* and *Mr. Dooley in the Hearts of His Countrymen*, which were followed by five other volumes. One of Dooley's observations was about Thanksgiving: "'Twas founded be th' Puritans to give thanks f'r bein' presarved fr'm th' Indians, and . . . we [Irish] keep it to give thanks we are presarved fr'm th' Puritans."

¶ St. Stanislaus Church, 1351 West Evergreen Ave.

This neo-Renaissance house of worship was designed by Patrick Keely and was completed in 1881 to serve a predominantly Polish parish.

Born in Kilkenny, Ireland, Keely was apparently trained by his architect father before immigrating to the United States and settling with other Irish newcomers near the Brooklyn Navy Yard. As he perfected his craft, he employed several styles: English Gothic at first, and Romanesque and Second Empire later. During a career that lasted more than four decades, Keely was the dominant figure in the field of Roman Catholic architecture in North America, designing sixteen cathedrals and an estimated 500 to 600 other churches (although explicit documentation has been found for only about 150). Among his more famous works are the Catholic cathedrals of Boston and Chicago. If his design for a Catholic cathedral in Brooklyn had been carried out, that church would have been larger than St. Patrick's in Manhattan.

DIXON

J Ronald Reagan Boyhood Home, 816 South Hennepin Avenue.

From 1920 to 1923, this two-story white frame house was the residence of young *Ronald Reagan, his older brother, and his parents. This was the first of five houses which the parents of the future president rented in Dixon between 1920 and 1939. The house features family memorabilia and a ten-minute film about Reagan's early life and later career. The president was born in nearby Tampico.

Although Reagan's father, Jack, never achieved his dream of own-

Statue of Ronald Reagan.
(Photo courtesy of the
Ronald Reagan Boyhood Home
Preservation Foundation.)

ing his own shoe store, he taught his son the importance of tolerance. The son enjoyed telling the story of how his father refused to stay in a hotel when he learned that it did not accept Jews. Before angrily leaving the hotel and spending the night instead in his car, the elder Reagan retorted that the managers probably did not like Catholics either.

§ Open March-November 31, Monday-Saturday 10-5, Sunday and holidays 1-4; December-February 28, Saturday 10-4, Sunday 1-4. Closed January 1, Easter, Thanksgiving, and December 25. Phone: 815-288-3404. A visitor center is located at 810 South Hennepin Avenue.

¶ An eight-foot-high bronze statue of President Reagan stands in a park south of his boyhood home. The statue was erected in 1988 and depicts the former president holding kernels of corn in his hand – a reminder of Illinois' agricultural production.

¶ A bronze plaque at the Loveland Community Building commemorates the fact that young Ronald Reagan saved seventy-seven lives during the seven years he was a lifeguard at Lowell Park.

EQUALITY

¶ **General Lawler Monument,** Calhoun Street.
This memorial honors Michael Kelly Lawler, a native of County Kildare, Ireland, who served in both the Mexican War and the Civil War. During the former conflict he was a cavalry captain, an experience which served him well when he raised the 18th Illinois Infantry at the beginning of the Civil War. Wounded at the battle of Fort Donelson, he led the attack on Vicksburg and was brevetted major general after the war. Before returning to his farm in Illinois, he followed a career as a horse trader in the South. He is buried in Hickory Hill Cemetery, two miles east on State 13.

GALENA

¶ **First Grant House,** 121 High Street. Private.
In 1860 *Ulysses S. Grant arrived from St. Louis with his wife and four children to take up residence in this brick cottage. When the Civil War broke out, this future commander of the Union army drilled recruits in Galena. Within seventeen months he was named colonel of the 21st Illinois Volunteer Regiment and brigadier general in command of the military post at Cairo, Illinois.

¶ **Galena Historical Society,** 211.5 Bench Street.
Among the items in the society's museum is Thomas Nast's life-size painting of General Lee's surrender to *Ulysses S. Grant at

Appomattox. One of the officers depicted on the canvas is *General John Rawlins, Grant's aide-de-camp during the Civil War. Rawlins, who was of Scotch-Irish descent, had been a lawyer in Galena prior to the war. He later served as Grant's secretary of war.

¶ **Grant Home State Historic Site,** 510 Bouthillier Street.

After the Civil War this two-story brick Italianate house was given to *General Ulysses S. Grant by the citizens of Galena. The former Union commander and his family lived here until 1867, when he moved to Washington, D.C., to become secretary of war for *President Andrew Johnson. He returned to the house in 1879, after two terms as president and a two-year tour of the world. He left Galena for New York City in 1881.

Besides family possessions, the house displays silver and china used in the White House while Grant was president.

§ Open April-December 31, daily 9-5; rest of the year, Thursday-Monday 9-5. Closed major holidays. Phone: 815-777-0248.

¶ **Grant Park,** on the east bank of the Galena River, via the Johnson Street Bridge.

In the park stands the statue *Grant, Our Citizen*, a memorial to *Ulysses S. Grant donated by a Chicago newspaper editor.

¶ **J. R. Grant Leather Store Site,** 120 South Main Street.

A plaque marks the site of the leather goods shop owned by *Jesse Grant, the father of the famous Civil War commander. In 1860 the younger Grant came to Galena with his family in order to work in his father's store.

• A reconstruction of a leather store of the period is located at 211 South Main Street.

¶ **Rawlins House,** 511 Hill Street. Private.

This was the home of *General John Rawlins, aide-de-camp to *General Ulysses S. Grant during the Civil War.

¶ **Vinegar Hill Lead Mine and Museum,** 6 miles north on State 84, at 8885 North Three Pines Road.

This bitterly named mine was discovered in 1824 by *John Furlong, who christened it for the site of a skirmish against the British garrison in Wexford, Ireland, in 1798. Furlong, who had participated in the ill-fated battle, was captured by the British and impressed into military service before being sent to Canada. While there, he heard about Julien Dubuque's excursions into this part of Illinois in search of lead.

Following his escape from the British army, Furlong lived in this area for several years and purchased property in Galena soon after Illinois achieved statehood. Six years later he and three friends struck a rich vein of lead ore in what is now Vinegar Hill. Furlong's descendants worked the mine until 1934. His great-great-grandson opened the mine to tourists in 1967. Today Mark Furlong, the discover's third-great-grandson, welcomes visitors to the mine.

§ Open June-August 31, daily 9-5; May, September, and October, Saturday and Sunday 9-5. Fee. Phone: 815-777-0855.

¶ Although a nearby Catholic church attended by early Irish settlers no longer exists, its cemetery contains the remains of many of those pioneers.

GLENVIEW

¶ **Theodore Roosevelt Memorial,** Glenview Country Club.

Known locally as the *Boy Scout Fountain*, this memorial honors *President Theodore Roosevelt for his support of the Scouting movement and its ideals. The monument, which consists of a reflecting pool, a fountain, and a bronze statuary group of four Boy Scouts, was designed by *Andrew O'Connor. The statues of the four boys were modeled from the artist's sons.

At the dedication of the memorial on July 4, 1919, one of the speakers offered his interpretation of the memorial's emphasis on nature: "The water in the fountain is a symbol of purity. A Scout is clean. This water rushes to serve freely those who thirst. A Scout is friendly and courteous and helpful. To this fountain little birds are coming already to drink and bathe and preen their plumage. A Scout is kind to animals. And as it catches the rays of the sun and makes a joyful noise on summer days this water will remind us that a Scout is cheerful."

HIGHWOOD

¶ **Fort Sheridan,** north on Sheridan Road.

Now a 725-acre U.S. Army post, the fort is located where military troops called to Chicago after the Haymarket Riot in 1886 encamped. The following year the camp was named for *General Philip Sheridan, the famous Civil War officer who had earned a reputation for maintaining order after the Chicago fire of 1871.

LINCOLN

¶ **Museum of the Presidents,** Lincoln College, 300 Keokuk.

The museum, located in the McKinstry Memorial Library, displays documents signed by every U.S. president, including, of course, the fourteen of Irish ancestry.

§ Open Monday-Friday 10-12 and 1-4:30, Saturday and Sunday 1-4:30.

MOUNT OLIVE

¶ **Mother Jones Burial Site,** United Miners' Cemetery, North Lake Street.

In 1936 a granite shaft was erected over the grave of Mary Harris "Mother" Jones, who wished to be buried here among the miners for whose cause she had struggled for more than fifty years as a labor organizer and agitator.

After emigrating from Cork, Ireland, where she was born in 1830, she first lived in Canada, where she received her formal education. Later, while teaching school in Memphis, Tennessee, she married an ironworker named Jones. Following his death and the deaths of their four children during a yellow fever epidemic, she returned to Chicago. Tragedy struck another blow when her possessions were destroyed in the Great Fire of 1871.

> After joining the Knights of Labor, Jones spent the rest of her life in the cause of labor and the struggle against social injustice. Almost forty years later, in testimony before a congressional committee, she expressed her life's mission: "wherever a fight is on against wrong, I am always there" – in Pittsburgh during the labor riots of 1877; in Chicago during the Haymarket strike of 1886; in Birmingham during the railroad strike of 1894; in Virginia, West Virginia, and Colorado during various coal strikes between 1900 and 1913; and in New York during the street car strike of 1915-16. A West Virginia prosecutor described her as the "most dangerous woman in America," at whose arrival "20,000 contented men lay down their tools and walk out."

Jones was known for both her fiery speech and her sense of the dramatic. On one occasion she organized the striking miners' wives into a "women's army" that scared off scabs with brooms and mops. Addressing strikers in Charleston, West Virginia, in 1912, she condemned the governor for not meeting with them ("You can expect no help from such a goddamned dirty coward") and warned that if the company's security "thugs" were not dismissed, "there is going to be one hell of a lot of bloodletting in these hills." During a period of martial law in West Virginia, she was arrested and sentenced to twenty years in prison for conspiracy to commit murder. Following a congressional investigation, however, she was soon released.

Mother Jones's most dramatic effort, however, was one to build support for a federal child-labor law. In 1903 she led a march of striking Philadelphia mill workers to the home of *President Theodore Roosevelt in Oyster Bay, Long Island. Although almost all the workers soon dropped out of the 125-mile trek, Jones continued to play to the press. At Princeton University, when a professor asked her to address one of his classes, she arrived with a stooped ten-year-old boy: "Here's a text book on economics. He gets three dollars a week and his sister who is fourteen gets six dollars. They work in a carpet factory ten hours a day while the children of the rich are getting their higher education." In Paterson she said about Roosevelt: "I am going to find out if he is the President of the capitalists only or whether he is the President of the workingman, too. If he is the President of the capitalists only, he will be wiped out at the next election." When the six remaining marchers – including three children – finally arrived at Oyster Bay, they were refused admission and informed by Roosevelt that child-labor legislation was a state responsibility rather than a federal one. Jones responded with her usual intensity: "He is a brave guy when he wants to take a gun and fight other grown people, but when those children went to him he would not see them."

PANA

§ **Abraham Lincoln Statue,** Rosemont Grove Cemetery.

This bronze statue of the martyred president was designed by *Charles Mulligan.

PEORIA

§ **John Flanagan House,** 942 Northeast Glen Oak Avenue.

Now the headquarters of the Peoria Historical Society, this 1837 Federalist and Italianate structure was the home of Judge John Flanagan, an early settler in the community. The house, Peoria's oldest standing residence, displays antique tools and toys and decorative arts and textiles.

Born in Philadelphia in 1806 to John and Jane Flanagan, the future judge studied and practiced law in that city until 1830, when he moved to Pottsville, Pennsylvania. There he combined his legal profession with a commercial enterprise dealing in coal. Flanagan first came to the Peoria region that year to settle his father's estate, which included 650 acres of land which the older man had acquired from local Indians six years before. By the end of 1837, John Flanagan had brought his mother and other family members to his newly acquired property in Peoria County, where he built this house for himself and his family on a bluff over-looking Lake Peoria. He subsequently developed his property in East Bluff. As a Peoria alderman he used his influence to secure the construction of a canal to drain that section of the city.

§ Open Monday-Friday 10-3. Fee. Phone: 309-674-1921.

QUINCY

¶ **George Rogers Clark Statue,** Riverview Park, Chestnut and 2nd streets.

This statue of the famous Revolutionary War soldier was designed by *Charles Mulligan while he was the director of sculpture at the Art Institute of Chicago.

¶ **Governor John Wood Mansion,** 425 South 12th Street.

Built in 1835 by John Wood, this twelve-room frame house is the headquarters of the Historical Society of Quincy and Adams County.

Wood was born in New York in 1798, the grandson of Timothy Wood of Longford, Ireland, and the son of a surgeon and captain during the Revolutionary War. After heading west in 1818, he formed a partner-ship to raise livestock thirty miles southeast of what is now Quincy. He later bought land in this area and with the help of Irishmen Peter Flynn and James Moffatt erected a log cabin in present-day Quincy, the first white man's house in this part of the state.

Wood subsequently enjoyed a sixty-year career as the town's fore-most leader, serving multiple terms as town trustee, alderman, and mayor and helping defeat a new state constitution that would have allowed settlers to bring their slaves into Illinois. From 1850 to 1854 he represented the district as a Whig in the state senate, and in 1856 he was elected lieutenant governor, succeeding to the governorship at the death of its incumbent three years later.

When a "peace convention" was held in Washington, D.C., in Feb-ruary 1861 in an effort to prevent the oncoming civil war, Wood was one of five delegates appointed by the governor. When war finally came, Wood was named quartermaster of the state and at age sixty-six was commissioned colonel of the 137th Illinois Volunteer Regiment. Dur-ing General Nathan Forest's raid on Memphis, Wood commanded a brigade at the front.

¶ A monument marks Wood's grave in Woodland Cemetery on South 5th Street.

¶ **Governor Wood Statue,** Washington Park.

This bronze statue of *John Wood, one of the founders of Quincy, was erected by the city and was unveiled on July 4, 1883.

SALEM

¶ **William J. Bryan Birthplace,** 408 South Broadway.

The "Great Commoner" – *William Jennings Bryan – was born in this house in 1860 and lived here until he was nineteen, when he left to attend Illinois College in Jacksonville. His first Scotch-Irish ancestor to reach America was William Smith Bryan, who settled in the foothills of the Blue Ridge Mountains in Virginia in 1650.

As a youngster William Jennings Bryan faced a religious dilemma: whether to join his father's Baptist church or his mother's Methodist congregation. Although he compromised by attending one church on Sunday morning and the other in the afternoon, he was later converted to Presbyterianism. By his own account, however, this conversion was not the *metanoia* one would expect: "Having been brought up in a Christian home, conversion did not mean a change in my habits of life or habits of thought. I do not know of a virtue that came into my life as a result of my joining the Church because all the virtues had been taught me by my parents."

Among the exhibits in the house are first editions of Bryan's books, his Spanish-American War uniform, and souvenirs of the 1896 Democratic Convention, at which he delivered his famous "Cross of Gold" speech.

§ Open daily except Tuesday. Closed holidays. Phone: 618-548-7791.

¶ **William J. Bryan Memorial Park,** north on State 37.

At the entrance to the park is a statue of *William Jennings Bryan by Gutzon Borglum.

At a dinner hosted in Bryan's honor by the mayor of Dublin in 1913, someone asked the famous American when he had dropped the "O" from his name. Bryan replied by asking the members of the audience whether they had ever heard of an O'Brian prior to the eleventh-century Irish king Brian Boru. When no one offered an answer, Bryan explained that "Bryan" had been the original name and that the "O" had been *added* by others, not eliminated by his ancestors.

SPRINGFIELD

¶ **State Capitol,** Capitol Street, between Spring and Second streets.

On the capitol grounds are the statues of five distinguished citizens of Illinois. The statue of Lincoln in front of a granite slab inscribed

Statue of Abraham Lincoln
by Andrew O'Connor,
on the grounds
of the Illinois state capitol.

with his farewell speech to the people of Springfield is the work of *Andrew O'Connor and was unveiled in 1918. The statue of Pierre Menard, the state's first lieutenant governor, was designed by *John Mahoney.

Inside the capitol are statues of *Governor John Wood, Chicago mayor *Richard Daley, and *David E. Shanahan. The last politician was a member of the Illinois House of Representatives from 1894 to 1936, the final sixteen years as Speaker.

TAMPICO

⚑ Ronald Reagan Birthplace, 111 Main Street.

President Ronald Reagan was born in this apartment above a bakery on February 6, 1911. Nine years later his father, John Edward Reagan, moved his family to Dixon, Illinois.

President Reagan's paternal line came from Ballyporeen, County Tipperary, Ireland. In 1847 his great-grandfather, Michael O'Regan, immigrated to London, where he married Catherine Mulcahy and adopted the present spelling of the family name. The couple moved to Canada with their sons in 1858 and later took up farming near Fairhaven, Illinois.

In 1984, when Ronald Reagan visited Ballyporeen, he was shown his great-grandfather's 1829 baptismal record, hoisted a pint in a pub named for the president, and learned that he was distantly related to *John F. Kennedy and Queen Elizabeth II.

§ Open Memorial Day-Labor Day, daily 10-12 and 1-4. Phone: 815-438-2815.

TROY GROVE

¶ "Wild Bill" Hickok State Monument, 1 block from U.S. 52.

Erected in 1929, this memorial commemorates the famous scout and lawman James Hickok, who was born here in 1837, the grandson of an Irish immigrant who had fought at Plattsburgh during the War of 1812.

Even as a youth "Wild Bill" Hickok was considered the best shot in this part of Illinois. At eighteen he headed for Kansas, where he joined the paramilitary forces intent upon bringing the territory into the Union as a free state and where he briefly served as a lawman. His first job as a stagecoach driver on the Santa Fe Trail was short lived, however, after he was attacked by a bear. Although he killed his attacker with a bowie knife, Hickok was injured so severely that he was not expected to recover. The young adventurer defied the odds, though, and recovered enough to work for the Overland Stage on the Oregon Trail. While in Nebraska in 1861, he was almost killed again, this time in a gunfight with the McCanles Gang.

With the outbreak of the Civil War, Hickok began his varied career as scout and lawman. During the war itself he served as a Union scout and was several times captured and sentenced to death as a spy but invariably escaped. After the hostilities he served as a scout and Indian fighter on the frontier for generals *Philip Sheridan, Winfield Scott Hancock, and George Custer. As deputy U.S. marshal at Fort Riley, Kansas, he was responsible for enforcing the law over a 200,000-square-mile territory. Although he killed many outlaws and recovered hundreds of stolen horses and mules, he never killed anyone except in self-defense or in the execution of his duties. His most famous act of self-defense occurred when he killed Phil Coe, the owner of a saloon and gambling house in Abilene, Kansas, where Hickok was the marshal. Although the lawman followed more peaceful pursuits for a while – touring with *"Buffalo Bill" Cody and his troupe – he returned to the Wild West, this time to Deadwood City, North Dakota, where he was killed by Jack McCall. Hickok is buried in Mount Moriah Cemetery in Deadwood City.

WHEATON

¶ Cantigny, 3 miles west on Roosevelt Road (State 38) and then south on Winfield Road.

This 500-acre estate was formerly the property of *Colonel Robert McCormick, the editor and publisher of the *Chicago Tribune*. Two museums are located on the property:

The First Division Museum honors U.S. military veterans, including those in the First Infantry Division (of which McCormick was a member during World War I).

The Robert R. McCormick Museum is the restored Georgian home of the colonel and his grandfather, an earlier owner of the *Tribune*.

§ Grounds open daily 9-dusk. Museums open Memorial Day-Labor Day, Tuesday-Sunday 10-5; February, Friday and Sunday 10-4; rest of the year (except January), Tuesday-Sunday 10-4. Closed Thanksgiving and December 25. Parking fee. Phone: 708-668-5161.

INDIANA

BUTLERVILLE

℈ Hannah Milhous Plaque, on the south side of U.S. 50, on the east side of town.

This plaque was dedicated in 1971 by President Richard Milhous Nixon in honor of his mother, Hannah Milhous. The president's mother was a descendant of Thomas Milhous and his wife, Quakers who had come to America in 1729 from Carrickfergus, County Antrim, Ireland.

President Nixon's mother was born in 1855 on a farm near Butlerville, in a large frame house that was destroyed by fire in 1968. When Hannah Milhous was twelve years old, her family moved to Whittier, California, the Quaker colony where her son Richard was born in 1913.

When President Nixon and his wife visited Ireland in 1970, they had mixed results when it came to meeting family relations. Although officials found and introduced the First Lady (née Patricia Ryan) to purported cousins, they failed to find a single Milhous. As a result, when the president was taken to Timahoe, a village northwest of Dublin, where his fifth-great-grandfather had once lived, he had to content himself with a visit to the Quaker cemetery where that ancestor was buried. Even that visit was anticlimactic, however, because the burial ground contained no individual grave markers but only a large slab with a list of those who were buried there. Nixon's dog at the time – an Irish setter called Timahoe – was named for the president's ancestral home.

℈ Hopewell Cemetery, 1 mile past the Baptist Church at the west end of town.

This quaint cemetery is the final resting place of many members of the Milhous family, the maternal ancestors of *President Richard Nixon.

CONNERSVILLE

℈ John Conner Trading Post Site, indicated by a marker in front of the Moose Lodge on Eastern Avenue.

This town of about 18,000 residents grew up around the trading post established here in 1808 by John Conner. Conner's paternal grandfather was one of three brothers who had immigrated to America from County Meath, Ireland. His father, Richard Conner, was probably born in 1718 and lived in Maryland before moving to the Ohio territory. After marrying Margaret Boyer, a white woman who had grown up among the Shawnee, Richard Conner and his wife took up residence among the Christian Delaware Indians at one of the Moravian missions in Ohio. The Conners' children were born and grew up at these Indian settlements in Ohio and Michigan.

Sometime before 1800 John headed west for Indian country in what is now Indiana, where he established himself as a fur trader. During the War of 1812, he served as a guide and an interpreter for General William Henry Harrison. (Many years later Conner's granddaughter recounted how he once disguised himself as Chief Tecumseh at an Indian council. As Conner prepared and smoked a pipe and handed it to the nearest chief, however, another elder recognized the imposter and exclaimed, "You no Tecumseh – you big John Conner.") Following the incorporation of Connersville in 1813, Conner was its first sheriff and the owner of most of its first commercial ventures: a gristmill, a sawmill, a tavern, a general store, and a distillery. He also owned two farms and two town lots in Noblesville, Indiana. After his death these enterprises were maintained by his brother William.

CRAWFORDSVILLE

¶ **Lew Wallace Study,** Wallace Avenue and East Pike Street.

On the property is a bronze statue of the Civil War general Lew Wallace by *Andrew O'Connor, a replica of the artist's marble work in the rotunda of the U.S. Capitol.

It was here that Wallace wrote *Ben Hur* following his return in 1885 from Turkey, where he had served as U.S. minister. Wallace's career as lawyer, state senator, military leader, and scholar are traced through various memorabilia on display.

§ Open April-October 31, Wednesday-Saturday 10-4:30, Tuesday and Sunday 1-4:30. Fee. Phone: 317-362-5769.

¶ **R. R. Donnelley and Sons Company,** John Sloan Street.

Since 1941 this factory in Crawfordsville has been the book manufacturing center of the nation's largest supplier of commercial printing services. This plant and another nearby handle the production of such world famous publications as *World Book Encyclopedia*, *World Book*, *The Holy Bible*, *Reader's Digest Books*, and *Time-Life Books*.

The history of Donnelley and Sons began with Richard R. Donnelley, a native of Ontario, Canada, whose parents had emigrated from northern Ireland. After serving an apprenticeship in the printing trade, the young Donnelley in 1857 accepted a managerial position with a New Orleans newspaper. Seven years later he became the managing partner of a printing firm in Chicago, which was subsequently purchased by a group of Chicago investors who hoped to create a publishing house capable of luring the western trade from the large eastern firms. The resulting merger was known as the Lakeside Publishing & Printing Co. As the firm's new building neared completion in the Windy City, however, the structure and most of its equipment were destroyed in the Great Fire of 1871. Donnelley immediately became one of the most active leaders in the city's relief effort, obtaining permission from *General Philip Sheridan to share army rations with the city's dispossessed.

Donnelley was equally timely in finding quarters for a new printing office and headed for New York to obtain the needed heavy equipment. Upon his return he superintended the operation of his own fledgling concern while successfully reviving the Lakeside Company's fortunes, until in 1873 the two businesses were merged. The resulting giant went on to print twenty-three periodicals as well as telephone directories for various municipalities.

When Donnelley acquired complete control of the enterprise, he brought his sons into partnership with him, a move that resulted in the company's current name. By the time of his death in 1899, the family business had become the largest commercial printing and binding operation in the United States. The Lakeside Press, the company's corporate headquarters in Chicago, today prints such national magazines as *Fortune, Life,* and *Time.*

FORT WAYNE

¶ **Anthony Wayne Monument,** on the northwest corner of Hayden Park, at Harmar Street and Maumee Avenue.

This heroic-size equestrian statue of *Anthony Wayne, the Revolutionary War general, was sculpted by *Charles Mulligan and was dedicated in 1918. Wayne established the first American fort in the area in 1794 after defeating the Miami Indians.

¶ **Historic Fort Wayne,** 211 South Barr Street.

This is a replica of the fort constructed in 1815-16 by *Major John Whistler. The fort replaced an earlier one which had been saved from a siege by the Shawnee chief Tecumseh in 1812. For guidance in constructing the replica, historians and architects consulted Whistler's diagram of the fort. The four-acre site, which includes the Old Fort and the adjacent Frontier Village, features eleven wooden structures. Among those in the stockade are barracks, officers' quarters, and a hospital.

Whistler was born in northern Ireland about 1756 and as a youngster ran away from home to join the British army. During the American Revolution, he served under General John Burgoyne and was captured at the battle of Saratoga. After the war he returned to America and joined the U.S. army. In 1791 he was severely wounded in a campaign against the Indians. A dozen years later he and his infantry company were sent to the southern shore of Lake Michigan, where they constructed Fort Dearborn.

§ Open Memorial Day-October 31, Friday-Sunday 10-5. Fee. Phone: 219-424-3476.

INDIANAPOLIS

One of the city's ethnic enclaves was Irish Hill, a community that grew up near the Kingan and Company slaughterhouse, opened in 1862 by Samuel Kingan and Thomas Kingan, brothers from Belfast, Ireland. They were among the first to introduce mechanical refrigeration in the processing and preserving of meat on a large scale. So confident were Irish immigrants that they would find work at Kingan's that they addressed their steamer trunks to the packing plant and simply arrived there for work. The plant remained in the Kingan family until it was sold to the Hygrade Food Products Corporation in 1952.

¶ Crown Hill Cemetery, 3402 Boulevard Place.

Among the well known figures buried here are *President Benjamin Harrison, three U.S. vice presidents, the gunman John Dillinger, and the poet James Whitcomb Riley (who mistakenly thought he was of Irish descent).

¶ Benjamin Harrison House, 1230 North Delaware, 1 mile north of Washington Street (U.S. 40).

Except for his terms as a U.S. senator and as president of the United States, *Benjamin Harrison lived in this house from 1874 until his death in 1901. The sixteen-room house contains his library, White House desk, hand-carved bed, and baby crib.

Harrison had come to Indianapolis in 1854 to practice law, a profession to which he returned after his defeat by *Grover Cleveland in the presidential race of 1892. Harrison's mother was descended from Archibald Irwin and William McDowell of Franklin County, Pennsylvania, both of whom were almost certainly from northern Ireland.

§ Open February-December 31, Monday-Saturday 10-3:30, Sunday 12:30-3:30. Closed major holidays except the Fourth of July. Fee. Phone: 317-631-1898.

¶ General Lawton Statue, Garfield Park, Raymond Street and Southern Avenue.

This bronze statue of General Henry W. Lawton, a casualty of the Spanish-American War, was sculpted by Daniel Chester French and *Andrew O'Connor. The heroic figure was completed in Paris and depicts its subject carrying a shield.

¶ **State Capitol,** between Capitol Avenue, Washington Street, Senate Avenue, and Ohio Street.

The eight colossal marble allegorical figures in the rotunda were sculpted by *Alexander Doyle.

§ Open Monday-Friday 9-3. Phone: 317-233-5293.

LAFAYETTE

¶ **Fort Ouiatenon Historical Park,** South River Road.

This twenty-acre park on the Wabash River was created in the 1920s on what was thought to be the site of a French fort. (A replica of a French blockhouse marks the site.) From 1717 to 1760 the fort was an important fur-trading post inhabited by up to 2,000 people. The British later garrisoned the fort when Chief Pontiac unsuccessfully tried to force back white settlement after the French and Indian War. In 1765 Pontiac ended his war against the British in negotiations at the fort with Indian agent George Croghan. The chief symbolized his pacific intentions by hurling his tomahawk to the ground, a gesture that gave rise to the phrase "bury the hatchet."

After leaving his native Dublin, Ireland, Croghan had settled in western Pennsylvania in the 1740s and had begun to establish trading posts throughout the upper Ohio Valley. Because of his knowledge of the Iroquois and Delaware languages and customs, he was made deputy superintendent of Indian affairs by *Sir William Johnson, Britain's chief Indian agent in the region. Once, while trying to open up the Illinois country to white settlement, Croghan was attacked by Indians. He took the tomahawking he received in stride, however: "I got the stroke of a Hatchet on the Head, but my skull being pretty thick, the hatchet would not enter, so you may see a thick skull is of service on some occasions."

In 1764 Croghan was in London, seeking reimbursement for financial losses which he and other traders had experienced during the previous decade. Despite its amusing misspellings, the letter which he wrote from there to Johnson reflects its author's disillusionment with the English Establishment: "[T]he Cheefe Study of the pople in power hear att present is To Lay Heavy Taxes on the Coloneys and tis Talkt of Laying an Internal Tax on them Next Cesion of parlament. . . . The pople hear spend thire Time on Nothing Butt abuseing one aNother & Striving who Shall be in power with a view to Serve themselves and thire frends, and Neglect the publick. . . . Was I to Spake My Mind I wold say they are all R-g-e-s (Rogues) aLike."

Like Johnson, Croghan was prominently involved in the formation of various land speculation companies. Early in his career he acquired and sold several thousand acres around Carlisle, Pennsylvania, before obtaining large tracts of land near Pittsburgh and another 250,000 acres in central New York. His most promising association appeared to be with the Grand Ohio Company, which hoped to establish Vandalia, south of the Ohio River, as the fourteenth British colony. The promise of his vast land holdings came to naught, however, with the outbreak of the Revolution, and he died in poverty.

• During the Feast of the Hunters' Moon in late September and early October, the local residents reenact the historic gathering of traders, frontiersmen, soldiers, and Indians at the fort in the mid-eighteenth century.

§ Open Memorial Day-Labor Day, Tuesday-Sunday 12-5; mid April-Memorial Day, and Labor Day-October 31, Saturday and Sunday 12-5. Fee. Phone: 317-423-9363.

LOWELL

¶ Buckley Homestead, 3606 Belshaw Road.

This 160-acre farm, settled by Dennis Buckley and his wife, Catherine, in 1849, has been turned into a living-history museum whose dozen buildings chronicle three periods of local Indiana history.

Having fled the Potato Famine in Ireland, the Buckleys and their four children moved to this area to be near their relatives, the Driscoll family. Despite the Buckleys' good fortune, Dennis died only two years after purchasing a seventy-nine-acre homestead. His eight-year-old son Patrick grew up to serve with the Indiana Volunteers during the Civil War, while his son John built the present house and raised grain and beef cattle on the farm.

§ Open May-October 31, grounds daily 7 a.m.-dusk, buildings Saturday and Sunday 10-5 (weekdays by appointment). Phone: 219-696-0769.

MADISON

¶ Jeremiah Sullivan House, 304 West 2nd Street.

This two-story Federal-style house was built in 1818 by Judge Jeremiah Sullivan, the son of an Irish immigrant from Charleville, County Cork.

The younger Sullivan was a graduate of William and Mary College in Virginia and served as a captain in the War of 1812. After moving to Indiana, he became Madison's first lawyer, was elected to the state legislature, and joined the Presbyterian Church in town (although his mother was a Methodist and his father a Catholic). From 1837 to 1846 Sullivan was a justice of the state supreme court and enjoyed the distinction of suggesting the name "Indianapolis" for the state capital. Later in his life he recalled a conversation with his son, at that time a

The Federal-style residence of Jeremiah Sullivan.
(Photo courtesy of Historic Madison, Inc.)

member of the state assembly: "Tommy sat with me an hour or two on Saturday night. He seems already to be disgusted with public life. He says he had seen more corruption and dishonesty during the last ten days of his life than he ever saw before. I think he has probably spoken the truth.

§ Open May-October 31, Monday-Saturday 10-4:30, Sunday 1-4:30. Fee. Phone: 812-265-2967.

NEW HARMONY

¶ **Workingmen's Institute,** 407 West Tavern Street.

When this building was constructed as a library in 1894, it was one of a number of buildings that made up the Workingmen's Institute. That educational enterprise had been founded in 1838 "to bring scientific and all other useful knowledge within the reach of Manual and Mechanical Laborers without the aid of professional men and teachers." Today this building still serves as a public library, but it also maintains a historical museum, an art gallery, and local archives.

That the library was ever built was due in large measure to the generosity of Dr. Edward Murphy, a successful New Harmony physician. Although born in Cork, Ireland, in 1813, he had been brought as a youngster to Louisville, Kentucky, by a brutal man who claimed to be his uncle. After running away from his "guardian," the young Murphy came under the tutelage of the New Harmony commune created in 1825 by Robert Owen, the British philanthropist and social reformer. Here Murphy was educated and unsuccessfully tried his hand at farming and haberdashery. He subsequently attended medical school in Louisville but returned to New Harmony to practice. From his medical practice and various investments, he acquired considerable wealth, a great portion of which he donated to the library and its art gallery. By the time of his death in 1900, he had bequeathed not only books and Italian paintings but also $155,000.

§ Open Tuesday-Saturday 10-noon and 1-4:30; also Sunday 1-4:30, May-October 31. Closed major holidays. Fee. Phone: 812-682-4806.

NOBLESVILLE

¶ **Conner Prairie Pioneer Settlement,** 4 miles south of Noblesville on Allisonville Road or 6 miles north of Indianapolis via I-465 exit 35.

Conner Prairie is a living-history museum that includes the Pioneer Adventure Area and a reconstructed 1836 village. The oldest portion of the museum is the Conner House, a Federal-style brick residence built in 1823 by the fur trader *William Conner, whose brother had founded Connersville sometime before 1813.

Conner had moved to this area in 1802 and constructed a log cabin and trading post before marrying Mekinges, the daughter of a Delaware Indian chief. In 1818 he served as an interpreter for the negotiators of a treaty which removed Native Americans from the central part of the state to Missouri. The treaty had an unexpected effect upon Conner's marriage when his wife decided to accompany her people west, taking their six children with her.

Conner, who chose to remain in this area, later married Elizabeth Chapman, a white woman with whom he had ten more children. It was for her that he built the house on display today. He and his wife lived here until 1837, when they moved to a 150-acre farm nearer to Noblesville, a community which Conner had helped found fourteen years earlier. From there he oversaw the management of a general store, a sawmill, a gristmill, and 3,000 acres of land in four counties. He later served three terms in the state legislature.

§ Open May-October 31, Tuesday-Saturday 10-5, Sunday 12-5; April and November, Wednesday-Saturday 10-5, Sunday 12-5. Fee. Phone: 317-776-6000.

OXFORD

❡ **Kelly's Livery Stable,** on State 352 south of State 55.

This white barn is easily identified by the words "Dan Patch 1:55" painted on the green roof. The words are a reference to the famous trotter which was foaled behind the barn in 1896 and which set the world's record for the mile nine years later, a record that stood for thirty-three years. During his ten-year racing career, Dan Patch earned more than $2 million for his owners. An autopsy showed that this famous horse had an enlarged heart weighing nine pounds, well above the five pounds of the average horse's heart.

RICHMOND

❡ **Andrew F. Scott House,** 126 North 10th Street. Private.

This was the boyhood home of Francis MacNutt, the American diplomat, papal courtier, and author who was born here in 1863 of Scotch-Irish ancestry.

Despite his Episcopalian upbringing and attendance at such WASP bastions as Phillips Exeter Academy and Harvard Law School, MacNutt converted to Roman Catholicism at the age of twenty and subsequently announced his intention to seek ordination. While studying at the Pontifical Academy of Noble Ecclesiastics in Rome, however, he discontinued his preparation for the priesthood and took up a diplomatic career. He first served with the U.S. legations in Constantinople and Madrid and then with the court of Pope Leo XIII, thereby becoming the first American to hold such a position in the papal government. After ten years at the Vatican, he resigned in 1905 and spent the rest of his life at his home in the Tyrol. Of his seven books, *Letters of Cortes* and *Bartholomew de las Casas* are of particular interest to American historians. Two other works are autobiographical – *Six Decades of My Life* and *A Papal Chamberlain.*

In 1904 MacNutt accompanied the papal legate to Ireland, on what he thought was probably the first visit to the Emerald Island by a papal representative since the time of Queen Mary Tudor in the sixteenth century. At Kingstown, when the legate prepared to impart a papal blessing to the huge crowds that had gathered at the harbor, a local clergyman with the papal entourage exclaimed, "But more than half of these people are Protestants! You can't give the Apostolic Blessing to Protestants – not in Ireland!" At the clergyman's urging, the legate instead announced that he would remember the crowd in his prayers. On another occasion on that trip, MacNutt went with the legate to an evening of entertainment sponsored by a local Gaelic language society – complete with men in kilts, women playing harps, and all singing

Gaelic songs. "While this was going on," MacNutt later wrote, "I told the Legate he must make a short speech and end it by shouting at the top of his lungs *Erin go bragh!* He got the three words by heart, and when he trumpeted them forth I really thought the roof would fall in on us" from the sound of the ovation he received.

RUSHVILLE

¶ **Laughlin Monument,** County Courthouse, Main and 1st Street.

The outdoor monument on the north side of the courthouse honors Dr. William Laughlin, a man of many talents who donated the land on which Rushville is located.

Laughlin, who was born in Pennsylvania in 1778 (most likely to Irish parents), studied medicine, law, and surveying at Jefferson College in Philadelphia. After coming to Indiana in 1816, he first taught school but then began to practice medicine and accepted a position as a government surveyor. Before long he had also opened a law practice and in 1818 was elected to the state legislature.

After surveying Rush County – which he named for Benjamin Rush, his college mentor and the famous signer of the Declaration of Independence – Laughlin purchased land where Rushville would soon be founded. His donation of seventy-five acres became the site of the new county seat, which the commissioners named Rushville. Laughlin eventually established the town's first school, was its first teacher, and built its first water-powered grist mill.

The mill, however, proved to be Laughlin's undoing. In 1823, when Rushville was ravaged by malaria, the citizens believed that the disease had been caused by the stagnant water above Laughlin's mill dam. An enraged mob soon destroyed the mill, an act of destruction for which later citizens of Rushville hoped to atone by erecting the memorial in front of the courthouse.

SOUTH BEND

¶ **City Cemetery,** Elm Street and Colfax Avenue.

James and Mary McKinley, the grandparents of *President William McKinley, are buried here.

¶ **University of Notre Dame,** Notre Dame Avenue.

Although the Notre Dame football team is today known as "the Fighting Irish," in earlier times it was called "Catholics" and "Hoosiers." (Its opponents used derogatory terms like "Dirty Irish," "Papists," and "Damn Micks.") One of the first references to the nickname "Fighting Irish" occurred in a sports article in 1909, although the name did not become universally established until the end of the 1920s. To the charge that the nickname was inappropriate because so many of the university's students were not of Irish descent, the team's Norwegian-born coach, Knute Rockne, said, "They all have the Irish spirit, and that's what counts." (In point of fact, about 50 percent of the football players who received varsity letters from Rockne had Irish surnames.)

❡ In 1914 the university was presented with the sword of *General Thomas Francis Meagher, at one time the commander of the Irish Brigade during the Civil War. Notre Dame's collection also includes a green flag of the Irish Brigade and the sword of *General James Shields, a hero of both the Mexican War and the Civil War.

❡ Corby Hall was named for Father William Corby, the Civil War chaplain of the Irish Brigade. In front of this residence hall is a bronze statue of the former Notre Dame instructor as he gave general absolution to the soldiers at Gettysburg. This statue was dedicated in 1911 and is a copy of the original on the Gettysburg battlefield. Both works were done by the sculptor *Samuel Aloysius Murray.

William Corby was born in 1833 in Detroit, where his father, Daniel Corby of King's County, Ireland, had settled. When he was twenty years old, the young Corby entered the University of Notre Dame and within a year had joined the Congregation of the Holy Cross, the teaching religious order which administered the university. After his ordination he combined pastoral work with his duties as a professor and the director of the Manual Labor School at the university. When the Civil War began, Corby was commissioned chaplain of the 88th New York Infantry, one of the many Celtic units in the Irish Brigade. After the war Corby returned to Notre Dame, first assuming administrative duties there and then serving as provincial general of the Holy Cross Congregation in the United States. During his tenure at the university, he oversaw an ambitious building program, the broadening of academic offerings, and the establishment of a law school.

The sculptor Samuel Murray, meanwhile, was the son of immigrants from Cork, Ireland. He most likely learned the art of sculpting from his father, who was a stonemason. After studying art under Thomas Eakins, the young man became the famous artist's assistant and subsequently spent a half century at the Moore Institute of Arts, Sciences and Industry in Philadelphia, teaching anatomy and modeling from life. In 1894 his entry in the Philadelphia Art Club exhibition earned him a gold medal, while ten years later he was awarded a silver medal at the Louisiana Purchase Exposition in Chicago. Besides his statues of Father Corby, Murray is best known for his statue of *John Barry in front of Independence Hall in Philadelphia and the Bishop Shanahan Memorial in St. Patrick's Cathedral in Harrisburg, Pennsylvania. Murray was a member of the Friendly Sons of St. Patrick in Philadelphia.

¶ O'Shaughnessy Hall is named for Ignatius Aloysius O'Shaugh-nessy, an oil company executive who donated $200,000 to the university for the creation of a fine arts foundation. The hall houses the College of Arts and Letters as well as the university's art gallery.

The grandson of an Irish immigrant who had settled in Massachusetts in the 1830s, O'Shaughnessy was graduated from the College of St. Thomas in St. Paul, Minnesota, in 1903. He worked in the insurance and banking fields before creating the Global Oil & Refining Company in 1917 and serving as president of its subsidiaries, the Lario Oil & Gas Company and the Globe Pipeline Company. In addition to being a director of the First National Bank of St. Paul and a member of the Chicago Yacht Club, he was a trustee of the University of Notre Dame, a Knight of the Holy Sepulchre, and a Knight of Malta. He also contributed $600,000 for the erection of a physical education building at St. Thomas College and for the library at St. Louis University in Missouri.

VINCENNES

¶ **Fort Knox II,** 3 miles north on Fort Knox Road, off State 41.

Named for *General Henry Knox, George Washington's secretary of war, the original fort on this site was constructed in 1802. The outline of the excavated fort is marked. Fort Knox was the second of three military garrisons on the Wabash River built to discourage Indian attacks against the American settlers in the region.

§ Open daily. Phone: 812-882-1776

ZIONSVILLE

¶ **Patrick H. Sullivan Foundation Museum,** 1 block west of State 334 at 225 West Hawthorne Street.

This museum, which houses historical displays and a genealogical library, was established through the generosity of Iva Etta Sullivan, a local librarian and teacher, in honor of her great-grandfather, Patrick Henry Sullivan.

Patrick Sullivan, a native-born Virginian of Irish descent, arrived in this part of Indiana in 1824, thereby becoming the first white settler in Boone County. He later served as a county commissioner and was the father of seventeen children. Sullivan and his second wife are buried in the old Sheets graveyard, a mile southeast of Zionsville.

§ Open Tuesday-Saturday 10-4. Closed major holidays and December 24 to early January. Phone: 317-873-4900.

¶ **Patrick H. Sullivan Memorial,** on the lawn of the Hussey Library, 250 North 5th Street.

MAINE

AUGUSTA

❡ **Blaine House National Historic Landmark,** at Capitol and State
streets.

From 1862 to 1893 this large Federal-style house was the residence
of James G. Blaine, who served as speaker of the House of Representatives, U.S. senator, and secretary of state under presidents Garfield and
Harrison. Blaine's descendants gave the house to Maine in 1919 for use
as the state's executive mansion. Besides period furnishings and an art
collection, the house features Blaine's restored study.

Blaine's first American ancestor was James Blaine, who had emi-
grated from Londonderry, northern Ireland, in 1745 and settled near
Lancaster, Pennsylvania. The later Blaine was the son of Maria Louise
Gillespie (an Irish Catholic) and Ephraim Lynn Blaine (a Scotch-Irish
Presbyterian).

Blaine's nomination for President in 1884 by the Republican Party
caused the Democrats to fear the loss of their traditional Irish allies.
The Republicans first played up their candidate's roots – his Irish Catholic mother and his Irish-American cousin (Sister Angela Gillespie, a
famous Civil War nurse). Blaine himself did his part, paying tribute to
"the ancient faith in which my mother lived and died" and referring to

The former Blaine House, now the state executive mansion.

Sister Angela as literally his sister. The Grand Old Party also reminded Irish voters about Blaine's generally aggressive stance toward Great Britain while serving as secretary of state. In Boston, meanwhile, the Irish Land League claimed that if Blaine was elected "Ireland would be free in thirty days." And in New York a huge rally for Blaine opened with an acknowledgment of the event's historic nature: "To think of thousands of Irish Democrats assembled together to endorse the nomination of the Republican Party."

Blaine's chances of winning the Irish vote *en bloc* disappeared, however, because of a famous slur and the withering attacks of the Irish-American press. The *Irish American* labeled the Republican "the tattooed candidate, who is charged with being a renegade to the faith of his mother, and whose whole political record is a foul blot on the reputation of the Irish race for honor and probity." The paper also reminded the voters of the Republican Party's "unvarying anti-Irish proclivities." Meanwhile, while making a pro-Blaine statement, the Reverend Samuel Burchard let slip an unfortunate allusion to the Democratic Party's historical connection with saloonkeepers, Catholic immigrants, and secessionists: "We are Republicans, and don't propose to leave our party, and identify ourselves with the party whose antecedents have been RUM, ROMANISM, AND REBELLION."

§ Open Monday-Friday 2-4. Phone: 207-289-2301.

¶ *Lady Wisdom,* State Capitol, State and Capitol streets.

The idealized statue of "Lady Wisdom" atop the dome of the state capitol was a gift of its sculptor, William Clark Noble. The twenty-foot-high copper repoussé work depicts a female figure holding a pine torch, the symbol of Maine, in her upraised right arm.

Noble, who was born in Gardiner, Maine, in 1858, was descended from an Irishman who had served as a British officer at Louisbourg, Nova Scotia, in 1744. Influenced by a biography of the Danish sculptor Thorwaldsen which he had read at age eight, Noble decided upon a career as a sculptor. To earn money to pay for art school, he became a prize fighter, boxing under the unlikely name "The Art Student" and saving $28,000 from a year's worth of prize money. After completing an apprenticeship in Boston, he began to do wax and clay modeling and decorative carvings in wood, stone, and plaster. Armed with this experience, he launched his career in Newport, Rhode Island, with commissions for interior carving and decoration.

Noble is known primarily as a sculptor, although he was also a painter of some note. Among his sculpted works are portrait busts of *William Cody, David Lloyd George, Alexander Hamilton, Nathaniel Hawthorne, Henry Cabot Lodge, Henry W. Longfellow, *John McCullough, Harriet Beecher Stowe, and *Theodore Roosevelt, and portrait reliefs of Edward Everett Hale, John Philip Sousa, and General Joseph Wheeler. His larger works include statues of *Governor Andrew Curtin (Bellefonte, Pa.); Robert Burns (Providence, R.I.); William Channing (Newport, R.I.); Bishop Phillips Brooks (New York City); Pius X, Leo XIII, and Benedict XV (the Vatican); and Thomas Jefferson, Napoleon, and *Anthony Wayne for the 1904 St. Louis Exposition.

Noble's most ambitious work, however, never came to fruition, although it brought him to financial ruin and physical collapse. For more than forty years, he had created models of a gigantic memorial to American womanhood which he hoped would be erected in the nation's capital. Envisioned as a stone monument standing 297 feet high, adorned with bronze statuary, and standing on a 300-foot oval base, the $20 million project aroused the interest of Daisy Calhoun of the Women's Universal Alliance. After working on the project for two more years and receiving only $2,000 for his efforts, Noble severed his relationship with Calhoun and attempted to obtain full compensation for his work. Instead, he ended up defending himself against Calhoun's charge of blackmail. A newspaper account described a sidelight of the resulting legal battle: "Noble had the court in gales of laughter as he mimicked Mrs. Calhoun. She wanted the model changed 'about every other day,' he said. She wanted the statues of the Arts, Science and Literature swept off the summit of the memorial, and a fifty-foot statue of herself put there, sitting on a throne, 'looking down on the poor mothers of the world.'" Although the judge dismissed the case against him, Noble was never compensated and his health was fatally ruined by the ordeal.

BANGOR

¶ St. John's Catholic Church, York Street.

This brick Gothic revival structure was designed by *Patrick Keely and was built in 1855 to serve the town's Irish community. The funds to construct the church came principally from James O'Donahue and Timothy Field, two Irishmen who had lived in Bangor before making their fortune in the California gold fields.

BELFAST

Founded in 1770, this town was named for Belfast, Ireland, by Protestant Scotch-Irish settlers who had earlier established Londonderry, New Hampshire. James Miller, a member of the group which had moved to the new site, insisted that it be named for Belfast, the place of his birth. When a dispute with the other colonists ensued, the question was decided by the toss of a coin.

DAMARISCOTTA

¶ **Matthew Cottrill House,** Main Street Historic District.

This private residence is named for Matthew Cottrill, the Irish immigrant who built it after becoming one of the town's most prominent merchants. The 1802 Federal-style house was designed by Nicholas Codd, another Irishman.

Cottrill had settled in Damariscotta about 1791 and with fellow Irishman James Kavanagh had become a successful shipbuilder and exporter of lumber to the West Indies. When Father John Cheverus visited the area about 1797, he preached in one of Cottrill's barns and celebrated mass in his house. Kavanagh later fitted up one of his stores as a place of worship for the Irish Catholics in the area until a church was constructed in 1803.

Cheverus mentioned the two Irish merchants in a letter to *Bishop John Carroll in 1801, at the same time mentioning one of the disabilities that still afflicted Catholics in Puritan New England. "Last Thursday," he wrote, ". . . the judges gave us here a little specimen of their good will toward the Catholic religion and its ministers. Mr. Kavanagh, a respectable merchant, living at Newcastle [Maine], has fitted up at his own expense a small neat chapel where I officiated last year for better than three months. Moreover, the same gentleman with his partner, Matthew Cottrill, has subscribed $1000 for our new church. He thought in consequence he would be free from paying taxes to the Congregational minister of his township, but the judges of the Supreme Court now sitting in Boston declared unanimously that he must pay for the support of the said minister, [for the Massachusetts] Constitution, said they, obliged every one to contribute for the support of Protestant ministers and them alone."

GARDINER

¶ **"For Humanity" Memorial,** South Gardiner Congregational Church.

This memorial tablet to the twenty-five men of Gardiner who served in World War I was a gift of its creator, *William Clark Noble. The artist was born in Gardiner in 1858.

The tablet depicts the battlefield scene of a dying soldier and a Red Cross nurse crouched beside an artillery piece. The young soldier clutches the robe of the Crucified Christ, whose image watches over the pair. Dedicated in 1923, the tablet compares the sacrifice of those who served during the war to that of Christ, who offered himself up "for humanity."

¶ **William Clark Noble Burial Site,** Mt. Hope Cemetery, Mt. Hope Cemetery River Road.

Despite his illustrious career, *William Clark Noble died a pauper and was buried in an unmarked grave. In 1983, however, a granite headstone with bronze lettering was erected over the burial site.

KITTERY

¶ **Fort McClary,** Kittery Point Road, off State 103.

The original eighteenth-century fortification here was named Fort William. Considered impregnable during the Revolution, the fort was spared a British attack and was renamed Fort McClary for *Major Andrew Clary, who had fought valiantly at the battle of Bunker Hill on June 17, 1775.

Fort McClary was garrisoned during every American military action prior to World War II. Today the fort's hexagonal wooden blockhouse, probably built in the 1840s, surmounts a cut-granite first story. Visitors can see the powder magazines, the rifleman's house, various perimeter walls, and the foundations of the original barracks.

§ Open June-September 30, daily 9-5. Phone: 207-493-2845.

MACHIAS

¶ **Burnham Tavern Museum,** Main and Free streets.

In this gambrel-roofed structure Captain Jeremiah O'Brien and other local patriots gathered in June 1775 to plan the capture of the British schooner *Margaretta*. The Americans who were wounded in the battle were brought here for treatment.

In 1770 O'Brien and his Dublin-born father had been among a group of settlers who were granted land in Machias on condition "that they build a suitable meeting house for the public worship of God and settle a learned Protestant minister and make provision for his comfortable and honorable support."

§ Open late June-Labor Day, Monday-Friday 9-5; rest of the year, by appointment. Fee. Phone: 207-255-4432.

MACHIASPORT

¶ **Fort O'Brien,** overlooking the Machias River.

The first fortification on this site was called Fort Machias and was built soon after the beginning of the Revolution. When the fort was destroyed by the British in 1814, the site remained unfortified until the construction of Fort O'Brien in 1863. Its remaining earthworks are part of a state historic park. The fort was named for *Jeremiah O'Brien, the local hero who captured a British schooner off the coast in 1775.

§ Open daily Memorial Day-Labor Day.

¶ **Gates House,** off State 92.

This Federal-style house displays models of the British schooner *Margaretta* and the sloop *Unity*, both of which were captured by *Jeremiah O'Brien and his brothers in the first naval encounter of the Revolutionary War.

In June 1775 the H.M.S *Margaretta* arrived off Machiasport with two sloops to take on lumber for the British barracks in Boston. Tempers flared when Captain Moore of the 100-ton British ship refused to heed O'Brien's warning to abandon his mission. Moore raised the ante by ordering the colonials to remove the Liberty Pole which they had erected in town only a month before. When O'Brien's brother John challenged the order, Moore repeated his demand that "That liberty pole must come down or it will be my painful duty to fire upon the town." In response, a heavily armed band of forty colonials – including Jeremiah and his five younger brothers – leaped aboard the eighty-ton *Unity* and seized it. After provisioning the captured sloop with twenty shotguns, a small cannon, hay forks, and axes, the colonials gave chase to the *Margaretta*. When O'Brien ordered Moore to surrender, the British commander opened fire, killing two of the American crew. The Irishman then maneuvered his ship next to the *Margaretta* and lashed the two together, thereby making it easier to subdue the British crew. After outfitting the *Unity* with the *Margaretta*'s guns, O'Brien rechristened her *Machias Liberty*, the first American armed cruiser of the Revolutionary War. This engagement prompted the Continental Congress to create an American navy.

In subsequent years Jeremiah O'Brien's name was further immortalized by the U.S. Navy. In 1900 the torpedo boat destroyer *O'Brien* was launched at Elizabethport, New Jersey, becoming the first American vessel to be christened with an Irish name. During World War II the *Jeremiah O'Brien* was one of almost 3,000 Liberty ships built in response to the massive German sinking of Allied shipping. The *Jeremiah O'Brien* is the last surviving Liberty ship and is berthed in San Francisco, where it serves as the National Liberty Ship Memorial.

§ Open June-Labor Day, Monday-Friday 12:30-4:30; rest of the year, by appointment. Phone: 207-255-8461.

NEW CASTLE

¶ James Kavanagh House.

This two-story Federal-style house was built in 1803 by Nicholas Codd for James Kavanagh, a wealthy merchant and fellow Irishman. Kavanagh had earlier fitted up one of his stores as a place of worship for the Irish Catholics in the area until a church was constructed.

Bishop Cheverus mentioned Kavanagh and his Irish business partner, Matthew Cottrill, in a letter to *Bishop John Carroll in 1801, at the same time mentioning one of the disabilities that still afflicted Catholics in Puritan New England. "Last Thursday," he wrote, ". . . the judges gave us here a little specimen of their good will toward the Catholic religion and its ministers. Mr. Kavanagh, a respectable merchant, living at Newcastle [Maine], has fitted up at his own expense a small neat chapel where I officiated last year for better than three months. Moreover, the same gentleman with his partner, Matthew Cottrill, has subscribed $1000 for our new church. He thought in consequence he would be free from paying taxes to the Congregational minister of his township, but the judges of the Supreme Court now sitting in Boston declared unanimously that he must pay for the support of the said minister, [for the Massachusetts] Constitution, said they, obliged every one to contribute for the support of Protestant ministers and them alone."

¶ St. Patrick's Catholic Church, 2.5 miles north on State 215.

This oldest remaining Catholic house of worship in New England was constructed in 1803 and was dedicated five years later. It was built from a design by Nicholas Codd, who reputedly was shanghaied from Ireland expressly for the purpose. St. Patrick's is also the only Catholic church in New England to possess a bell cast by Paul Revere. A gift of *Matthew Cottrill, the bell is one of the ninety-three Revere bells which remain of the original 400.

One of the tombstones in the churchyard is that of Edward Kavanagh, whose Irish-born father was an early benefactor of the church. The son attended Collège de Montréal, Georgetown College in the District of Columbia, and St. Mary's College in Baltimore. Following the ruin of his father's business during the War of 1812, the son abandoned plans to enter the Catholic priesthood in order to revive the family mercantile and shipbuilding enterprise. He subsequently entered state politics and was the first Irish Catholic elected to a New England state legislature, the first elected to Congress from New England, and the first to be a New England governor.

§ Open daily 9-dusk. Phone: 207-563-3240.

St. Patrick's Church
near New Castle.

NORTH WHITEFIELD

¶ St. Denis Catholic Church, State 218.

Built in 1833 to serve the Irish immigrants who had settled in this area in the early nineteenth century, this is the second oldest Catholic church in Maine and one of the oldest in New England. The earliest Irish arrivals were fishermen from Newfoundland who settled on farms in Whitefield.

PROSPECT

¶ Fort Knox State Historic Park, east on State 174 from Prospect or north from U.S. 1 west of the Waldo-Hancock Bridge.

The first of Maine's granite forts was begun during the Aroostook War, a series of disputes with Great Britain in the 1840s over the Maine-New Brunswick boundary. The fortification measures 350 by 250 feet and was named for *Henry Knox, the famous hero of the American Revolution. The fort was used as a troop training site during the Civil War and the Spanish-American War. Visitors can see original cannon, hot-shot furnaces, soldiers' quarters, powder magazines, and parade grounds.

§ Open May-October 31, daily 9-dusk. Fee. Phone: 207-469-7719.

THOMASTON

¶ **Montpelier,** on High Street (State 131).

This mansion is a reconstruction of the 1795 home to which *Henry Knox retired after serving as President Washington's first secretary of war. The eighteen-room Federal-style house was designed by Boston architect Charles Bullfinch, who complied with Knox's request by incorporating such features as a flying staircase, clerestory windows, and an oval parlor.

§ Open Memorial Day-Labor Day, Wednesday-Sunday 9-5:30. Fee. Phone: 207-354-8062.

A reconstruction of "Montpelier," the 1795 home to which Henry Knox retired after serving as the first U.S. secretary of war.

MARYLAND

ADELINE

¶ **Taney Place,** 5 miles south on State 508. Private.

Built about 1750, this two-story house was where Roger Taney, the famous chief justice of the U.S. Supreme Court, was born in 1777. He was descended from Michael Taney, an indentured servant who was probably Irish and who had arrived in America in 1660.

In 1819 the house was the site of a quarrel between Michael Taney V and John Magruder over a woman. After Magruder slapped the thirty-five-year-old Taney, the master of the estate stabbed his assailant through the heart and fled into Virginia. When Taney died, his body was returned to Maryland for burial, but as the body lay in the coffin awaiting interment one of the Magruders smashed the corpse's face with a stone.

ANNAPOLIS

¶ **Roger Taney Statue,** State House, State Circle.

A seated statue of *Roger Taney, chief justice of the U.S. Supreme Court from 1836 to 1864, is located in front of the State House, the oldest in continuous use in the nation.

¶ **St. Anne's Church,** Church Circle.

Built in 1859, this is the third church on this site since the parish was founded in 1692. In the churchyard are the graves of Thomas Lynch and Charles Carroll "Barrister."

• Thomas Lynch was the grandson of the family's first American ancestor, Jonack Lynch, a native of Ireland who had come to South Carolina soon after the first settlement of that colony about 1670. From his father, Thomas Lynch inherited extensive tracts of land and early became a spokesman for colonial rights against the British Parliament and the Crown. While attending the Continental Congress, he was described by another delegate as a man who "wears the manufacture of this country, is plain, sensible, above ceremony, and carries with him more force in his very appearance than most powdered folks in their conversation. He wears his hair strait, his clothes in the plainest order, and is highly esteemed." His son was one of the Irish-American signers of the Declaration of Independence.

• Charles Carroll "Barrister" is memorialized on a plaque in the church: "In Grateful Memory of Charles Carroll, Barrister. Vestryman of St. Anne's Church. Born at Annapolis the 22nd of March 1723. Died the 23 of March 1783 at his home Mount Clare. Patriot and Leader in the Cause of America's independence. Eminent Jurist and Churchman. President of the Convention of 1776 Which gave the State of Maryland its Bill of Rights and First Constitution. Honored by his Country for his outstanding Talents and Virtues. He lived to see the Attainment of his High Endeavors. He died Respected and Beloved."

¶ St. John's College, King George Street.

• The Carroll-Barrister House on campus was the birthplace of Charles Carroll, nicknamed "Barrister" to distinguish him from his father, Charles, a surgeon. This 1722 structure is now used as an administration building.

The Carrolls were descended from a long-established Catholic family in King's County, Ireland, that traced its ancestry to that country's ancient Celtic kings. The family's first American ancestor was Charles Carroll, a friend of Lord Baltimore's who came to the colony in 1689.

• McDowell Hall was named about 1860 for John McDowell, who served as president of St. John's College for the first sixteen years of its existence.

McDowell was the grandson of an Irish immigrant who had settled in Chester County, Pennsylvania, soon after coming to America about 1715. A graduate of the College of Philadelphia, McDowell moved to Maryland in 1782 to teach and to study law. Although he engaged in a successful legal practice there, he was still attracted to teaching and, when the newly formed St. John's College offered him a professorship in mathematics, he readily accepted. He also served as the president of the fledgling institution until 1806, when he accepted a position teaching natural philosophy at the University of Pennsylvania. Although poor health forced him to return to Maryland, he declined the principalship of St. John's when it was offered to him again.

During McDowell's tenure as president of St. John's, one of its students was George Washington's step-grandson. In a letter to McDowell, the former president acknowledged that George Washington Parke Custis on occasion lacked motivation but otherwise described him as one would expect in a letter of recommendation: "From drinking and gaming he is perfectly free, and if he has a propensity to any other impropriety it is hidden from me. He is generous and regardful of the truth." The following summer Custis acknowledged that he had fallen in love with a young woman whom he would have married if she had not refused him. At the beginning of the next school year, Washington again wrote to the college president, this time urging him to act *in loco parentis*: "Prevent as much as it can be done, without too great a restraint, a devotion of his time to visitations of the families in Annapolis, which, when carried to excess or beyond a certain point, can not but tend to direct his mind from study and lead his thoughts to very different objects."

¶ United States Naval Academy, entrance at King George and Randall streets.

Several of the structures on the sprawling campus bear the names of famous Irish-American naval officers:

• Macdonough Hall was named for Commodore Thomas Macdonough, the victor of the battle of Plattsburgh in 1814.

• Mahan Hall honors Admiral Alfred Thayer Mahan, the 1859 graduate of the Academy whose most famous work was *The Influence of Sea Power upon History, 1660-1783.* Between 1886 and 1890 he was president of the U.S. Naval War College in Newport, Rhode Island.

• Maury Hall was named in honor of Matthew Fontaine Maury, an oceanographer of Irish and French Huguenot descent. He first received major recognition during his thirty-six-year career in the U.S. Navy with a published work on navigation.

Later as superintendent of the Naval Observatory in Washington, D.C., Maury published his research on winds and currents and accompanying sailing directions. His fame was assured when he accurately predicted that use of his charts and directions would reduce sailing time appreciably. (Ten to fifteen days were shaved off a voyage from New York to Rio de Janeiro, for example, while the average New York-San Francisco run was reduced by an incredible forty-five days.) Faced with such impressive results, the world's navies and merchant marines adopted the uniform system of recording oceanographic data which Maury had advocated. In the mid 1850s he published the first textbook on modern oceanography and was consulted about both the route and the best time for laying the Atlantic cable.

With the outbreak of the Civil War, however, Maury resigned his naval office and accepted a commission in the Confederate navy. During the war he served as the Confederacy's special agent to Britain, where he helped obtain ships for the Southern cause. When he was excluded from the postwar amnesty, he proposed to the Mexican government a plan to colonize former Confederates and their families in that country, a scheme that came to nothing, however. After two years in England, he returned to Lexington, Virginia, to accept the professorship of meteorology at the Virginia Military Institute.

Thoroughly modern in his educational views, Maury advocated replacing the traditional classical curriculum based on the study of Latin and Greek with courses in mathematics and science. He regarded the military academy at West Point as "the only tolerable institution in the United States because of the absence there of the humbuggery of the Learned Languages." He is buried in Hollywood Cemetery in Richmond, Virginia.

Memorial Hall displays the flag which *Commodore Oliver Hazard Perry flew during his victorious engagement against a British fleet on Lake Erie in September 1813. The blue flag had originally belonged to Captain James Lawrence, whose famous words – "Don't give up the ship!" – Perry had sewn on the flag prior to his own sea battle.

§ The academy is open daily 9-5. Closed January and December 25. Phone: 410-267-3363.

BALTIMORE

¶ Basilica of the Assumption of the Blessed Virgin Mary, Cathedral and Mulberry streets.

This is the oldest cathedral in the United States and was begun in 1806 by *John Carroll, the country's first Roman Catholic bishop. Carroll is buried in the church crypt, as is *Cardinal James Gibbons, archbishop of Baltimore from 1877 to 1921. A portrait bust of Carroll is located in the nave of the basilica.

A member of Maryland's most prominent Irish family, John Carroll was the brother of Daniel Carroll, one of the framers of the Constitution, and the cousin of *Charles Carroll of Carrollton, the only Catholic signer of the Declaration of Independence. During the Revolution John Carroll was instrumental in obtaining the support of the French government for the patriot cause, a contribution which George Washington acknowledged in extremely flattering terms: "Of all men whose influence was most potent in securing the success of the Revolution, Bishop Carroll of Baltimore was the man."

As the first Catholic bishop in a country that was generally hostile to and ignorant of Catholicism, Carroll argued for the use of the vernacular in the liturgy. His suggestion was based on the premise that Protestants were deprived of a proper understanding of the Catholic Church because of the use of Latin. Despite the fact that his views were attacked by the archbishop of Dublin, Carroll expressed his hope that the Church would allow the clergy in Ireland, England, and America to celebrate the liturgy in the vernacular, "for I do indeed conceive that one of the most popular prejudices against us is that our public prayers are unintelligible to our hearers. Many of the poor people, and the negroes generally, not being able to read, have no technical help to confine their attention."

Two years after Carroll's elevation to the episcopacy, the Baltimore Synod of 1791 instructed priests to read the Sunday Gospel in the vernacular and recommended the vernacular for the Our Father, the Hail Mary, and the Apostles' Creed. However, no permission was granted for the use of the vernacular for the mass or in the administration of the other sacraments.

§ Open Monday-Friday 7-2, Saturday and Sunday 7-6:30. Phone: 410-727-3564.

¶ Baltimore & Ohio Railroad Museum, 901 West Pratt Street.

This museum incorporates the nation's first passenger and freight train station, the Mount Clare. The museum's thirty-seven acres exhibit more than a hundred historic rail cars (including the *Tom Thumb*) as well as various types of engines and telegraph and telephone equipment.

The station was built in 1830 on land given the Baltimore & Ohio Railroad by *Charles Carroll of Carrollton, a shrewd businessman and a major force in many of the nation's early industrial and commercial enterprises. Besides being a member of the Chesapeake & Ohio Canal Company, he was a director of the Baltimore & Ohio Railroad. In 1828, at the age of ninety-three, he performed the groundbreaking for construction of the B & O Railroad and watched as the company's first line was completed to Ellicott's Mills. (The silver spade which he used is on display in the museum.)

In May 1830 Carroll was among the passengers who made the first trip on the new railroad. The thirteen-mile ride in the horse-drawn car *Pioneer* took sixty-five minutes. The following August the first American-built steam engine – the *Tom Thumb* – ran the distance to Ellicott's Mills in seventy-five minutes, although the return trip, which was on the downgrade and included a four-minute water stop, took only sixty-one minutes. In 1844 the world's first official telegraph message was received at Mount Clare station when Samuel Morse sent the words "What God hath wrought" from the Supreme Court building in Washington, D.C.

§ Open daily 10-5. Closed January 1, Thanksgiving, and December 25. Fee. Phone: 410-752-2490.

¶ Carroll Park, Washington Boulevard and Monroe Street.

This property was once part of "Georgia," the 2,300-acre plantation of Dr. Charles Carroll, whose branch of the family was Protestant due to his renunciation of Catholicism when he arrived in Maryland from Ireland in 1715. Near the center of the park is "Mount Clare," the mansion completed in 1760 as the home of Dr. Carroll's son Charles, dubbed "Barrister" to distinguish him from other men of the same name in the extended family. The house is the oldest pre-revolutionary mansion in Baltimore and contains portraits of Charles and his wife by Charles Wilson Peale.

§ Open Tuesday-Friday 10-4:30, Saturday and Sunday 12-4:30. Closed holidays. Fee. Phone: 410-837-3262.

"Mount Clare," the home of Charles Carroll "Barrister."

℥ Carroll Viaduct, Gwynn's Falls near Carroll Park.

The cornerstone of this bridge – the first constructed of masonry in the United States – was laid in 1829 by *Charles Carroll of Carrollton. The viaduct, which is still in use, was built for the Baltimore & Ohio Railroad, of which Carroll was a director.

℥ Charles Carroll Mansion, Duke of Gloucester Street.

This was the birthplace of *Charles Carroll of Carrollton, the only Catholic signer of the Declaration of Independence. Here he was married, lived during the Revolution, and entertained George Washington. Because Maryland law forbade public Catholic worship, local Catholics attended mass in the mansion's private family chapel. Nearby is St. Mary's Church, built on property deeded to the parish by Carroll's granddaughters.

℥ Charles Carroll Mansion, 800 East Lombard Street.

Noted for its winding staircase when the house was built in 1808, this was the winter home of *Charles Carroll of Carrollton. Following the deaths of John Adams and Thomas Jefferson, Carroll was the last surviving signer of the Declaration of Independence. At the time of his death here in 1832 at the age of ninety-five, he was the wealthiest man in the country.

Two years earlier a visitor had recorded what was perhaps the se-

---

cret of Carroll's longevity: "He takes a cold bath every morning in the summer, plunging headlong into it; rides on horseback from eight to twelve miles; drinks water at dinner, had never drunk spiritous liquors at any period of his life, but drinks a glass or two of madeira wine every day, and sometimes champagne and claret; takes as much exercise as possible; goes to bed at nine o'clock, and rises before day."

§ Open April-October 31, Tuesday-Saturday 10-5, Sunday 12-5; rest of the year, Tuesday-Saturday 10-4, Sunday 12-4. Fee. Phone: 410-396-3524.

¶ Daniel Dulany Burial Site, St. Paul's Cemetery, Lombard Street and Fremont Avenue.

Daniel Dulany was born in Annapolis in 1722 and was named for his father, a native of Queen's County, Ireland, and a descendant of the medieval O'Dulaney family. Daniel the younger was educated at Eton College and studied law at the Middle Temple in London. After three years in the Maryland legislature, he was appointed to the governor's council and later to the secretaryship of the province. His professional ability prompted *Charles Carroll to comment that Dulany was "indisputably the best lawyer on this continent."

Following Parliament's passage of the Stamp Act in 1765, Dulany published a pamphlet in which he contended that the American colonies were not – and could not realistically be – represented in Parliament and that taxation without representation violated English common law. This work was widely quoted by William Pitt when that British statesman attempted to persuade Parliament to repeal the hated tax. When relations between the colonies and the mother country turned violent, however, Dulany had no stomach for revolution and retired to his estate near Baltimore, where his continued loyalty to the Crown resulted in the confiscation of his property in 1781.

¶ Edgar Allan Poe Burial Site, Westminster Burying Ground, on the southeast corner of Fayette and Greene streets.

*Edgar Allan Poe was so little known at the time of his death that the mourners at his funeral "filled a single carriage." Although he was originally buried in the rear of the adjoining Presbyterian Church, a campaign by Baltimore school teachers and students in 1875 raised enough money to move his body to its present location. The poet's grave is marked by a stone with his likeness on one side and a bronze plaque (given by French admirers) on the other.

Also buried here is Poe's grandfather, David Poe, who had emigrated from Londonderry, northern Ireland, and settled about 1748 in Pennsylvania, where he married Elizabeth Cairnes, also of an Irish family. James McHenry, a native of northern Ireland, a signer of the U.S.

Constitution, and President Washington's secretary of war, is also interred in this cemetery.

§ Open daily April-November 30, dawn-dusk. Tours available first and third weekends of each month, Friday at 6:30 p.m. and Saturday at 10 a.m. Phone: 410-328-7228.

¶ **Edgar Allan Poe Monument,** 29th Street, between Maryland Avenue and Oak Street.

This bronze statue depicts the poet *Edgar Allan Poe wearing a dressing gown and listening to the Muses. The monument contains a slightly inaccurate quotation from "The Raven": "Dreaming Dreams no Mortals Ever Dared to Dream Before." In 1930 a Poe admirer insisted that city authorities singularize the offending word "Mortals." When officials ignored his demand, he said he would remove the "s" himself on the night of May 30. Learning that police were preparing to guard the monument that night, the admirer appeared the evening before to chisel the letter from the text. Although he was arrested, the authorities did not prosecute when supporters came to his defense.

¶ **Edgar Allan Poe National Historic Landmark,** 203 North Amity Street.

This small three-story brick building was the home of *Edgar Allan Poe from 1832 to 1835, a period which some biographers call his "dark and mysterious years." Here he wrote "MS in a Bottle," "Berenice" (his first sensational horror story), and his only play, *Politan*. At the time, he was living with his grandmother, his aunt, his brother, and two cousins, one of whom – Virginia Clemm – he later married, although she was only thirteen years old.

In 1835 the novelist *John Pendleton Kennedy recommended Poe for a position on the *Southern Literary Messenger* in Richmond. Fourteen years after leaving this house, Poe was found in the gutter in Lombard Street and was carried to what is now Church Home Hospital, 100 North Broadway, where he died. A marker at that location memorializes his death.

§ Open April-July 31 and September to mid December, Wednesday-Saturday 1-4. Fee. Phone: 410-525-1274 or 410-396-7932.

¶ **Fort McHenry National Monument and Historic Shrine,** at the east end of Fort Avenue.

Constructed between 1798 and 1803, this star-shaped fort was named for James McHenry, President Washington's secretary of war. Born in northern Ireland in 1753, McHenry had received a classical education in Dublin before coming to Philadelphia in 1771. During the Revolution he served as a surgeon in the Continental Army, and in 1787 he was a delegate to the Constitutional Convention.

§ Open daily June-Labor Day, 8-8; rest of the year, 8-5. Closed January 1 and December 25. Fee. Phone: 410-962-4299.

¶ Johns Hopkins Hospital, 600 North Wolfe Street.

• The Outpatient Center – at 601 North Caroline Street – was originally known as the Brady Urological Institute, founded in 1912 with a $600,000 donation by *James Brady, the famous "Diamond Jim." Brady made the gift after receiving treatment at the Johns Hopkins Hospital for long-standing urological problems.

• The Welch Library – 1900 East Monument Street – houses *Four Doctors*, an oil painting by John Singer Sargent depicting the hospital's four most prominent early physicians. The four men had been entrusted by the benefactor Johns Hopkins with the duty of carrying out his wish that the hospital advance the cause of medical science. One of the four doctors was *Howard Kelly, who was associated with the hospital from 1889 until 1919.

¶ Johns Hopkins University, off Charles and 34th streets.

The 140-acre campus of this internationally renowned private liberal arts institution was originally the estate of *Charles Carroll Jr., the son of Charles Carroll of Carrollton, a signer of the Declaration of Independence.

§ Tours available Monday-Friday at 10, 12, and 3 from the admissions office at 140 Garland Hall. Phone: 410-516-8171.

¶ One of the points of interest on the campus is "Homewood," a brick Georgian mansion built in 1809 by the elder Charles Carroll as a wedding gift for his son. Charles Carroll Jr., however, was an alcoholic whose drinking marred domestic bliss at the $40,000 mansion. The extent of the family's embarrassment about Carroll's drinking is revealed in a remark by his nephew, who wrote that "we can't get him to shoot himself, so must bear with this degradation still longer." From 1897 to 1910 Homewood was a boys' school, a fact that accounts for the graffiti-covered brick outhouse behind the mansion.

Homewood was the birthplace of John Lee Carroll, the governor of Maryland from 1875 to 1880. This great-grandson of Charles Carroll of Carrollton grew up at the family's ancestral home, Doughoregan Manor, near Ellicott City, Maryland, and received his legal training at Harvard Law School. Although he moved to New York City in 1859 to practice law, he soon returned to his native state, both because of his father's poor health and his own Southern sympathy in the emerging sectional conflict. After his father's death he purchased Doughoregan Manor from his brother and made it his country estate.

Carroll later served two terms in the state senate and in 1875 was elected governor of Maryland despite exceptional controversy about his Roman Catholicism. Although he promoted policies designed to improve the state's commercial and agricultural interests, his reputation among the working class suffered from his intervention in a strike by employees of the Baltimore & Ohio Railroad over a wage reduction. When the strikers resorted to violence to protest the use of "scabs," the governor sent in the state militia. He was forced to call for federal troops when rioting and destruction of property began in Baltimore.

§ Homewood is located at 3400 North Charles Street. Open Monday-Friday 11-3, Sunday 12-3. Phone: 410-516-5589.

¶ **Lafayette Statue,** Mt. Vernon Park, in the 500 block of North Charles Street.

This equestrian statue of the Marquis de Lafayette is the work of *Andrew O'Connor.

¶ **Lee and Jackson Statue,** Wyman Park, at the corner of Howard Street and Park Drive.

This memorial, reputedly the only double equestrian statue in the world, depicts the final meeting of Confederate generals Robert E. Lee and *Thomas "Stonewall" Jackson, just before the latter was killed at Chancellorsville, Virginia.

¶ **Patterson Park,** Eastern and Patterson Park avenues.

The original portion of this park was a gift to the city by William Patterson, a native of County Donegal, Ireland, who as a teenager had come to Philadelphia to work for the Irish shipping merchant Samuel Jackson. The foundation of Patterson's fortune was made during the American Revolution, when he sold French munitions to the rebel colonists. In the last year of the war, he was among the Baltimore merchants who gave the Marquis de Lafayette 10,000 guineas with which to obtain supplies for the Yorktown campaign.

In 1803 Patterson's eighteen-year-old daughter, Elizabeth, married Jerome Bonaparte, Napoleon's youngest brother, in a ceremony witnessed by *Bishop John Carroll. When the emperor expressed his opposition to the marriage, the couple sailed to Europe aboard the *Erin*, one of Patterson's ships, intent upon pleading their case. Although Pope Pius VII refused to grant Napoleon's demand that the marriage be annulled, the French Senate and the Maryland Assembly passed decrees of annulment. Elizabeth at first refused Napoleon's offer of $12,000 to stop referring to herself as Madame Bonaparte, but she later accepted a pension of 60,000 francs. Her tombstone in Greenmount Cemetery is inscribed with the words, "After life's fitful fever, she sleeps well."

¶ **Roger Taney Statue,** Washington Place, just north of the Washington Monument.

This statue of *Chief Justice Roger Taney is a duplicate of that in front of the State House in Annapolis.

¶ **U.S. Frigate** *Constellation,* Constellation Dock, at Pratt and Light streets, on Pier 1 in Inner Harbor.

When it was launched in 1797, the *Constellation* was the U.S. Navy's first commissioned ship. During its heyday it saw action against a variety of foes: France in 1798-1800, the Tripoli pirates in 1802, the British in the War of 1812, and the Confederates in the Civil War.

In February 1841 the *Constellation* came under the command of *Lawrence Kearny, the newly appointed commander of the East India Squadron. At the time of his promotion, both Kearny and the ship were in Rio de Janeiro. From Rio, Kearny sailed to Table Bay, near the Cape of Good Hope, arriving there in twenty-eight days. After spending three months at Saldanha Bay – to fix the rudder – he rounded the Cape, entered the Mozambique Channel, and proceeded to Sumatra, Singapore, Manial, and finally Macao, which he reached by March 1842.

§ Open mid June-Labor Day, daily 10-8; mid May to mid June and day after Labor Day-Columbus Day, daily 10-6; rest of the year, daily 10-4. Closed January 1, Thanksgiving, and December 25. Fee. Phone: 410-539-1797.

¶ **Walters Art Gallery,** 600 North Charles Street.

The nucleus of the gallery's 25,000 *objets d'art* was the personal collection of Henry Walters, a railroad entrepreneur in the South and the Southwest and a descendant of Scotch-Irish stock. In 1920 he enriched his museum's holdings by purchasing the Marcello Massaranti collection of Italian art for $1 million. When he died in 1931, he left his museum and its works to the city. Among the gallery's most treasured possessions is the original manuscript of the *Star Spangled Banner*.

§ Open Tuesday-Sunday 11-5. Closed January 1, July 4, Thanksgiving, and December 24-25. Fee. Phone: 410-547-9000.

BROOKLANDVILLE

¶ **Brooklandwood,** Falls Road. Private.

Erected in the mid 1790s, this was once the home of *Charles Carroll of Carrollton and of *George Brown, a banker in the firm of Alex Brown & Sons.

CAMBRIDGE

❡ Holy Trinity Church, 7 miles south on State 16.

Many members of the famous Maryland Carroll family are buried in the cemetery next to the church, including *Anna Ella Carroll, an unofficial advisor to President Lincoln and the female strategist who allegedly designed the Union's successful Tennessee campaign during the Civil War.

§ Church open Monday-Saturday 9-5, Sunday 2-5. Cemetery open daily 24 hours. Phone: 410-228-2940.

ELLICOTT CITY

❡ Baltimore & Ohio Railroad Station Museum, 2711 Maryland Avenue at Main Street.

The museum is the restored first terminus of the B & O Railroad, built in 1830 at the end of the company's first stretch of track, a thirteen-mile line from Baltimore. Visitors can see the stationmaster's quarters, a waiting room, an engine house, and a freight house. The last building displays a model of the original stretch of track.

When the B & O Railroad was organized in 1827, one of its most influential founders was Alexander Brown, a native of County Antrim, Ireland, where he had been a linen auctioneer and the proprietor of a linen store in Belfast. In 1800, however, he immigrated to Baltimore with his wife and the oldest of his four sons. Almost immediately he announced in a Baltimore newspaper the opening of his linen warehouse on North Gay Street: "The subscriber, lately arrived from Ireland, has brought with him a most complete assortment of 4-4 & 7-8 wide Irish Linen, which upon examination, will be found much lower [in price] than any inspected for three years past, & which will be sold low by the box or piece for cash or good acceptance in the city on the usual credit." When his three other sons arrived in Baltimore two years later, "They landed on a hot Sunday morning in July, dressed in thick woolen Irish suits and heavy plaid stockings, and created quite a sensation among the good people of Baltimore, quietly wending their way to church. Thither their mother took them also, with a heart thankful for their safe arrival, after she had borrowed from her neighbors thinner clothing better suited to the American climate."

Although Brown had begun his American career as an importer of Irish linen, he quickly moved into the export business. At first he sent cotton and tobacco to Great Britain, but eventually he handled a full range of commodities, from champagne to indigo. In due time his sons established branches of the business in Liverpool, Philadelphia, and New York. The task of overseeing these operations as well as the movement of the family's ships and capital led quite naturally to the creation of an international merchant banking business. The firm,

Alexander Brown & Sons, is the oldest banking house in the United States and is still headquartered in Baltimore. Although Brown suffered temporarily from the War of 1812, he steadfastly adhered to the principle that established his reputation for integrity: "It is essential for us in all our dealings not only to be fair but never to have the appearance of unfairness." At his death his wealth was estimated at $2 million.

§ Open Memorial Day-Labor Day, Wednesday-Monday 11-4; rest of the year, Friday-Monday 11-4. Fee. Phone: 410-461-1944.

¶ **Doughoregan Manor,** 8 miles west on Manor Lane. Private.

Built about 1727, this two-story mansion was the home of *Charles Carroll of Carrollton. (Today the home belongs to Philip Carroll, a direct descendant of its original owner.) On either side of the manor's 300-foot façade is an ell, one containing servants' quarters and the other a Catholic chapel. The original estate of more than 13,000 acres included farm buildings and quarters for almost a thousand slaves. The estate was held intact until 1870, when all but 3,000 acres was sold.

Charles Carroll was born in Annapolis and received his early schooling at Bohemia Academy, a school in Warwick, Maryland, operated by Jesuit priests. After six years at a Jesuit institution in St. Omer, France, he completed his education by studying law in London. Despite his legal training, Carroll was ineligible for public office in Maryland because of restrictions against Catholics. As relations between the official British government and the Maryland colonists deteriorated, however, Carroll was able to play an increasingly influential role in the extralegal institutions which the Americans created. Besides serving in the Maryland convention in 1776, he was a member of the Continental Congress and was the only Catholic to sign the Declaration of Independence. By committing treason against the British, Carroll placed his considerable wealth in jeopardy. When he took up the pen to sign the famous document, one of the other delegates alluded to the precarious nature of Carroll's fortune by reportedly saying, "There goes a few millions!"

EMMITSBURG

¶ **John Hughes Cabin,** Mount St. Mary's College.

John Hughes, who became the first archbishop of New York City, lived in this small log cabin in 1820 while receiving instruction at the college. In return for room and board, he worked as a gardener.

From his youth in County Tyrone, Ireland, Hughes had always wanted to be a priest, but his father, a poor tenant farmer, could afford to give his son no more than a rudimentary education. About his feelings at the time, the younger Hughes said, "Many a time have I thrown down my rake in the meadow, and kneeling behind a hayrick, begged of God and the Blessed Virgin to let me become a priest." In 1817 he immigrated to America, where he worked as a laborer, a road mender, a quarry hand, and a garden digger in southern Pennsylvania. Still intent upon becoming a priest, he applied for admission to nearby Mount St. Mary's College but was repeatedly rejected because there was no vacancy. After actually moving to Emmitsburg, he worked as a laborer on a millrace and as a mason's helper on a bridge-building project. The young man's persistence paid off at the end of 1819, when the president of the college hired him as superintendent of the institution's garden in return for board and instruction.

Many years later, as bishop of New York, the nation's most populous Irish diocese, Hughes condemned the clannishness of many of his flock and insisted that they adopt the predominant American culture as soon as possible. His own allegiance to his adopted country was never in doubt: "My feelings, my thoughts, have been so much identified with all that is American, that I have almost forgotten I am a foreigner." He disliked professional Irish politicians and the tendency of the Democratic party to monopolize and pander to the Irish vote.

Yet, when necessary, Hughes defended the Irish against the attacks of anti-immigrant forces. In response to the destruction of a convent in Charleston, Massachusetts, he warned that "if a single Catholic Church were burned in New York, the city would become a second Moscow." In 1844, when anti-Irish and anti-Catholic speakers announced their intention to hold a public rally, Hughes feared that the church burnings which had occurred in Philadelphia the month before might be repeated in New York. Through the Catholic press he urged Catholics to remain calm but to prepare to act in self defense if necessary. After forming cadres of between 1,000 and 2,000 men to protect each Catholic church in the city, Hughes urged the mayor to determine whether the police force had available "a company or so of artillery, and a squadron of horse" that could be used to intimidate any prospective rioters. As a result, city officials canceled the meeting.

§ The interior of the cabin can be viewed through the windows. Phone: 301-447-6122.

FREDERICK

⚑ Barbara Fritchie House, 154 West Patrick Street.

Although Barbara Fritchie was not of Irish descent, she figured prominently in a story involving the Scotch-Irish Civil War general Thomas "Stonewall" Jackson. According to the version of the story rendered in John Greenleaf Whittier's poem "Barbara Fritchie," Jackson had ordered his men to fire on the Union flag should they encounter it on their march through Frederick in 1862. Nevertheless, the ninety-five-year-old Fritchie defiantly waved the Stars and Stripes, adding, "Shoot if you must this old gray head, / But spare your country's flag." Jackson, in turn, countermanded his order: "Who touches a hair of yon gray head / Dies like a dog! March on!"

§ Open April-September 30, Monday and Thursday-Saturday 10-4, Sunday 1-4; October and November, Saturday and Sunday 1-4. Fee. Phone: 301-698-0630.

¶ Evangelical Reformed Church, West Church Street.

While attending a service here before the battle of Antietam, Confederate general *Thomas "Stonewall" Jackson slept through a sermon whose sentiments were favorable to the Union.

¶ Mount Olivet Cemetery, at the end of Market Street.

• Near the entrance of the cemetery is a sixteen-foot monument marking the grave of Francis Scott Key, the author of the "Star Spangled Banner." The memorial was designed by *Alexander Doyle and includes a nine-foot statue of Key. The bronze standing figure depicts the composer holding the text of his famous anthem in his left hand as he points with his right arm to the Stars and Stripes atop a nearby flag pole. The monument was dedicated in 1898.

• The medallion on the monument over the grave of Barbara Fritchie, the heroine of Whittier's famous Civil War poem, was designed by *James Edward Kelly and includes a profile portrait of the heroine of Whittier's famous Civil War poem.

¶ Roger Taney House, 123 South Bentz Street.

From 1835 to 1864 this was the home of *Roger Taney, best known for his ruling in the Dred Scott case while he was the chief justice of the U.S. Supreme Court.

Taney was described by a contemporary as "a tall square-shouldered man, flat-chested . . . with a stoop that made his shoulders even more prominent, a face without one good feature, a mouth unusually large, in which were discolored and irregular teeth, the gums of which were visible when he smiled, dressed always in black, his clothes sitting ill upon him . . . . And yet, when he began to speak, you never thought of his personal appearance, so clear, so simple, so admirably arranged were his low-voiced words. . . . There was an air of so much sincerity in all he said, that it was next to impossible to believe he could be wrong.

§ Open April-December 31, Saturday 10-4, Sunday 1-4. Phone: 301-663-8703.

❡ Roger Taney Law Office, Court Street.

From 1801 to 1823 this building was the law office of *Roger Taney, who had come to Frederick to practice law with Francis Scott Key, whose sister he later married.

Despite his ruling in the Dred Scott case that African Americans were not considered citizens under the Constitution, Taney had earlier declared his antislavery views. In defending a Methodist minister charged with inciting insurrection for delivering an antislavery sermon, Taney had said, "Slavery is a blot upon our national character[,] and every lover of freedom confidentially hopes that it will be effectually wiped away. And until that time shall came when we can point without a blush to the language held in the Declaration of Independence, every friend of humanity will seek to lighten the galling chains of slavery."

❡ Roger Taney Statue, in front of City Hall, 101 North Court Street.

A bronze bust of *Roger Taney rests on a pedestal to which is attached a plaque summarizing his career: "Chief Justice of the United States 1836-1864. Secretary of the Treasury 1833-1834. Attorney General of the United States 1831-1833. Attorney General of Maryland 1827-1831. Citizen of Frederick and Lawyer Practicing in the Frederick County Court 1801-1823. Born in Calvert County March 17, 1777. Died in Washington, D.C. October 12, 1864. Buried in St. John's Catholic Cemetery, Frederick, Md."

Statue of Chief Justice Taney.

❡ St. John the Evangelist Church, 116 East 2nd Street.

This church was built in 1837 by Irish immigrants who labored on a nearby canal. Construction of the church was completed under the direction of *Father John McElroy, who served the parish for two decades. During that time he established a boys' school, an orphanage, a convent, a girls' free school, and a Jesuit novitiate. He later founded Boston College.

❡ Chief Justice Roger Taney is buried next to his mother in St. John's Cemetery at 4th and East streets.

HAVRE DE GRACE

¶ **Havre de Grace Lighthouse,** on Concord Point.

Built in 1827, the lighthouse was first manned by *Lieutenant John O'Neill, who had been rewarded with the post because of his bravery during a British raid in May 1813. His descendants served as keepers for many years after his death.

KINGSTON

¶ **Kingston Hall,** on the west side of State 667. Private.

This late eighteenth-century brick mansion once belonged to Thomas King Carroll, a governor of Maryland and a member of the famous Irish-American family of Carrolls. Following his inauguration in 1830, Governor Carroll supported efforts to improve the state's educational and penal institutions and used his influence to expedite the completion of the Baltimore and Ohio Railroad. Although he worked his plantation at Kingston Hall with slaves, he opposed the "peculiar institution" and was fearful of its growth in the country. As a result, he supported the colonization of freed blacks to Africa.

Governor Carroll's daughter, Anna Ella Carroll ("Princess Anne"), was raised in her father's Protestant faith and became an outspoken champion of the anti-Catholic and antiforeign Know Nothing Party. Her most ambitious publication was *The Great American Battle*, a 365-page book praising the Know Nothings and condemning "the Papal system."

With the outbreak of the Civil War, Anna Carroll became an equally vigorous champion of the Union. When Senator John Breckinridge of Kentucky urged the border states to secede, she distributed 50,000 copies of a pamphlet in which she charged Southern leaders with having prepared for war since the 1830s. In this and two other tracts, she argued that, since secession was unconstitutional, the Confederacy was a rebel government which could be dealt with by the president rather than by Congress. During the war she authored a pamphlet in which she argued that President Lincoln possessed implied powers not directly conferred upon him by the Constitution, a position that may have influenced his decision to issue the Emancipation Proclamation as a military tactic.

Carroll also passed on to the War Department a plan for a Union invasion of the Tennessee River Valley, a strategy that would bypass the more heavily fortified Mississippi. (*General Ulysses S. Grant successfully employed the strategy, breaking Confederate power in the West through his capture of Fort Donelson and Fort Henry.) Although at first Carroll gave credit for this plan to a river pilot and amateur strategist, she later claimed that the idea was hers. For many years after the war, she unsuccessfully petitioned Congress for proper compensation for the strategy. In the 1880s she became a symbol for woman suffragists of alleged male injustice. She is buried in the graveyard of Old Trinity Church in Cambridge, Maryland.

PERRYVILLE

As early as 1680 an 80,000-square-mile tract of land in this part of Maryland was known as "New Ireland." That same year Lord Baltimore, the proprietor of the Maryland colony, granted 32,000 acres of that land to George Talbot, a native of Castle Rooney, County Roscommon, Ireland. On that land was Susquehanna Manor, which Talbot renamed New Connaught. Three years later an adjoining tract of 7,000 acres – known as New Munster – was granted to a group of Irishmen, among whom was Edmund O'Dwyre of Tipperary. At about the same time, a tract called New Leinster was patented by Bryan O'Daly of County Wicklow, Ireland. In 1684 Lord Baltimore proclaimed these territories the County of New Ireland.

Although Talbot subsequently carried out the terms of his land grant, he inexplicably fell afoul of the law. As was expected of him, he brought over a hundred Irish settlers and built block houses and signal towers for protection against the Native Americans. Soon after his appointment as deputy governor, though, he precipitated a quarrel on board the *Quaker*, during which he mortally stabbed the tax collector Christopher Rousby. According to Thomas Allen, the captain of the ship, Talbot first tried to kiss him (Allen) and then "hit me a blow on the heart and a box on the ear." Talbot later approached Rousby below deck and said, "'Rousby, you son of a whore, you dog, give me your hand,' but Rousby refused unless he gave him better words. And Talbot said again, 'Rousby, you dog, give me your hand. Don't you know that I am your Governor and can do you a kindness.' Rousby answered, 'I don't value anything you can do to me.' And with that Talbot started up and pulled Rousby's cravat to pieces. Rousby said nothing, but rose up to go, and Talbot started up and met him, and clapped him on the right shoulder with his left hand, saying, 'dear Rousby,' with his dagger under his coat in his right hand, and then stabbed him in the right breast.'" Rousby died within a half hour.

Talbot was promptly arrested and sent to Jamestown for trial, but he was soon rescued by his wife and a group of "red haired" Irishmen and taken back to Maryland. According to tradition, one of his hiding places was a cave on the Susquehanna River near Perryville, where two trained falcons brought him food until he surrendered in July 1685. At his trial in Jamestown, he tried to exonerate himself by saying that he had killed "without any manner of premeditated malice in the height of his passion for which he most heartily beg'd God and the King's pardon." Although the jury found him guilty, he was later pardoned by the King.

ROCKVILLE

¶ **F. Scott Fitzgerald Burial Site,** St. Mary's Cemetery, Veirs Mill Road and Rockville Pike.

The paternal ancestors of F. Scott Fitzgerald were descended from prominent figures in Maryland's colonial history, while his maternal grandfather was Philip McQuillan, an Irish immigrant from County Fermanagh. Despite the fact that this grandfather had made a fortune in the wholesale grocery business in St. Paul, Minnesota, Fitzgerald felt embarrassed by his McQuillan ancestry, describing it as "straight 1850 potato-famine Irish." Before his death in 1940, the famous author requested to be buried with his Maryland ancestors in the Catholic Cemetery in Rockville. The local bishop denied permission, however, probably because of Fitzgerald's defection from the Catholic Church. Instead, he was buried in Rockville Union Cemetery.

(When Fitzgerald was laid out in a Hollywood funeral home, one of the few people who came to pay their respects was Dorothy Parker. Rarely at a loss for the right phrase, she judged the dead author with the words he had used to describe the protagonist in his masterpiece, *The Great Gatsby*: "The poor son of a bitch.")

In 1975, after St. Mary's Cemetery had been declared a historic monument, Fitzgerald's daughter – Scottie – obtained permission to transfer his remains to the site. In a gesture of reconciliation, the archbishop of Baltimore said: "F. Scott Fitzgerald came out of the Maryland Catholic tradition. He was a man touched by the faith of the Catholic Church. There can be perceived in his work a Catholic consciousness of reality. He found in his faith an understanding of the human heart caught in the struggle between grace and death. His characters are involved in this great drama, seeking God and seeking love. As an artist he was able with lucidity and poetic imagination to portray this struggle. He also experienced in his own life the mystery of suffering and, we hope, the power of God's grace."

SAMPLES MANOR

¶ Kennedy Farmhouse, Chestnut Grove.

This farmhouse was the unlikely staging point for the attack by the abolitionist John Brown on the federal arsenal in Harpers Ferry, five miles away across the Potomac River. Brown hoped that the attack would led to an armed uprising of black slaves.

In July 1859 Brown leased this house and an adjoining cabin from the heirs of **Robert "Booth" Kennedy, who had died the previous April. Kennedy had bought the house and twenty-five acres around it in the 1840s. Although altered since then, the original house had a store-room and a kitchen in the basement, bedrooms and a living room on the first floor, and an attic. Here the abolitionist, his daughter, two of his sons, and at least one associate spent several weeks in preparation for the assault. (One of the people killed during Brown's attack was Luke Quinn, a nineteen-year-old Irish immigrant.) Although the aboli-tionist succeeded in capturing the arsenal, his quixotic scheme was crushed with the arrival of U.S. marines under Colonel Robert E. Lee.

§ Open by appointment. Phone: 301-963-3300.

SHARPSBURG

¶ Antietam National Battlefield, on State 34/65.

Here on September 17, 1862, Union forces stopped the Confederate advance into Maryland and Pennsylvania, but at a cost to both sides of 23,000 dead and wounded. Although the Irish Brigade played a con-spicuous part in this victory by pushing the enemy back to its second line, one Irish regiment lost half its men while another lost a third. According to one eyewitness, "The rebels seemed to have a special spite against the [Brigade's] green flag, and five color-bearers were shot down successively in a short time. . . . 'Big Gleason,' . . . six feet seven, sprang forward and snatched it up. In a few minutes a bullet struck the staff, shattering it to pieces; Gleason tore the flag from the broken staff, wrapped it around his body . . . and went through the rest of that fight untouched."

¶ One of the many memorials on the battlefield is a shaft in honor of *William McKinley, who was attached to the Union commissary at the time of the battle. Realizing that the men in his brigade had eaten only a scant breakfast before the engagement, he drove a mule team loaded with food rations and hot coffee right into the thick of the fight-ing. For this unusual attention to duty, he was promoted to second lieu-tenant. Rutherford B. Hayes, a major at the time, described McKinley's action as "a thing that had never occurred under similar circumstances in any other army in the world."

William McKinley Memorial on the Antietam battlefield.

¶ The Irish Brigade will be honored with a proposed memorial next to the observation tower overlooking the "Bloody Lane," a sunken road where the brigade lost 500 men. The memorial, which will be ten feet high, will include two bronze sculptures embedded in Irish granite. The bronze on the front will depict the Irish Brigade on the battlefield, while a bust of Thomas Meagher, the brigade's commander, will adorn the back. (See Gettysburg, Pennsylvania.)

§ Battlefield and visitor center open 8:30-5. Fee. Phone: 301-432-5124.

SILVER SPRING

¶ **Old St. John the Evangelist Church,** 9700 Rosensteel Avenue.

Erected in 1894, this brick structure marks the site of the first frame church built here in 1774 by *John Carroll, the Maryland native who became the first Catholic bishop in the United States. Today the church is known as Our Lady, Queen of Poland.

¶ In the cemetery nearby is the grave of Daniel Carroll, the bishop's cousin and one of the signers of the Constitution. The graveyard was originally part of a land grant made in 1680 to an ancestor of the Carroll family.

TANEYTOWN

¶ Antrim, 30 Trevanion Road.

Recently restored as a bed and breakfast establishment, this antebellum mansion was built in 1844 by Andrew Ege as a wedding gift for his daughter. The house, once the center of a 450-acre plantation, was named for Ege's birthplace, County Antrim, Ireland.

§ Phone: 800-858-1844.

UPPER MARLBORO

¶ Darnall's Chance, 14800 Governor Oden Bowie Drive.

Constructed between 1694 and 1713, this brick residence was owned for almost forty years by the prominent Darnall and Carroll families. Although the two families were cousins, they became even more intertwined through the marriage of *Charles Carroll of Carrollton to Mary Darnall in 1768. The house is the probable birthplace of Bishop John Carroll and his cousin Daniel Carroll, a signer of the U.S. Constitution.

§ Open Monday-Friday 9-4, Sunday 12-4. Phone: 301-952-8010.

WARWICK

¶ St. Francis Xavier (Old Bohemia) Church, Eastern Shore.

The first Catholic congregation on this site was formed in 1704 by the Jesuits, who by 1745 had also established Bohemia Academy. Among its students were *John Carroll and *Charles Carroll of Carrollton. Because at that time Catholics were denied opportunities for political and educational advancement in Maryland, the two Carroll cousins were sent by their fathers to France, where they attended a school run by English Jesuits.

Among the priests buried in the church is Father Charles Whelan (Friar Maurice), an Irish-born Capuchin priest who was the first pastor of St. Peter's Church in New York City. Although born in Ireland in 1741, he had escaped the Irish penal laws by spending much of his life in France. In 1780, however, he joined the French fleet as a chaplain and accompanied it to Newport, Rhode Island, as it prepared to assist the Americans in their revolution against Great Britain. After being imprisoned by the British for a time, he arrived in New York City in October 1784.

Whelan immediately lamented "That Catholics here are very poor, but very zealous, being for the most part Irish. They are not able to build a chapel, nor even to buy a place for saying Mass, only a Portuguese gentleman has allowed us a part of his house for that purpose." He later wrote to the papal nuncio in Paris about the polyglot nature of his parishioners: "It is necessary for a priest in this place to know at least Irish, English, French and Dutch, since our congregation is composed of people of these nationalities as also of Portuguese and Span-iards." After serving as pastor for two years, Whelan became a mis-sionary in Kentucky but by 1790 had returned to New York State. He finally settled at Bohemia Manor, where he died in 1806.

§ Mass is said here on the third Sunday of April, May, September, and October. The rectory museum is open Sunday 12-3 (summer only). Phone: 410-737-5191.

WESTOVER

¶ Rehobeth Presbyterian Church, 5757 Coventry Parish.

Built in 1705-06 through the efforts of the Reverend Francis Makemie, this is the oldest Presbyterian church in the United States.

Makemie was born in County Donegal, Ireland, most likely in 1658. Following his graduation from the University of Glasgow, he was or-dained by the presbytery in Laggan, Ulster. Between 1683 and 1698 he served as a missionary in the American colonies – first in North Caro-lina, Virginia, and Maryland and then in Barbados. During his minis-try he was a well known controversialist, defending Presbyterian prac-tices and beliefs against the attacks of Quakers and Anglicans. While visiting England in 1704-05, Makemie laid the foundation for the Pres-byterian Church in America by persuading the Presbyterian and Inde-pendent ministers of London to send two of their number to America. The following year these two joined Makemie and four other ministers to form the first American presbytery, a move generally ascribed to Makemie's leadership.

At the beginning of 1707, however, Makemie was arrested in New York for preaching without a license from the royal governor, Lord Cornbury. After having been denied permission to preach publicly in the Dutch Church in New York City, Makemie had responded by preach-ing instead in a private house "though in a public manner, and with open doors." In the ensuing controversy Cornbury called Makemie a "Jack of all Trades . . . a Preacher, a Doctor of Physick, a Merchant, an Attorney, or Counsellor at Law, and which is worse of all, a Disturber of Governments." (Cornbury himself frequently caused a stir, appear-ing at public ceremonies coiffed like a woman and wearing a dress, silk stockings, and high-heeled shoes.)

At his trial the embattled minister argued that "if our liberty . . . de-pended upon [either] a license or certificate from the Bishops of En-gland, or the Governors of America, we should soon be deprived of our liberty of conscience secured to us [nonconformists by the Tolera-tion Act]." The jury agreed with Makemie's logic and acquitted him.

§ Phone: 410-957-0949.

MASSACHUSETTS

ADAMS

¶ **President McKinley Monument,** 92 Park Street, in front of the public library.

This eight-foot-high bronze statue of *President William McKinley rests on a pedestal decorated with reliefs depicting episodes from the former president's life: as a congressman addressing the House of Representatives, as a commissary sergeant risking his life to bring food to troops during the battle of Antietam, and as president taking the oath of office. The fourth relief is inscribed with an excerpt from his last speech, given in Buffalo, New York, just before his assassination: "Let us remember that our interest is in Concord, not Conflict, and that our real Eminence is in the Victories of Peace, not those of War."

BOSTON

¶ **Ann Glover Memorial,** Our Lady of Victories Shrine, 27 Isabella Street.

In the church is a plaque memorializing Ann Glover, an Irishwoman who was hanged as a witch near the site of this church on November 16, 1688. The tablet describes her as the first Catholic martyr in Massachusetts because the Puritans' notorious anti-Catholic sentiments probably were a factor in their prosecution of her.

During the summer of 1688, in a prelude to the more famous witchcraft trials of Salem, Massachusetts, four children of John Goodwin of Boston were the victims of what was believed to be demonic possession. Goodwin's thirteen-year-old daughter, Martha, was the first of the children to exhibit the customary symptoms – after she had accused the family's washerwoman of stealing linens. According to the Puritan minister Cotton Mather, the washerwoman's mother – Ann Glover – had "bestowed very bad Language" upon the Goodwin daughter. Before long, Martha was "visited with strange Fits," allegedly through the witchcraft of Glover, whom Mather described as an "ignorant and a scandalous old Woman" and whom even her husband sometimes described as a witch. Within a few weeks three other Goodwin children were seized with similar afflictions. Sometimes they would be deaf, blind, or dumb, while at other times they appeared to be swallowing their tongues. However, following a day of prayer and fasting observed specifically for the benefit of the afflicted children, the youngest was permanently freed from his torment.

In the meantime, Ann Glover was questioned by the authorities and jailed. According to Mather, she could speak only Gaelic at the trial, although she was known to speak English well. In court she said that she and her husband had been sent from Ireland to Barbados during Cromwell's time. Mrs. Glover stated that while in Barbados her husband was "scored to death and did not give up his religion [probably Roman Catholicism], which same I hold to." When asked whether she was a Papist, and when shown "an idol [statue of a saint?] that was diabolical," she said, "I die a Catholic!" Perhaps because she not could fully comprehend the questions put to her, she admitted that she had tormented the children by stroking small rag dolls that were produced during the trial. When she took up one of these dolls in court, one of the afflicted children was seized with fits.

In addition, the night after her trial Glover was heard explaining to the devil that she had confessed everything because he had deserted her. Upon examination by court-appointed physicians, Glover acknowledged her Roman Catholicism and recited the Lord's Prayer "very readily." After the doctors had declared her of sound mind, the magistrates signed her death warrant, although reluctantly. As Glover predicted from the scaffold, her death brought no cessation to the sufferings of the Goodwin children. They continued to exhibit signs of affliction for many months.

¶ **Boston Athenaeum,** 10.5 Beacon Street.

Among the library's holdings are the book collections of George Washington and General Henry Knox, the Revolutionary War hero and the first president's secretary of war. Knox was descended from a member of a Scotch-Irish congregation from Londonderry, Ireland, who had come to Boston in 1729 and established the "Church of the Presbyterian Strangers."

Many of the books in the Knox collection are from the "New London Book Store," which he opened on Washington Street (near Court Street) in 1771. In his first newspaper advertisement, he announced "A large and very elegant assortment of the most modern Books in all branches of Literature, Arts and Sciences . . . to be sold as cheap as can be bought at any place in town."

Despite Knox's support of the Patriot cause, his bookstore became "a great resort for the British officers and Tory ladies." One of these "high-tone" ladies was Lucy Flucker, the daughter of the colony's royal secretary, who, despite her family's prohibition, married the young Knox. To lure him to the Loyalist persuasion, Lucy's father tempted him with a commission in the British Army, although unsuccessfully.

§ Open Monday-Friday 9-5:30; tours available Tuesday and Thursday at 2:30. Phone: 617-227-0270.

¶ **Boston Massacre Location,** marked by a circle of cobblestones at the intersection of State and Congress streets.

On March 5, 1770, a lone British sentry outside the Customs House was attacked by a gang of rowdy youths, a disturbance that attracted a growing crowd. After moving a detachment of eight Redcoats to the scene, Captain Thomas Preston (himself an Anglo-Irishman) attempted to pacify the crowd, although he told his men to load their weapons. When a bystander hit one of the soldiers with a stick, the Redcoat accidentally discharged his gun as he fell to the ground. The other soldiers immediately fired into the mob, killing four and wounding seven others. Among the wounded who later died was the Irish immigrant Patrick Carr.

On the night of the violent confrontation between Boston "ruffians" and British soldiers, Carr was living in Queen (now Court) Street in the household of his employer, a leather-breeches maker. When Carr responded to the clamor of bells announcing the initial commotion, he started to leave the house with a small cutlass hidden under his coat until a neighbor persuaded him to leave the weapon at home. By the time the Irishman approached the center of the disturbance, the "Lobster Backs" had begun firing into the crowd of taunting citizenry. As he crossed King Street, he was hit by a bullet that "went through his right hip & tore away part of the backbone & greatly injured the hip bone." A companion carried him into a nearby house and then ran for a doctor. Carr was later moved to his master's house in Queen Street. Although at least two doctors tried to save his life, the young apprentice died on March 14. Three days later – on St. Patrick's Day – Carr was laid to rest in the Old Granary Burial Ground on Tremont Street, where four of the other victims of the "Massacre" had already been buried.

At the trial of the British soldiers, several witnesses gave compelling testimony about Carr's apparent intentions on the night of the violence. Carr's landlady explained how the Irishman had originally intended to go to the scene of the disturbance carrying a concealed weapon. Dr. John Jeffries, who had gone to see Carr the morning after the "Massacre," repeated what he purported was his conversation with the wounded man: "I asked him whether he thought the soldiers would fire. He told me he thought the soldiers would fire long before. I asked him whether he thought the soldiers were abused a great deal, after they went down there. He said, he thought they were. I asked him whether he thought the soldiers would have been hurt, if they had not fired. He said he really thought they would, for he heard many voices cry out, kill them. I asked him then . . . whether he thought they fired in self-defense, or on purpose to destroy the people. He said he really thought they did fire to defend themselves; that he did not blame the man whoever he was, that shot him." In answer to the question whether he thought Carr was aware of the danger he was in at the time of the disturbance, Jeffries replied somewhat equivocally: "He was told of it. He told me also, he was a native of Ireland, that he had frequently seen mobs, and soldiers called upon to quell them." Jeffries again paraphrased Carr's assertion that the British soldiers had shown unusual patience in the face of the taunting they received. According to Jeffries, Carr claimed "that he had seen soldiers often fire on the people in Ireland, but had never seen them bear half so much before they fired in his life." In a final conversation with Jeffries, the Irishman allegedly forgave "whoever he was that shot him, he was satisfied he had no malice, but fired to defend himself."

¶ **Boston Massacre Monument,** the Boston Common, near the Oliver Wendell Holmes Walk.

This twenty-five-foot granite shaft contains the names of the five "massacre" victims: Crispus Attucks, Samuel Maverick, Jonas Caldwell, Samuel Gray, and *Patrick Carr.

In front of the shaft is a seven-foot bronze female figure holding a broken chain in her right hand and a flag in her left. An eagle beside

Monument to the victims of the Boston Massacre, one of whom was the Irishman Patrick Carr.

her has just landed, while her right foot rests on a twisted crown about to fall off the plinth. Around the apex of the shaft are thirteen stars. A bronze bas-relief on the base depicts the Massacre on King (now State) Street. On the relief are two quotations: "From that Moment we may date the Severance of the British Empire" (Daniel Webster) and "On that night the Foundation of American Independence was laid" (John Adams).

In a speech at the dedication of the monument in 1888, Hugh O'Brien, Boston's Irish-born mayor, said: "The Boston Massacre was one of the most important and exciting events that preceded our Revolution . . . . I rejoice . . . that the erection of the Attucks Monument on Boston Common ratifies the words of the [Declaration of Independence] that all men are free and equal; and that the memory of the martyrs whose blood was shed in the cause of liberty in 1770 will thus be preserved and honored for all time."

¶ **Boston Public Library,** 666 Boylston Street, Copley Square.

This Italian Renaissance structure is noted for several pieces of art work by Irish or Irish-American artists:

• a bust of the goddess Athena and the seal of the library (with the words "Free to All"), both of them by Augustus Saint-Gaudens and located on the façade of the building;

• a medallion portrait of Robert C. Billings (a benefactor of the library) by Augustus Saint-Gaudens;

• a pair of lions by Louis Saint-Gaudens in honor of the men of two Massachusetts regiments who died in the Civil War. (The names of the campaigns and the battles in which the regiments participated are inscribed on the pedestals.)

• bronze busts of Boston mayor *Hugh O'Brien and journalist *John Boyle O'Reilly, both by John Donoghue.

Donoghue was born in Chicago in 1853 to parents from western Ireland and attended the Chicago Academy of Design and the Ecole des Beaux-Arts. His most notable classical works are the bust *Phaedra* and the statues *Young Sophokles*, *Hunting Nymph*, *Hannibal*, and *Kypris*. While in Rome, he also modeled a colossal figure called *The Spirit*, intended for exhibition at the Chicago World's Fair. Officials refused to accept the statue, however, because they feared that it would be blown down by the elements in the Windy City. As the model for his statue *The Boxer*, Donoghue used the famous pugilist *John L. Sullivan.

§ Open Monday-Thursday 9-9, Friday and Saturday 9-5. Closed holidays. Phone: 617-536-5400.

¶ **Bunker Hill Monument,** Monument Square, Charlestown.

This 221-foot granite obelisk commemorates the battle of Breed's

Hill on June 17, 1775. Among the Americans who participated in the battle were 694 men with Irish surnames, among them Coughlan, Lyons, McGaffey, and Savage. In addition, seven of the American officers were natives of Ireland, five had Irish immigrant parents, and another five were of Irish descent. Seventy percent of the companies that suffered casualties had Irishmen or sons of Irishmen in them; fifty-four casualties had Irish surnames, and twenty-two were natives of Ireland. The names of the Americans killed in the battle are on the Memorial Tablets in Winthrop Square in Charlestown.

> One of the unfortunate officers cut down that day was Major Andrew Clary, the son of an immigrant from County Tyrone, Ireland. During the battle Clary commanded a battalion in John Stark's New Hampshire regiment and fought valiantly, but later that day he was struck by a chance shot from a British frigate in the Charles River. The major was described as "a favorite officer, six and a half feet in height, with a Herculean form in perfect proportions, a voice like a Stentor and the strength of Ajax; ever unequalled in athletic exercise and unsubdued in single combat, whole bodies of men had been overcome by him and he seemed totally unconscious that he was not equally unconquerable at the cannon's mouth." Fifty years later, in an address to mark the laying of the cornerstone of the Bunker Hill Monument, Daniel Webster made note of Clary's valor during the battle.

Another colorful participant in the battle was the clergyman John Martin. Born in Ireland in 1750 and living in the west country until the age of seven – "speaking and hearing nothing but old Irish" – he attended a Catholic seminary in West Meath before coming to Rhode Island in 1771. During the battle on Breed's Hill, he supervised about a thousand men as they labored to finish building the entrenchments. His clerical dress and his ministrations to the dead and wounded guaranteed him no quarter, however, for the British soldiers "damned him for a clerical dog" and fired upon him as he carried off the American casualties: "The soldiers rushed on him with their bayonets, [but] he defended himself with his sword and killed his adversaries, [and then] brought off his wounded." For his bravery he was rewarded with a chaplaincy in a Rhode Island regiment. Later during the war he crossed the British lines as a spy for the Americans.

§ Open daily 9-4:30. Phone: 617-242-5641.

¶ **Cardinal Cushing Memorial,** in a small triangular park opposite the Saltonstall Building in old Bowdoin Square.

This bronze bust of Richard Cushing, the archbishop of Boston from 1944 to 1970, was erected from contributions made by the Catholic clergy of the Boston archdiocese. At its dedication in 1981, Cardinal Humberto Medeiros described his predecessor as a leader who "never lacked the common touch."

The son of an Irish blacksmith, Cushing felt buoyed by the openness in the Catholic Church which was initiated by Pope John XXIII. In 1961 the cardinal expressed his belief that "the Church is a dynamic, not a static institution. . . . It cannot be frozen in set forms. There are essentials of its life, but beyond these there must always be innovation, enterprise, new vision." Although very interested in the issues of religious liberty and ecumenism discussed at the Second Vatican Council, he participated in the proceedings only minimally, apparently because of difficulty in understanding the Latin in which the discussions were conducted.

Cushing later broke new ground by speaking in synagogues and Protestant churches and served as a panelist in a Catholic-Protestant conference at Harvard University. In response to criticism about these actions, he replied: "I'm all for Catholics being identified with Protestants and Jews . . . in every possible friendly way. Nobody is asking them to deny their faith, and they shouldn't be asking anybody to deny their faith." In 1963, when he left to participate in the election of a successor to John XXIII, he expressed his hope that "the new Pope will be living in the twentieth . . . and not the fourteenth or sixteenth century." His own modern vision of the Church was seen in the fact that he established the first Catholic chapel at an airport and the first diocesan center for radio and television.

Through his association with the Kennedy family, Cushing became a friend and admirer of *John F. Kennedy. During the latter's presidential campaign, the cardinal countered critics who charged that Kennedy would be obliged to follow Vatican policies as president. "Whatever may be the custom elsewhere," Cushing pointed out, "the American tradition . . . is satisfied simply to call to public attention moral questions with their implications, and leave to the conscience of the people the specific political decision which comes in the act of voting." Cushing gave the invocation at Kennedy's inauguration and later conducted the funeral of the assassinated president at St. Matthew's Cathedral in Washington, D. C.

¶ **Cardinal O'Connell Way,** in the West End, north of Cambridge Street and between Blossom and Staniford streets.

After graduating from Boston College, *William O'Connell studied for the priesthood at the North American College in Rome. Several years after his ordination in 1884, he was named rector of his Roman alma mater, in which capacity he doubled the school's enrollment and put its finances in order. After the Russo-Japanese War he was named papal envoy to the Japanese emperor, who subsequently awarded him the Grand Cordon of the Sacred Treasure. The Vatican later adopted all the archbishop's recommendations with regard to Japan: the development of a native clergy, the introduction of more religious orders, and the creation of a Catholic university in Tokyo.

After becoming archbishop of Boston in 1907 and cardinal four years later, O'Connell oversaw an administration that recorded phenomenal growth. He created 128 new parishes, introduced twenty religious communities into the archdiocese, doubled the number of elementary schools, and tripled the number of high schools. In addition, three women's colleges were founded under his auspices, enrollment at the archdiocesan seminary tripled, and Catholic charities benefited from his disbursement of a $2.5 million bequest which he had received from an American theater impresario.

In 1937 even Harvard University – founded 300 years before as a bulwark of Puritan orthodoxy – recognized O'Connell's work for the people of Boston by awarding him a doctoral degree, the first by Harvard to a member of the American Catholic hierarchy. Two years later he became the first American prelate to attend a papal conclave.

¶ **Charlestown Navy Yard,** off I-93 in Charlestown.

The U.S.S. *Constitution*, the oldest commissioned ship in the American navy, was launched near here in 1797. It earned the name "Ironsides" because of its exploits during the War of 1812.

The nickname "Ironsides" was shared with Father William Henry Reaney, one of the first Catholic chaplains in the U.S. Navy. Reaney was appointed chaplain in 1892 and received his nickname because of his birth aboard the U.S.S. *Constitution* as it lay in New York harbor. Noted for his friendliness and Irish wit, he loved athletics of all kinds, especially boxing. He was, in fact, a sparring partner of *President Theodore Roosevelt. During his chaplaincy he served on the U.S.S. *Charleston, Baltimore,* and *Olympia.*

¶ **Church of the Immaculate Conception,** Harrison Avenue and Concord Street.

Designed by *Patrick Keely, this edifice was built as the collegiate church of Boston College, founded in 1863 on adjacent property by Father John McElroy, a native of Ireland. The Jesuit college, New England's first such Catholic institution, began with a faculty of six Jesuits and a student body of twenty-two. The school remained on this site until 1913, when it was relocated in Chestnut Hill, a Boston suburb.

McElroy had come to America in 1803 from Enniskillen, County Fermanagh, Ireland. After working as a bookkeeper at Georgetown College for a number of years, he joined the Society of Jesus. While a seminarian at Georgetown during the War of 1812, he witnessed the burning of the nation's capital by the British from his dormitory window. After his ordination he served as an instructor at Georgetown College and then as pastor of St. John's Church in Frederick, Maryland.

In 1846 the Irish priest was appointed by *President James K. Polk as a chaplain to the American army at Matamoros, Mexico, where he served for eleven months and earned the highest praise of General Zachary Taylor. Returning to Boston after the war, the priest foresaw the need of an institution of higher learning to serve the increasing numbers of Catholics in the city. After much effort he finally obtained the property on Harrison Avenue, in the city's South End.

¶ **Colonel Cass Statue,** in the Public Garden, along Boylston Street.

Born in Ireland in 1822, Thomas Cass immigrated to Boston, where he conducted a real estate and brokerage business. In 1854 he became captain of a militia unit known as the Columbian Artillery Company, which by then had a largely Irish Catholic membership. The following year, however, the governor disbanded all militia companies made up of persons of foreign birth.

At the outbreak of the Civil War, Cass formed and commanded the Ninth Massachusetts Infantry, composed entirely of Irish immigrants. Colonel Cass was killed while leading his men at the battle of Malvern Hill in Virginia on July 1, 1862.

The statue of the colonel was dedicated in 1899 in the presence of veterans of the "Fighting Ninth."

¶ **Commodore Barry Bust,** near the information center on the Boston Common.

This bust honors John Barry, a native of Ireland who became known as the "Father of the American Navy."

¶ **Copley Square,** at Boylston and Dartmouth streets.

This expansive urban plaza was named for John Singleton Copley, the son of Irish immigrants and America's most outstanding colonial artist.

Although Copley had secured a reputation – and a commensurate income – as a Boston portrait painter before the age of thirty, he felt uncomfortable with the growing political unrest on the eve of the Revolution. (His wife's family was loyalist in its sentiments.) He therefore found it opportune to travel to London, where, during his subsequent expatriate career, he became known for his heroic-sized historical paintings. His most famous works in this genre are *The Death of the Earl of Chatham, The Siege of Gibraltar, The Arrest of Five Members of the Commons by Charles I,"* and *The Death of Major Pierson."*

Copley's own political leanings were revealed shortly after George III recognized American independence, when the artist painted the Stars and Stripes over a ship in the background of a portrait of Elkanah Watson. About the pictorial sleight of hand, Watson later wrote: "This was, I imagine, the first American flag hoisted in Old England."

¶ The site of Copley's Boston studio is marked with a plaque on the Somerset Club, 42 Beacon Street.

¶ **Dorchester Heights National Historic Site,** Thomas Park, Dorchester Heights, South Boston (near the intersection of Broadway and G Street).

Completed in 1902, the 215-foot monument on this site commemorates the actions taken by the Continental Army in May 1776 to dislodge the British from Boston after a yearlong siege.

Extraordinary efforts to drive out the British had begun in November 1775, when *General Henry Knox and his men began a 300-mile trek from upstate New York to Boston, dragging in the dead of winter the fifty-nine cannon they had captured at Fort Ticonderoga. On the night of March 4, 1776, American soldiers and volunteers moved the artillery into position on these heights south of Boston. Although the British launched an attack on the American position, they were unsuccessful and evacuated their troops and local Tories on March 17.

§ Open daily 9-9 in summer; abbreviated times the rest of the year.

¶ **Faneuil Hall,** Faneuil Hall Square, Merchants Row.

The assembly hall on the second floor is dominated by the huge oil painting *Liberty and Union, Now and Forever* by *George Healy. The work depicts the famous debate which took place in the U.S. Senate on January 25, 1830, in which Daniel Webster of Massachusetts argued the issue of nullification and states' rights with Robert Haynes of South Carolina.

In painting the huge work for King Louis-Philippe of France, Healy included either in the Senate chamber or in the gallery the most prominent politicians and members of Washington society of the day. The Irish-American artist worked on the painting for seven years, only to see his royal patron deposed in 1848. Healy later sold the work to a group of Boston businessmen, who presented it to the city in 1851.

§ Open Monday-Friday 10-4. Closed January 1, Thanksgiving, and December 25. Phone: 617-635-3105.

¶ **Great Hunger Memorial,** at the Atlantic Avenue end of the Faneuil

Hall Marketplace.

This temporary stone marker is the only memorial in the United States to the victims of the Irish famine in the middle of the nineteenth century. The memorial was dedicated in 1993 by Boston mayor *Raymond Flynn to commemorate the sesquicentennial of the famine.

J Holy Cross Cathedral, Washington and Malden streets.

Because by 1860 the area in which the original Church of the Holy Cross was located had become increasingly commercial, *Bishop John Fitzpatrick decided to sell that church and erect the present structure at this site. The cathedral was designed by *Patrick Keely and was constructed between 1866 and 1876. It is one of the largest Gothic cathedrals in the world and one of about thirty churches which Keely designed in the Boston area.

J James Family House, 131 Mt. Vernon Street, Beacon Hill. Private.

During the mid 1880s, this address was the home of Henry James Sr. and two of his children, Alice and Henry Jr. It was here that the latter child wrote a dramatization of his novel *Daisy Miller.*.

The family was descended from William James, an emigrant from County Cavan, Ireland, who eventually settled in Albany, New York. The fortune which he made through investments in numerous business enterprises, including the Erie Canal, allowed his son and grandchildren to travel and pursue intellectual interests. During a visit to the ancestral home in 1837, William's son, Henry Sr., was "so intoxicated with the roads and lanes and hedges and fields and cottages and castles and inns that I thought I should fairly expire with delight."

J John Boyle O'Reilly House, Winthrop Street, toward the lower end of Common Street.

The last house before the fire station was once the home of John Boyle O'Reilly, the Irish-born patriot, political prisoner, author, editor, and civic leader.

J John Boyle O'Reilly Memorial, Boylston Street, near the Brookline Avenue bridge over the Back Bay Fens.

A bronze bust of John Boyle O'Reilly stands atop a tapering stone pedestal. To the rear is a female personification of Erin flanked by allegorical figures of her sons, Poetry and Courage. The work of Daniel Chester French, the monument was dedicated in 1896, six years after O'Reilly's death.

Born near Drogheda, Ireland, in 1844, O'Reilly became active in the Fenian movement to overthrow British rule in Ireland even while he was a member of a British regiment. When his efforts to recruit other

John Boyle O'Reilly Memorial.

Irish soldiers to the cause were uncovered, he was court-martialed and found guilty of conspiracy and failure to inform the authorities of "an intended mutiny." Although he was sentenced to death, that penalty was commuted to life imprisonment and finally to twenty years of penal servitude. During a two-year period he was imprisoned at six different locations throughout England. At Mountjoy Prison he wrote three poems on the walls of his cell: "The Irish Flag," "For Life," and "The Irish Soldiers." Beneath the last was scratched the remark: "Written on the wall of my cell with a nail, July 17, 1866. Once an English soldier; now an Irish felon; and proud of the exchange." In October 1867 he was transported to a penal colony in Western Australia to serve the rest of his sentence.

In 1871, however, with the help of *Father Patrick McCabe, the prison colony's chaplain, O'Reilly made his escape, ultimately to America. He first took passage on an American whaling ship commanded by Captain David Gifford, who treated him kindly during the six-month cruise to Java and who lent him twenty guineas when they separated off the Cape of Good Hope. (While still on Gifford's ship, O'Reilly was almost killed during the pursuit of a whale but was rescued by the second mate, Henry Hathaway.) At Good Hope, O'Reilly boarded another American ship bound for Liverpool, where he shipped aboard the *Bombay* as "third mate" and headed for Philadelphia, arriving nine months after his escape from Australia. In 1873 O'Reilly dedicated his first book – *Songs of the Southern Seas* – to Captain Gifford, but news of the dedication arrived two hours after his death. O'Reilly's memorial to the good captain was the poem "A Tribute Too Late."

After moving to Boston, O'Reilly began a literary career that made him one of the most popular writers and commentators on the Irish-American scene. His editorial influence grew steadily, initially after he obtained a position with the *Pilot*, the most influential "Irish paper" in America, and later when he joined with *Cardinal William O'Connell of Boston to purchase that publication. Through this vehicle, as well as through his articles in the major publications of the period, O'Reilly became a spokesman for racial and religious tolerance, American patriotism, Irish nationalism, and the ideals of the Democratic Party.

Despite his support for the rights of Irish-American citizens, O'Reilly condemned sectarianism and efforts to create an Irish political party. After the 1871 Orange Riots (generally between Catholic and Protestant Irish in New York City), he thundered on the editorial page of the *Pilot*: One way to end this discord is "when Americans, tired out and indignant with her squabbling populations, puts her foot down with a will and tells them all – Germans, French, Irish, Orange – 'You have had enough now. There is only ONE flag to be raised in this country and that flag is the Stars and Stripes.'" He later urged reconciliation between Orangemen and Catholic Irish: "No matter if we do differ in religious belief: that is no reason why we should be enemies and ready to fly at each other's throat. The best Irishmen in our country's history were North of Ireland Protestants. Twine the flags – they are both Irish. The Orange is the oldest national color. Let us be sensible, friends on both sides, and not carry our island bickerings into the view of America's friendly cities." And even in the face of a growing xenophobic nativist movement, he attacked efforts to establish an "Irish" political party to counter anti-immigrant measures: "The Irishman who would proscribe a native American, and the native American who would proscribe an Irishman, are guilty of the same crime against the principles of the Constitution. . . . All that was good and beautiful in our dear native island, we should cherish forever. . . . But we cannot, as honest men, band together in American politics under the shadow of an Irish flag."

O'Reilly acknowledged, however, that most of his fellow Irish Americans joined him in their steadfast devotion to the Democratic Party. In defending this loyalty, he wrote that "Every assault on their rights as citizens in this country has come from the Republican party and its predecessors . . . ." Yet it is interesting to contrast the following excerpts of his essentially Jeffersonian Democratic creed with its modern Rooseveltian expression: "Democracy means to us the least government for the people, instead of more or most. It means that every atom of paternal power not needed for the safety of the Union and the intercourse of the population should be taken from the Federal Government and kept and guarded by the States and the people . . . . It means antagonism to all men, classes and parties that throw distrust and discredit on the . . . common people . . . ."

An indication of the esteem in which this naturalized American was held by his contemporaries is evident in the frequency with which he was called upon to provide the appropriate patriotic sentiment on various civic occasions. Before a gathering of the Grand Army of the Republic in 1886, for example, he delivered a Memorial Day oration entitled "The Common Citizen Soldier," usually regarded as his best speech. Two years later he read his poem "Crispus Attucks" at the dedication of the Boston Massacre Monument on the Boston Common, and in 1889 he read a poem at the dedication of the Pilgrim Monument at Plymouth. He also wrote "Liberty Lighting the World" for the unveiling of the Statue of Liberty.

Following his death in 1890, O'Reilly was universally praised for his ability to foster cultural understanding. One eulogist described him thus: "Loving and loyal to the land of his adoption, and ever ready to work for her good and her glory . . . he never forgot the land of his birth; he always battled for her against scurrilous enemies, here and abroad. . . . Here he made friends for Ireland by his genius, his tenderness for oppressed humanity, his 'love for justice and hatred of iniquity' . . . ." Other eulogists emphasized his ability to abolish the old distinction between English American and Irish American: "This man, this Roman Catholic, on New England soil, in daily association with the sons of Puritans, – the sons of men who hated the Papacy as the instrument of Satan, and whose descendants have not entirely got beyond the narrowness of their forefathers, – could yet describe in fitting terms, and show the appreciation of his mind and soul for, the achievements of the founders of New England."

❡ John Fitzgerald House, 4 Garden Court Street. Private.

A marker identifies the location of the house in which *John "Honey Fitz" Fitzgerald lived with his family between 1886 and 1894. His daughter Rose – the mother of President John Fitzgerald

Kennedy – was born here in 1890.

Fitzgerald's twenty-five-year political career was one of the most colorful in Boston history. Following his election to the Massachusetts Senate, he became a spokesman for the rights of the Irish and of immigrants in general. During the mayoral campaign of 1905, he promised a "Bigger, Better, Busier Boston" and raised eyebrows by conducting the city's first political motorcade and spending $120,000, twice as much as his blue-blood Republican opponent.

Once in the mayor's office, Fitzgerald supported industrial development and harbor expansion and built vocational schools, public baths, and playgrounds. He permitted graft in the awarding of city contracts, however, and created such sinecures as city dermatologist and municipal tea warmer. Ever the extrovert, he attended 1,500 dances, 1,200 dinners, and a thousand meetings – all during his first term alone. Before long, his mellifluous eloquence and singing voice had earned him the nickname "Honey Fitz." In the 1910 campaign he first sang "Sweet Adeline," which eventually became his trademark.

Although he ran for a third term in 1914, he withdrew from the race because of attacks by challenger *James Curley, who threatened to expose Fitzgerald's alleged affair with a woman known as "Toodles." In a bid for the U.S. Senate two years later, Fitzgerald unsuccessfully ran against Henry Cabot Lodge; in 1952 the ex-mayor's grandson – John Fitzgerald Kennedy – won a Senate seat in a race against Lodge's grandson.

Of John Fitzgerald's six children, Rose was his favorite. After graduating from Dorchester High School (where she was elected the prettiest senior), Rose studied music at the New England Conservatory before attending the Convent of the Sacred Heart in Boston and the Manhattanville College of the Sacred Heart in New York. Although her father attempted to prevent her from marrying Joseph P. Kennedy, she was persistent and finally won her father's grudging permission. (Fitzgerald won a partial victory, however, by denying Kennedy a lavish wedding, arranging instead a private ceremony in *Cardinal William O'Connell's chapel.)

Although Rose's marriage to "the lone wolf" banker of Wall Street promised her a charmed life, it was regularly punctuated by more than its share of tragedies involving her children. The mental retardation of her daughter Rosemary was followed by the deaths of Joseph Jr. during World War II, of Kathleen in a plane crash in France in 1948, and of John and Robert at the hands of political assassins. "I just made up my mind that I wasn't going to be vanquished by anything," she once said. "If I collapsed, I knew it would have a very bad effect on other members of the family." Her life was summed up in her personal motto: "I know not age, nor weariness nor defeat."

❡ The Rose Fitzgerald Kennedy Garden, near the birthplace, contains a granite fountain inscribed with a quote from the Kennedy matriarch: "If God were to take away all his blessings and leave me but one gift, I would ask for faith."

❡ **John F. Kennedy Federal Building,** on the north side of City Hall Plaza.

This modern building was named in honor of *John F. Kennedy, who served as a congressman from Charlestown before being elected to the U.S. Senate from Massachusetts.

❡ **John F. Kennedy Statue,** State House, Beacon Street and Park Street.

A bronze life-size standing statue of *President John F. Kennedy is located on the south side of the State House. The statue catches the president in his stride, with his right hand in his coat pocket.

❡ **Mayor Collins Monument,** Commonwealth Avenue, between Clarendon and Dartmouth streets.

This memorial to Mayor Patrick Collins consists of a plinth flanked by allegorical female figures of Erin and Columbia and topped by a bust of the Irish native.

After accompanying his mother from County Cork to Boston in 1848, the young Collins faced harassment by his Yankee peers because of his religion and race, frequently being beaten up and once suffering a broken arm. As a youngster he held a variety of jobs, including fishmongering, farming, coal mining, and upholstering. (He even helped organize an upholsterers' union.)

While still pursuing his education, Collins began the political career that would earn him the nickname "one of Boston's greatest Irishmen." Even before his graduation from Harvard Law School, he was elected to the Massachusetts House. Later in the state senate he advocated the removal of various anti-Catholic disabilities and fought for the introduction of Catholic chaplains in jails and public hospitals. Beginning in 1901, he was elected to two successive terms as mayor of Boston. He reduced the city's tax levels and generally opposed what he called "benevolent Socialism" – excessive municipal spending and borrowing. He also served three terms in the U.S. House of Representatives.

Despite his political reliance on Boston's Irish, Collins tried to discourage ethnic politics, emphasizing the *unum* more than the *pluribus* in the American motto. During the 1876 election he told the voters: "I kneel at the altar of my fathers, and I love the land of my birth, but in American politics I know neither color, race nor creed. Let me say here and now that there are no Irish voters among us. There are Irish-born citizens, like myself, and there will be many more of us, but . . . Americans we are, Americans we will remain . . . ."

¶ **Mayor Curley Memorial,** near Faneuil Hall, in the park between North and Congress streets.

This memorial consists of two life-size bronze statues of colorful Boston mayor James Curley, one of him seated on a park bench as if talking to a companion, and the other standing with his hands behind his back.

Curley, the son of immigrants from Galway, Ireland, early tried his hands at politics, sometimes showing an unappreciated independence by campaigning against his ward boss's candidate. In one electoral contest, although Curley won by 500 votes, the party bosses stole the election from him by "counting him out." Nevertheless, the determined Curley was successively elected to the city council, the state assembly, the board of aldermen, the House of Representatives, the governorship, and the mayoralty.

During his four terms as mayor between 1914 and 1949, Curley was known as the "mayor of the poor" and a champion of the Irish.

*One of two statues
near Fanieul Hall
in honor of Mayor
James Curley.*

His administrations were marked by increased expenditures for public works, a policy whose increasing tax assessments caused many of the city's business interests to oppose him. He failed to be reelected in 1917 when a rival ward boss split the Irish vote by running two phoney candidates with Irish surnames.

Although previous Irish mayors had refrained from attacking Yankee culture and tradition, Curley lambasted the WASP Establishment. In a letter to the Harvard Board of Overseers, he exulted: "The Massachusetts of the Puritans is as dead as Caesar, but there is no need to mourn the fact. Their successors – the Irish – had letters and learning, culture and civilization when the ancestors of the Puritans were savages running half-naked through the forests of Britain. It took the Irish to make Massachusetts a fit place to live in." On another occasion he attacked wealthy Yankees as descendants of scoundrels who "got rich selling opium to the Chinese, rum to the Indians, or trading in slaves."

Despite his active campaigning for Franklin Roosevelt in 1932, Curley was disappointed in his hope of securing in return a suitable political appointment. Although the Irish American had hoped to be named secretary of the navy, F.D.R. suggested the Italian ambassadorship, adding that Curley would be the first Catholic ambassador to Rome. After asking for time to think it over, Curley sent telegrams to the King of Italy, Premier Mussolini, and the Vatican to obtain their reaction to the proposal. When the former mayor returned to Roosevelt ready to accept the ambassadorial spot, the president claimed that the appointment had run into objections from the Italian monarch. After Curley proffered the affirmative telegram from the Italian government, F.D.R. changed his story and said that it must have been Mussolini who objected. Curley called Roosevelt's bluff by producing the telegrams which expressed approval by both the Italian premier and the Holy See and then stormed out of the office. (The former Boston mayor later learned that his name had never been submitted for the position.)

❡ Mayor Curley Residence, 350 Jamaicaway at Moraine Street.

Mayor James Michael Curley began construction on this brick colonial mansion – appropriately enough – on St. Patrick's Day, 1915. The twenty-one-room house is notable for its chandeliers, Italian marble fireplaces, and shamrock-decorated shutters. It was here that Curley died in 1958, just short of his eighty-fourth birthday.

During his political career Curley survived both personal tragedy and political scandal. Although he and his wife had nine children, only two survived to adulthood. In fact, in 1950 two of their children died of cerebral hemorrhage the very same day. During his first term in the state legislature, he spent sixty days in jail for impersonating someone else in a civil service exam. (Always trying to win political advantage, he said about the incident, "I did it for a friend!") Later, while mayor in the 1930s, he was charged with defrauding the city and was ordered to repay almost $43,000. Finally, after his last term as mayor, the seventy-two-year-old Curley served five months in jail for mail fraud stemming from a charge of influence-peddling in Congress.

A fictionalized version of his career is portrayed in Edwin O'Connor's 1956 novel *The Last Hurrah*, although because of what Curley described as inaccuracies the former mayor responded in a 1957 autobiography, *I'd Do It Again*. Even one of his most outspoken critics admitted that Boston "would be a shabby place without having had him."

§ Although the house is generally not open to the public, it can be viewed by appointment. Phone 617-635-4105.

¶ **McCormack Building,** Bowdoin Street and Ashburton Place.

This state office building was named for John McCormack, the first Catholic to be elected Speaker of the U.S. House of Representatives.

McCormack was a native of South Boston, one of thirteen children born to an Irish bricklayer and his wife, themselves the children of emigrants fleeing the Irish potato famine in the 1840s. During a long career in the House of Representatives, McCormack fervently supported the New Deal and earned the nickname "the fighting Irishman" for his aggressive debating style. Because of his close ties with many Catholic clerical leaders, he was dubbed "the Archbishop" by his enemies, although many Jewish voters in his district called him "Rabbi John." Noted for his anti-Communist stance, he was appointed chairman of the first House Committee on Un-American Activities. With the election of Sam Rayburn to the speakership in 1940, McCormack served as his deputy until he himself assumed the Speaker's chair in 1962. After warning the nation about the importance of the scientific race with the Soviet Union, he sponsored the bill to create the National Aeronautics and Space Administration. He died in 1980.

¶ **The Museum at the John F. Kennedy Library,** on the campus of the University of Massachusetts, State 3/I-93 exit to Morrissey Boulevard (in Dorchester).

Dedicated in 1979, the library contains many Kennedy memorabilia, including the president's rocking chair and a copy of his desk inside a replica of the Oval Office in the White House. A thirty-minute film chronicles the former president's life. The museum also commemorates the political career of *Robert Kennedy.

§ Open daily 9-5. Closed January 1, Thanksgiving, and December 25. Fee. Phone: 617-929-4523.

¶ **Museum of Fine Arts,** 465 Huntington Avenue.

The museum's galleries exhibit American, Asian, Classical, Egyptian, and European sculpture and painting. Among its sculpted pieces are works by *Thomas Crawford, including *Adam and Eve, Hebe and Ganymede, Orpheus and Cerberus, Shepherdess, Aurora, Mercury and Psyche, Pandora, Boy Playing Marbles, Children in the Wood, Dancing Jenny, Flora, Indian Hunter,* and a bust of Josiah Quincy. The museum also contains Celtic ornaments, Irish silver, portraits by *John Singleton Copley, and the 1853 painting of Daniel Webster by *George Healy.

§ Open Tuesday-Sunday 10-4:45 (Wednesday until 9:45). Closed January 1, July 4, Thanksgiving, and December 24-25. Fee. Phone: 617-267-9300.

¶ **Nichols House Museum,** 55 Mt. Vernon Street.

Between 1885 and 1960 this brick mansion was the home of Rose Standish Nichols, author and pacifist and the country's first female landscape architect. The museum contains two works by *Augustus Saint-Gaudens: the bronze statue *Diana of the Crossroads* and a bronze relief of Robert Louis Stevenson.

§ Phone: 617-227-6993.

¶ **Old City Hall,** School Street (next to King's Chapel).

The present building was completed in 1865 and was used until the new city hall in Government Center was opened in 1968. Today the Old City Hall serves various commercial uses.

Boston's first Irish Catholic mayor was Hugh O'Brien. After arriving in Boston with his immigrant parents, the youngster learned the printing trade and at age sixteen set himself up as editor and publisher of the *Shipping and Commercial List.* He later served as an officer of the Franklin Typographical Society and the Charitable Irish Society.

In 1875 O'Brien launched his political career by serving the first of six terms as city alderman. Nine years later he was first elected mayor, continuing the city's tradition of businessmen-amateur politicians. By the end of his first term, his advocacy of mayoral control of the budget, limits on municipal spending and taxing, and tax incentives to attract manufacturing interests to the city had gone far to dispel Yankee mistrust of an Irish Catholic mayor. Nevertheless, he was unsuccessful in his fourth mayoral bid, partly because of opposition from the American Protective Association, which had stirred up anti-Catholic and anti-immigrant sentiment.

¶ **Old Granary Burial Ground,** Tremont Street.

Among those buried here the victims of the Boston Massacre (including the Irishman Patrick Carr), John Hancock and Robert Treat

Paine (both regarded by some authorities as descendants of emigrants from Ulster), and James Sullivan (a governor of Massachusetts and the first Irish justice of the state's supreme court).

§ Open daily 8-4

⚓ O'Neill Building, Causeway Street and Lomasney Way.

This state government building was named for Thomas "Tip" O'Neill, the Speaker of the House of Representatives from 1977 to 1987.

The grandson of an immigrant bricklayer from County Cork, the young O'Neill was nicknamed for a baseball player renowned for hitting foul tips. During his senior year at Boston College, the young political aspirant narrowly lost a bid for a seat on the Cambridge City Council. Following his election to the state legislature, he became the youngest majority leader in the state's history and an advocate for the "Little New Deal," a program of social legislation on the state level.

Newly elected to the U.S. House in 1952 to replace *John F. Kennedy, O'Neill generally supported the liberal Democratic agenda. Although he almost immediately became part of the congressional power structure – thanks to House Democratic whip *John McCormack – the novice congressman never forget his ties to his constituents. His regular Saturday walks through the ethnic neighborhoods in his district became legendary and reflected his belief that "All politics is local." He generally backed Lyndon Johnson's domestic programs but broke with the president on the Vietnam War. Following the congressional Watergate hearings, O'Neill publicly called on *President Richard Nixon to resign, fully expecting him to do so "for the good of the country" before impeachment proceedings began.

During the presidency of *Ronald Reagan, O'Neill used his influence as Speaker to oppose the conservative president's policies. Convinced of government's ability to ameliorate social ills, O'Neill opposed a balanced budget because it would "dismantle the programs that I've been working for as an old liberal." During his political wrangling with Reagan, the Speaker once called him the most ignorant man who had ever occupied the White House and referred to him as "a cheerleader for selfishness" and "Herbert Hoover with a smile."

⚓ Lomasney Way is named for Martin Lomasney, the son of an Irish immigrant tailor and for thirty years the head of Boston's Democratic political machine. He once described the machine's philosophy: "I think there's got to be in every ward somebody that any bloke can come to – no matter what he's done – and get help. Help, you understand; none of your law and your justice, but help." *Mayor John "Honey Fitz" Fitzgerald later acknowledged Lomasney as his "political grandfather," from whom he had learned that "the politician who thinks he can get away from the people who made him, usually gets what is coming to him – a swift kick in his political pants."

¶ St. Joseph's Cemetery, 990 La Grange, West Roxbury.

This cemetery is the final resting place of *John "Honey Fitz" Fitzgerald, one Boston's most colorful mayors and the grandfather of President John Fitzgerald Kennedy.

§ Phone: 617-327-1010.

¶ St. Stephen's Catholic Church, Hanover Street, at the east end of the Paul Revere Mall.

The present church stands on the site of the second Congregational house of worship in the North End. In 1802 that structure was torn down and replaced by a larger one designed by Charles Bulfinch. The Unitarian congregation that was using the church in 1862 sold it to the Roman Catholic Archdiocese, which sought it as a place of worship for the teeming numbers of Irish living in the area. In 1965 *Cardinal Richard Cushing restored the church to conform to its original design by Bulfinch. Fifteen years later Cushing was honored by the Boston Society of Architects for his leadership in the restoration effort.

• In 1863 John Fitzgerald – the future mayor of Boston – was born in a slum-tenement not far from St. Stephen's (where he was baptized). He was one of eleven children born to Irish Famine immigrants who had come to Boston in the 1840s. Fitzgerald was the first Irish boy and the first Catholic to attend Boston Latin School, where he overcame the prevailing bigotry to be chosen captain of two athletic teams and the editor of the school newspaper. His matriculation at Harvard Medical School was cut short, however, by the obligation to support his family after his father's untimely death. Fitzgerald later married *Mary "Josie" Hannon, who bore him six children. The oldest, Rose Fitzgerald, married *Joseph P. Kennedy and was the mother of President John Fitzgerald Kennedy.

• On January 22, 1995, St. Stephen's was crowded with mourners attending the funeral of *Rose Fitzgerald Kennedy after her death at the age of 104.

¶ Shaw Memorial, Beacon Street, across from the State House.

Designed by *Augustus Saint-Gaudens, this monument honors Colonel Robert Gould Shaw and the other officers and men of the 54th Massachusetts Regiment. The memorial, which was dedicated in 1897, depicts Shaw and his men as they passed the State House on May 28, 1863, after receiving their regimental colors from Governor John Andrew. The back of the monument is inscribed with the names of the men of the regiment who were decorated for bravery.

Although Shaw and his officers were white, the enlisted men in

The Robert Gould Shaw Memorial by Augustus Saint-Gaudens.

this regiment were all free African Americans who had volunteered to fight during the Civil War. The 54th fought bravely during the attack on Fort Wagner, South Carolina, on July 18, 1863, but Shaw and many of his men were killed in the assault and were buried near the fort. In his memoir Saint-Gaudens explained why the memorial to Shaw and his men had taken him so long to complete: "My own delay I excuse on the ground that a sculptor's work endures for so long that it is next to a crime for him to neglect to do everything that lies in his power to execute a result that will not be a disgrace. There is something extraordinarily irritating, when it is not ludicrous, in a bad statue."

In 1910, when the National Institute of Arts and Letters presented Mrs. Saint-Gaudens with its gold medal in honor of her husband's work, the ceremony included a reading of the following excerpt from Robert Underwood's poem "Saint-Gaudens: An Ode":

> So, on the traveled verge
> Of storied Boston's green acropolis
> That sculpted music, that immortal dirge,
> That better than towering shaft
> Has fitly epitaphed
> The hated ranks men did not dare to hiss!
> When Duty makes her clarion call to Ease
> Let her repair and point to this:
> Why seek another clime?

Why seek another place?
We have no Parthenon, but a noble frieze, -
Since sacrifice than worship nobler is.
It sings – the anthem of a rescued race;
It moves – the epic of a patriot time,
And each heroic figure makes a martial rhyme.
How like ten thousand treads that little band,
Fit for the van of armies! What command
Sits in that saddle! What renouncing will!
What portent grave of firm-confronted ill!
And as a cloud doth hover over sea,
Born from its waters and returning there,
Fame, sprung from thoughts of mortals, swims the air
And gives them back her memories, deathlessly.

¶ **Soldiers' and Sailors' Monument,** the Boston Common.

Dedicated in 1877, this monument is considered the greatest work of Martin Milmore, a native of Sligo, Ireland, where his father was a schoolmaster. The centerpiece of the memorial is a granite shaft topped by a bronze figure of "Liberty." Around the pedestal are statues representing Peace, the Sailor, the Muse of History, and the Soldier. Between the projections on which the statues stand are four bas-reliefs depicting the Battle of Fort Sumter, the Departure of the Forces for the War, the Work of the Boston Sanitary Commission, and the Return from the War.

Milmore was educated in Boston schools, learned woodcarving from his brother, and in his first effort at sculpting modeled a bust of himself with the help of a mirror. While living in Rome, he executed busts of Pius IX, Ralph Waldo Emerson, and Wendell Phillips. He was also known for his portrait busts of *Ulysses S. Grant, Abraham Lincoln, Henry W. Longfellow, *Cardinal John McCloskey, Charles Sumner, and Daniel Webster. Milmore's other larger works are the Soldiers' Monument in Roxbury, Massachusetts, the statue of General Sylvanus Thayer at the U.S. Military Academy, and the *Sphinx* in Cambridge, Massachusetts.

According to Daniel Chester French, "Milmore was a picturesque figure, somewhat of the Edwin Booth type, with long dark hair and large dark eyes. He affected the artistic . . . , wearing a broad-brimmed soft black hat, and a cloak. His appearance was striking, and he knew it."

¶ **Trinity Church,** Copley Square.

Some of the frescoes in this Romanesque church were painted by *Augustus Saint-Gaudens and John LaFarge. Although the statue of

Episcopal bishop Phillips Brooks outside the church was designed by Saint-Gaudens, it was sculpted by his assistants after the artist's death.
§ Open daily 8-6. Phone: 617-536-0944.

BROOKLINE

¶ Holyhood Cemetery, Heath Street. Phone: 617-327-1010.
Holyhood is the final resting place of many Boston Irish, including:
   • Patrick Collins, the mayor of Boston from 1901 to 1905, whose funeral was attended by 100,000 people.
   • Patrick Guiney, a native of County Tipperary, Ireland, who served in thirty Civil War engagements, succeeded to command of the Ninth Massachusetts Volunteers, and was partially blinded at the battle of the Wilderness. Guiney's death in March 1877 occurred on a public street in Boston, after he had removed his hat, knelt on the pavement, and crossed himself.
   • John Boyle O'Reilly, the famous editor, poet, and Irish nationalist, whose grave is marked by a huge boulder.
   • James Jeffrey Roche, author, journalist, and poet.
Born in Queen's County, Ireland, Roche grew up in Canada, where his father had resettled and conducted a school. In 1883 the younger man became assistant editor of the *Boston Pilot* and seven years later succeeded to the editorship of that paper, the country's leading Catholic Irish journal. Besides contributing to the nation's major publications and producing several collections of poetry, he wrote the adventure novel *The Story of the Filibusters* and a biography of John Boyle O'Reilly, his friend and fellow Irish patriot and American citizen. He also collaborated with Douglas Hyde and Lady Gregory in preparing a ten-volume work entitled *Irish Literature.*
   The huge granite memorial on Roche's grave was a gift of the John Boyle O'Reilly Club. In 1909 the monument was inscribed as follows: "A writer – he gave freely of his genius to humanity that the strong might be restrained, the weak strengthened and right might reign; a poet – patriotism, heroism and justice were the burden of his song; and author – his kindly wit and gentle satire were turned on folly and hypocrisy; and editor – his pen fought stoutly for the oppressed and persecuted of all races and creeds; a man – he never surrendered his principles to temptation, keeping his conscience clear and his mind free."

¶ Kennedy National Historic Site, 83 Beals Street.
   This frame house was the birthplace in 1917 of *President John F. Kennedy, whose father, Joseph P. Kennedy, had purchased it just before his marriage to *Rose Fitzgerald in 1914. (The elder Kennedy, the

son of a prosperous East Boston family, had graduated from Harvard two years before and was well on his way to financial success via real estate, banking, and the stock market.) Two other Kennedy children – Rosemary and Kathleen – were born in this house. In 1966 the Kennedy family repurchased the residence, which the president's mother restored to its 1917-21 appearance. Visitors can listen to a tape recording of Rose Kennedy describing various aspects of the house as well as incidents from the family's history.

§ Open daily 9-4:45. Phone: 617-566-7937.

¶ **Kennedy Residence,** on the northeast corner of Abbotsford and Naples roads. Private.

Joseph and Rose Kennedy moved to this house in 1921. During their six-year residence here, their children Eunice, Patricia, and Robert were born in the house.

CAMBRIDGE

The first official recognition of St. Patrick's Day during the Revolution was by General George Washington himself. On March 16, 1776, Washington informed the members of the Continental Army encamped in Cambridge that the parole for the next day would be "Boston" and the countersign "Saint Patrick." As "Brigadier of the Day" he named *General John Sullivan. On the 17th the army marched into Boston and took possession of the city from the British.

¶ **John F. Kennedy School of Government,** Harvard University, Boylston Street (also known as John F. Kennedy Avenue).

Following the assassination of *President John F. Kennedy in 1963, the Kennedy family offered Harvard University $3.5 million if its Graduate School of Public Administration was renamed the John F. Kennedy School of Government. The Kennedy Institute later donated $10 million to a Kennedy Institute of Politics within the J.F.K. School of Government.

¶ **Longfellow National Historic Site,** 105 Brattle Street.

This Georgian residence was the home of the famous American poet from 1837 until his death in 1882. Among the paintings in the house are three by *George Healy: *Fanny Appleton* (Henry Wadsworth Longfellow's wife), *Mary Appleton* (Mrs. Longfellow's sister), and *Franz Liszt*. The last portrait was done in 1868 following a visit by Longfellow and Healy to the Convent of San Francesco Romano in Rome, where the famous pianist was living at the time. Longfellow was so impressed by the inspired expression on Liszt's face as the musician held a candle to light his guests' way that he asked Healy to portray that look just as they had seen it.

§ Open daily 10-4:45. Closed January 1, Thanksgiving, and December 25. Fee. Phone: 617-876-4491.

¶ Massachusetts Institute of Technology.

Originally known as Boston Tech, M.I.T. had its beginnings in 1865 in downtown Boston. When the new Cambridge campus was officially opened in 1916, a domed and porticoed edifice was erected in honor of William Barton Rogers, the founder and first president of the institution.

Rogers, one of four extraordinary brothers who went on to distinguished careers in science, was born in Philadelphia in 1804, the son of an immigrant from County Tyrone, Ireland. He attended the College of William and Mary, where his father, Dr. Patrick Kerr Rogers, taught chemistry and natural history. At the age of twenty-three, the younger Rogers succeeded to his father's chair. In 1835, however, he accepted the professorship in natural philosophy at the University of Virginia. Although he remained there for eighteen years, he disliked the racial and religious bigotry and intolerance he encountered in Charlottesville. After moving to New England and marrying into a wealthy Yankee family, he became a well-known public speaker on science and its role in the educational curriculum.

In 1859 Rogers and a similarly inclined group formed the Massachusetts Conservatory of Arts and Sciences and sought incorporation from the state for the Massachusetts Institute of Technology, "having for its objects the advancement of the Mechanic Arts, Manufactures, Commerce, Agriculture and the applied sciences generally, together with the promotion of the practical education of the industrial classes. . . ." It was not until 1865, however, that the school actually opened – with fifteen students attracted by the prospect of learning "the various professions of the Mechanician, the Civil Engineer, the Builder and the Architect, the Mining Engineer and the Practical Chemist." Except for a nine-year period, Rogers served as the institute's president until 1881.

§ Tours leave from 77 Massachusetts Avenue, Monday-Friday 10 and 2. Phone: 617-253-4795.

¶ Mount Auburn Cemetery, 580 Mount Auburn Street.

Mount Auburn is regarded as the country's first garden cemetery and contains the graves of such illustrious Americans as Oliver Wendell Holmes, Julia Ward Howe, Henry Wadsworth Longfellow, and James Russell Lowell. Some monuments in the cemetery have an "Irish connection":

• The tombstone of the Civil War officer *Thomas Cass is inscribed with the following: "In Memory of Colonel Thomas Cass, Organizer and First Commander of the Famous Ninth Regiment of Infantry and Massachusetts Volunteers. Born in Farnley, Queens County, Ireland, 1821. Mortally wounded at the Battle of Malvern Hill, Virginia, July 1st, 1862, while leading his Regiment. Died in Boston, July 12th, 1862."

• *The Sphinx* was sculpted in 1872 by the Irish-born brothers Martin and Joseph Milmore and is inscribed with the words "American Union Preserved / African Slavery Destroyed / By the Uprising of a Great People / By the Blood of Fallen Heroes."

• The cemetery chapel contains a life-size statue of the Revolutionary patriot James Otis by *Thomas Crawford.

§ Open daily June-August 31, 8-7; rest of the year, 8-5. Phone: 617-864-9646.

CHESTNUT HILL

¶ **Boston College,** 140 Commonwealth Avenue.

Boston College was founded in 1863 by *Father John McElroy on property in Boston's South End. The Jesuit college began with a faculty of six Jesuits and a student body of twenty-two. In 1913 the school was relocated to its present site.

The earliest buildings on campus were designed by architect *Charles Maginnis in the English Collegiate Gothic style. Today the campus covers 200 acres on three levels.

• On the campus is the John J. Burns Library, which contains religious and art objects, Hibernian regalia, stained glass windows with Irish themes, and more than 6,000 books and journals on Ireland. Open Monday-Friday 9-5. Appointment recommended. Phone: 617-552-3282.

COHASSET

¶ **The *St. John* Memorial,** Central Cemetery, Joy Place, off North Main Street.

In 1914 the Ancient Order of Hibernians dedicated this twenty-foot Celtic cross to mark the burial place of about forty-five of the ninety-nine Irish immigrants killed in the wreck of the brig *St. John* in 1849. The monument was unveiled by Theresa St. John of Cohasset, the granddaughter of James St. John and Mary Cole, one of the Irish survivors.

On October 7, 1849, as the British brig *St. John,* loaded with emigrants from Galway, Ireland, approached the coast of Massachusetts, it was driven upon the rocks near Cohasset. Ninety-nine of its 121 passengers and crew members were lost. Henry David Thoreau captured the emotional impact of the incident in "The Shipwreck," a chapter in

The St. John *Memorial, marking the burial place of forty-five Irish immigrants killed in a shipwreck off Cohasset in 1849.*

his book *Cape Cod*.

CONCORD

❡ Walden Pond Reservation, 0.5 mile south on State 126.

On the north shore of the pond is a replica of the cabin which Henry David Thoreau built here in 1845. In *Walden* he explained that the boards for his dwelling place had come from the shanty of James Collins, an Irishman who worked on the Fitchburg Railroad. After paying Collins $4.25 for the shanty, Thoreau tore it down and removed it to the side of the pond, where he spread the boards on the grass so the sun could bleach and warp them back into shape. Thoreau added that an Irish lad ("a young Patrick") later told him that "neighbor Seeley, an Irishman," had stolen some of the usable nails from the boards while Thoreau was busy transporting the wood to the new site.

EAST BROOKFIELD

❡ Connie Mack Birthplace, Maple and Main streets. Private.

This was the birthplace of baseball player *Connie Mack (né Cornelius McGillicuddy), the manager of the Philadelphia Athletics. (See Cooperstown, New York.)

FALL RIVER

¶ **Battle Cove,** off I-95 exit 5.

On exhibit is a variety of U.S. Navy vessels, including a battleship, a submarine, two PT boats, and the destroyer U.S.S. *Joseph P. Kennedy Jr.* The destroyer, named for the older brother of John F. Kennedy, was built in 1945 and saw action in the Korean War, the NASA space recovery missions, and the 1962 Cuban blockade.

Joseph Kennedy Jr. was killed in 1944 while flying a top secret mission across the English Channel in an attempt to destroy what was believed to be the launching site of Hitler's V-1 rockets. Just before the flight, he made a phone call to a friend in London: "I'm about to go into my act. If I don't come back, tell dad . . . that I love him very much." After his death his nineteen-year-old brother Robert took his place by enlisting in the Navy and later served aboard the U.S.S. *Joseph P. Kennedy Jr.*

§ Open daily July 1-Labor Day, 9-8; rest of the year, 9-5. Closed January 1, Thanksgiving, and December 25. Fee. Phone: 508-678-1100.

HULL

¶ **Public Library,** 9 Main Street.

The library was originally the summer home of John Boyle O'Reilly, the Irish-born patriot, author, editor, and civic leader. The Queen Anne-style house was designed by O'Reilly's wife and was built on the site of Hunter House, Hull's first parsonage (built in 1644 and razed in 1888). O'Reilly's original house had a foyer, a living room, two reception rooms, and four bedrooms. The structure was purchased by the town of Hull in 1913 to be used as its public library.

• The John Boyle O'Reilly Memorial, on the grounds of the library, was unveiled on August 10, 1917, by the author's daughter. Among the guests that day was Henry Hathaway, who had saved O'Reilly's life in an incident that occurred after the Irishman's rescue from a British penal colony in Australia.

§ Phone: 617-925-2295.

HYANNIS

¶ **John F. Kennedy Memorial,** Ocean Street, on Lewis Bay.

This memorial consists of a bronze medallion of the president's profile set in a twelve-foot curved stone wall, in front of which are a fountain and pool.

¶ John F. Kennedy Museum, Town Hall Building, 397 Main Street.

This museum features five rooms of photographs capturing the life and times of the Kennedys and their friends at Hyannis. A seven-minute film describes life at the "Summer White House."

§ Open Monday-Saturday and holidays 10-4, Sunday 1-4. Fee. Phone: 508-790-3077.

¶ Kennedy Compound National Historic Landmark.

This five-acre property includes three large frame houses that have belonged to various members of the Kennedy family. The largest and oldest dates from 1904 and belonged to Joseph and Rose Kennedy. To the rear of the "Big House" is the two-story shingle home of John F. Kennedy, while the twelve-room house to the right belonged to Robert Kennedy.

When Joseph and Rose Kennedy's children visited their parents' estate here, they were expected to follow a strict regimen. Every morning at 7 a.m. all the children were required to report promptly on the lawn for calisthenics with their own physical education instructor. After breakfast came swimming, sailing, and tennis lessons, followed by competitions in all three sports later in the day.

§ The compound is not open to the public, although local boat tours offer a view of the summer homes.

LOWELL

¶ Cardinal O'Connell Bust, Cardinal O'Connell Parkway, near City Hall.

A granite birdbath in the middle of the parkway is surmounted by a bust of William O'Connell, who was born in Lowell in 1859 and went on to become Boston's third Catholic cardinal. He was the youngest of the eleven children of John and Brigid O'Connell, natives of County Cavan, Ireland.

As the Irish population of Lowell continued to increase, prejudice against them grew, particularly in the public schools. Although in 1835 the Catholic Irish population in Lowell was only 12 percent of the total, within eight years it had climbed to 20 percent." By 1861 the Irish constituted perhaps half of the town's inhabitants. According to O'Connell, his early years in the Lowell public schools in the 1860s was "a perfect torture," characterized by the feeling that his teachers held a "bitter antipathy" toward the Catholic Irish students. He added that the Irish youngsters were made to feel inferior to Protestant children of English ancestry. And he complained that, when the teachers discussed the English Reformation, they portrayed the Protestant leaders – even the bloody Cromwell – as saints, while belittling the "glorious name of Thomas More."

¶ Lowell National Historical Park and Heritage State Park.

Drawn to Lowell by the prospect of harnessing the water power created by the Concord and the Merrimack rivers, a group of investors began construction of textile mills and power canals in 1822. The restored textile mills, workers' houses, and five-mile canal system in the park commemorate the city's place in the American Industrial Revolution. Guided tours by foot, trolley, and boat are offered several times daily in the summer.

§ The visitor center at 246 Market Street provides exhibits and a slide show about Lowell's industrial development. Open daily 8:30-5. Closed January 1, Thanksgiving, and December 25. Phone: 508-970-5000.

¶ Outside the visitor center is a bronze statue of a canal construction worker applying his strength to a lever in order to move a huge granite block. The statue could easily represent Hugh Cummisky or one of the many other Irishmen who labored to construct the earliest local canals.

A native of County Tyrone, Cummisky was one of the first and most successful Irish in Lowell. Having come to Lowell from Boston – where he had been the construction foreman and general supervisor on the docks in Charlestown – he became the leader of a work gang whose loyalty he could use as leverage with his Yankee employers. He and his men worked first on the Middlesex Canal (connecting Lowell with Boston Harbor), then on the Pawtucket Canal, and finally on the construction of St. Patrick's Catholic church in Lowell.

Cummisky's purchase of property at Merrimack and Lowell streets in 1830 was the first recorded land transaction with an Irishman in Lowell, and within ten years he had bought additional property on four other streets. While in Lowell, he developed friendships with the local Yankee leaders and served as town constable. In 1860 he listed himself as a "gentleman" who owned $6,000 in real estate and $1,000 in personal property.

¶ A restored 1835 boarding house at 25 Shattuck Street features an exhibit on the daily life of the mill workers and describes the role of immigrants in the development of the city.

Because of expanded production in Lowell's textile mills, by the late 1840s the mill owners employed more than 10,000 workers. The recession of 1848, however, resulted in the dismissal of hundreds of workers, many of them Yankee women. When the economy revived, the mills hired Irish girls, who worked for whatever they could get. Harriet Hanson Robinson, who was employed in the Lowell mills between 1836 and 1848, wrote that the first Irish women worked as scrubbers and waste pickers: "They were always good natured, and when excited used their own language. . . . These women, as a rule, wore peasant cloaks, red or blue, made with hoods and several capes, in summer . . . to 'kape cool,' and in winter to 'kape warrum.' They earned good wages, and they and their children . . . very soon adapted themselves to their changed conditions of life and became 'as good as anybody.'" In 1851 the Prescott Corporation changed its recruitment practices altogether, no longer hiring Yankee women but employing Irish women exclusively, a shift that was adopted by other employers to varying degrees.

§ Open Labor Day-June 30, Tuesday-Saturday 10-4; rest of the year, Wednesday-Sunday 10-4. Closed January 1, Thanksgiving, and December 25.

¶ St. Patrick's Catholic Church, 282 Suffolk Street.

The first Catholic church on this site was erected in 1831. The present structure was built at a cost of $60,000 and was dedicated in 1854. The memorial in the pavement in front of the church marks the graves of three Irish-born priests whose pastorates and the later pastorate of their younger cousin are known as the "O'Brien Dynasty" (1848-1922). A plaque in honor of the O'Briens is located in the church vestibule.

St. Patrick's is located in what during the 1820s began to be called "The Acre," one of two Irish settlements or "paddy camps" in Lowell. While "The Acre" was settled by emigrants from southwestern Ireland, the other camp – "The Half Acre" – was inhabited by Connaught Irish. Factional tempers flared routinely between the two groups, causing one peaceful citizen to ask the mayor to help "preserve the peace, and maintain order and quiet in the neighborhood of the Catholic Church, on Sunday." As late as 1849 Corkonians and Connaughtmen fought a sporadic three-day battle. On the last day Irish women worked "like beavers, lugging bricks & stones in their aprons for the contending parties" before the city guards put an end to the violence. Ironically, this riot occurred only hours before the arrival in Lowell of *Father Theobald Mathew, the famous temperance crusader from Ireland.

That demon rum was not without influence in causing these melees never escaped the notice of hostile Yankees. On the heels of the 1849 riot, the *Lowell Tri-Weekly American* thundered: "[T]hese disgraceful riots . . . almost universally commence over a glass of liquor. *Rum* is the prime mischief-maker, and under its influence the sectional differences of the old country are magnified into huge proportions." Other anti-Irish sources that year provided unsettling statistics: More than 75 percent of the unlicensed saloons in Lowell were run by Irish, and 90 percent of the inmates in the city almshouses were Irish; the number of arrests for one month in 1848 equalled the number for a whole year in the early 1840s.

Middle-class Yankees in Lowell were also outraged by the proverbial uncleanliness of their Irish neighbors. In 1848 a Protestant minister described the frequent living arrangements of the Irish: "Their rooms are generally not ventilated at all. Some six to ten persons frequently sleep in a single room, and sometimes in one bed . . . . The . . . little uncovered ground [is] the receptacle of dirty water, rubbish, and corrupt vegetable matter; and numerous outhouses of necessity near to the windows, sometimes filling every room, and the whole neighborhood with noxious exhalations." As late as the 1880s another observer described the Lowell camps as "an Irish village, with the real Irish cabins and shanties, built of board, sod, and mud – much as can be seen in Ballyshannon" – or built of slabs, stones, and turf. Other commentators railed against the Irish custom of housing the pigs in the shanties.

¶ **Whistler House Museum of Art,** 243 Worthen Street.

The museum includes the birthplace of James McNeill Whistler and a gallery that displays examples of mid nineteenth- and twentieth-century American art, including prints by Whistler.

Descended from an Irish branch of an old British family, Whistler denied that he was a native of Lowell ("I shall be born when and where I want, and I do not choose to be born at Lowell . . . ."). Instead, he claimed to have been born in St. Petersburg, Russia, where his American-born father superintended the building of the St. Petersburg-Moscow Railroad and where the youngster first took drawing lessons. After returning to the United States for his education, he spent three years at the U.S. Military Academy before heading for Paris in 1855, never to return to America.

During his subsequent career Whistler was noted for his portraits, marine scenes, and landscapes. His most famous work – *Portrait of My Mother* (originally called *An Arrangement in Grey and Black*) – is now in the Louvre. While in London, he become known for his acerbic wit and eccentric dress. His artistic creed is summed up in his notion that a painting had "no mission to fulfill" but was a "joy to the artist, a delusion to the philanthropist, and a puzzle to the botanist." Although he disdained critics, he conceded their usefulness because "they keep one always busy . . . either fighting or proving them idiots." When art critic John Ruskin mocked him for asking 200 guineas for one particular painting – "for flinging a pot of paint in the public's face" – Whistler successfully sued him for slander, although the artist was awarded only a farthing.

§ Open March-December 31, Wednesday-Saturday 11-4, Sunday 1-4. Fee. Phone: 508-452-7641.

MARBLEHEAD

¶ **Eugene O'Neill House,** Point O'Rock's Lane at Marblehead Neck. Private.

Built about 1900, this six-room Victorian cottage was the last home of *Eugene O'Neill, where he and his third wife, Carlotta Monterey, lived from 1948 to 1951.

MILFORD

¶ **Irish Round Tower,** Catholic Cemetery, State 85.

This sixty-foot granite tower was erected by *Father Patrick Cuddahy, who discovered pink granite here and opened the area's first quarry in the middle of the nineteenth century.

NEW BEDFORD

¶ *Catalpa* **Memorial,** on the grounds of the Registry of Public Deeds Building, Pack and 6th streets.

This granite monument was erected in 1976 to commemorate the rescue of six Fenian prisoners from an Australian penal colony a hundred years before. Their names are listed on the granite stone: Richard Cranston, Thomas Darragh, Michael Harrington, Thomas Hasset, Martin Hogan, and James Wilson.

The unusual rescue was conceived by *John Boyle O'Reilly, the editor of the *Boston Pilot*. Replicating the scheme that had effected his own escape from the same prison only seven years earlier, O'Reilly and his supporters hired a New Bedford whaler, the *Catalpa*, under the command of Captain George Anthony. With the groundwork laid by two Fenian leaders who had preceded the ship to Australia, the prisoners deserted their work detail and made their way to the shore, there to await the arrival of the *Catalpa*. Although the six successfully boarded the whaleboat sent out by the larger ship, stormy weather prevented it from immediately returning to the *Catalpa*. After a storm-tossed night at sea, they sighted the American ship and gratefully boarded her.

The Fenians' escape had not gone unnoticed, however, as the arrival of the British gunboat *Georgette* proved. Even before the British ship fired a warning shot, Captain Anthony realized that he would easily be bested in a shooting match. Perhaps believing that patriotism is the last refuge of outlaws – as well as scoundrels – Anthony ordered his men to hoist the Stars and Stripes. "That's the American flag.," he cried to the British officer. "I am on the high seas. My flag protects me. If you fire on this ship, you fire on the American flag." Although the captain of the *Georgette* allowed the *Catalapa* to sail on, he continued to follow the ship for some time but eventually returned to Australia. The six Fenians arrived safely in New York City in 1876. In a speech marking their return, O'Reilly said, "The Irishman who could forget what the Stars and Stripes have done for his countrymen, deserves that in the time of need that flag shall forget him."

§ Original documents and photographs associated with the *Catalpa* rescue are on display in the New Bedford Whaling Museum on Johnny Cake Hill in the historic part of town. Open Monday-Saturday 9-5, Sunday 1-5. Fee. Phone: 508-997-0046.

PROVINCETOWN

¶ **Provincetown Playhouse,** Town Hall, Commercial Street.

This playhouse has been located in the Town Hall since 1977, when fire destroyed its predecessor, the Wharf Theater. The earlier theater, literally on the town wharf, had seen the debut of many plays by *Eugene O'Neill while he was a member of the Provincetown Players. Each summer the playhouse produces at least one of O'Neill's plays.

O'Neill's debut as a performed playwright occurred with the production of *Bound East* in the Wharf Theater in July 1916. The author incorporated in the play some of the "life experiences" he had enjoyed since leaving Princeton University during his freshman year: steamship voyages as a seaman; life as a derelict in Argentina, Liverpool, and New York; an attempted suicide; and newspaper work on the *New London Telegraph.* O'Neill appeared in the play as the second mate – with only one line.

ROXBURY

¶ **Forest Hills Cemetery,** 95 Forest Hills Avenue.

This cemetery is noted for two memorials associated with the Irish-born sculptor Martin Milmore:

• The Soldiers' Monument in honor of the Civil War slain depicts a soldier resting on his rifle as he gazes on the graves of his fallen Union comrades. Milmore also designed war monuments for Boston, Charlestown, and Fitchburg, Massachusetts; Canaan and Keene, New Hampshire; and Erie, Pennsylvania.

• Milmore's grave is marked by one of the most famous pieces of sculpture in the United States – *Death and the Young Sculptor* by Daniel Chester French.

§ Phone: 617-524-0128.

SPRINGFIELD

¶ *The Puritan,* State and Chestnut streets.

This imposing statue, sculpted by *Augustus Saint-Gaudens in 1885, depicts Deacon Samuel Chapin, one of Springfield's founders. The sculpture was commissioned by Chester Chapin, a sixth-generation descendant of the minister and a later president of the Boston and Albany Railroad. Since no likeness of Deacon Chapin was available to Saint-Gaudens, he sculpted the head of *The Puritan* from a bust he had made of the younger Chapin in 1881.

¶ *Titanic* **Historical Society Museum,** 207 Centre Street.

This museum tells the story of the ill-fated luxury liner *Titanic,* which was constructed in Belfast, Ireland, between 1909 and 1911. More than 900 feet long and as high as an eleven-story building, the *Titanic* was considered unsinkable. Yet less than five days out on its maiden voyage in April 1912, it struck an iceberg and sank in less than an hour. Of the 2,227 passengers and crew, 705 escaped in twenty rafts and lifeboats. One of the survivors of that fateful day was *Margaret Tobin Brown ("Molly" Brown), who earned the nickname "Unsinkable" after taking command of the other survivors in lifeboat number six.

§ Directions: I-90 exit 7, 1 mile south on State 21, 1 mile west on State 141 (Main Street), 1 block north on Pinevale Street, and a half block west to 207 Centre Street. Open Monday-Friday 10-4, Saturday 10-3. Closed holidays. Phone: 413-543-4770.

TAUNTON

¶ **Robert Paine Statue,** in the square opposite City Hall, 15 Summer Street.

Unveiled in 1914, this bronze statue honors Robert Treat Paine, a signer of the Declaration of Independence and a patriot regarded by some authorities as of Irish ancestry.

According to those sources, Paine was descended from Robert O'Neill of Dungannon, Ireland. O'Neill had changed his name to Paine in order to preserve his estates following the victory of William III at the battle of the Boyne. Paine's grandson Robert Treat Paine was born in Boston in 1731 and prosecuted the British soldiers indicted after the "Boston Massacre" in 1770.

WESTON

¶ **Cardinal Spellman Philatelic Museum,** Regis College, 235 Wellesley Street.

The museum houses the private stamp collection of *Cardinal Francis Spellman, the archbishop of New York from 1939 to 1967. Changing exhibits of stamps and postal memorabilia are displayed in the museum's two galleries.

Spellman's interest in philately began when he was a student at the North American College in Rome. He acquired many of the volumes in his collection as gifts from heads of government during World War II. In an address to the National Federation of Stamp Clubs, he remarked that "Stamps are miniature documents of human history . . . . They delineate cultural attainments, industrial works, domestic, civil and social life."

Over the years the following Irish or Irish Americans have been recognized on U.S. postage stamps: Chester A. Arthur, John Barry, William Jennings Bryan, James Buchanan, Nellie Cashman, "Buffalo Bill" Cody, Grover Cleveland, George M. Cohan, David Crockett, Bing Crosby, Father Edward Flanagan, Stephen Collins Foster, Robert Fulton, Ulysses S. Grant, Horace Greeley, Father John Harrington, Joel Chandler Harris, Benjamin Harrison, Victor Herbert, James Hoban, Sam Houston, Charles Evans Hughes, Andrew Jackson, Thomas "Stonewall" Jackson, Andrew Johnson, Casey Jones, Stephen Kearny, Helen Keller, John F. Kennedy, Robert Kennedy, Henry Knox, Thomas Macdonough, Edward MacDowell, John McCormack, Cyrus McCormick, Ephraim McDowell, William McKinley, John McLaughlin, Andrew Mellon, Margaret Mitchell, Thomas Nelson Sr., Thomas Nelson Jr., Eugene O'Neill, Matthew C. Perry, Oliver H. Perry, Edgar Allan Poe, James K. Polk, George Read II, Theodore Roosevelt, Edward Rutledge, Augustus Saint-Gaudens, Philip Sheridan, Annie Sullivan, John Sullivan, and Charles Thomson.

Soon after Spellman's appointment as archbishop of New York, the collection was moved to Regis College. Unhappily, however, in 1959 some of the stamps in the collection were stolen from the college library. Following the burglary, the collection was moved to the newly built Cardinal Spellman Museum, the gift of Mabel Gilman Corey. In 1969 another theft resulted in further loss to the collection. The following year authorities discovered that a volunteer at the museum had systematically pilfered stamps worth $40,000 over a period of years.

The burglar eventually made full restitution in the form of stamps of equivalent quality and value.

§ Open Tuesday-Thursday 9-4, Sunday 1-4, and by appointment. Phone: 617-894-6735.

WORCESTER

¶ College of the Holy Cross, 1 College Street.

• The Dinand Memorial Library houses the Richard O'Flynn Collection, which includes records of Irish societies, cemeteries, and military units like the Jackson and Emmet Guards.

• The Healy Building is named for James Augustine Healy, the first African-American Jesuit priest and Catholic bishop in the United States. Healy was one of ten children born to Irish immigrant Michael Morris Healy and a mulatto slave on his plantation near Macon, Georgia. Like his four brothers, the younger Healy attended Holy Cross College, where his father had enrolled them as a way of securing their emancipation.

Upon graduation James Healy pursued a career in the Catholic priesthood. After studying at seminaries in Montreal and Paris, he was ordained in the Cathedral of Notre Dame in 1854. Returning to Boston, he served first as chancellor to *Bishop John Fitzpatrick and then as pastor of Holy Cross Cathedral and St. James Church. He was especially devoted to the welfare of orphans and delinquents and succeeded in persuading public charitable and correctional institutions in Boston to permit Catholic clergy to perform religious services in them.

As bishop of Portland, Maine, Healy won the nickname "The Children's Bishop" because of his efforts against child labor abuses and on behalf of children of men killed in the Civil War. He was equally mindful of the poor and sick in his diocese, often paying their doctor bills and delinquent taxes. In addition, he was an active member of the Catholic commission for Negro and Indian missions.

Two of Healy's brothers also became priests, while two of his sisters became nuns. A third brother – Michael – was an agent with the U.S. Revenue Cutter Service and was reputedly one of the sea captains upon whom Jack London based his fictional Captain Larsen in *The Sea Wolf*. In 1886 Michael Healy began his career as the federal government's principal law enforcement officer in the waters around Alaska. On both the high seas and in remote coastal villages, he was revenue officer, federal marshal, grand jury, judge, and chief warden. Among the Eskimo, in fact, he was a legend. When one of them was asked, "Who is the greatest man in America?" he replied, "Why, Mike Healy. He is the United States. He holds the power here for the whole country."

MICHIGAN

BEAVER ISLAND

Beginning in 1847, this island was settled by 2,600 Mormons who hoped that the island's remoteness would protect them from the usual hostility which the sect encountered. This expectation was unrealized, however, and open violence broke out between the Mormons and local inhabitants, who destroyed some of the sect's buildings.

A group of Irish fishermen from Mackinaw City later settled on the island, rebuilding the destroyed structures, establishing their base at St. James, and claiming some of the farm land. After these Irishmen received legal title to their holdings, they invited many of their friends and relatives from northern Ireland to join the settlement. Many of these later immigrants came from Aranmore Island off the west coast of County Donegal and surely must have spoken Irish.

One of these immigrants was Charles O'Donnell. While working on a railroad construction job in Toronto, he ran off with the payroll which his gang foreman had entrusted to him. The Irishman later came to Beaver Island – which he thought was remarkably like Aranmore – to help build the lighthouse known as Harbor Light. After returning to Toronto to repay the sum he had stolen, he came back to Beaver Island with his wife and as many other Irish as he could persuade.

❡ The tombstones in the cemetery attached to St. Mary's Church in St. James reveal the names of those early settlers, listed here in order of frequency: O'Gallaghers, Boyle, O'Donnell, McDonogh, Green, Floyd, McCann, McCauley, Bonner, Martin, Dunleavy, Mooney, Malloy, and O'Brien.

❡ Southwest of St. James is a log and clapboard cabin built about 1860 by an Irish settler named Philip Connelly. It was later the home of Feodor Protar, a Russian immigrant who schooled himself in medicine and offered free medical services and supplies to the inhabitants of the island.

BUCHANAN

❡ **Joseph Coveney Burial Site,** Oak Ridge Cemetery, Front Street.
The cemetery contains an unusual monument over the grave of Joseph Coveney, a native of Ireland who settled here in 1836. Because he was an atheist, the monument is inscribed with atheistic sentiments. The grave marker had to be made in England, however, because no local stonecutter would carve the inscription.

DEARBORN

¶ **Henry Ford Estate-Fair Lane,** off Evergreen Road and U.S. 12, on the campus of the University of Michigan.

Built by Henry Ford in 1915 for $2 million, this fifty-six-room mansion was the permanent home of the famous automotive pioneer and industrialist. He selected the name "Fair Lane" after the name of the street in County Cork where his maternal grandfather had been born.

Besides a powerhouse which Ford and his friend Thomas Edison devised to allow the estate to produce its own power, light, and heat, the house had a bowling alley, a heated indoor swimming pool, and a $30,000 organ. Each of the eight fireplaces in the mansion is inscribed with an appropriate epigram (e.g., "Chop your own wood and it will warm you twice."). Among the guests who stayed here were President Herbert Hoover, Charles Lindbergh, and the Duke of Windsor.

Now located on only 72 of the estate's original 1,369 acres, Fair Lane is owned by the University of Michigan.

§ Tours depart April-December 31, Monday-Saturday at 10, 11, 1, and 2, Sunday 1-4:30; other months, Monday-Friday at 1:30. Closed January 1, Easter, Thanksgiving, and December 25. Fee. Phone: 313-593-5590.

Fair Lane Mansion, the home of Henry Ford.
(Photo by Matthew Winquist. From the collections of the Henry Ford Estate-Fair Lane.)

¶ **Henry Ford Museum,** Village Road and Oakwood Boulevard.
This twelve-acre museum chronicles America's transition from an

agricultural society to an urban one. It also traces the life of the famous automotive pioneer through photographs, letters, and artifacts. Among the items on display are Ford's 1896 Quadricycle (his first automobile) and the fifteen-millionth Model-T, constructed in 1927. The museum also displays one of the largest collections of *Eclectic Readers* by *William McGuffey.

The museum's exhibit on the American automobile displays five vehicles used by nine U.S. presidents. One of the automobiles here is the 1961 Lincoln Continental convertible in which *John F. Kennedy was killed while in Dallas. This car was subsequently rebuilt with a permanent roof and armor plating that added a ton to its weight.

§ Open daily 9-5. Closed Thanksgiving and December 25. Fee. Phone: 313-271-1620 or 800-TELL-A-FRIEND.

¶ Greenfield Village, Village Road and Oakwood Boulevard.

This eighty-one-acre complex is designed to recreate American history as a living experience rather than "book history" heavy on dates and facts. Henry Ford's experiential sense of history was summed up in the opinion that "Our history has depended more on harrows than on guns or speeches. I thought that a history which excluded harrows and all the rest of daily life is bunk . . . ."

Begun in 1920, Ford's collecting program brought to this site an unequaled array of tools, machines, and buildings from America's past, including his own birthplace. The village also contains the homes of Noah Webster and the Wright brothers as well as the birthplaces of *William McGuffey and Harvey Firestone.

¶ The two-story log cabin in which *William McGuffey was born in 1800 was moved here from Washington, Pennsylvania, in 1934. McGuffey's famous series of readers was used in American schools for a century.

¶ The birthplace of Henry Ford is a two-story clapboard farmhouse originally located on his parents' forty-acre farm in Dearborn. The eleven-room house, where Ford lived until age sixteen, was moved to Greenfield Village in 1944. Ford's paternal grandfather, John Ford, had been a Protestant tenant farmer near Clonakilty in County Cork, Ireland. In 1847 he left his homeland for America, bringing with him his wife and their seven children. One of the sons, William, subsequently met and married the daughter of Patrick O'Hern, also a native of Cork. Their son Henry was born in 1863.

In the early 1920s this son – now a famous car manufacturer – visited Ireland to open his company's first factory outside the United States. During the visit he pledged £5,000 for the Hospital Building Fund in Cork. The next day, however, the local press reported that he had promised to donate £10,000. When officials from the hospital fund offered to correct the error with a new headline ("Henry Ford Did Not Give £10,000 to Hospital"), the American manufacturer realized that he had been "taken in" and promised to make the larger donation. His only condition was that he be allowed to choose the biblical quotation that would adorn the hospital: "I came among mine own – and they took me in."

DETROIT

¶ **Edsel and Eleanor Ford House,** 1100 Lake Shores Road, Grosse Pointe Shores.

Reflecting the architectural style found in the English Cotswolds, the mansion on this sixty-three-acre estate was completed in 1929 as the home of Edsel Ford, the only child of industrialist *Henry Ford. The house contains an art collection of Old Masters and Impressionist paintings.

§ Open Wednesday-Sunday 12-4. Fee. Phone: 313-884-4222.

¶ **Father Casey Burial Site,** St. Bonaventure Friary Chapel, 1740 Mt. Eliott Street.

On the left hand side of the chapel is the grave of Father Solanus Casey, a Capuchin priest declared "venerable" by Pope John Paul II in July 1995. Casey is the first man born in the United States to be recognized by the Catholic Church for his "heroic virtues," the first step on the road to possible canonization.

Born in a log cabin near Prescott, Wisconsin, in 1870, Bernard Casey – as he was baptized – was the son of Famine immigrants from counties Monaghan and Armagh. One of sixteen children, "Barney" dropped out of school to help support his family, working in succession as a lumberjack, a streetcar conductor, and a prison guard. Although he first entered the Milwaukee archdiocesan seminary, his difficulty with the German and Latin in which the courses were conducted forced him to leave. He encountered additional difficulties with his studies after joining the Capuchin Franciscan Order in Detroit (accepting the religious name "Solanus"). Although ordained in 1904, he was denied permission to preach and hear confessions.

After serving for fourteen years in various parts of New York, Casey was assigned to St. Bonaventure Friary in Detroit. There he tried to satisfy the needs of those who sought food and financial assistance, and he was one of the founders of the soup kitchen that now serves more than 1,000 people each day. His reputation for prophecy and healing brought busloads of people to see him. Local church authorities are investigating two possible miracles attributed to him.

Casey's cause for sainthood is being advanced by *Father Michael

Crosby, who wrote most of the 1,300 pages of documentation about Casey's life presented to the Vatican. According to Crosby, the Detroit priest was an ardent advocate of Irish home rule. "[He] took on a couple of bishops who were not as strong as he thought they should be in supporting Ireland," Crosby said. "He wrote very strong articles to the editor of the *Irish World* newspaper about Irish independence."

§ Open daily 8:30-5.

HARBOR BEACH

¶ Frank Murphy Birthplace Museum, 142 South Huron Street.

This nineteenth-century house was the birthplace of Frank Murphy, governor of Michigan, U.S. attorney general, and associate justice of the U.S. Supreme Court.

All four of Murphy's grandparents were Irish immigrants who had fled their homeland between 1847 and 1849. His father, who at sixteen was imprisoned for his part in the Fenian invasion of Canada, settled in Harbor Beach, where he practiced law and was known for his unorthodox views, being staunchly anti-British and a follower of *William Jennings Bryan. His son Frank, meanwhile, after serving as a lieutenant in World War I, briefly studied law at Trinity College, Dublin, where he took particular interest in the Sinn Fein movement, so recently catapulted into prominence because of the 1916 Easter Uprising.

Murphy's subsequent political career was colored by the challenges caused by the Great Depression. As mayor of Detroit he complemented the city's public relief efforts with the creation of an employment agency and public housing for homeless men. When the city's resources were stretched to the limit, Murphy convened a series of mayoral conferences which sought federal aid for the nation's struggling cities. (Murphy was elected the first president of the resulting U.S. Conference of Mayors.)

Later, as governor of strike-racked Michigan, he refused to use the National Guard to expel sit-down strikers from the factories. Through his preference for negotiating, he was able to achieve peaceful settlements in six major strikes. (He once said that the sit-down strike was a "reassertion of the personality – the dignity of the offended human reasserting itself after the frightening experience of the Depression.") His refusal to use the National Guard to break up a sit-down strike in a General Motors plant in Flint caused the automobile manufacturer to recognize the United Auto Workers.

Following his appointment to the Supreme Court, Murphy was a consistent defender of civil liberties, although he was criticized for allowing his personal philosophy to influence his interpretation of constitutional law. Perhaps his most famous dissent was in the 1944 case which upheld the detention of Japanese Americans on the West Coast after the attack on Pearl Harbor.

❡ Frank Murphy is buried in Rock Falls Cemetery, just south of Harbor Beach.

HOLLY

During the late 1800s and the beginning of the twentieth century, the area off Saginaw Street in Holly was infamous for its brothels and taverns. In 1908 the town was visited by the intemperate temperance crusader Carrie Nation. After delivering a lecture on the evils of liquor, she "did a hatchet job" on some of the saloons in this part of town. Holly commemorates the appearance of this "visiting angel" during the Carry Nation Festival on the weekend after Labor Day.

Carry Moore Nation was born in Bryantsville, Kentucky, in 1846. Her father, George Moore, was descended from a pioneer Irish settler in the area, while her mother was a manic-depressive who fancied that she was Queen Victoria. Carrie Moore later used her own mystic experiences to justify her temperance mission as divinely inspired. In 1877 she married David Nation, a minister, lawyer, and newspaper editor, but when, after twenty-five years of marriage, she moved to Kansas to become the pastor of a church, he divorced her on the grounds of desertion.

As a member of the Woman's Christian Temperance Union, she was known throughout the world for her hatchet, which she used without mercy in her saloon-smashing sprees. These were all the more threatening because of her 175-pound, almost six-foot physical presence. In Wichita, for example, she trashed the Hotel Carey and other distinguished saloons, destroying quantities of liquor worth thousands of dollars. She justified her hellion habits on the theory that, wherever saloons were illegal, any citizen had the right to destroy not only their demon rum but also their furniture. She, in turn, was the victim of violence, often being shot at, clubbed, or cut. Although she was arrested about thirty times, she was able to pay her fines from the proceeds of her lectures and the sale of souvenir hatchets. She lies buried in Belton, Missouri, under a monument inscribed, "She hath done what she could."

IRISH HILLS

The lakes and the rolling hills of this region along State 12 thirty-five miles southwest of Ann Arbor so reminded a clergyman by the name of Lyster that he named the area for his native land. The area's topography can be viewed from the Irish Hills Towers, one mile west of the junction of U.S. 12 and State 124.

¶ On Route 12 near Brooklyn is St. Joseph's Catholic Church, an enlargement of a chapel which Irish settlers built in 1854. The church-yard contains the graves of those Irish pioneers and their children.

MUSKEGON

¶ **Hackley Park,** Webster Avenue between 3rd and 4th streets.

The park contains memorials to three Irish Americans: statues of Philip Sheridan and Ulysses S. Grant and a monument in honor of William McKinley. The bronze figure of McKinley was the nation's first memorial to the president after he was assassinated in 1901.

¶ **Muskegon Museum of Art,** 296 West Webster Avenue.

In addition to a European collection, the museum features the works of *James McNeill Whistler and includes the painting *Tornado Over Kansas* by *John Steuart Curry.

§ Open Tuesday-Friday 10-5, Saturday and Sunday 12-5. Closed major holidays. Phone: 616-722-2600.

NILES

¶ **Carey Mission Site,** Grant Street, on the west bank of the St. Joseph River.

The mission was founded in 1822 by the Reverend Isaac McCoy, the first Protestant missionary in this part of the state and the grand-son of an Irish immigrant who had come to America in 1760. At its height the mission boasted twenty-seven buildings and provided for the instruction of seventy Native American pupils in agriculture and scholastic subjects.

During his ministry toward the Indians in this area, McCoy traveled hundreds of miles and endured the usual physical hardships of a frontier missionary as well as the unusual grief of losing five of his children while he was away. (He lost five more children at other times.) As more and more settlers and traders visited the mission, bringing with them pernicious influences (especially "demon rum"), McCoy concluded that only segregation from the white man would allow for the civilization and Christianization of the Native Americans. He accordingly waged a campaign to popularize his colonization concept and to win from Congress the creation in 1830 of the "Indian Country" in what is now Oklahoma.

OLD MISSION PENINSULA

¶ Old Mission Church, Grand Traverse Bay.

The present structure is a replica of the log church built here in 1839 by the Reverend Peter Dougherty, a Presbyterian missionary of most likely Irish descent who labored among the Ottawa and Ojibwa Indians in this area. Omena, on the west side of Grand Traverse Bay, was named from the Indian word *Omenah?* ("Is it so?"), which Dougherty used to reply to every statement made by a native American.

ROYAL OAK

¶ Shrine of the Little Flower, Woodward Avenue (U.S. 1) and Twelve Mile Road.

Although this shrine to St. Thérèse of Liseux is noted for its 111-foot crucifixion tower (dubbed "the silo" by the irreverent), it is more well known as the site of the radio broadcasts of Father Charles Coughlin, the first pastor to use radio as a regular feature of his ministry.

Coughlin's first broadcast occurred in October 1926, a century after his great-grandfather had arrived in America and joined other Irish immigrants in building the Erie Canal. During the radio program Coughlin contrasted the message of St. Thérèse (the "Little Flower") with the racial hatred espoused by the Ku Klux Klan. When local Klan members responded by burning a cross outside the priest's original shrine, the radio preacher raised the ante, predicting that someday he and his followers would "raise a cross so high to the sky that neither man nor beast can burn it down."

By 1933 Coughlin had kept his promise, as the finishing touches were added to his 111-foot tower. (The sculpted image of the crucified Christ on the tower is twenty-eight feet high, large enough, presumably, to intimidate the most zealous White Robe.)

Coughlin continued to express controversial views during the 1930s, but now against different targets. He argued, for example, that atheism and materialism had led to socialism and communism and that laissez-faire economics had led to the Depression. As the unofficial spokesman for the downtrodden, he condemned President Hoover as "the banker's friend, the Holy Ghost of the rich, the protective angel of Wall Street."

The orator-priest initially embraced Franklin Roosevelt's economic prescriptions for the country, in 1933 hailing the New Deal as "Christ's Deal" and urging support for specific elements in the president's overall program. By the middle of the decade, though, Coughlin was opposing Roosevelt's internationalism and engaging in personal vituperation against the president. He called F.D.R. a "liar," "communistic," and "Franklin Doublecross Roosevelt," adding that the difference between the Republicans and the Democrats was simply a matter of degree: "between carbolic acid and rat poison."

By now the controversial priest was noted for a singularly unpriestly oratorical style: tearing off his Roman collar in public and screaming invective and haranguing audiences. In response to Coughlin's personal attacks on President Roosevelt, *Archbishop Edward Mooney of Detroit tried to restrain the priest's inflammatory remarks. Using his authority under canon law to censor a priest's public addresses, Mooney appointed a panel to review Coughlin's radio broadcasts before delivery, although, strangely, the members of the panel were priests sympathetic to Coughlin.

§ Open Monday-Friday 6:30-3:15, Sunday 7:30-2:30, holidays 7:30-noon. Phone: 810-541-4122.

MINNESOTA

ELK RIVER

¶ **Oliver H. Kelley Farm,** on U.S. 10, 2.5 miles southeast, at 15788 Kelly Farm Road.

This 189-acre farm was the property of Oliver Kelley, the founder of the National Grange of the Patrons of Husbandry, formed to promote and protect the interests of the country's farmers. The large Italianate farmhouse on the property was built about 1875 and was occupied by Kelley's daughters, who operated the farm while he served with the Department of Agriculture in Washington, D.C. Today the farm is a living-history center, whose costumed interpreters demonstrate the use of nineteenth-century farming implements and practices.

Kelley, the great-grandson of an Irish immigrant who had come to America in 1755, arrived in Minnesota in 1849. He thereafter became an enthusiastic promoter of the region and hoped to attract settlers through his letters to the eastern press. Beginning in 1865, while a clerk for the Bureau of Agriculture in the nation's capital, he surveyed agricultural conditions throughout Minnesota and the South. He and six associates subsequently founded the National Grange. Although as the new organization's secretary Kelley stressed its social benefits, others hoped to use the Grange in the farmers' battle against monopolies, especially the railroads. By 1874 the organization numbered 20,000 granges, primarily in the South and Middle West.

§ Farm open May-October, Monday-Saturday 10-5, Sunday noon-5. Interpretive center open November-April, Saturday 10-4, Sunday noon-5. Fee. Phone: 612-441-6896.

GRACEVILLE

¶ **John Ireland Marker,** on the western end of town on the north side of State 28.

This memorial plaque commemorates the role played by Father John Ireland in establishing several Irish farming communities throughout the state.

Beginning in the 1870s, just before he was elevated to the episcopacy, Ireland threw his support behind the colonization of Irish immigrants to the west. Appalled by the conditions which his fellow Irish immigrants endured in the eastern cities, he believed that these newcomers should be encouraged to adopt a rural way of life. In this way, he hoped, they would be freed from the squalor and temptations in the slums (chief of which, in his view, was Demon Rum). To help achieve this end, he became an agent for the St. Paul & Pacific Railroad, thereby becoming eligible to purchase large tracts of land relatively cheaply.

After acquiring almost 400,000 acres in the state, Ireland helped establish nine colonies – the most successful such effort conducted under Catholic auspices in the United States. Four of the new communities were christened with typically Irish names (Avoca, Clontarf, Fulda, and Iona), and four of the nine are still in existence. The settlement at Clontarf, for example, was created in 1876 by a "prohibition colony" from Pennsylvania. After arriving at Benson, Minnesota, at that time the western terminus of the Great Northern Railroad, the group treked north to a tract of land which they named for a watering place near Dublin. In a pamphlet entitled *Invitation to the Land*, Ireland later described Clontarf as one of the "wide open opportunity-waiting spaces of the west."

The St. Paul churchman quickly learned, however, that the story of one failure could counteract a string of successes. Such seems to have been the case with the creation of the Connemara colony near Graceville. The group – composed of 300 Irish fishermen and peasants from the west coast of Ireland – arrived there in 1880. At once they were provided with clothing, two months' worth of provisions, houses already constructed, and offers of work from farmers in the local area. Despite these auspicious beginnings, the colony soon failed. To fishermen and subsistence farmers from Ireland, the cultivation of wheat on a large scale proved beyond their ability, especially the ability of the slackers and former paupers who composed a large portion of the group. Many of the colonists died that first winter because they had been too lazy to sod their shanties and to dig cellars to protect their potatoes.

Despite the extent of Ireland's achievements at resettlement, the number of Irish immigrants to the Great Plains was much lower than he had hoped. In 1898 he looked back over the history of colonization somewhat ruefully, declaring that, if greater efforts had been made during the previous decade, the western states would have been peopled by many more Catholics and "tens of thousands of Catholic families would have gained happy homes and an honorable competence upon the land, instead of having gone down to ruin in the fierce maelstrom of large cities."

GRAND RAPIDS

❡ Judy Garland Childhood Home, 2727 Highway 169 South.

Judy Garland, the famous star of *The Wizard of Oz*, lived in this partially restored house until she was four years old, when she and her vaudevillian parents moved to California. Although she frequently referred to her father's Irish charm, it is unlikely that he had much Irish ancestry, if indeed any. The future entertainer's undoubted Irish roots came from her maternal grandmother, Eva Fitzgerald.

Garland, whose real name was Frances Gumm, was born in 1922 and made her theatrical debut in vaudeville at the age of two or three – encoring "Jingle Bells" seven times. At the age of thirteen she broke into motion pictures when Metro-Goldwyn-Mayer Studios offered her a contract. During the next fifteen year she appeared opposite some of the biggest names in the industry: with *Mickey Rooney in the Andy Hardy films, *Babes on Broadway*, and *Girl Crazy*; with *Gene Kelly in *For Me and My Gal, Summer Stock*, and *The Pirate*; and with Fred Astaire in *Easter Parade* and *Royal Wedding*. For her performance as Dorothy in *The Wizard of Oz*, she received a special award from the Academy of Motion Picture Arts and Sciences in 1939.

§ Open daily 10-5. Suggested donation. Phone: 218-327-9276.

• In late June each year Grand Rapids honors its famous daughter with the three-day Judy Garland Festival, which includes a talent show and a series of film seminars.

¶ **Judy Garland Historical Center,** Central School Heritage and Arts Center, at the junction of State 2 and U.S. 169.

A yellow brick road leads to the entrance of this heritage and arts center. The Judy Garland collection on the third floor contains memorabilia from the actress's life and movie career.

§ Open Monday-Friday 9:30-5, Saturday 9:30-4. Also open Sunday 10-4 Memorial Day-Labor Day. Admission. Phone: 218-326-6431.

HASTINGS

¶ **Ignatius Donnelly House Marker,** on the grounds of the Nininger Town Hall, 1.5 miles northwest on County 42 (Nininger Road).

A metal marker commemorates the site of Ignatius Donnelly's home, originally located just north of the town hall. Donnelly, the son of an Irish physician, was an internationally known author, orator, politician, social reformer, and prophet and lived in the Nininger house until his death in 1901.

Despite efforts to save the house and make it the centerpiece of a state park, the structure was razed in 1949, but not before the beautiful cherry paneling in Donnelly's library was saved. The library was temporarily reconstructed in 1981 as part of an exhibit in honor of Donnelly at the Minnesota Historical Society in St. Paul.

The plaque in front of the town hall reads in part: "Donnelly, a lawyer from Philadelphia, moved west to Minnesota and launched a national campaign to attract settlers to Nininger City, a promising village of more than 500 residents when it was laid out around this site in 1856. After the town melted away during the panic and depression of 1857, Donnelly turned his astonishing energy to politics, serving one term as lieutenant governor and three terms in Congress. For nearly 40 years his restless search for fair and effective social and economic institutions led him to play a role in virtually every agrarian reform movement of the late nineteenth century. In addition to his fiery campaigns on behalf of farmers and workers, Donnelly wrote several unconventional and widely read books of popular science, including *Atlantis, The Great Cryptogram, Ragnarok,* and *Caesar's Column,* in which he predicted the collapse of American society in the year 1988."

Although Donnelly was a staunch Republican while he served in Congress both during and immediately after the Civil War, he gradually turned his back on a party which he felt served privileged special interests through its support of hard-money principles and a protective tariff. In a nation faced with the tremendous upheaval brought about by industrialization, he believed that politics would increasingly become a conflict "between the few who seek to grasp all power and wealth, and the many who seek to preserve their rights as American citizens and freemen." He accordingly moved more and more to the left – from Liberal Republican to Granger to Greenbacker to Populist.

As a motivating force behind the formation of the Populist Party, Donnelly authored the preamble of that party's 1892 platform, generally regarded as the most radical ever proposed by a major party. ". . . We meet in the midst of a nation brought to the verge of moral, and political, and material ruin," he warned. "Corruption dominates the ballot-box, the legislature, the Congress, and touches even the ermine of the bench. . . . The fruits of the toil of millions are boldly stolen to build up colossal fortunes for a few . . . ." He also helped formulate and promote the party's agenda: direct election of U.S. senators, restriction of immigration, the initiative and referendum, a graduated income tax, low-interest government loans, a silver standard, and government ownership of the railroads.

Although more generally known for his political career, Donnelly earned a reputation as an iconoclastic author. In *The Great Cryptogram,* for example, he attempted to prove that the works attributed to Shakespeare were actually written by Francis Bacon. In a later novel entitled *Caesar's Column: A Story of the Twentieth Century* (1891), he described America as he envisioned it a century into the future. Writing under the pseudonym "Edmund Boisgilbert" and using the eyes of a young traveler, he depicted a nation of extreme contrasts: a world of physical comforts and technological marvels (e.g., airships and communications and transportation systems), on the one hand, and, on the other, "a degraded society . . . with the rich in complete control, the laboring classes reduced to a horrible quasi-barbaric poverty, ending in a revolution more bloody and violent than any that had preceded it." To Donnelly, this "brave new world" was the result of "the reduction, by competition, of the wages of the worker to the least sum that will maintain life and muscular strength to do the work required . . . . I do not know if there is a hell in the spiritual universe, but if there is not, one should certainly be created for the souls of the men who originated, or justified, or enforced that damnable creed." (Donnelly was equally trenchant in his anticlericalism, although amusingly alliterative: "It was a black and bloody and bitter and dreadful world when the black gowns controlled it – both in Europe and America.") Elsewhere in *Caesar's Column* he pleaded "for a renewal of the bond of brotherhood between classes; for a reign of justice on earth that shall obliterate the cruel hates and passions which now divide the world." And to the churches he made some pointed suggestions: "The world to-day clamors for deeds, not creeds! for bread, not dogma; for charity, not ceremony; for love, not intellect." Although the establishment press ignored the book, by the end of the decade it had sold almost 700,000 copies in Europe and the United States.

MINNEAPOLIS

¶ **Dowling Urban Environmental Center,** 3900 West River Road.

Although it originally housed the Michael Dowling School for Crippled Children, this building is still named for the Minneapolis banker and lecturer whose achievements in the face of personal hardship made him a national figure.

Born in 1866 in Massachusetts, Dowling was the son of an Irish immigrant journeyman carpenter. As a youngster the son supported himself by working as a Mississippi steamboat hand, as a farmer in the Northwest, and as a paperboy in Chicago. During a blizzard in Minnesota, however, extreme exposure led to the loss of both his legs, his left arm, and most of his right hand. Having in the meantime become an orphan, he was declared a public charge, although he persuaded the authorities to finance his education at Carleton College in return for dispensation from their obligation to support him.

Following his graduation from college, the young Dowling followed a variety of careers – teaching school, selling books, operating a skating rink, and serving as a school principal. He later established a weekly newspaper and was chief clerk of the Minnesota legislature and secretary of the National League of Republican clubs. In this last capacity he came to the attention of *President William McKinley, who sent him to the Philippines to report on the condition of the school system there.

After election to the Minnesota House of Representatives, Dowling served as its Speaker, although he continued to pursue a career in real estate, banking, and insurance. After World War I he visited disabled soldiers throughout the United States and England, hoping to rouse their spirits with his own life story and positive attitude. Dowling and his wife were married for twenty-five years and had three children.

℥ **Minneapolis Institute of Arts,** 2400 Third Avenue South.

Considered one of the region's finest art museums, the institute has more than 80,000 *objects d'art* from as far back as 2000 B.C. In addition to ancient Greek and Roman statuary, the museum's collection includes Italian, Dutch, and French paintings. Its American collection includes works by *John Singleton Copley, Thomas Eakins, *Georgia O'Keeffe, John Singer Sargent, Benjamin West, and Grant Wood.

§ Open Tuesday, Wednesday, Friday, and Saturday 10-5, Thursday 10-9, and Sunday noon-5. Closed July 4, Thanksgiving, and December 25. Phone: 612-870-3131.

NORTHFIELD

℥ **Northfield Historical Society Museum,** 408 Division Street.

The museum was formerly the First National Bank of Northfield, the target of a bank robbery attempt on September 7, 1876, by the James-Younger Gang. When the bandits were unable to open the safe, they shot indiscriminately into the street, killing two townspeople and wounding a third. Two of the would-be robbers were also wounded, however, when hastily armed merchants near the bank returned fire. After only seven minutes in town, the remaining six members of the gang escaped, but just ahead of a small posse. By nightfall the number of pursuers had grown to 200, and within a few days to a thousand. Although *Jesse and Frank James eluded the posse, Charlie Pitts was killed and the three Younger brothers were captured and sentenced to life imprisonment.

• Each year on the weekend after Labor Day the town of Northfield celebrates the Defeat of Jesse James Day, complete with a parade, a rodeo, and a reenactment of the robbery attempt.

OWATONNA

℥ **Norwest Bank,** East Broadway and North Cedar Street.

Designed by *Louis H. Sullivan, this 1908 bank is regarded as one of the Chicago architect's finest structures. The local bankers who commissioned the work were impressed with Sullivan's rejection of the typical Revival architecture of the period and gave him a free hand. The one-story brick and stone bank is known for its decorative ironwork, large arched windows, and mosaic ornamentation. Its vibrantly decorated interior – largely the work of George Grant Elmslie, Sullivan's chief designer – features stained-glass windows, chandeliers, stenciled walls, and plasterwork incorporating more than 200 shades of color.

℥ **"Old No. 201" Engine,** in front of a former depot at the intersection of I-35 and U.S. 14.

This 1880 locomotive was driven by Jonathan Luther "Casey" Jones during his railroading career in the southern Mississippi Valley. (Jones's mother was probably Irish.)

The engine is similar to the *Cannon Ball Express*, which Jones was driving when he was killed in a collision with a freight train. The famous engineer lost his life in 1900 while trying to stop his passenger train from crashing into a line of railroad cars stopped on the tracks near Vaughan, Mississippi.

ST. PAUL

¶ **Cathedral of St. Paul,** 239 Selby Avenue.

Patterned after St. Peter's Basilica in the Vatican, this Catholic cathedral was constructed between 1905 and 1915 under the leadership of Archbishop John Ireland. The city of St. Paul commemorated the Irish-born immigrant by naming the boulevard between the cathedral and the State Capitol in his honor.

Archbishop Ireland was born in Kilkenny, Ireland, in 1838 and came to America with his parents. While still a youngster in St. Paul, he showed an aptitude for polemics, often arguing theology with the Presbyterian minister on his milk route. Following his ordination, he served in the Civil War as chaplain of the Fifth Minnesota Volunteers until he was stricken with fever at Vicksburg. As a pastor in St. Paul he campaigned against political corruption and the influence of liquor interests, going so far as to defenestrate whiskey bottles during house-to-house inspections in the Irish community. He subsequently became the leader of the temperance movement in this part of the country after three drunken men presented him with a piece of paper signed by a saloon keeper and his patrons and containing the plea, "For God's sake organize a temperance society." For his zeal in this effort, he was called the "Father Mathew of the West" and "the Consecrated Blizzard" of the Old Northwest.

Like his contemporary *Cardinal James Gibbons of Baltimore, Ireland sought to dispel the notion that Catholicism was incompatible with American institutions. In a major address during the Third Plenary Council in 1884, for example, the bishop of St. Paul insisted that "the principles of the church are in thorough harmony with the interests of the Republic . . . ." He later lent his influence to prevent the Vatican from officially condemning the Ancient Order of Hibernians and the Knights of Labor, although his need to do so called into question his thesis about the compatibility of the Church and America's democratic ideals. Whatever the case, his liberalism on Church-State matters, on the one hand, and his political identification with the Republican Party, on the other, energized his enemies within the hierarchy. Despite the best efforts of *Theodore Roosevelt and Secretary of State John Hay on his behalf, Ireland was never awarded the red hat.

§ Open Monday-Tuesday and Thursday-Friday 8-6, Wednesday 8-4, Saturday 8-8, Sunday 1-6. Phone: 612-228-1766.

¶ **F. Scott Fitzgerald Birthplace,** 481 Laurel Avenue. Private.

This was the birthplace in 1896 of F. Scott Fitzgerald, the famous novelist whose love-hate relationship with the wealthy formed the basis of much of his work, including *This Side of Paradise* and *The Great Gatsby*.

Fitzgerald's dual American and Irish ancestry seems to have been the cause of the identity crisis that plagued him for most of his life. Through his paternal forebears, Fitzgerald was descended from prominent figures in the history of colonial Maryland. (He was named, in fact, for Francis Scott Key, the author of the "Star Spangled Banner" and a cousin of his paternal grandmother.) His maternal grandfather, Philip McQuillan, had emigrated from County Fermanagh, Ireland, in 1843, settling first in Galena, Illinois, and then in St. Paul, where he operated a wholesale grocery business and left a fortune worth more than $125,000. Yet despite this grandfather's financial success, Fitzgerald regarded his maternal ancestry as "straight 1850 potato-famine Irish."

The author's cultural schizophrenia is evident in his remark that "I am half black Irish and half old American stock. . . . The black Irish half of the family had the money and looked down upon the Maryland side of the family who . . . really . . . had 'breeding.' So . . . spent my youth alternately crawling in front of the kitchen maids and insulting the great."

An example of Fitzgerald's iconoclasm occurred in St. John the Evangelist Episcopal Church in St. Paul one Christmas Eve. After "suppering heavily" while home from Princeton in 1913, the young college student expressed a desire to sing Christmas carols. Entering the church after the service had begun, he swayed down the aisle until he reached the foot of the pulpit. "Don't mind me, go on with the sermon," he said to the minister directly above his head. Fitzgerald later commented that the St. Paul press was so eager to report his impropriety that the local papers "had the extra out before midnight."

¶ **F. Scott Fitzgerald Residence,** Summit Terrace, 599 Summit Avenue. Private

In 1918 F. Scott Fitzgerald was living with his parents in the three-story apartment at this address, on a street which he later called "a museum of American architectural failures."

It was here that the twenty-two year old worked on the final version of *This Side of Paradise* after the manuscript – originally called *The Romantic Egotist* – had been rejected twice by Scribner's. He worked on the third floor of the apartment, pinning to the curtains the chapters he intended to keep in the revision. By the end of that July he told his editor that while his earlier book had been "a tedious, disconnected casserole this is a definite attempt at a big novel and I really believe I have it." When his publisher finally accepted the manuscript, he wrote to a friend at Smith College:

> In a house below the average
> On a street above the average
> In a room below the roof
> With a lot above the ears
> I shall write Alida Bigelow . . .
> Scribner's has accepted my book. Ain't I smart!

¶ **General Shields Memorial,** second floor rotunda, State Capitol, Aurora and Constitution avenues.

At the insistence of the Grand Army of the Republic, this memorial statue in honor of General James Shields was erected by the state of Minnesota in 1914.

A native of County Tyrone, Ireland, Shields enjoyed a number of distinctions: He challenged Abraham Lincoln to a duel, served in three conflicts (the Black Hawk War, the Mexican War, and the Civil War), and was the only American to represent three states in the U.S. Senate (Illinois, Minnesota, and Missouri).

While serving as auditor for the state of Illinois in the late 1830s, Shields was attacked in a pseudonymous letter submitted to the *Springfield Journal* by Abraham Lincoln. Using the pen name "Rebecca of the Lost Townships," Lincoln criticized Shields for requiring that taxes be paid in gold or silver. The letter, in the form of a dialogue between Rebecca and a farmer, called Shields "a fool, as well as a liar. With him truth is out of the question. . . . If I was deaf and dumb and blind I could tell him by the smell." A second letter, written in part by Mary Todd, Lincoln's future wife, playfully attempted a reconciliation with Shields: "I have long expected to die a widow, but as Mr. S is rather good looking than otherwise, I must say I don't care if we compromise the matter by – . . . maybe sorter let the old grudge drop if I was to consent to - be - be - h-i-s w-i-f-e? . . . I never fight with anything but broomsticks or hot water, or a shovelful of coals or some such thing, the former of which, bein' somewhat like a shillalah, may not be very objectionable to him."

When the Irishman demanded to know the author of the letters, Lincoln accepted responsibility but failed to respond to the Irishman's demand for a retraction. Insulted by the silence, Shields challenged the lawyer to a duel. Only then did Lincoln offer his apologies: "I had no intention of injuring your personal or private character, or offending you as a man or a gentleman, and I did not then think . . . that that article could produce . . . that effect against you. . . . And I will add that your conduct toward me . . . had always been gentlemanly, and that I had no personal

*Statue of James Shields
in the Minnesota State Capitol.*

grudge against you and cause for any." Perhaps unexpectedly, Shields and the future president become lifelong friends.

Shields went on to serve with extraordinary distinction in the Mexican War. At the Battle of Cerro Gordo, his right lung was pierced by a cannon grapeshot an inch and a third in diameter, although luckily the missile exited before hitting his spine. His life was saved when an Irish physician named McMillan removed the coagulated blood from the wound by forcing a bandaged ramrod through the general's body. At Churubusco, Shields led the charge of New York Irish and South Carolina volunteers. Later at the battle of Chapultepec in September 1846, he fought on foot, with sword in hand, after his horse had been shot out from under him. Although he subsequently suffered a fractured arm during the assault on Mexico City, the men under his command were the first to plant the Stars and Stripes over the city. For his exploits he was honored by the states of Illinois and South Carolina. From the former he received a $3,000 sword, whose scabbard was engraved with the words: "Presented by the State of Illinois to General James Shields for gallant services at Vera Cruz, Cerro Gordo, Contreras, Churubusco, Chapultepec, and the Garita of Belen, City of Mexico." The diamond-studded sword which South Carolina presented him was worth $5,000.

An example of James Shields' romantic daring was evident in an episode which occurred on the eve of the capture of Mexico City. That night an English boy entered the general's tent and informed him that his – the boy's – sister was being held captive in the city by a Mexican desperado. Although Shields acknowledged that he had no authority to command any of his men to participate in a rescue attempt, more men volunteered than were needed. With Shields in the lead, he and his men stealthily followed the boy back into Mexico City, rescued the woman, and had almost returned to camp when the Mexicans opened fire on them, although without effect. The next morning when General Winfield Scott reprimanded Shields for his unauthorized expedition, the Englishwoman pleaded her rescuer's case. Scott was unyielding, however, and threatened the Irishman: "Shields, I shall court martial you; I shall have you dishonorably discharged, and disgrace you." Shields nobly replied: "General Scott, you can court martial me, you may have me dishonorably discharged, but no one, except myself, can disgrace me." The possibility of a court-martial disappeared the next day when his troops were the first to raise the American flag over the Mexican capital. Soon after her return to England, the object of the general's rescue sent him a diamond and emerald breastpin.

After representing Illinois in the U.S. Senate at the beginning of the 1850s, the Mexican War veteran settled on his land grant in Minnesota Territory. While there, he became an energetic promoter of Irish colonization and was influential in establishing the townships of Erin, Kilkenny, Montgomery, and Shieldsville. By 1857 the last-named community had almost 300 residents, more than half of them natives of Ireland and most of the rest of Irish parentage. That same year he became one of Minnesota's first U.S. senators.

§ Open Monday-Friday 9-5, Saturday 10-4, Sunday 1-4. Closed Easter, Thanksgiving, December 25 and 31. Phone: 612-296-2881.

¶ **Ignatius Donnelly Burial Site,** Calvary Cemetery, Front and St. Albans streets, Block 32, lot 8.

A large headstone marks the graves of *Ignatius Donnelly and his wife, Katherine, and their daughter, Mary, and her husband, George Giltinan. (The Donnelly name is on the north side of the stone and is not visible from the road.) Donnelly was a prominent state and national politician, author, and social reformer. (See Hastings, Minnesota.)

¶ **James J. Hill House,** 240 Summit Avenue.

Constructed between 1889 and 1891, this 36,000-square-foot Victorian house belonged to James J. Hill, the founder of the Great Northern Railroad. The three-story house was built at a cost of $200,000 and has a three-story pipe organ, twenty-two fireplaces, stained-glass windows, and an art gallery.

Hill, whose ancestors had come from northern Ireland, abandoned plans to become a doctor when an accident with an arrow caused the loss of sight in one eye. After arriving in St. Paul at the age of seventeen, he found work as a clerk for a steampacket line and soon learned all aspects of the freight business. By 1867 he had contracted to supply the St. Paul & Pacific Railroad with fuel. Realizing that coal would soon replace wood as the railroad's chief fuel, he completed a survey of the nation's coal sources and markets and formed the Northwestern Fuel Company. Through his subsequent development of the Great Northern Railroad system between St. Paul and Puget Sound, he was soon on his way to gaining monopoly control of the rail freight between Chicago and the Pacific Northwest. (Between 1891 and 1906 the G.N.R. network expanded with the construction of an average of one mile of railroad per day.) By 1901 Hill and his associates had secured controlling interest in both the Northern Pacific and the Chicago, Burlington & Quincy lines.

In the administration of his railways, Hill insisted that his officers follow a simple maxim: "Intelligent management of railroads must be based on exact knowledge of facts. Guesswork will not do." While at the height of his railroad career, he was also a director of several banks, including Chase National. In the last year of his life, his friends honored him with the endowment of the James J. Hill Professorship of Transportation at Harvard University.

§ Open Wednesday-Saturday 10-3:30. Closed holidays. Fee. Phone: 612-297-2555.

¶ James J. Hill Reference Library, 80-90 West 4th Street.

Located in an Italian Renaissance building shared with the St. Paul Public Library, the Hill Library was established through a $1 million endowment created by the railroad magnate *James J. Hill. The interior of the two-story hall, which opened in 1921, is lined with Ionic columns.

¶ Minnesota Historical Society, 345 Kellogg Boulevard West.

The society's holdings include approximately half the volumes in the personal library of *Ignatius Donnelly, the famous author, politician, and social reformer. His collection originally numbered several hundred books – 200 on Shakespeare and Bacon alone – and was housed in the cherry paneled library of his home in Nininger, Minnesota. During his lifetime, the collection was one of the largest in the state. Because Donnelly made marginal notations in many of his books, it is possible to trace the source of his social and political ideas. Long after Donnelly's death, however, when the house lay in disrepair, "souvenir hunters" stripped the library of many of its fine volumes. The remaining works – as well as the library itself – were rescued before Donnelly's house was razed in 1949. The volumes which the historical society today possesses are in the Reserve Room and are accessible through prior arrangement.

In 1981 the Minnesota Historical Society reconstructed Donnelly's paneled library as part of an exhibit. The library was later disassembled and today is held in storage by the historical society.

¶ O'Shaughnessy Plaza and Auditorium, 143 West 4th Street.

This plaza and civic auditorium are named for Ignatius Aloysius O'Shaughnessy, an oil company executive and a benefactor of the University of St. Thomas in St. Paul.

The grandson of an Irish immigrant who had settled in Massachusetts in the 1830s, O'Shaughnessy was a 1903 graduate of St. Thomas College (the predecessor of today's university). He worked in the insurance and banking fields before creating the Global Oil & Refining Company in 1917 and serving as president of its subsidiaries, the Lario Oil & Gas Company and the Globe Pipeline Company. In addition to being a director of the First National Bank of St. Paul and a member of the Chicago Yacht Club, he was a trustee of the University of Notre Dame, a Knight of the Holy Sepulchre, and a Knight of Malta. He also donated $200,000 to Notre Dame university for the creation of a fine arts foundation.

¶ St. Paul Seminary, Mississippi River Boulevard between Summit and Goodrich avenues.

This Catholic seminary was established in 1894 by *Archbishop John Ireland following a bequest by *James J. Hill. Although raised by a Baptist father and a Methodist mother, the famous railroad magnate had married Mary Theresa Mehegan, the daughter of Catholic Irish immigrants. Hill's other benefactions to the archdiocese of St. Paul were numerous and generous, including $50,000 toward the construction of the cathedral.

¶ St. Thomas Academy, 949 Mendota Heights Road.

This college preparatory and military academy was created in 1963 as an offshoot of St. Thomas College, originally founded in 1885 by *Archbishop John Ireland.

The campus chapel is built in the style of a Byzantine basilica, and the school library contains impressive holdings of French and Celtic literature.

¶ University of St. Thomas, 2115 Summit Avenue.

The life of Archbishop John Ireland is commemorated in two memorials at this Catholic institution: a stained-glass window in St. James Church and a statue in the lower quadrangle of the campus.

At first known as St. Thomas College, this institution was founded in 1885 by Ireland, for almost two decades the archbishop of St. Paul. The property on which the college was built originally belonged to William

*Statue of Archbishop Ireland
at the University of St. Thomas.
(Photo courtesy of the
University of St. Thomas.)*

Finn, an Irish-American soldier stationed at nearby Fort Snelling. Finn had acquired the land as a pension when he was discharged from military service after blowing off one of his fingers in a gun accident. He later sold the property to Archbishop Ireland.

The college was initially both a seminary for the training of priests and a liberal arts institution for lay students. In 1894, however, the theological school was moved to a new site, now occupied by St. Paul Seminary.

Today the St. Thomas campus boasts several buildings erected through the generosity of *Ignatius Aloysius O'Shaughnessy, a 1903 graduate of the college and a prominent oil company executive. The school's library, educational center, and athletic building and stadium bear the name of their donor. A bust of O'Shaughnessy is located in the library, while his regalia as a Knight of Malta and of the Holy Sepulchre are on display in the educational center.

SANBORN

¶ McCone Sod House Exhibit, 1 mile east of junction U.S. 71 and then 0.25 mile south on a gravel road.

These two sod houses were built in 1987 by Stan McCone to honor his Irish ancestors who lived in such houses in Tulare, South Dakota, in the 1880s.

One of the sod houses contains a dirt floor and is simply furnished, while the other has a wooden floor, is appointed more amply, and can be rented out to bed and breakfast guests.

§ Open May 1-Labor Day, Monday-Saturday and holidays 9-5, Sunday 2-5. Fee. Phone: 507-723-5138.

SHAKOPEE

¶ **Historic Murphy's Landing,** 1 mile east on State 101.

This eighty-eight-acre site is an outdoor living-history museum that features forty period buildings, including two farmsteads, a fur trading post, and a schoolhouse. The structures represent the various ethnic groups which settled in the Minnesota River Valley between 1840 and 1890: Czech, Danish, English, French, German, Irish, Norwegian, Polish, and Scandinavian. The site also includes sixteen Native American mounds dating from the first century B.C.

¶ Historic Murphy's Landing occupies the site of a nineteenth-century inn and ferry landing owned by Richard Murphy, who arrived in this area in 1853.

Presumably of Irish background, Murphy was born in Tennessee sometime between 1801 and 1804 but moved to Illinois at the age of seventeen. After serving in the Black Hawk War, he was elected to the Illinois legislature. In 1848, however, *President James K. Polk appointed him Indian subagent for the St. Peter Indian Agency in what later became the state of Minnesota. He was stationed for about four years at Fort Snelling before being transferred to the Dakota reservation agency.

After taking up this new position, Murphy moved to Eagle Creek, a small town east of Shakopee. In 1856 the state legislature granted him a fifteen-year charter to operate a ferry on the Minnesota River, a concession that prompted him to build a two-story inn to accommodate the travelers for whom he expected to play boatman. Before long, however, plans were afoot to build a bridge across the river in order to provide a direct route from Shakopee to St. Paul. According to the plan, the bridge would be built at a site near Murphy's hotel. Although at first the prospect of a bridge seemed to threaten Murphy's ferry business, he soon realized that the railroads would connect with the river at Eagle Creek, forming a juncture with the steamboat lines already there or likely to develop. As a result, he visualized the emergence of a large settlement on his very doorstep. Unfortunately, however, the rail line was not built for a decade, during which time the Shakopee landing was preferred to Murphy's. Murphy used the hotel as a home for his family and lived there until his death in

1875.

The stone inn was subsequently used for a variety of purposes, including a homeless shelter during the Depression. In 1963, however, the building was destroyed by fire, caused by either a defective chimney or faulty wiring. The twelve members of the family that lived there at the time escaped the flames but suffered the other extreme – a temperature of thirty degrees below zero. The foundations of the inn are still visible and are located near the center of Murphy's Landing Village.

¶ The second site in Murphy's Landing with an Irish connection is the O'Connor House, built in 1865 by an immigrant named John O'Connor.

O'Connor and his wife, Catherine, were born in Ireland in 1825 and 1835, respectively. After immigrating to the United States, they eventually made their way to Minnesota, arriving in Glendale in 1855. After service as a private in the Minnesota Volunteers for three years during the Civil War, O'Connor returned to the state but soon moved with his wife and four children to Shakopee. There in 1865 he built the house on display in Murphy's Landing Village.

At the time of its construction, the house was located on a highly desirable corner, but the value of the residence declined precipitously when the St. Paul & Sioux City Railroad ran its tracks down the middle of Second Street. Although railroad officials claimed that O'Connor had granted them permission to build the tracks in front of his house, the Irishman sued. (The result of the suit is unknown.)

The nature of O'Connor's employment or occupation remains a mystery. Since the census records give no such evidence, it has been presumed that he was a handyman who worked for his neighbors whenever he could. With the birth of his seventh child in 1871, O'Connor and his wife must have been living a precarious existence, a conclusion justified by the fact that the Irishman mortgaged his home eight times during the next seven years. In addition, on at least two occasions the house was sold to pay off debts or back taxes, although in each case O'Connor redeemed the property. His situation must have been desperate when his wife was fined $30 for assaulting a neighbor, Anna May Hilgers.

§ Historic Murphy's Landing is open Memorial Day-Labor Day, Tuesday-Sunday 10-5; September and December, Monday-Friday 10-5. Fee. Phone: 612-445-6901.

NEW HAMPSHIRE

AMHERST

¶ **Horace Greeley Birthplace,** Horace Greeley Road.

A stone monument and plaque stand in front of the birthplace of Horace Greeley, the founder of the *New York Times* and coiner of the advice "Go west, young man." The house, which has four fireplaces, dates from about 1775.

Greeley, who was descended from Scotch-Irish stock on his mother's side, set a new standard in American journalism by replacing the usual interest in the lurid with an emphasis on social and political reform. Through his editorials he attacked slavery and economic monopolies, opposed capital punishment, supported the rights of labor, and advocated the free distribution of government lands to western settlers. The focus of his efforts was summarized in his remark that newspapers should be "as sensitive to oppression and degradation in the next street as if they were practised in Brazil or Japan."

As the slavery issue intensified during the 1850s, Greeley favored disunion rather than complicity in the extension of the "peculiar institution" into the western territories. When civil war finally came, he insisted that Congress and President Lincoln emancipate the slaves, partially in the belief that the Union could not "afford to repel the sympathies and reject the aid of Four Millions of Southern people." As war dragged on, however, he urged Lincoln to negotiate a peace with the South, arguing that "our bleeding, bankrupt, almost dying country . . . shudders at the prospect of fresh conscriptions, of further wholesale devastations, and of new rivers of human blood."

CANAAN

¶ **Soldiers' Monument,** Broad Street Park.

This traditional Civil War memorial was designed by *Martin Milmore. A duplicate stands in the town common in Peterborough, New Hampshire.

CORNISH

¶ **Saint-Gaudens National Historic Site,** off State 12A between Cornish and Plainfield.

After purchasing this summer home and studio in 1883, Augustus Saint-Gaudens remodeled it and named it "Aspet" after his father's birthplace in France. Two studios on the property display bas-reliefs, busts, portraits, and models of his statuary (including the Admiral

Farragut Statue, the Adams Memorial, *The Standing Lincoln*, and *Amor Caritas*). The sculptor's grave is marked by a small Ionic temple on the property.

Saint-Gaudens was born in Dublin to a French father and an Irish mother (Mary McGuiness), but within six months of his birth his family sailed for America, eventually settling in New York City. There the youngster first showed his artistic bent by sketching the shoemakers in his father's shop. He later studied drawing at Cooper Union and the National Academy of Design.

By 1867 Saint-Gaudens was working as a cameo cutter in Paris and attending a small art school, where, as he reported, "I modeled my first figures from the nude." Within a year he was studying sculpture at the Ecole des Beaux-Arts and startling his comrades by singing the "Marseillaise." Although he suffered from illness and financial worries after moving on to Rome, he designed *Hiawatha* there and received various commissions, among them requests for copies of busts of Demosthenes and Cicero. The hold which the Eternal City had on him at that time is evident when – once again living in New York – he would "turn on the water at the little wash-basin, let it run continuously with a gentle tinkle, and thus recall the sound of the fountain in the garden at Rome."

After returning to the United States, Saint-Gaudens received a variety of commissions. His most famous were *Admiral Farragut* (New

"Aspet," the home of the Dublin-born sculptor Augustus Saint-Gaudens.

York City), *The Puritan* (Philadelphia), *Lincoln* (Chicago), *General John Logan* (Chicago), the *Shaw Memorial* (Boston), *General William Sherman* (New York City), the *Adams Monument* (District of Columbia), and *Diana* (for the tower of the original Madison Square Garden). He was also commissioned to design statues of Robert Louis Stevenson (Edinburgh, Scotland) and Charles Stewart Parnell (Dublin, Ireland). In 1905 he created designs for several U.S. coins, including a rendering of "Liberty" for the twenty-dollar gold piece.

Saint-Gaudens was a founder of the Society of American Artists, received honorary degrees from Harvard, Princeton, and Yale, and was elected to the Royal Academy. As a teacher at the Art Students' League, he advised his pupils "to develop technique and then to hide it." On one occasion, as he wended his way through a studio full of the accouterments of his "trade" – scaffolds, plaster casts, and clay models – he remarked that "People think a sculptor has an easy life in a studio. It's hard labor, in a factory."

§ Open Memorial Day-October 31, grounds daily 8-dusk, buildings daily 8:30-4:30. Fee. Phone: 603-675-2055.

¶ Saint-Gaudens House and Studio, Dingelton Hill and Whitten roads.

Although this two-and-a-half-story house was originally built about 1794 for Shakers in Enfield, New Hampshire, it was bought and moved to this site by Louis Saint-Gaudens, the younger brother of the more famous sculptor Augustus Saint-Gaudens.

Louis Saint-Gaudens was born in New York City in 1854 and studied sculpture first under his brother and then at the Ecole des Beaux-Arts in Paris. After returning to the United States, he became part of the "Cornish Colony" and helped his brother in many of his works. Louis, who suffered from alcoholism, occasionally climbed a windmill on the property, pulled up the ladder after himself, and nursed a bottle of bourbon in that secluded spot.

In 1901 the younger brother exhibited at the Pan-American Exposition in Buffalo, New York. His most famous work is probably his pair of lions in the Boston Public Library, sculpted to honor the men of two Massachusetts regiments who died in the Civil War.

DERRY

Scotch-Irish Presbyterians arrived in this area in 1719, although apparently they were at first taken for Catholic Irish. In 1722 the area now occupied by Derry and Londonderry was granted to John Moor and named for the famous Ulster city. The earliest settlers cultivated potatoes – the first grown in North America – and introduced Irish linen-making. The products of this latter industry became so brazenly imitated that by 1748 the town officials ordered that the end of each quantity of cloth produced here be stamped with the words "Londonderry in New Hampshire."

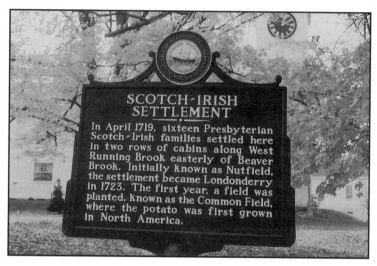

Historical marker in Londonderry, New Hampshire.

❡ Matthew Thornton House, 2 Thornton Street.

A granite boulder in front of this clapboard house memorializes Matthew Thornton, the Irish-born signer of the Declaration of Independence who bought the house in 1757.

Thornton was a native of Limerick, Ireland, and arrived in Boston in 1718. Although he was a physician in Derry from 1740 to 1778, there is little evidence about the nature of his medical practice. It is known, however, that on at least two occasions he was paid extremely large sums by the New Hampshire Assembly for rendering medical services: £25 for attending a man injured in a riot, and £94 for caring for a sick soldier.

Apparently interested in the new medical developments of his time, Thornton allowed himself to be inoculated against the small pox. He used his recovery experience as the basis of a satire on members of his profession: "Dr. Cash . . . was the [inoculator], and for a few days, visited us [but] we saw no more of him, till I paid his bill of 18 dollars. Dr. Surly came two or three times each day . . . , viewed us through his glasses, and then, with a smiling grin, softly said, 'What, no worse yet? this is but trifling to what you will feel, before all is over.' Dr. Critical Observer . . . came once in two or three days, and stayed about a minute each time. Dr. Gay . . . tripped round and sung a tune, and told us 'all would end well.' Dr. Experience, a merchant, who has had the Small Pox, visited us every day, and gave a much truer account of the Small Pox than all the doctors." Thornton's later criticism of the medical corps in the Continental Army lacked the humor of his satire but was just as biting: "An inexcusable Neglect in the Officers, want of Fidility, Honour, and Humanity, in the Drs and averice in the Suttlers, has Slain ten Soldiers to the Enemies one, and will Soon prevent every man of Common Sense from putting his Life and Fortune in the Power of Such as Destroy both without pity and mercy."

Both before and after the Revolution, Thornton served New Hampshire in a variety of positions. In 1775 he was elected president of the provincial congress and was the chairman of the committee which drafted the state's first constitution – the first adopted by any of the thirteen former colonies. Although he was not appointed to the Continental Congress until four months after the Declaration of Independence was adopted, he was permitted to sign the document on November 19, 1776.

Some years later, while Thornton served as a state judge, an incident in his court gave rise to an amusing anecdote. According to the story, when the defense attorney found Thornton reading a book and the associate justice asleep during the trial of a particular case, the lawyer told the jury: "Gentlemen, my unfortunate client has no hope but in *your* attention, since the Court in their wisdom will not condescend to hear this case!" Thornton replied by saying, "When you have anything to offer, Mr. _____, which is pertinent to the case on trial, the Court will be happy to hear you. Meantime I may as well as resume my reading."

𝕵 Pinkerton Academy, Pinkerton Street.

This educational institution was founded by Major John Pinkerton and Elder James Pinkerton, whose father had come from Ulster to Londonderry about 1738. In 1814 these two prosperous merchants endowed the school with $14,500 "for promoting piety and virtue, and for the education of youth in such of the liberal arts and sciences or languages as the Trustees . . . shall direct." Today the academy offers a college preparatory curriculum as well as agricultural, commercial, and scientific courses of studies to 2,600 students in grades nine through twelve.

DUBLIN

The original land grant in this area was given to William Thornton and thirty-nine other colonists about 1750. The first settler in Dublin was Thornton's brother Matthew Thornton, a native of Limerick, Ireland,

and a signer of the Declaration of Independence. Many of the other early settlers were Scotch-Irish.

DURHAM

♫ General John Sullivan Memorial Bridge, across the Bellamy and Piscataqua rivers.

This bridge on the route from Durham to Portsmouth was named for *John Sullivan, the Revolutionary War general and governor of the state.

♫ John Sullivan House, 23 New Market Street.

This eighteenth-century structure was the home of *John Sullivan, who purchased it in 1764. His grave is in the cemetery behind the house. A monument in front of the house marks the site of the meetinghouse where Sullivan and a band of colonials hid the arms and gunpowder which they had seized from the British at Fort William and Mary in 1774.

According to tradition, when Sullivan's mother was on her way from Ireland to America, someone asked her what she was going to do among the colonists there. She replied, "Raise governors for them," a prediction that bore fruit when her sons James and John became the respective governors of Massachusetts and New Hampshire.

The Matthew Thornton House in Merrimack.

MERRIMACK

❡ Matthew Thornton Home and Grave, State 3 (Daniel Webster Highway).

This private residence was formerly the home of *Matthew Thornton, who purchased it in 1780 after its confiscation from a Tory who had fled the state. Three years later the legislature granted Thornton the exclusive right to ferry passengers across the river near his house. This area is still known as Thornton's Ferry.

• Thornton's grave is located across the highway and is marked by a monument dedicated in 1892.

NEW CASTLE

❡ Fort Constitution, in a small park east of the town square.

Known in revolutionary times as Fort William and Mary, this fortification was the object of an attack by colonials under *Major John Sullivan on December 15, 1774. During this raid and another the day before, the Americans captured five tons of gunpowder, fifteen cannon, and a large quantity of arms. Sullivan must have relished the irony of his victory when he thought of his grandfather Philip O'Sullivan, who had fled Ireland after the victory of King William III at the battle of the Boyne in 1690.

Occurring four months before the battles of Lexington and Concord, the attacks on Fort William and Mary constituted the first overt act of aggression against British authority in the colony. Some of the captured munitions were turned against the British at the battle of Bunker Hill the following spring. In a letter to John Adams in 1775, Sullivan urged Congress to declare independence from Great Britain at once: "Have we any encouragement from the people of Great Britain? Could they exert themselves more if we had shaken off the yoke and declared ourselves independent? Why, then, in God's name is it not done? Do the members of your respectable body think that [the British] will throw their shot and shells with more force than at present? . . . . Could they have treated our prisoners worse had we been in open and avowed rebellion than they do now?"

PETERBOROUGH

❡ MacDowell Colony National Historic Landmark, north on MacDowell Road off U.S. 202.

In 1896 the Scotch-Irish composer Edward Alexander MacDowell turned his sixty-acre farm here into a working retreat with the erection of a log studio to complement "Hillcrest," his farmhouse. His widow later opened the "colony" to other musicians as well as to writers and painters. Today the colony's 500-acre property consists of approximately thirty-five studios and outbuildings. Visitors are welcome at Colony Hall and can visit the library and MacDowell's grave.

Although MacDowell's initial musical training in the United States was from South American instructors, his subsequent musical preparation was decidedly European. In 1876 he was admitted to the Paris Conservatoire, but, after developing a dislike for French music, he decided to pursue his education in Germany. He was soon appointed head piano instructor at the Darmstadt Conservatory. On a later visit to Franz Liszt to play his (MacDowell's) First Piano Concerto, the American musician was so nervous that he could not ring the bell to the famous European's house. For the next two years MacDowell concentrated on composing orchestral pieces and symphonic poems.

Following his return to Boston with his new wife, MacDowell realized that he must devote his time to performance and instruction rather than composition. He was soon lionized as the foremost American composer and pianist and saw his larger compositions more frequently performed by both American and European orchestras. In addition, he developed a growing clientele of piano and composition students. This increasing fame may have been influential in his appointment in 1896 to the first professorship of music at Columbia University. Although he established a male chorus and a university orchestra, he was distressed by the realization that his music classes carried no academic credit and that few of his students were prepared for the calibre of musical instruction he hoped to give them. In this latter regard, he vainly requested that the academic world place greater emphasis on the fine arts. He hoped that music would become the nucleus of a fine arts department that would also include belles lettres, painting, and sculpture.

After suffering a carriage accident in 1905, the forty-four-year-old musician began to show signs of mental illness. During periods of lucidity, however, he expressed his hope of turning his summer estate at Peterborough into an artists' colony. Leonard Bernstein, Aaron Copland, and Virgil Thomson were among the composers who subsequently spent time in residence here. Since 1960 the MacDowell Medal has been awarded annually to a distinguished composer, artist, or writer.

§ Open Monday-Friday 1-4.

NEW JERSEY

ATLANTIC CITY

¶ **John F. Kennedy Bust,** opposite the Atlantic City Convention Center, on the Boardwalk between Mississippi and Florida avenues.

BARNEGAT LIGHT

¶ **Barnegat Lighthouse State Park,** on the north end of Long Beach Island, off Broadway Avenue.

Historic 167-foot Barnegat Lighthouse warns seafarers of Barnegat Shoals, the site of more than 200 shipwrecks. The lighthouse was built in 1857-58 under the direction of *George Gordon Meade, who at the time was an engineer but who later was the Union commander at Gettysburg. The structure was used as a lighthouse until 1927.

§ Park open daily dawn-dusk. Lighthouse open Memorial Day-Labor Day, daily 10-4:30; October and other times in May and September, Saturday and Sunday 10-4:30. Fee. Phone: 609-494-2016.

BRIDGEPORT

¶ **Commodore Barry Bridge,** over the Delaware River between Bridgeport, New Jersey, and Chester, Pennsylvania.

The bridge is named for John Barry, the Irish-born "Father of the American Navy."

CALDWELL

¶ **Grover Cleveland Birthplace,** 207 Bloomfield Avenue (State 506).

Grover Cleveland, the only U.S. president to serve two nonconsecutive terms, was born here in 1837 and lived here until his family moved to Fayetteville, New York, four years later. Cleveland's maternal grandfather was Abner Neal, who had immigrated to Baltimore from Ireland in the late 1700s. A great-great-grandfather was Richard Lamb of Dublin, who died about 1736 on his way to New England.

During the presidential campaign of 1876, Cleveland became the object of attacks against his character. A Buffalo newspaper first published the insinuation that Cleveland was the father of an illegitimate son, the issue of a relationship with a widow named Mrs. Halpin. Although Cleveland never knew for sure that he was the father of the child, he agreed to take responsibility for him when Halpin claimed that Cleveland was the boy's father. When the mother began drinking while nursing the child, Cleveland indirectly took steps to have the boy committed to the care of an orphan asylum, the expenses of which Cleveland agreed to pay. After Halpin kidnapped the child, the authorities intervened and recommitted him to the orphanage, although he was later adopted by a distinguished New York family. During the campaign Cleveland's detractors titillated the voters with the jeer: "Ma, Ma, where's my Pa? Gone to the White House, Ha, Ha, Ha!"

§ Open Wednesday-Saturday 9-12 and 1-5, Sunday 1-5. Closed holidays. Phone: 201-226-1810.

ELIZABETH

¶ **Caldwell Burial Sites,** First Presbyterian Church, Broad Street, south of Caldwell Place.

A seventeen-foot monument in the churchyard marks the graves of the Reverend James Caldwell and his wife. Caldwell was the most famous colonial pastor of this church.

The inscription on the monument reads: "Sacred to the memory of the Rev. James Caldwell and Hannah his wife, who fell victims to their country's cause in the years 1780 & 1781. He was the zealous and faithful pastor of the Presbyterian Church in this Town, where by his evangelical labors in the gospel vineyard, and his early attachment to the civil liberties of his country, he has left in the hearts of his people a better monument than brass or marble."

Born in Virginia of Scotch-Irish and Huguenot descent, James Caldwell was graduated from the College of New Jersey (now Princeton) in 1759 and within two years was ordained and installed here as pastor. Because of his militancy for the Patriot cause and his service as a chaplain during the war against Britain, Loyalists called him the "high priest of the Revolution" and offered rewards for his capture.

In 1781 Caldwell met his death during an unfortunate incident with a Patriot guard, an Irishman named James Morgan. Having gone to meet an acquaintance who had arrived by boat at De Hart's Point, Caldwell went aboard the vessel to pick up a package belonging to the woman. As the minister returned to his carriage, Morgan ordered him to stop, apparently with the intention of questioning him about the package. When Caldwell failed to obey the command quickly enough, the sentry shot him through the heart. At Morgan's trial another soldier testified that he had heard the Irishman express his intention to "pop" Caldwell off whenever he had the chance, while still another soldier claimed that Morgan had been bribed to kill the parson.

FREEHOLD

¶ Monmouth Battle Monument, Monmouth County Courthouse, Monument and Court streets.

This eighty-five-foot shaft is crowned with a representation of "Liberty Triumphant." The statue of Molly Pitcher and the five large panels on the base of the monument were designed by *James Edward Kelly. The bas-relief panels depict scenes from the battle of Monmouth in 1778: Colonel Nathaniel Ramsey defending his guns, Washington rallying his troops, Molly Pitcher at the cannon, the council of war at Hopewell, and the charge of *Anthony Wayne.

¶ Old Tennent Church, Main and Tennent streets.

Built in 1731 for a predominantly Scottish and Scotch-Irish congregation, this church was served during the middle of the eighteenth century by two eminent Irish-born pastors – William Tennent and his brother John Tennent. William, who was pastor here for forty-four years, was buried beneath the church floor after his death in 1777.

William Tennent had come to America as a boy from his native County Armagh with his father, a Presbyterian minister. After attending his father's "Log College" in Neshaminy, Pennsylvania, the young man studied theology in New Brunswick, New Jersey, where he was almost buried alive. It seems that, after intense study had broken his health, one day he fell into unconsciousness while conversing with his brother in Latin. After his body had become as "cold and stiff as a stake," he was prepared for burial – but suddenly he came back to life. He later reported having experienced a state of perfect bliss, although for a year he had no memory of his former life. After recovering sufficiently, he succeeded his brother as pastor of the Freehold church.

Apparently because Tennent's inattention to financial affairs had led to some difficulties, a friend of his suggested that he find a wife "to attend to his temporal affairs, and to comfort his leisure hours by conjugal endearments." When the ingenuous minister replied that he did not know how to go about obtaining a wife, the friend introduced him to his sister-in-law. The two were married within a week.

§ Phone: 908-446-6299.

HALEDON

¶ American Labor Museum/Botto House National Landmark, 83 Norwood Street.

During the 1913 textile workers strike in nearby Paterson, the Botto House, the home of an Italian immigrant weaver, was the headquarters of a monstrous labor rally.

Among the labor agitators who addressed the thousands of strikers who gathered here was Elizabeth Gurley Flynn, whose Irish immigrant working-class parents had had a long association with political and social radicalism. She recalled that she "drew in a burning hatred of British rule" with her mother's milk and that before she was ten she knew of the great Irish heroes – Robert Emmet, Wolfe Tone, Michael Davitt, Charles Stewart Parnell, and Jeremiah O'Donovan Rossa. She proudly proclaimed that her ancestors had participated in every rebellion against the British and that her father, who lived past eighty, never mentioned the word "England" without adding the curse, "God damn her!"

Flynn was a labor activist for almost her entire life. Even as a youngster she was closely involved with socialist activities in the Bronx and quit high school in 1907 after joining the recently formed Industrial Workers of the World. During the next twenty years, she participated in various labor struggles, among them the free speech movement in Montana and Washington; strikes by textile workers in Lawrence, Massachusetts, and Paterson and Passaic, New Jersey; and the Mesabi Range miners' strike in Minnesota. During these crusades she became friends or associates of the major labor and radical leaders in the country, including Eugene V. Debs, *William Z. Foster, and Bill Haywood. She was even the subject of a song – "The Rebel Girl" – written in her honor by an imprisoned labor leader in Utah.

Following World War I, Flynn redirected her efforts. For the next four years, she was engaged in helping defend political and economic dissidents, many of whom had been arrested during the 1919-20 Red Scare. She was a founder of the American Civil Liberties Union and remained on its board of directors until she was expelled for being a member of the Communist Party. In 1953 she was convicted of violating the Smith Act – for advocating the overthrow of the government – and served a two-and-a-half-year prison term. Among her writings was a 1950 work entitled *Horizons of the Future for a Socialist America.*

§ The museum features exhibits on the labor movement and immigrant life. Open Wednesday-Sunday 1-4. Closed holidays except Labor Day. Fee. Phone 201-595-7953.

KEARNY

This town of about 35,000 residents was named for Major General Philip Kearny, who lost his left arm in the Mexican War and was the commander of the First New Jersey Brigade during the Civil War. His earliest paternal ancestor in America was Michael Kearny, who had emigrated from Ireland in 1704 and settled in Perth Amboy, New Jersey.

LONG BRANCH

¶ Long Branch Historical Museum, 3 miles north at 1260 Ocean Avenue.

This was formerly the Church of the Presidents, so called because it was attended by seven U.S. presidents when they summered in this famous resort community: *Ulysses S. Grant, Rutherford B. Hayes, James Garfield, *Chester A. Arthur, *Benjamin Harrison, *William McKinley, and *Woodrow Wilson.

§ Open by appointment. Phone: 908-229-0600.

McGUIRE AIR FORCE BASE

This Air Force facility was named for *Major Thomas McGuire, the winner of the Medal of Honor for his heroic actions in World War II.

Born in New Jersey in 1920, McGuire joined the Army Air Corps in 1941 and while serving in the Pacific theater downed thirty-eight Japanese aircraft, a tally that was the second highest of any American fighter pilot during the war. McGuire was killed when his plane crushed in the Philippines in 1945 while he covered a fellow pilot under attack.

MORRISTOWN

¶ Kemble Estate, Tempe Wick Road, near State 202. Private.

In 1781 this mid-eighteenth-century mansion was occupied by *General Anthony Wayne, whose Pennsylvania Line was encamped in nearby Jockey Hollow with other units of the Continental Army.

¶ Morristown National Historic Park.

General George Washington and the Continental Army encamped in this area during the winters of 1777-78 and 1779-80. Today the park includes Washington's headquarters, a library and historical museum, Fort Nonsense, and Jockey Hollow.

Aware of the sizable numbers of Irish soldiers in his ranks, Washington in 1780 ordered that St. Patrick's Day be celebrated among his men at the Morristown encampment. He ordered "that all Fatigue and Working Parties cease for tomorrow, the 17th, a day held in particular Regard" by the Irish. The camp parole on March 16 was "Saint," and the countersign was "Patrick" or "Sheila." According to a newspaper account, "the Day was ushered in with music and hoisting of colors exhibiting the thirteen stripes, the favorite harp and an inscription, 'The Independence of Ireland.'"

Almost a year later, however, on January 1, 1781, Jockey Hollow was the scene of a mutiny by the eleven regiments of the Pennsylvania Line. Long feared by the line's commander, *General Anthony Wayne, the mutiny was sparked by long-standing grievances concerning supplies, pay, and terms of enlistment. After seizing the guns and ammunition in the camp and after refusing to heed the words of Wayne and a hundred other officers, approximately half of the line's 2,500 men headed off to Philadelphia to present their grievances to the Continental Congress in Philadelphia.

The overall composition of the Pennsylvania Line may have been reflected in the Eleventh Regiment's high percentage of Irish-born recruits: 28 percent of its sergeants and 45 percent of its rank and file. That a considerable number of Irish soldiers were involved in the mutiny can be surmised from the fact that Wayne selected two officers of Irish descent to accompany him to Princeton, New Jersey, where he hoped to negotiate with the leaders of the rebellion. One of the officers was Richard Butler, a native of Ireland, whose brother William was commandant of the Fourth Regiment and whose three younger brothers were officers in the line. The other brigade commander to go with Wayne was Walter Stewart, a Pennsylvania native of Irish descent who was so handsome that the ladies of Philadelphia referred to him as "the Irish Beauty." Irish-born Colonel Stephen Moylan was later permitted by the mutineers to join the negotiations.

It was probably during the mutiny of the Pennsylvania Line that General Wayne was accorded his nickname, "Mad Anthony." After Wayne ordered the arrest of his trusted spy – the Irishman "Jemmy the Rover" – for disorderly conduct, the bold subordinate asked whether Wayne was "Mad" or "in Fun." When told that he would receive twenty-nine lashes for any future misconduct, Jemmy replied, "Then Anthony is mad! Farewell to you! Clear the coast for the Commodore 'Mad Anthony's' friend."

§ Open daily 9-5. Closed January 1, Thanksgiving, and December 25. Fee. Phone: 201-539-2085.

ℐ Schuyler-Hamilton House, 5 Olyphant Place.

During Washington's encampment in Morristown in 1779-80, this private residence was used as the headquarters of Dr. John Cochran, the chief physician and surgeon general of the Continental Army.

Born in Pennsylvania to immigrants from northern Ireland, Cochran had studied "physic and surgery" at Lancaster, Pennsylvania, and had served with the British medical corps during the French and Indian War. At the outbreak of the Revolution, he volunteered for the American hospital services and helped draft a plan to create military hospitals for the American troops. General Washington was so impressed with Cochran's care for smallpox victims and for his wounded men that he recommended him for the post of physician and surgeon-general in the middle department of the Continental Army. Later as the army's physician-in-chief, Cochran regularly complained of the bureaucratic delays that hampered his work. "It grieves my soul," he wrote in a private letter, "to see the poor, worthy, brave fellows pine away for want of a few comforts, which they have dearly earned. I shall wait on the Commander-in-Chief, and represent our situation, but I am persuaded it can have little effect, for what can he do? He may refer the matter to Congress; they to the Medical Committee, who will pow-wow over it awhile and nothing be heard of it."

§ Open Tuesday-Saturday 2-5 and by appointment.

NEWARK

Three Catholic churches in Newark were designed by *Patrick Keely: St. Patrick's Pro-Cathedral (1846-50,) Washington Street and Central Avenue; St. Mary's Abbey Church (1856), High and William streets; and St. James Church (1863-66), Lafayette and Jefferson streets.

¶ **Essex County Courthouse,** Springfield Avenue and Market Street.

The façade of this 1906 French Renaissance structure is adorned with eleven statues by sculptor *Andrew O'Connor. In addition to representations of Truth and Power on either side of the entrance, statues of Adam, Eve, Cain, Thais, Wisdom, Learning, Justice, Maternity, and Light adorn the cornice.

¶ **Military Park,** bounded by Broad Street, Park Place, Rector Street, and Raymond Boulevard.

In the park are a bust of *John F. Kennedy and a statue of *Major General Philip Kearny (the commander of the New Jersey volunteers during the Civil War). The pedestal of the Kennedy memorial is inscribed with an excerpt from the president's inaugural address: "Let every nation know, whether it wishes us well or ill, that we shall pay any price, bear any burden, meet any hardship, support any friend, oppose any foe, in order to ensure the survival and success of liberty. This much we pledge – and more."

¶ **Monsignor Doane Statue,** Doane Park, north of Military Park.

This bronze statue by *William Clark Noble honors Monsignor George Hobart Doane, a Civil War chaplain and the rector of St. Patrick's Cathedral in Newark.

PATERSON

¶ **Dean McNulty Statue,** St. John the Baptist Catholic Church, 381 Grand Street.

This bronze statue in front of the church marks the grave of Dean

William McNulty, Paterson's most famous churchman and philanthropist. The statue shows McNulty seated on a bench, with his head tilted, listening to a young orphan boy.

McNulty, who was born in Ballyshannon, County Down, Ireland, in 1829, served as a pastor in Paterson for fifty-eight years. During that time he founded hospitals, orphanages, and homes for the aged. After his death at the age of ninety-three, his funeral was probably the biggest public demonstration of its kind in New Jersey until that time.

⚓ **Paterson Museum,** Thomas Rogers Building, 2 Market Street.

Among the museum's exhibits are two submarines built by John Holland – the shell of his original fourteen-foot submarine built in 1878 and his second thirty-foot submarine constructed three years later.

Holland was born in Liscanor, County Clare, Ireland, in 1841, where he learned English at St. Macreehy's National School. After joining the Christian Brothers, he taught at several of the religious congregation's schools in the country. While teaching in Dundalk, he pursued the study of submarine navigation, reading the works of others in the field and constructing a successful model of an underwater apparatus. Plagued by ill health, however, he sought permission to leave the Christian Brothers and subsequently immigrated to Boston in 1873.

Despite his new surroundings, Holland never abandoned his hope of perfecting a submarine boat. In 1875 he submitted a refined design to the U.S. Navy, only to have it dismissed as a "lunatic scheme of a civilian landsman." His hopes were buoyed, however, when the Irish Republican Brotherhood (also known as Fenians) offered to finance an experimental craft. In 1878 Holland tested his one-man boat in the Passaic River. (The steam-powered, fourteen-foot-long craft was recovered from the river bottom in 1927 and is now in the Paterson museum.)

Impressed by the possibility that submarine power could pose a serious threat to British naval supremacy, the Fenians commissioned Holland to build a full-size submarine. The resulting *Fenian Ram* was constructed at the Delamater Iron Company in New York City and was thirty-one feet in length, displaced nineteen tons, was powered by a one-cylinder internal-combustion engine, and was equipped with an underwater cannon fired by compressed air. After its launching in 1881, the $23,000 vessel frequently sailed under New York Harbor, on one occasion remaining on the bottom for an hour. The vessel was able to dive by inclining its axis and being propelled forward by its motor rather than being pushed up and down by vertical action. The Fenians, however, were never able to make practical use of Holland's invention. For many years the *Fenian Ram* was kept in storage, but in 1916 it was placed on exhibit to raise funds for victims of the Easter Rising in

Dublin that year.

Although several of Holland's plans were finally accepted by the U.S. Navy Department, they were never carried to completion because of unavailable appropriations. In 1895 the J. P. Holland Torpedo Boat Company obtained a $150,000 government contract to construct a submarine according to Navy specifications, which, however, virtually ignored Holland's ideas. The Irishman must have felt vindicated, though, when the *Plunger*, as the craft was called, was abandoned as a failure.

Finally, using private capital, Holland proceeded to build a submarine of his own. Bearing its inventor's name, the vessel was constructed in Elizabeth, New Jersey, and was launched in 1898. Measuring fifty-three feet in length and having a displacement of seventy-five tons, the *Holland* was armed with a dynamite gun and several torpedoes. Surface propulsion was provided by an internal combustion engine, while electric storage batteries and a motor provided underwater propulsion, making the *Holland* the first submarine able to cruise for any significant distance while submerged. Like the earlier *Fenian Ram*, it could dive by inclining its axis. After receiving the support of *Theodore Roosevelt, the secretary of the navy, and undergoing a series of tests, the *Holland* was finally purchased by the U.S. government, which soon ordered six more like it. Holland's Torpedo Boat Company subsequently constructed submarines for Great Britain, Russia, and Japan.

In 1910 the Japanese government honored Holland with the Mikado's Order of the Rising Sun. He died four years later, just before the submarine warfare of World War I shattered forever his hope that the submarine would be used only for peaceful purposes.

§ Open Tuesday-Friday 10-4, Saturday and Sunday 12:30-4:30. Closed holidays. Fee. Phone: 201-881-3874.

℟ William Hughes Statue, in front of Passaic County Courthouse, Hamilton Street.

This statue was erected by citizens of the state to honor William Hughes, who represented New Jersey in the U.S. Senate from 1913 to 1918.

Born in Drogheda, Ireland, in 1872, Hughes had come to the United States as a youngster. After working in the Paterson silk mills, he followed a career in law and made a specialty of representing various unions throughout the city. In 1902 he won a seat in the U.S. House of Representatives, ironically beating the influential owner of the mills in which he had worked as a boy. In Congress he supported an eight-hour work law, antitrust legislation, and direct election of U.S. senators. During his subsequent term in the Senate, he called for railroad regulation, female suffrage, creation of a labor department, and improvement of the Passaic River. It was said of him that "Billy Hughes always spoke for 20,000,000 laboring people when he addressed the senate."

¶ **William Paterson Statue,** in front of City Hall, 155 Market Street.
     This statue honors William Paterson, a member of the Constitutional Convention, a senator in the first Congress, and a governor of New Jersey. He was born in County Antrim, Ireland, in 1745 and was brought to America as an infant two years later.

PENNSAUKEN

¶ **Peter McGuire Burial Site,** Arlington Cemetery, Cove Road (State 616), just past Bethel Park Cemetery.
     A six-foot polished granite tombstone marks the grave of Irish-American Peter McGuire, generally regarded as the "Father of Labor Day."
     A wood joiner by trade, McGuire was a member of the International Workingmen's Association and the Social Democratic (later Socialist Labor) Party and helped organize the United Brotherhood of Carpenters and Joiners. He was also instrumental in laying the groundwork for the formation of the Federation of Organized Trades and Labor Unions in 1881. Eventually becoming involved in the eight-hour day movement, he went on to become one of the founders of the American Federation of Labor. He served the A.F.L. as first secretary and vice president. He is usually credited with the idea of establishing a holiday in honor of the working class.
     The first Labor Day parade was held in New York City on September 5, 1882. Five years later Oregon became the first state to designate a Labor Day holiday, while the U.S. government followed suit for its employees in 1894.

PERTH AMBOY

¶ **Kearny Cottage Museum,** Hayes Park, 63 Catalpa Street.
     Built in 1781, this was the birthplace and lifelong home of *Lawrence Kearny, the motivating force behind efforts to open up China to American trade. The four-room museum on the first floor of the clapboard

house displays such personal items as Kearny's sabre and sea chest.

After joining the U.S. Navy in 1807, Lawrence served in a variety of capacities aboard ships engaged in protecting American shipping from piratical raids. As commander of two expeditions, for example, he captured bandit ships off Cuba and in the Mediterranean. In 1840, however, he was appointed commander of the East India Squadron and charged with protecting U.S. interests in China. From the start he made a favorable impression upon the leaders of the Middle Kingdom, particularly in his fairness and insistence that the United States "does not sanction 'the smuggling of opium' on this coast under the American flag, in violation of the laws of China." His most important role in cultivating Sino-American relations was his call that China open five of its ports to American trade as it had recently done for the British. Within a year of his request, the Chinese complied, eventually formalizing the new relation by signing the 1844 Treaty of Wanghia. During his later career Kearny served as commandant of the New York Navy Yard and mayor of Perth Amboy.

§ Open Tuesday and Thursday 2-4; last Sunday of the month 2-4. Phone: 908-826-1826.

The Kearny Cottage, the birthplace of Commodore Lawrence Keanry.
(Photo courtesy of the Kearny Cottage Historical Association.)

❡ **St. Peter's Episcopal Church,** Rector and Gordon streets.

Throughout the church are wall plaques in memory of various members of the Kearny family, whose first American ancestor emigrated from Ireland in 1704 and eventually settled in Perth Amboy. Among those honored are Philip Kearny, the famous Civil War general, and his cousin, Lawrence Kearny, who served as vestryman of St. Peter's Church.

PLEASANTVILLE

❡ **Alfred E. Smith Monument,** St. Peter's Elementary School, Chestnut Street.

On the grounds is a statue of St. Thomas More, the sixteenth-century English statesman and martyr, erected in 1937 by members of the legal profession in honor of *Alfred Smith. The monument recognizes Smith's role as legislator, Catholic lay leader, governor of New York, and presidential candidate. Smith's nickname – "the Happy Warrior" – is recalled in verses from Wordsworth inscribed on the statue's base:

> Who, if he rise to stations of command,
> Rises by open means;
> And there will stand on honorable terms;
> Or else retire, and in himself possess his own desire,
> Find comfort in himself and in his cause.
> And, while the mortal mist is gathering,
> Draws his breath in confidence of Heaven's applause.
> This is the Happy Warrior;
> This is he whom every man in arms should wish to be.

PRINCETON

❡ **Grover Cleveland Burial Site,** Princeton Cemetery, 29 Greenview Avenue.

A square monument topped by an urn-shaped finial marks the grave of former president *Grover Cleveland, who died in 1908.

❡ **Westland,** 15 Hodge Road and Cleveland Lane. Private.

This two-and-a-half story stone residence was the home of *Grover Cleveland from 1897 until his death in 1908.

❡ **Woodrow Wilson House,** 25 Cleveland Lane. Private.

This was the home of *Woodrow Wilson while he was governor of New Jersey (1910-12).

❡ **Woodrow Wilson School of Public and International Affairs,**

Princeton University.

Made possible by a $35 million donation in 1961, the school was named for *Woodrow Wilson, a Princeton alumnus who became president of the university, governor of New Jersey, and president of the United States.

While president, Wilson saw his foreign policy toward Great Britain complicated by the failure of the Easter Rising in Dublin in 1916 and by the policy of national self-determination which he proclaimed in his Fourteen Points. Although Irish-American politicians condemned Britain for crushing the rebellion and executing its leaders, Wilson refrained from doing anything that would jeopardize the Anglo-American war effort. (Wilson's Presbyterian Scotch-Irish roots often placed him at odds with the Catholic Celtic Irish.) He did, however, suggest to the British that American public opinion would never be satisfied short of some degree of Irish independence.

While on the surface Wilson's call for self-determination seemed to encompass Irish independence, the president believed that the Irish Question was an internal matter to be resolved by the British. Once, when a delegation of Irish Americans requested to see the president in order to press the case of Irish home rule, Wilson ordered his Secret Service man to eject the delegation's leader from the building. Wilson was further embarrassed when more than 5,000 supporters of Irish freedom sent a delegation to France to state their case at the Paris Peace Conference. Although Wilson received the delegation, he admitted that his "first impulse was to tell the Irish to go to hell." Despite a resolution by the U.S. Senate requesting that the Irish-American delegates get a hearing at the Versailles conference, Wilson refused to accommodate them further, thereby causing American Hibernophiles to join forces with Wilson's enemies.

SOUTH ORANGE

⚓ Seton Hall University, 405 South Orange Avenue.

• The McManus Collection in the McLaughlin Library contains 4,000 volumes on Irish history, politics, and literature.

• The carriage house on the campus was built in 1887 for Eugene Kelly, an Irish immigrant who became a successful merchant and investor and a patron of Seton Hall University.

A native of County Tyrone, Kelly began a career in the dry-goods business soon after his arrival in America in the 1830s. First employed with Donnelly & Company, New York City's largest dry-goods business, he quickly went off on his own, making a small fortune selling merchandise in Kentucky and St. Louis before heading for San Francisco. Although he arrived in the booming California city too late to reap the rewards of trade with the "Forty-Niners," Kelly and two other Irishmen founded what later became the leading dry-goods company on the West Coast. He and other Irish partners went on to establish a banking house, which opened a branch in New York City when Kelly returned there in 1856. Thirty-five years later the San Francisco branch became a joint-stock company known as the Donohue-Kelly Banking Company. Kelly was a director of several banks, including the Emigrant Savings Bank.

While living in New York, the multimillionaire devoted his energies to philanthropy and civic affairs. He served on the New York Board of Education for more than a decade, was a trustee and patron of the Metropolitan Museum of Art, and was a member of the committee that organized the dedication of the Statue of Liberty. Besides being a major benefactor of St. Patrick's Cathedral and Seton Hall College, he was one of the founders of Catholic University in America in Washington, D.C. To that last institution he donated $100,000 to endow chairs in ecclesiastical history and Holy Scripture named, respectively, for himself and his wife, Margaret Anna Hughes, the niece of *Archbishop John Hughes.

SPRINGFIELD

⚑ First Presbyterian Church, 37 Church Mall.

A monument in front of the church commemorates the battle of Springfield on June 23, 1776, and the part played in it by the *Reverend James Caldwell, the chaplain of Dayton's New Jersey Brigade. During the battle, when the American soldiers ran out of wadding for their rifles, Caldwell broke open the church doors and began to distribute to the men copies of the Watts hymnbooks. "Now put Watts into them, boys!" he cried. The initiative of the "Soldier Parson" is immortalized in the poem "Caldwell at Springfield" by Bret Harte and in a painting by John Ward Dunsmore at Fraunces Tavern in New York City.

TRENTON

⚑ Trenton Battle Monument, Five Points (the intersection of North Broad Street, North Warren Street, Martin Luther King Jr. Boulevard, Pennington Avenue, and Brunswick Avenue).

The thirteen-foot bronze statue of George Washington and the bust of General William Stryker on this 137-foot-high monument were sculpted by William O'Donovan.

O'Donovan was born in 1844 in what is now West Virginia and enlisted in the Confederate army at the age of eighteen. In the 1870s, after establishing a studio in New York City, he achieved recognition for his bas-reliefs and portrait busts of well known Americans, among them the bust of *Archbishop John Hughes at St. John's College, Fordham, New York. O'Donovan's many military works include equestrian reliefs of Lincoln and Grant for the Soldiers' and Sailors' Arch (Brooklyn, N.Y.), a monument to the captors of Major André (Tarrytown, N.Y.), a statue of General Daniel Morgan (Schuylerville, N.Y.), and additional statues of Washington in Newburgh, New York, and Caracas, Venezuela.

¶ **Washington Crossing State Park,** 8 miles northwest on State 29, then northeast on State 546.

Although this park is the site of the landing by George Washington and his troops after they crossed the Delaware River from Pennsylvania on Christmas Eve 1776, the park is also the site of a less famous crossing in the opposite direction. Following Washington's defeat at the battle of Long Island, the American general was pursued by Lord Cornwallis west across New Jersey. When Washington reached Trenton on December 8, 1776, he used the boats and rafts of Patrick Colvin, the owner and operator of the only ferry between Trenton and the Pennsylvania side of the Delaware. Three and a half weeks later, the Irish Catholic Colvin helped ferry Washington and his men back across the Delaware River when they launched their surprise attack against the British at Trenton on Christmas Eve.

§ Open Memorial Day weekend-Labor Day, daily 8-8; rest of the year, daily 8-4:30. Phone: 609-737-0623.

¶ The Ferry House, at the south end of the Continental Line in the park, belonged most likely to *Patrick Colvin at the time of the crossing.

On two other occasions in his life, Colvin rendered patriotic services to George Washington. In 1781, when the general crossed New Jersey on his way to join Lafayette in Virginia, his army was again ferried across the Delaware by Colvin. Eights year later, when the newly elected president passed through Trenton on his way to New York City for his inauguration, Colvin took charge of the presidential party.

§ Open Wednesday-Sunday 9-4:30. Phone: 609-737-2515.

UNION

¶ **Caldwell Parsonage Museum,** 909 Caldwell Avenue.

During the colonial period this was the parsonage of Connecticut Farms Presbyterian Church, which still stands a few blocks away. Among those living here in June 1780 was the family of the *Reverend James Caldwell, known as the "Soldier Parson" because of his active support of the Patriot cause during the Revolution.

Although Caldwell's family had fled here for safety from British troops, the dangers of war followed. In the battle of Connecticut Farms that June, Caldwell's wife, Hannah, was killed by a random bullet, and the parsonage was burned by the enemy. From then on, Caldwell always preached with pistols close at hand. After he himself was killed the following year, his nine children were placed with foster parents.

§ Open the third Sunday of the month.

WESTFIELD

¶ **Gallows Hill,** Broad Street, to the northeast.

Here in 1781 was hanged James Morgan, the Irishman found guilty of shooting the "Fighting Parson," the *Reverend James Caldwell. The day on which Morgan was scheduled to be hanged for his crime was unusually cold, and when the execution was delayed he snapped at his guards, "Do your duty and don't keep me here shivering in the cold."

NEW YORK

ALBANY

¶ **Cathedral of the Immaculate Conception,** Eagle Street and Madison Avenue.

This Gothic Revival cathedral was completed in 1852 from a design by *Patrick Keely for Bishop John McCloskey, who was born in Brooklyn in 1810, the son of immigrants from County Derry, Ireland.

§ Open Monday-Friday 6-4, Saturday 8-11, Sunday 8-6. Phone: 518-463-4447.

¶ **Dongan's Charter,** Albany County Hall of Records, 20 South Pearl Street.

Each year on the Saturday closest to July 22, the city of Albany celebrates its chartering in 1686 by Thomas Dongan, the first colonial governor of New York. The 300-year-old charter is preserved in the Albany County Hall of Records and can be viewed by special arrangement.

Although born in 1634 in Castletown, County Kildare, Ireland, Dongan grew up in France, where his father had taken his family following the fall of Charles I and the victory of the parliamentary forces in the English Civil War. After joining the Irish Regiment in France, the young Dongan served in several campaigns with the French army and eventually attained the rank of colonel.

With the restoration of the Stuarts in 1660, Dongan was recalled to England and was subsequently appointed governor of New York. In that capacity he did a creditable job protecting the interests of the Catholic proprietor (the Duke of York) and attempting to guarantee the rights of the colony's inhabitants. He successfully defended the boundaries of the colony against French incursions and cemented an alliance with the Iroquois.

Following instructions from the duke, Dongan convened in 1683 the first representative assembly ever held in New York. At Dongan's urging, this assembly later adopted "The Charter of Liberties and Privileges granted by His Royal Highness to the Inhabitants of New York and its Dependencies." When the Duke of York succeeded to the throne as King James II, however, the new monarch refused to accept Dongan's charter in every particular, although he did recognize the document's grant of religious freedom to all Christians. Three years later the governor granted a charter to Albany, the event which is recognized in the city's annual celebration.

Dongan also opened the first free common school in the colony during the British regime. Established in New York City in 1685, the school was administered by Father Henry Harrison, an Irish Jesuit. With the end of James's short reign in 1688, Dongan returned to England, where he tried to regain his ancestral home, which had been confiscated during the civil war. Following the death of his brother (the Earl of Limerick) in 1696, Dongan succeeded to the title.

§ Open Monday-Friday 9-5. Phone: 518-447-4500.

¶ **General Sheridan Statue,** on the grounds of the state capitol, bounded by Washington Avenue and Swan, State, and Eagle streets.

This equestrian statue honors *Philip Sheridan, a cavalry commander under *General Ulysses S. Grant during the Civil War.

Although Sheridan's memoirs claim that he was a native of Albany, he actually may have been born aboard the ship which carried his parents from Ireland to America. According to one theory, he may have invented an American birth in order to be eligible for the presidency of the United States.

Guy Park, built in the eighteenth century by Sir William Johnson.

AMSTERDAM

¶ **Guy Park Historic Site,** 366 West Main Street at Henrietta Street.

Although now a museum, this house was built in 1766 by Sir William Johnson for his daughter Mary and her husband, Colonel Guy Johnson, Sir William's nephew. A native of Ireland, Sir William was superintendent of Indian affairs in this region for the British in the mid 1700s. (See Johnstown, New York.)

§ Open Monday-Friday 8:30-4:30. Phone: 518-842-8200.

BUFFALO

In May 1866 Buffalo was one of three staging areas for a planned invasion of Canada by the Fenians, an American offshoot of the Irish Revolutionary Brotherhood pledged to the use of force to free Ireland from British rule.

The Fenians had received their name from *John O'Mahony, who likened the new revolutionary group to *Fianna Eireann*, the heroic band of warriors whose leader was the legendary Finn McCool. Besides being a student of ancient Gaelic culture, O'Mahony had been a rebel leader in the abortive 1848 uprising in Ireland before fleeing to France and then to New York.

To serve as their secretary of war, the Fenians had chosen General Thomas Sweeny, an Irish-born hero of the Mexican War and a Civil War infantry commander. Sweeny proceeded to plan a three-pronged invasion of Canada which the Fenians hoped would result in the capture of Canada as a bargaining chip for the independence of Ireland.

The Fenian invasion force at Buffalo was under the command of Captain John O'Neill, a native of County Monaghan, Ireland. O'Neill had moved up the ranks in the Union army during the Civil War, leaving the service as captain of the 17th U.S. Colored Infantry. After becoming involved in the Fenian cause, he crossed the Niagara River into Canada in May 1866 with a force of about 600 men – another 200 were too drunk to get into the boats – and captured the village of Fort Erie, where they raised the Fenian flag on British soil. After defeating a larger Canadian force two days later, O'Neill and his men returned to Fort Erie to await the arrival of 3,000 more Fenians from Buffalo. In the meantime, the U.S. gunboat *Michigan* prevented the arrival of supplies and reinforcements to O'Neill. The next day the Fenians were captured and arrested by American authorities as they fled back into the United States. In all, the Fenians suffered eight killed and twenty wounded; the Canadians, twelve killed and forty wounded.

¶ **Albright-Knox Art Gallery,** Elmwood Avenue, near State 198.

This Greek Revival building is flanked by two side porches, each with four caryatids designed by *Augustus Saint-Gaudens and based on those of the Erechtheum in Athens, Greece.

§ Open Tuesday-Saturday 11-5, Sunday 12-5. Closed January 1, Thanksgiving, and December 25. Phone: 716-882-8700.

¶ Naval and Servicemen's Park, 1 Naval Park Cove.

Among the ships on display here is the cruiser *The Sullivans*, named in honor of the five Sullivan brothers who were killed during the battle of Guadalcanal in November 1943.

The brothers – Albert, Madison (Matt), Joseph (Red), Francis, and George Sullivan – ranged in age from twenty to twenty-nine and were natives of Waterloo, Iowa. The five had enlisted in the U.S. Navy together in January 1942 on condition that they not be separated during the war. The brothers perished after their ship, the U.S.S. *Juneau*, was sunk by Japanese fire in the Solomon Islands. George, the eldest brother, died while trying to escape on a raft, while the other four went down with the ship. A spokesman for the Navy said that the loss of the Sullivan brothers was the heaviest blow suffered by any American military family.

The brothers were honored by a mass at St. Patrick's Cathedral in New York City and by the announcement that a newly built destroyer would be named in their honor. In April 1943 the Sullivans' mother christened the ship in San Francisco. That same month the Sullivans' sister, Genevieve, took her brothers' place in the war effort by joining the WAVES, while their forty-three-year-old uncle, Patrick Henry Sullivan, joined the crew of the new destroyer.

§ Open April-October 31, daily 10-dusk; November, Saturday and Sunday 10-dusk. Fee. Phone: 716-847-1773.

¶ Oliver H. Perry Statue, central plaza.

This monument was erected in 1915 in honor of *Oliver Hazard Perry, the commander of the victorious American fleet at the battle of Lake Erie in 1813. In reporting his victory over a British fleet, he said, "We have met the enemy, and they are ours."

¶ President McKinley Assassination Site, in the middle of Fordham Drive, between Elmwood Avenue and Lincoln Parkway.

A bronze tablet marks the spot where *President William McKinley was killed as he was shaking hands with visitors to the Temple of Music at the Pan-American Exposition on September 6, 1901. The assassin – Leon Czolgosz – had approached the chief executive with a handkerchief covering the revolver in his hand. McKinley died eight days later at the Milburn House, at 1168 Delaware Avenue.

¶ President McKinley Monument, Niagara Square.

This 120-foot-high obelisk monument was dedicated in 1907 in memory of *President William McKinley. A marble lion stands at each corner of the base.

J Theodore Roosevelt Inaugural National Historic Site, 641 Delaware Avenue.

Following the assassination of *President William McKinley in 1901, it was in this house that *Vice President Theodore Roosevelt took the oath of office as the twenty-sixth president of the United States. This 1838 Classical Revival house features a slide show and memorabilia related to Roosevelt and McKinley.

At the time of McKinley's assassination, Roosevelt was in Vermont but rushed to Buffalo by train. When it appeared that McKinley was recovering after surgery, the vice president left on an outing to the Adirondacks with his family. Three days later, however, after receiving a message that the president was dying, Roosevelt returned to Buffalo but arrived after McKinley's death.

§ Open April-December 31, Monday-Friday 9-3, Saturday and Sunday 12-5; rest of the year, Monday-Friday 10-5, Sunday 12-5. Closed holidays. Fee. Phone 716-884-0095.

CAMBRIDGE

J Philip Embury Burial Site, Woodland Cemetery.

A monument marks the burial place of Philip Embury, the Irish-born founder of American Methodism. Under his leadership Irish immigrants erected the first Methodist church in America on John Street in New York City in 1768.

Two years later Embury moved to upstate New York, where he farmed, preached, served as a magistrate, and formed a Methodist society in the town of Ashgrove. Sixty years after his death in 1772, his remains were removed from his farm to Ashgrove, although in 1866 they were reburied in Woodland Cemetery in Cambridge.

CANASTOTA

J Old Erie Canal State Park, State 5/46 or I-90 exits 33 and 34.

Visitors can see portions of the old Erie Canal, including the towpath, change bridges, and aqueducts.

Conceived by Irish-born Christopher Colles and advocated by Governor DeWitt Clinton, himself of Irish descent, the canal was built between 1817 and 1825. Because the canal provided work for increasing numbers of Irish immigrants, it was called "a capital road from Cork to Utica." At the time of its completion, it stretched 350 miles from Albany to Buffalo, and almost 50,000 Irish lived along the route, most of them the men who had worked on the huge undertaking.

Three Irish workers were singled out for special recognition because of their herculean feat: finishing fifty feet of canal – including banks and towpaths – to a depth of four feet in five and a half days, for the "very liberal wages" of $1.87 per day.

§ Open dawn-dusk. Phone: 315-687-7821.

¶ Canal Town Museum, 122 Canal Street.

This 1874 structure displays local memorabilia as well as items associated with the construction of the Erie Canal.

§ Open Monday-Friday 9-5. Closed holidays. Phone: 315-697-3451.

COOPERSTOWN

¶ National Baseball Hall of Fame and Museum, Main Street.

Exhibits include the Ballparks Room, the Baseball Today display, the Grandstand Theater, the Great Moments Room, and the World Series Room.

When the museum was opened on June 12, 1939, *U.S. Postmaster General James Farley and seventy postal clerks were on hand to sell half a million commemorative stamps recognizing the centenary of American baseball. Among the Irish-American members of the Baseball Hall of Fame are "Duke of Tralee" Roger Bresnahan, "Mickey" Cochrane, Charles Comiskey, Ed Delahanty, Hugh Duffy, Michael "King" Kelly, "Iron Man" Connie Mack, Joseph McGinnity, and "Orator" Jim O'Rourke.

• Charles Comiskey, the son of a Famine Irish immigrant father, began his career with the Milwaukee team and went on to become the founder of the American League. In 1900 he established the Chicago White Sox, a team which he owned until his death in 1931. The team's home stadium, Comiskey Park, is named for him. His stinginess in refusing to pay for the laundry of his team's uniforms caused his players to protest by wearing their increasingly dirty uniforms for several weeks and calling themselves the "Black Sox."

• Ed Delahanty was one of five brothers in Cleveland to play for the major leagues. Between 1888 and 1903 he played for the Philadelphia Phillies and the Washington Senators and was the only player to win the batting championship in both the National and the American leagues. His career ended when he was suspended for heavy drinking. A week later he was found drowned near Niagara Falls, presumably because of a fall from a train.

• At the age of twenty-four, Connie Mack (né Cornelius McGillicuddy) parlayed his skill as a baseball player into $200 a month in the Connecticut League. He popularized overhand pitching and was one of the first catchers to take up a position directly behind the batter. After stints with the Washington Senators and the Pittsburgh Pirates, in 1901 he became manager and part owner of the Philadelphia Athletics. Over the next thirty years, his team won nine pennants, five World Series titles, and a record 3,776 wins. In 1914 and again during the Depression, falling attendance and rising salary demands from his "$100,000 infield" forced Mack to sell or release his star players, a move that caused his critics to call him a pennypincher. Nevertheless, the white-haired Mack, who always appeared in a business suit and a straw hat, was regarded as the "Grand Old Man" of baseball and was elected to the sport's Hall of Fame in 1937.

> Michael "King" Kelly did duty as catcher, shortstop, and outfielder with the Cincinnati Reds, the Chicago White Stockings, the Boston Beaneaters, and the New York Giants. His sale to Boston for $10,000 caused an uproar and earned him the nickname the "Ten Thousand Dollar Beauty."
>
> As the number one idol of his day, he achieved immortality with his base-stealing record (84) and with his base-running slide, the subject of the popular song "Slide, Kelly, Slide." Known for his disregard of the rules both on and off the field, when asked if he drank while playing, he replied, "It depends on the length of the game."
>
> Toward the end of his life, when he slid from a stretcher during his final illness, Kelly reputedly observed that "This is my last slide." At the time of his death, he was playing the lead role in Casey at the Bat on the Boston stage. He was the author of Play Ball: Stories of the Diamond Field.

• A visit to the National Baseball Hall of Fame would be incomplete without a reference to "Casey at the Bat," the classic expression of the sport's ethos. Although the poem was first recited publicly in 1888, it was not until almost a half century later that its author revealed the identity of the "Mighty Casey." According to Ernest L. Thayer, the author, the poem's slugger was named for Daniel Henry Casey, a high school classmate in Worcester, Massachusetts. When Thayer needed a name for his mythical ballplayer, he thought of the 200-pound, six-foot-two-inch teenager, who had almost beaten him up for remarks he had made in a newspaper article. Thayer described his choice of Casey's name as "a taunt thrown to the wind. God grant he never catches me." In subsequent years "Casey at the Bat" was the inspiration for one song, numerous verse parodies, three motion pictures (one starring *Michael "King" Kelly), two Disney cartoons, and an opera. Like some of the other spin-offs from the original, the opera gave Casey a personal history: He was born in Mudville in 1859 to John and Mary (O'Toole) Casey.

§ Open May-October 31, daily 9-9; rest of the year, daily 9-5. Closed January 1, Thanksgiving, and December 25. Fee. Gift shop. Phone: 607-547-9988.

EAST DURHAM

Nicknamed the "Irish Catskills," "Ireland's 33rd county," and the "Irish Music Capital of America," East Durham is a center of Irish and Irish-American culture. The area is host to noted musicians and athletic events, including hurling, Gaelic football, and the Irish-American Golf Open.

Visiting the town is like visiting Ireland, as is apparent in the names of some of its motels and shops: O'Neill House, McKenna's House, Guaranteed Irish, McGraths, Shamrock House, Gavin's, Fitzsimons, Keogh's, Kennedy's, Erin's Melody, and Bernie O's.

¶ East Durham Irish Cultural and Sports Centre.

This sixty-acre site is home to the following:

• The Irish American Heritage Museum. Open Memorial Day-Labor Day, Tuesday-Sunday 10-4; Labor Day-Columbus Day, Friday-Sunday 10-4; or by appointment. Fee. Phone: 518-634-7497.

• The John E. Lawe Memorial. A bronze bust and an inscribed plaque honor the "Champion of the Working Man," who "stood tall in the U.S. labor movement. A union man all his working life, 35 years with the Transport Workers Union of America, AFL-CIO as a dues-paying member, officer and international president (1985-1989). He was a dynamic local union leader, forceful negotiator, forward looking labor statesman and thoughtful labor spokesman. This emigrant from Kilgass, Strokestown, County Roscommon, Ireland, befriended and helped all struggling emigrant peoples. A proud Irish American (chosen Grand Marshal of New York City's 1987 St. Patrick's Day Parade), John was faithful to and supportive of both his native land and his adopted country. He was a dutiful husband, loving and protective father, an involved and much-honored community citizen, a concerned Roman Catholic gentleman. He passed this way and left it better for his passing."

• The John E. Lawe Memorial Sports Stadium, a professional playing field constructed to the same dimensions (95 x 160 yards) as Croke Park in Dublin. This field is the first of its size in North America and was dedicated on September 24, 1990.

• The Outdoor Pavilion, for performances and festival use

• The Patrick Kellegher Little League Baseball Field, home to the East Durham Little League

• The Peter J. O'Neill Library, open to the public by appointment and

• The Michael J. Quill Cultural Centre Building (under development), a performing arts and sports facility that will contain a theater, a banquet hall, exhibition space, and covered sports bleachers.

¶ National Shrine of Our Lady of Knock, on the grounds of St. Mary's Catholic Church, State 145, just south of town.

This shrine was constructed in the 1980s through the efforts of *Father Jeremiah Nunan and *Father John Mallon, the pastor of St. Mary's Church. The shrine commemorates an apparition which occurred in the small Irish village of Knock on August 21, 1879. The interior of the church is decorated with an Irish motif: stained glass windows depicting favorite Celtic saints, an altar screen resembling the church wall in Knock on which the apparition appeared, and, of course, the Irish tricolor.

National Shrine of Our Lady of Knock.

ELMIRA

¶ Sullivan (Newtown Battlefield) Monument, Battle Mountain, Newton Battlefield Reservation Road.

The tall obelisk on this site commemorates *General John Sullivan, whose destruction of the Iroquois settlement at Newtown (now Elmira) in 1779 brought to fourteen the number of such villages which he had destroyed in an effort to crush Britain's Indian ally.

The monument reads: "Near this site, Sunday, August 29, 1779, was fought the Battle of Newtown between Continental troops commanded by Major General John Sullivan and a combined force of Tories and Indians under Colonel John Butler and Joseph Brant, avenging the massacre of Wyoming and Cherry Valley, destroying the Iroquois Confederacy, ending attacks on our settlements, and thereby opening westward the pathway of civilization."

One episode in the battle of Newtown is described in these excerpts from "Sullivan 1779," a poem by Joseph Clarke read at the dedication of the monument in 1912:

> Thus Sullivan, with battle-flag outflung,
> Marched grimly by the banks of the Chemung;
> Vengeance his mission, a mandate to destroy:
> Death to the slinking murderers who crept
> By night upon our settlers as they slept,
> And slew them – woman, girl and boy –
> By the blazing of their log-built homes,
> Carved from the age-old wilderness
> Where the Susquehanna foams.
>
> . . . .
>
> The column writhes along its hard-won trail
> In swelter in the noonday heat,
> When a forest scout comes hurrying down
> On noiseless moccasined feet.
> "At the river's bend an Indian town,
> A score of rough-hewn huts tricked out
> With barbarous colors, blue and brown,
> But none makes answer to our shout."
> And Sullivan's force went death-like pale,
> On his brow a deepened frown.
> "Burn it to ashes; let the flames outspread
> Till their fields are bare," he hoarsely said.
> 'Twas quickly done,
> And the smoke still hung o'er the blasted vale,
> When Sullivan gloomily rode ahead
> In the blood-red setting of the sun.

FAYETTESVILLE

§ **Grover Cleveland House,** 109 Academy Avenue. Private.
    This was the boyhood home of *Grover Cleveland, the only U.S. president to serve two nonconsecutive terms (1887-91 and 1895-99).

FORT JOHNSON

¶ **Fort Johnson,** near the junction of State 5 and 67.

Now the Montgomery County Historical Society Museum, this gray stone structure was built in 1749 as the home of Sir William Johnson, his third in the Mohawk Valley. The fort contains original furnishings and displays on the Mohawk Indians and local history.

Johnson, a native of County Meath, Ireland, had been sent to America by his parents in the hope that such a trans-Atlantic move would break up his romance with an Irish girl. At first he worked as overseer of his uncle's estate in the Mohawk Valley, but within a year he made the first of many land purchases which helped him become one of the largest property owners in the British colonies. As a trader he was on good terms with the Six Nations Indian tribes, and it was through his influence that they were kept from siding with the French during the colonial struggles that ravaged the region in the 1740s and 1750s.

During the French and Indian War, Johnson defeated a French force at Lake George, where he subsequently built Fort William Henry. For his services the King made him a baronet and "Sole Agent and Super-intendent" of the Six Nations. Although he successfully pressured these tribes to grant him large tracts of land – seemingly in violation of his duty to superintend their interests – he apparently had a sincere concern for their welfare and frequently protected them from more rapacious white settlers. The Indians' esteem for him is preserved in their tribute that "He never deceived us." With his adoption into the Mohawk nation, be became the first European to be allowed to speak before the Iroquois confederation's longhouse council.

§ Open May-October 31, Wednesday-Sunday 1-5. Fee. Phone: 518-843-0300.

FORT STANWIX

¶ **Fort Stanwix,** 112 East Park Street.

The site of this reconstructed fort was the scene of a gigantic "summit meeting" in 1768 between *Sir William Johnson and some 2,000 Native Americans. By the resulting Treaty of Fort Stanwix, the Indians granted possession to the British of large tracts of land in what is now New York, Pennsylvania, West Virginia, and Kentucky – all for twenty boatloads of gifts worth about $50,000.

§ Open April-December 31, daily 9-5. Closed Thanksgiving and December 25. Fee. Phone: 315-336-2090.

¶ **Oriskany Battlefield,** 6 miles east.

On August 6, 1777, as 600 Mohawk Valley militiamen marched to relieve Fort Stanwix, they were ambushed by a force of local Tories and Native Americans. Two hundred militiamen were killed in the six-hour battle that ensued.

The site of the bloodiest battle of the Revolution is marked by a ninety-three-foot granite obelisk erected in 1883. Two of the bronze bas-reliefs on the memorial were designed by sculptor *William O'Donovan. One of his reliefs depicts General Nicholas Herkimer, the leader of the American troops, seated on the ground with his wounded leg extended. He seems to be emphasizing with his outstretched left arm a command to a young aide on his right side. The other bas-relief portrays hand-to-hand combat between a German-American soldier dressed in buckskins and an Indian with an uplifted tomahawk. The advancing foot of each combatant rests on the breast of a dead soldier on the ground.

§ Open Memorial Day-Labor Day, Wednesday-Saturday and Monday holidays 10-5, Sunday 1-5. Audiovisual presentation and tours available. Phone: 315-768-7224.

FORT TICONDEROGA

¶ **Fort Ticonderoga,** 1 mile northeast on State 74.

In a bloodless surprise attack in 1775, the fort was seized from the British garrison by Ethan Allan and his Green Mountain Boys. That winter some of the fort's cannon were transported overland by oxcart to Boston. Two reminders of that grueling feat – performed under the command of *Henry Knox – are located on the parade ground within the fort:

• The inscription on the Knox Monument reads: "From this fortress went General Henry Knox in the winter of 1775-76 to deliver to General George Washington at Cambridge the train of artillery from Fort Ticonderoga, used to force the British Army to evacuate Boston." The bronze plaque on the monument depicts oxcarts pulling cannon through the forests.

• The Knox Gun is one of the artillery pieces which were seized from Fort Ticonderoga and which were intended to help General Washington dislodge the British from Boston. While in transit, however, this gun fell through the frozen Mohawk River, where it remained until 1800. After its recovery it stood in front of the city hall in the village of Mohawk Valley for twenty years and was fired each time local Federalists won an election. When the Democrats were finally victorious at the polls, they consigned the hated cannon to the bottom of the river. The gun was rescued once and for all just prior to World War II.

§ Open July and August, daily 9-6; Memorial Day weekend-June 30, 9-5; September to mid October, 9-5. Fee. Phone: 518-585-2821.

GLEN FALLS

¶ Charles Evans Hughes Birthplace, 20 Center Street. Private.
    Built about 1850, this clapboard house was the early home of Charles Evans Hughes, New York governor, chief justice of the U.S. Supreme Court, presidential candidate, and secretary of state. Hughes was born here in 1910 to a Welsh father and an Irish mother (Mary Catherine Connelly).

GREAT NECK

¶ F. Scott Fitzgerald House, 6 Gateway Drive. Private.
    In 1922 this large colonial mansion on Long Island was rented by *F. Scott Fitzgerald, who worked on *The Great Gatsby* in a room over the garage. With his wife, Zelda, and countless weekend guests, he played the role of Trimalchio. On mornings after a typical bash, neighbors usually found him in a Bacchanalian sleep on the lawn.

HORSEHEADS

This small town of 7,000 inhabitants received its name from the 300 horse skulls which the first settlers in this region discovered in 1789. The skulls were the remains of the pack horses which had been used to transport the troops under *General John Sullivan from Pennsylvania to western New York to fight the Iroquois. Sullivan and his men had killed their starving and worn-out horses for food and left the heads behind.

INDIAN CASTLE

¶ Indian Castle Church, State 5S. Museum.
    This clapboard house was built about 1770 by *Sir William Johnson as a mission church for the Indians in the area. The land for the church had been donated by the famous Mohawk chief Joseph Brant. Johnson was a superintendent of Indian affairs for the British in the mid 1700s.

JOHNSTOWN

¶ Burke's Tavern, West Montgomery and Williams streets. Private.
    Built in 1765, this tavern was operated by innkeeper James Burke. The structure was moved to this site in 1788 from a nearby lot owned by *Sir William Johnson.

¶ Drumm House, West Green Street.
    Built in 1763 by *Sir William Johnson, this was at one time the home of Edward Wall, who taught in the free school established by Johnson.

℥ Johnson Hall State Historic Site, 0.25 mile west on Hall Avenue.

This Georgian mansion was built in 1763 by *Sir William Johnson. Between then and the American Revolution, it served as the center of his commercial and diplomatic relations with local Indian tribes. The house was designed by a Boston architect and although made of wood has the appearance of stone. The original stone house next to the main building displays a diorama and period exhibits.

Although Johnson usually conformed – at least externally – to the canons of the Anglican Church, he apparently never entered into either a sacramental or a civil marriage. By his first "wife," a German servant, he had three children. Following her death, he successively took into his home two Indian women – one the niece of a Mohawk chief and the other the sister of the famous Chief Joseph Brant – with whom he had eleven children.

§ Open mid May-October 31, Wednesday-Saturday 10-5, Sunday 1-5. Closed holidays except Memorial Day, July 4, and Labor Day. Phone: 518-762-8712.

℥ William Johnson Burial Site, St. John's Episcopal Church, North Market Street.

The construction of the original church on this site was supervised by *Sir William Johnson, who was buried in its chancel in 1774. When that structure was burned in 1836, it was replaced by the present building. Johnson's grave is marked by a large stone memorial behind the church.

℥ William Johnson Statue, next to Johnson Hall State Historic Site.

Erected in 1904, this memorial is inscribed with a tribute to *Sir William Johnson, described as "a man strong in character, a colossal pioneer, sole superintendent and faithful friend of the Six Nations . . . founder of Johnstown . . . ."

KINGSTON

℥ George Clinton Burial Site, Dutch Reformed Church, Main Street, between Wall and Fair streets.

George Clinton, the first governor of New York after independence from Britain, is buried in the churchyard. A monument was dedicated to his memory when his remains were reinterred here after their removal from Washington, D.C.

The grandson of an immigrant from Longford, Ireland, George Clinton was first elected to the governorship in 1777. The strong political machine which he developed served him well during his seven terms in the statehouse. He was opposed to the federal constitution – because he knew it would shift power from the states – and he hoped to block its adoption by presiding over the New York ratifying convention. He abandoned his opposition, however, when the necessary nine states approved the union. When his presidential aspirations were dashed in 1808, he agreed to accept the vice presidency under James Madison, for whom, however, he showed public disdain.

LAKE GEORGE

¶ Fort William Henry Museum, Canada Street (U.S. 9).

This stockaded structure is a reconstruction of the fort built on this site in 1756 by *Sir William Johnson to protect the portage between Lake George and the Hudson River. The original fort featured prominently in *The Last of the Mohicans* by James Fenimore Cooper.

§ Open May, June, September, and October, daily 10-5; July and August, daily 9 a.m.-10 p.m. Fee. Phone: 518-668-5471.

¶ William Johnson and King Hendrick Monument, Lake George Battleground Park, 0.5 mile south off U.S. 9.

This large monument consists of two bronze statues, one of the Mohawk chief King Hendrick and the other of *Sir William Johnson. The statues depict an episode in September 1755 when King Hendrick advised Johnson against attacking the nearby French.

After dismissing the chief's advice, Johnson sent 1,200 colonial and Indian troops to prevent the French from cutting his lines of communication with Fort Edward. When the British were repulsed in a clash with the French, the latter engaged Johnson's troops on this site but were thrown into retreat, suffering the loss of their commander and the capture of many prisoners.

MALONE

¶ Flanagan Hotel, Main and Elm streets.

In 1870 this hotel was the headquarters of the Fenian leaders who planned to lead their troops in the seizure of Canada to force the British to grant independence to Ireland. Although *President Ulysses S. Grant sent *General George Gordon Meade to prevent an invasion, Meade arrived too late to stop the initial incursion but was able to prevent 1,300 reinforcements from setting out from Malone.

The Fenians had been only moderately more successful four years earlier. In response to the arrival of about 2,000 Irish-American Fenians in Malone, the Canadians at that time had stationed gunboats in the St. Lawrence River and troops along the New York border. Although the

Fenians crossed the international boundary on June 2, 1866, and exchanged shots with Canadian troops, the undisciplined and poorly provisioned Fenians retreated almost immediately.

MENANDS

¶ Chester A. Arthur Burial Site, Albany Rural Cemetery, Cemetery Avenue, off Broadway.

Following his death from a massive cerebral hemorrhage in 1886, former president *Chester A. Arthur was buried here next to his wife.

§ Open daily 8-4:

MIDDLEBURG

¶ Timothy Murphy Monument, Middleburg Cemetery, Huntersland Road, off State 145.

This monument marks the grave of Timothy Murphy, the Irish-American rifleman whose legendary marksmanship during the Revolutionary War earned him the nickname "Sure-shot Tim."

The inscription on the monument reads: "To the Memory of Timothy Murphy, Patriot, Soldier, Scout, Citizen, Who served in Morgan's Rifle Corps, fought at Saratoga and Monmouth, and whose bravery repelled the attack of the British and their Indian allies upon the Middle Fort, October 17, 1780, and saved the colonials of the Schoharie Valley."

NEWBURGH

¶ George Clinton Statue, Clinton Square, off Fullerton Avenue.

This statue honors *George Clinton, a member of the Continental Congress, the first governor of New York, and vice president under Jefferson and Madison.

¶ Knox's Headquarters State Historic Site, Quassaick Avenue (State 94) and Forge Hill Road in Vails Gate.

Built in 1754, this two-story stone structure was the home of John Ellison, a local mill operator. During the later years of the Revolutionary War, it was used as the headquarters of several American commanders. *General Henry Knox lived here in the summer and fall of 1779 until he departed to prepare for the siege of Yorktown, Virginia. He resided here again from May to September 1782, when General Washington was headquartered in Newburgh. For the next year and a half, Knox was the commander of nearby West Point. He later served as President Washington's secretary of war.

§ Open Memorial Day-Labor Day, Sunday 1-5; other times by appointment. Phone: 914-561-5498/1765.

¶ **Temple Hill Monument,** New Windsor Cantonment State Historic Site, 1 mile north of Vails Gate on Temple Hill Road.

A tall fieldstone monument was erected on this site in 1892 to honor the 7,000 American troops who were quartered here in the fall of 1782, at what was the last encampment of the Continental Army. A tablet on one of the sides commemorates the Society of the Cincinnati, an hereditary fraternal organization of Continental Army officers. The society was created here on May 10, 1783, and was based on a constitution drafted by *General Henry Knox.

§ Open late April to mid November, Wednesday-Sunday 10-5. Phone: 914-561-1765.

¶ **Washington's Headquarters State Historic Park,** Liberty Street, between Washington and Lafayette streets.

For sixteen months after the Revolutionary War, the Hasbrouck House on this site was General Washington's headquarters. Exhibits about the Continental Army are on display in an adjacent museum.

This six-acre park also contains the Peace Monument, erected in 1883 to mark the disbanding of the Continental Army a century before. The four bronze statues on the fifty-three-foot monument were created by *William O'Donovan and represent the four types of soldiers who served in the Revolution: artillerymen, cavalrymen, riflemen, and officers. O'Donovan's life-size statue of George Washington originally stood inside the monument but is now located in front of the museum.

§ Open April-December 31, Wednesday-Saturday, 10-5, Sunday 1-5; rest of the year, Saturday 10-5, Sunday 1-5. Phone: 914-562-1195.

NEW YORK CITY

¶ **Admiral David Farragut Statue,** Madison Square Park, 23rd Street and Broadway.

This bronze statue by Augustus Saint-Gaudens was the Dublin-born sculptor's first major success. The work honors the commander of the Union fleet which captured New Orleans and defeated the Confederate fleet at Mobile in 1864. Farragut is depicted as a wind-buffeted figure flanked by female representations of Courage and Loyalty. The Union naval officer was famous for his command, "Damn the torpedoes, full speed ahead!"

¶ **Alfred E. Smith Boyhood Home,** 25 Oliver Street, Lower Manhattan.

A plaque on this three-story brick row house marks the fact that the future governor of New York lived here from 1909 until 1924. Despite Smith's reputation as the "quintessential Irish American," his father was of German and Italian background, while his mother – Catherine Mulvehill – was only half Irish.

¶ Alfred E. Smith Park, Catherine Street, near the boyhood home.

This park is adorned with a statue of the famous politician, dedicated in 1945 and showing Smith in a speaking pose behind a podium. The base of the statue is inscribed with the title of his political theme song, "The Sidewalks of New York.

In 1928 Smith was the unsuccessful Democratic nominee for U.S. president, the first Irish Catholic since Charles O'Conor in 1872 to be nominated for the U.S. presidency.

¶ American Irish Historical Society, 991 5th Avenue.

The library contains more than 15,000 volumes about Irish and Irish-American topics as well as photographs, personal items, musical instruments, and religious and art objects.

The society's headquarters is adorned with statues or portrait busts of the following Irish or Irish-American personalities: Eamon De Valera, a native of New York and the first president of Ireland; President John F. Kennedy; Dr. William MacNeven; Admiral Richard Meade, the first president of the American Irish Historical Society; attorney Charles O'Conor (by sculptor *Augustus Saint-Gaudens); sculptor William O'Donovan; and President Theodore Roosevelt, a founding member of the American Irish Historical Society.

§ Open Tuesday-Saturday 10-5 (appointment necessary). Phone: 212-288-2263.

¶ Bayard-Condict Building, 65 Bleecker Street, Lower Manhattan.

Erected between 1897 and 1899, this extremely ornate building is the only one in New York City designed by *Louis Sullivan and was one of the city's first skyscrapers.

¶ Bennett Park, between 183rd and 185th streets, Pinehurst and Fort Washington avenues, Upper Manhattan.

This was once the estate of James Gordon Bennett, the publisher of the *New York Herald*, and his wife, Henrietta Agnes Crean, a native of Ireland. The property and its house were maintained by their son, James Gordon Bennett Jr., who became chief executive officer of his father's paper in 1867.

The younger Bennett increased the *Herald*'s circulation by promoting several news exploits of his own making. One such effort was Henry

Stanley's expedition to Zanzibar in search of David Livingstone. Another was Bennett's sponsorship of an expedition in search of the Northwest Passage, an unsuccessful venture which received full coverage in the *Herald*, however, through the reporting of *Aloysius MacGahan. Bennett also attracted favorable attention for the paper through the Herald Relief Fund for victims of agrarian dislocation and violence in Ireland, subscribing $100,000 to the fund himself.

¶ **Bishop Brooks Statue,** Church of the Incarnation, 209 Madison Ave., Lower Manhattan.

This life-size statue of Bishop Phillips Brooks was sculpted by *William Clark Noble.

¶ **Broadway**

The "Great White Way" was first paved by Daniel Crimmins, who as a boy had worked for his Irish-born father's construction company. During his own contracting career, he constructed more than 400 buildings in the city, dug the tunnels for underground gas lines and electric wires, constructed much of the elevated-railway trackage, and built miles of viaducts and streets. He sometimes had as many as 12,000 men working for him at one time, and because of his generally good labor-management relations he was often asked to arbitrate wage disputes.

For his generosity to various charitable institutions in the city, Crimmins was named a Knight Commander of the Order of St. Gregory by Pope Leo XIII. A member of the Friendly Sons of St. Patrick and the American Irish Historical Society, Crimmins is also remembered as the author of *St. Patrick's Day – Its Celebration in New York and Other American Places, 1737-1845* (1902) and *Irish-American Miscellany* (1905).

¶ **Brooklyn Bridge,** Lower Manhattan.

One of the forces behind the building of the Brooklyn Bridge was William Kingsley, a second-generation Irishman who argued for a bridge across the East River to Brooklyn and who persuaded the engineer John A. Roebling to undertake the job.

Born in 1833 to Kilkenny emigrants living in Franklin County, New York, Kingsley was baptized William Kinsella but later changed his surname, presumably to hide his Celtic origins. After coming to Brooklyn in 1857, he formed a contacting business, which over the years paved Brooklyn's streets and built many of its reservoirs, waterworks, and sewers. At the time of his death, Kingsley was a director of the *Brooklyn Eagle*, the American District Telegraph Company, and the Metropolitan Gas Light Company. He was buried in Greenwood Cemetery in New York City.

¶ **Cardinal Hayes Place,** Pearl and Duane streets, Lower Manhattan.

This site is named for Patrick Joseph Hayes, the fifth archbishop of New York, who was born near here in 1867 to immigrants from Killarney, Ireland.

Soon after the American entry into World War I, Hayes was given the responsibility of ministering to the spiritual needs of Catholic chaplains and personnel in the U.S. military forces. (Within a year the U.S. military increased the number of its chaplains from twenty-five to almost 900.) In his new position Hayes visited military bases in the United States but was prevented from going to the European front partly because of the illness of *Cardinal John Farley of New York. Soon after succeeding Farley as archbishop, Hayes founded Catholic Charities.

¶ **Castle Clinton National Monument,** Battery Park, Lower Manhattan.

Originally known as West Battery, the first fort on this site was designed by John McComb Jr. as a circular formation with walls eight feet thick. Renamed in 1815 for *DeWitt Clinton, the city's longtime mayor, the fortress was later turned into Castle Garden, featuring a fountain and a promenade. From 1855 to 1890, however, the site was an immigrant landing station, processing more than eight million newcomers to America. The station provided fair currency exchange, medical care, and information about housing, job opportunities, and travel to different parts of the country. Today Castle Clinton is a point of departure for ferry boats to Ellis Island and the Statue of Liberty.

During the 1880s an Irish immigrant named Charlotte Grace O'Brien persuaded the Irish Catholic Colonization Society to establish a depot at Castle Garden to care for Irish immigrant women. There more than a 100,000 Irish women and girls found a temporary home, employment, counseling, and a chapel.

§ Open daily 8:30-5:30. Closed December 25. Phone: 212-344-72220.

¶ **Central Park,** extending from 59th to 110th streets and from 5th Avenue to Central Park West.

Central Park contains two Irish-American landmarks of note:

• Thomas Moore Bust, 59th Street and 5th Avenue entrance. This portrait bust by *Denis Sheahan honors the famous Dublin-born poet whose extremely popular *Irish Melodies* (1807-1834) expressed the glories of Gaelic civilization.

• Victor Herbert Statue, on the Mall. This bronze bust by *Edmond Quinn honors Victor Herbert, the Dublin-born musician who wrote more than forty operettas, among them *Babes in Toyland* and *Naughty Marietta*. The memorial is located near the Guggenheim bandstand, where Herbert used to play with the 22nd Regiment. After leaving Vienna, where he had been the first cellist with the Strauss orchestra, he played in the New York Metropolitan Opera Orchestra.

Herbert became an active exponent of Irish sensibilities when he was elected president of the Society of the Friendly Sons of St. Patrick in 1914. The following year he founded the society's glee club and addressed the organization's annual meeting in especially chauvinistic terms: "I do not wish to brag about the achievements of the Irish race, but is it not a fact that on every page of the World's history and particularly the history of this country, you will find the names of some of the most illustrious sons of Erin, and have we not in generous measure helped to build up this wonderful country since its earliest development? But we have become grateful sons of the Goddess of Liberty, enjoying the blessings of Freedom denied us in our own land. Unbounded as is our loyalty to the country of our adoption . . . we are still fond lovers of that Green Isle beyond the Sea."

Following the abortive 1916 Easter Uprising in Dublin, Herbert presided at a mass meeting to protest Britain's iron-fisted crushing of the revolt. He called on the attendees to remember the "Irish martyrs of 1916" and to contribute to a fund for the families of the executed rebels. The following October he opened the Irish Relief Fund Bazaar at Madison Square Garden, taking the opportunity to pay tribute to those who died in the uprising: "Those men paid the penalty of their convictions and won for themselves imperishable fame."

On the heels of this political activity, Herbert wrote the opera that he called the effort of his life. According to its creator, *Hearts of Erin* (later known as *Eileen*) contained no traditional Irish airs but, rather, "'Irish' numbers" which he had written "in the characteristic spirit of the music of my native country." So successful was Herbert in this task that a reviewer later wrote that the composer had expressed in music the very heart of a nation. Although *Eileen* was probably inspired by events in Dublin the previous spring, the opera actually takes place during an unsuccessful rebellion in 1798. After returning from the Continent to prepare for an uprising supported by the French, the opera's protagonist, Barry O'Day, falls in love with Eileen Mulvaney. Despite the military and political rout that follows, love conquers all as the amorous pair live happily ever after. The opera concludes with the hymn "When Ireland Stands Among the Nations of the World."

❡ **Charles O'Conor Birthplace Site,** 129 Front Street, Lower Manhattan.

On this site in 1804 was born Charles O'Conor, the New York attorney who held the distinction of being the first Catholic nominated for the presidency of the United States.

The son of an Irish political refugee, O'Conor received the nomination in 1872 from the "Straight-Out" Democrats, a group of dissidents who had bolted the Democratic Party after its selection of *Horace Greeley as its standard bearer. His popularity with these Southerners may have been due to his earlier opposition to abolition and to his belief that slavery was a "just, benign and beneficent" institution. He had also expressed the South's fear of becoming a minority in the federal government: "If we continue to fill the halls of legislation with abolitionists, and permit to occupy the executive chair men who declare themselves to be enlisted in a crusade against slavery, . . . what can we reasonably expect from the people of the South but that they will pronounce the Constitution . . . [and] this Union . . . unendurable evil . . . ." Although O'Conor refused the nomination, he and the dissidents' vice presidential candidate, John Quincy Adams, won 29,408 votes in twenty-three states.

❡ **Charles O'Conor Portrait Bust,** Appellate Division of the New York State Supreme Court, near Madison Square Park, Lower Manhattan.

During a legal career that lasted half a century, *Charles O'Conor was recognized as the ablest lawyer in America. One of the legal cases which brought him much attention involved the defense of *Jefferson Davis following the Civil War.

In late May 1865, Northerners sympathetic to Davis contacted O'Conor to request that he serve as the former Confederate president's counsel, most likely against a charge of treason against the United States. A year later, while Davis was still imprisoned at Fort Monroe, Virginia, O'Conor petitioned the U.S. attorney general to release Davis on $1 million bail posted by Northern businessmen Cornelius Vanderbilt, Gerrit Smith, and *Horace Greeley. The request was denied, however, because Davis was still a military prisoner and thus not eligible for bail. But on May 4, 1867, the attorney successfully sought a writ of habeas corpus requesting the military authorities at Fort Monroe to remand Davis to civil authorities in the state.

When O'Conor subsequently learned that the government prosecutor was not ready to proceed with the case, he again requested bail for his client. This time Davis was released after Greeley and several others pledged $100,000 in sureties. At the end of November, O'Conor petitioned that the indictment for treason be dismissed on the theory that

Davis had already been punished for his alleged crime by the provision in the Fourteenth Amendment which stripped him of his United States citizenship. The next month Chief Justice Salmon P. Chase agreed, quashing the indictment and ruling that the case could not be tried ex post facto.

Toward the end of his career, O'Conor achieved additional fame for his prosecution of the notoriously corrupt "Tweed Ring." Although he was successful in breaking up New York City's most infamous machine, he feared that his legal victory would provide no lasting protection against future corruption. O'Conor's pessimism in this regard is evident in public appeals he made soon after the Tweed litigation. In a pamphlet entitled *Democracy*, he argued that "in the main[, government] should be unfelt and unseen, or at least unperceived" and that "every positive regulation, not indispensable to the public and general welfare . . . violates the spirit of the Constitution." In an address in 1877, he said that "to be left alone by politicians and intermeddling officials is all that society needs." He warned that, while the U.S. Constitution guarantees liberty, "little, if anything, towards insuring perpetuity, or controlling the will of the popular majority, was affected by the device of a written constitution. The endurance, vigor, virtue of those fundamental principles which, in fact, are in the Constitution, depend wholly upon the intelligence and patriotism of our people."

¶ **Chester A. Arthur House,** 123 Lexington Avenue, Lower Manhattan.

Although this address now houses stores and apartments, it was formerly the residence of *Chester A. Arthur for most of his adult life. Following President Garfield's death in 1881 at the hands of an assassin, Vice President Arthur took the oath of office here on September 20. A bronze plaque on the building was dedicated in 1964 to mark the eighty-first anniversary of Arthur's signing of the Pendleton Civil Service Act.

¶ **Chester A. Arthur Statue,** Madison Square Park, Broadway and 23rd Street, Lower Manhattan.

Unveiled in 1899, this statue honors *President Chester A. Arthur.

¶ **Church of the Ascension,** 5th Avenue and 10th Street, Lower Manhattan.

The marble altar relief in this Gothic Revival brownstone church was created by *Augustus Saint-Gaudens.

¶ **City Hall,** Broadway and Park Row, Lower Manhattan.

The city hall was constructed in 1811 through the influence of New

York mayor DeWitt Clinton, whose grandfather had emigrated from Ireland to America in 1731. Besides serving ten annual terms as mayor and two terms as governor, Clinton was a state legislator, a U.S. senator, and the principal advocate for building the Erie Canal. In the New York legislature, he was a spokesman for Irish immigrants and drafted the law removing franchise restrictions against Roman Catholics.

• On the east side of City Hall is a bronze seated statue of *Horace Greeley, the founder of the *New York Times* and coiner of the advice "Go west, young man." Ever the eccentric, he was known for his squeaky voice, white socks and overcoat, broad-brimmed hat, throat-whiskers, and shapeless pants.

Despite his earlier unsuccessful attempts to win political office, Greeley tried again in 1871, this time as the nominee of both the Democratic Party and the Liberal Republicans. Although the latter group supported him because of his opposition to the renomination of *President Ulysses S. Grant, he had little prospect of gaining many Democratic votes because of his frequent attacks against the Democratic Party over the years. During the campaign he was called a fool, a crank, and a traitor and was an easy object of ridicule in political cartoons of the day. He was personally hurt by the invective hurled against him and lamented that he sometimes thought he was running for the penitentiary rather than for the presidency. After carrying only six Southern and border states, he felt that he was "the worst beaten man who ever ran for high office."

ℐ Christopher Colles Residence, 6 State Street.

This was the home of Christopher Colles, the Dublin-born engineer who designed New York City's water system and proposed what became the Erie Canal. He is buried in Greenwood Cemetery in New York City.

ℐ Claremont Avenue, Upper Manhattan.

This street was named for "Claremont," the mansion house of Michael Hogan, a native of County Clare, Ireland, and a wealthy New York businessman and philanthropist. The house was built in the early 1790s by George Pollock, an English linen merchant, and until 1953 stood on Strawberry Hill, north of Grant's Tomb.

Hogan, who began his career as a sea captain, first arrived in New York in 1804. With him was his wife, who was described as "a dark Indian princess" (possessed of a dowry of £40,000 in gold) and for whom he purchased Pollock's mansion. Hogan christened *la grand maison* either for his native County Clare or for the castle of his longtime friend, the Duke of Clarence, the future "Sailor King" of England, William IV. A memorial plaque in Hogan's honor is in Grace Church in Lower

Manhattan.

¶ Conference House, Hylan Boulevard, Tottenville, Staten Island.

On September 11, 1776, this structure was the site of an unsuccessful peace conference between Admiral Richard Howe (the commander of British naval forces in America) and three representatives of the Continental Congress (John Adams, Benjamin Franklin, and *Edward Rutledge). During the conference with Howe, Rutledge insisted that nothing short of complete independence would satisfy the Americans.

¶ Dominick Lynch House, 36 Broadway, Lower Manhattan.

This was the residence of Dominick Lynch, a successful merchant and a native of Galway, Ireland, who counted eighty-four mayors of that city among his ancestors.

In 1780, while still in Ireland, Lynch opened a branch of his father's trading business in Bruges, Flanders. His subsequent wealth was based on the purchase and shipment of flax seed to Ireland and on other trade during the continental wars of the period. (It was joked that he was the only Irishman to come to America with his fortune already made.)

After arriving in the United States, Lynch became involved in a number of enterprises of varying success. With his business partner, Thomas Stoughton, he opened a commercial house in New York City, for which he provided two-thirds of the $7,500 capitalization. He subsequently invested in bank stocks, real estate, and the China trade. He also acquired a tract of 2,000 acres near Fort Stanwix on the Mohawk River in New York State. Although he originally named his property Lynchville, sometime before the turn of the century he changed the name to Rome. Over the next twenty years, he built there a woolen factory, a cotton factory, and a sawmill.

In the meantime, mutual dissatisfaction had led to a dissolution of his partnership with Stoughton in 1795. As a result of litigation that continued for two decades, however, Lynch had to pay his former partner $25,000. While living in New York City, Lynch was a generous benefactor of St. Peter's Catholic Church.

¶ Duane Street, City Hall area.

This street was named after James Duane, the son of a prosperous New York merchant of Irish birth who arrived in New York soon after 1700. The younger Duane was a member of the Continental Congress, the first mayor of New York following the Revolution, a member of the New York state convention which adopted the Constitution, and the first federal judge of the district of New York.

¶ Edgar Allan Poe Cottage, Poe Park, 2640 Grand Concourse and

Kingsbridge Road, the Bronx.

This frame farmhouse was the last residence of any duration of *Edgar Allan Poe. Though well known when he arrived here in 1846 with his wife, Virginia, and his mother-in-law, Maria Clemm, he was impoverished. "Eddie rarely left his beautiful home," Mrs. Clemm recalled. "I attended to his literary business; for he, poor fellow, knew nothing about money transactions." Here Poe wrote his poems "Annabel Lee" and "The Bells," and here Virginia died of tuberculosis the next year. Her bed and Poe's rocking chair are on exhibit, as is a portrait bust of the author by *Edmond Quinn. The museum shows an audiovisual presentation about Poe's life.

§ Open Wednesday-Friday 9-5, Saturday 10-4, Sunday 1-5. Closed holidays. Fee. Phone: 718-881-8900.

Edmond Quinn, a native of Philadelphia of Irish descent, first studied art under Thomas Eakins at the Pennsylvania Academy of Fine Arts. At age twenty-five the student spent several months in Spain, where he was influenced by the work of Velazquez. He later studied modeling and sculpting in Paris.

Among Quinn's other sculpted works are a statue of John Howard (Williamsport, Pa.), the reliefs on the battle monument at King's Mountain (South Carolina), a bronze statue of Edwin Booth as Hamlet (Gramercy Park, New York City), the female figure of "Victory" for the war memorial at New Rochelle (N.Y.), and busts of Henry Clay, Cass Gilbert, *Victor Herbert, Edwin Markham, and *Eugene O'Neill. His busts of Edwin Booth, Dr. Oliver Wendell Holmes, and *James McNeill Whistler are in the Hall of Fame of New York University.

Although Quinn was said to have had a Celtic sense of humor, melancholia was evidently more predominant in his personality, for he ended his life by drowning in 1929.

¶ **Edgar Allan Poe House,** 45 West 3rd Street, Greenwich Village.

The famous poet lived here for a brief time and received medication for a cold at the Northern Dispensary (at Christopher Street and Waverly Place).

¶ **Edgar Allan Poe Street,** West 84th Street, between Broadway and Westend Avenue.

This renamed portion of West 84th Street marks the general location of the home and farm owned by *Patrick Brennan, where *Edgar Allan Poe lived in 1844 and where he completed "The Raven."

When Poe first met Brennan and his wife and their six children, he described the pair as "a hospitable agriculturalist and his consort." Poe later described their farm as "a perfect paradise," where he hoped that his consumptive wife, Virginia, would soon regain her health. As the poet revised his earlier drafts of "The Raven," he doubtless incorporated into it the statue of the goddess Athena – the "pallid bust of Pallas" – which stood above one of the doors in the Brennan home. Years later the Brennans recounted their observations about the sensitive poet: of the papers strewn over the floor of the room with the bust, of his daydreaming on a bench near the pond or at the summit of Mt. Tom, and his vigils with Virginia as they enjoyed the sunsets across the Hudson. Poe described his experience with the Brennans as "playing hermit in earnest, nor have I seen a living soul out of my family."

¶ **Ellis Island,** New York Harbor.

The island can be reached by ferry from Battery Park in lower Manhattan and from Liberty Park in Jersey City.

In 1890 Congress chose Ellis Island as the site of a new federal immigration center. The facility was built at a cost of $500,000 and contained a two-story processing building, a hospital, a boiler house, a laundry, and a utility plant – all constructed of wood. It also had telegraph and railroad ticket offices, a money exchange office, and an information bureau for the benefit of those seeking friends and relatives among the immigrants. Two military structures on the island were converted into dormitories for detainees.

On January 1, 1892, the Ellis Island Immigration Center formally opened to process steerage passengers coming into the country. More than twelve million immigrants – 500,000 of them Irish – were processed here before the center was closed in 1954.

¶ The outdoor American Immigrant Wall of Honor contains panels engraved with the names of 200,000 immigrants who arrived in the United States between 1892 and 1924.

¶ The Annie Moore Statue in the main building was erected in 1992 to commemorate the centennial of Ellis Island's opening and to honor the first immigrant registered at the new center. An identical statue stands in Queenstown in Cobh, County Cork, Ireland, the port from which Annie and her two younger brothers set sail.

Described as a fifteen-year-old "little rosy cheeked Irish girl," Annie Moore was among the 148 steerage passengers who arrived in New York Harbor aboard the steamship *Nevada*. On the morning of January 1, 1892, the passengers were placed aboard the immigrant transfer boat *John E. Moore*, which landed at the wharf on Ellis Island "amid a clang

Statue of Annie Moore,
the first immigrant
to register at Ellis Island.

of bells and din of shrieking whistles."

By a prearranged plan Annie was escorted to a registry desk, where her name was the first to be registered at the new landing bureau. The next day the *New York Times* described her arrival: "When the little voyager had been registered [the superintendent] presented her with a ten-dollar gold coin and made a short address of congratulations and welcome. It was the first United States coin she had ever seen and the largest sum of money she had ever possessed. She says she will never part with it, but will always keep it as a pleasant memento of the occasion."

Annie was accompanied by her two younger brothers, Anthony and Philip. The trio had come to join their parents, Matt and Mary Moore, who had immigrated to the United States three years earlier and had left the three children with an aunt until they could earn passage money for the rest of the family. The three youngsters arrived with a single piece of baggage among them.

On June 8, 1988, the Ellis Island Restoration Commission revealed its intention to establish a computerized genealogical center on Ellis Island. The system would contain information about seventeen million immigrants obtained from the original ship manifests.

One of the guests of honor that day was Margaret O'Connell

Middleton of Tucson, Arizona, Annie Moore's granddaughter. During the ceremony she returned the ten-dollar gold piece given to her grandmother when she arrived at Ellis Island. She in turn was given another gold piece by Ellis Island's superintendent in honor of the center's opening.

§ Open daily 9-5. Closed December 25. Phone: 212-264-8711.

¶ **Emigrant Savings Bank,** 51 Chambers Street, City Hall area.

Although now used for other purposes, the building at this site was once the Emigrant Savings Bank, founded in 1817 by *William MacNeven to help Irish immigrants.

¶ **Father Duffy Statue and Square,** Broadway and 43rd Street, Midtown Manhattan.

In front of a Celtic cross stands a bronze statue of Father Francis Duffy, the pastor of nearby Holy Cross Catholic Church. Within his parish were the slums and gangs of "Hell's Kitchen," the dance halls and burlesque houses of Times Square, and the legitimate theaters of Broadway.

Duffy is more generally known as chaplain of the "Fighting 69th" Regiment, a unit predominantly Irish since 1860, when it refused to march in honor of the visiting Prince of Wales. During World War I, the unit became the 165th Regiment of the American Expeditionary Force fighting in France. For his service on the battlefield, Duffy was awarded the Distinguished Service Cross, the Cross of the Legion of Honor, and the *Croix de Guerre*. At the time of his funeral in St. Patrick's Cathedral, he was eulogized by President Franklin Roosevelt as "a great Samaritan, a great Catholic, a great soldier."

The statue was erected in 1937 by his many friends in the theatrical profession. Among the 30,000 people at the dedication were members of the 69th Regiment band (playing "Onward, Christian Soldiers") and Irish Americans James Farley, Alfred E. Smith, and James Tunney.

¶ **Fifth Avenue**

Despite conflict over social and political issues in recent years, organizers of the St. Patrick's Day Parade continue a long tradition with their annual march down Fifth Avenue. The first St. Patrick's Day Parade in New York City took place in 1779 and was composed of Irish soldiers serving in the British army which occupied the city at that time.

¶ **Five Points,** Park, Baxter, and Worth streets, Lower Manhattan.

As early as the 1820s this area of the city had a large Irish population and may have been one of the country's earliest slums. The Five Points area was notorious for its bars, whorehouses, foul-smelling tanneries, and criminal gangs (one of them composed mostly of natives from County Kerry, Ireland).

¶ **Foley Square,** at the intersection of Duane, Lafayette, Pearl, and Centre streets, City Hall area.

The square was named for *Thomas Foley, a Tammany Hall politician known for his influence in New York state politics.

Born in 1852, Foley at age thirteen began work as a butcher's delivery boy and a blacksmith's helper but eventually opened several saloons. (His rules for such establishments forbade the admission of women and the encouragement of drunkenness by his bartenders.) In the meantime, he became a Tammany operative, first as a district captain, then as a city council member, and finally as New York County sheriff. He could have been nominated for state senator or become the outright leader of Tammany, but because he felt that he was better suited for politics rather than officeholding he declined the offers. As the unofficial head of Tammany, he was known for his generosity – and gullibility – to those in need. Angered by newspaper attacks against him by *William Randolph Hearst, Foley helped frustrate the famous publisher's attempts to win election as governor and U.S. senator.

The Tammany "kingmaker" is best remembered as being the political godfather of *Alfred E. Smith and for throwing his support behind his successful gubernatorial bid. After Foley's death in 1925, Governor Smith acknowledged his affection for his political mentor and offered the following tribute: "Tom had one great piece of advice that he gave to everyone when he started them off. He used to say: 'When anybody comes to see you about anything, tell them the truth. They won't like it at the time you tell it to them, but six months afterwards they will be your friend because they will find it out.'"

¶ **Ford Foundation Building,** 320 East 43rd Street, Midtown Manhattan.

This cube-shaped building faced with acres of glass was designed by Roche, Dinkeloo & Associates in the late 1960s.

Kevin Roche, a native of Dublin, received a bachelor's degree in architecture from the National University of Ireland in 1945. After moving to the United States, he studied at the Illinois Institute of Technology.

¶ **Fordham University,** 3rd Avenue and Fordham Road, the Bronx.

This Jesuit university was founded in 1841 by *John Hughes, New York City's first archbishop. A statue of Hughes by *William O'Donovan is located on the lawn in front of the university buildings.

¶ Fort Clinton, McGowan's Pass, Central Park.

Named in honor of *DeWitt Clinton, the longtime mayor of the city, the fort was built to defend nearby McGowan's Pass, reputedly named for Captain Daniel McGowan, a native of Ireland and a Revolutionary War soldier who owned a farm here.

¶ Fraunces Tavern, 54 Pearl Street, at Broad.

Among the items on display in the museum is a painting by John Ward Dunsmore depicting a scene from the battle of Springfield, New Jersey, in June 1776. During the battle, when the American soldiers ran out of wadding for their rifles, the *Reverend James Caldwell – the "Soldier Parson" – broke open the doors of the Presbyterian church and began to distribute to the men copies of the Watts hymnbooks. "Now put Watts into them, boys!" he cried.

On December 3, 1932, Fraunces Tavern was the site of a memorial meeting to commemorate a famous breakfast which occurred here in 1783. Following George Washington's return to New York City that year, the former American commander had breakfast with *Hercules Mulligan, a haberdasher by trade who had served as Washington's personal spy during the Revolution. This historic meal was celebrated in the poem "Breakfast with Hercules Mulligan" by Shaemus O'Sheel, who read the poem at the 1932 memorial. The last twenty-one lines of the poem are quoted here:

> Over the Bowling Green they ride,
> Washington, Mulligan, side by side;
> Thus the Chieftain, in all men's view
> Proves Hercules Mulligan staunch and true.
>
> For Washington knows the Irish breed;
> They sprung to arms in the hour of need,
> Sullivan, first to strike on land,
> O'Brien, first to strike at sea,
> Knox and Moylan and Wayne and Hand,
> Barry, Magaw and Shee.
> They proved their mettle on many a field,
> First to charge and last to yield,
> In the cause of Liberty.
>
> Washington smiles and bows to his host;
> "Hercules Mulligan, here's a toast:
> If the land we have seen this day set free
> Ever shall be in danger
> From foe within or stranger,
> May Heaven grant, to save us then,

The hearts and the hands of Irishmen."
And the shout rings 'round the board, "Amen"![1]

With the arrival of peace and the creation of a new nation, Mulligan seems to have continued his haberdashery business, one that now boasted among its clients the new president of the United States. According to Washington's account books, between May 1789 and May 1790 he paid Mulligan £288 for tailoring services and quantities of gingham, flannel, velvet, and other materials.

§ Open Monday-Friday 10-4. Closed major holidays except July 4. Fee. Phone: 212-425-1778.

¶ **Frawley Circle,** at the northeast corner of Central Park (110th Street).

This area is named for *James Frawley, a Tammany Hall politician, public administrator, and state senator.

¶ **General Grant National Memorial,** Riverside Drive and 122nd Street, Upper Manhattan.

*Ulysses S. Grant and his wife are buried in this circular Greek Revival tomb, the largest mausoleum in the United States. The white marble interior resembles that of Les Invalides, Napoleon's tomb in Paris, and is adorned with heroic bronze busts of five other Civil War generals, including *Philip Sheridan. Along the south façade are engraved Grant's words "Let us have peace."

Following Grant's death in 1885, his funeral procession through New York City was seven miles long and attracted a million people. His body was originally placed in a temporary vault in Riverside Park until the national memorial was completed in 1897.

§ Open Wednesday-Sunday 9-5. Closed holidays. Phone: 212-666-1640.

¶ **General Porter Statue,** Van Cortlandt Park, the Bronx.

This statue of General Josiah Porter was sculpted by *William Clark Noble.

¶ **George M. Cohan Statue and Square,** Broadway and 45th Street, Midtown Manhattan.

This square is dedicated to George M. Cohan, one of America's most famous composers and musical comedy stars, an entertainer who com-

---

[1]1995 Official Catholic Directory, P. J. Kenedy & Sons, in association with R. R. Bowker, a Reed Reference Publishing Company, New Providence, New Jersey. Written permission granted to publish data. All rights reserved.

posed more than 500 songs, helped produce about 150 plays, and either wrote or collaborated on the writing of forty plays.

When the statue in Cohan's honor was dedicated in 1959, Oscar Hammerstein II and George Jessel presided at the event. The crowd of 45,000 people in attendance closed the ceremonies by singing "Give My Regards to Broadway." The sides of the pedestal are inscribed with the names of Cohan's four most famous songs.

The grandson of Michael Keohane, an immigrant from County Cork, George Cohan was born into a traveling vaudevillian family and made his first stage appearance literally as an infant. As one of "The Four Cohans," the youngster acted, sang, danced, and recited in his father's sketches. His first great success was as the lead character in *Peck's Bad Boy*, a role that reputedly came naturally for the mischievous Mick. It was during these early years that he developed his trademark style – singing out of the corner of his mouth, thrusting his head forward as he strut across the stage, and ending each performance with his ingratiating *gracias*: "My mother thanks you, my father thanks you, my sister thanks you, and I thank you."

After succeeding to the role of sketch writer and business manager, Cohan formed a production partnership that produced many hits. The first success was *Little Johnny Jones*, a musical by Cohan about an American jockey accused of throwing the English Derby. Although critics were less than enthusiastic – some labeling it "flag-waving" – the public excitedly took up two of its songs – "Give My Regards to Broadway" and "Yankee Doodle Boy." (Although Cohan was born on July 3, his father invented the story that his son had been born on Independence Day, thus making him a "real live nephew of [his] Uncle Sam, born on the Fourth of July.") Other patriotic musicals followed, among them *George Washington, Jr.*, in which Cohan sang "You're a Grand Old Flag." But Cohan's greatest hit song – selling one and a half million copies – was "Over There," inspired by America's entry into World War I.

Years later President Franklin Roosevelt presented Cohan with the gold medal which Congress had voted to award him for the song. At his funeral in St. Patrick's Cathedral, the organist played "Over There" as a dirge, the first time a secular piece of music had ever been played in the Catholic cathedral.

¶ **Gramercy Park,** between 3rd & Park avenues and East 20th & East 21st streets, Lower Manhattan.

During the Dutch period this area was known as Crommessie ("small, crooked knife," for a nearby brook). A later owner of the property was *James Duane, the first mayor of New York after the Revolution. He named the area Gramercy Seat.

• In the park is a bronze statue of the actor Edwin Booth as Hamlet, the work of the sculptor *Edmond Quinn and a gift of the Players' Club.

ℐ Greenwich Village, Lower Manhattan.

This area was once the estate of Irish-born Sir Peter Warren, an illustrious naval commander during the colonial wars of the 1740s.

Born on the Warren estate at Warrenstown, County Meath, in 1703, Warren joined the British navy as a midshipman at the age of twelve and spent a dozen years cruising the West Indies and the North American coast. In 1730 he sailed to New York City as the captain of a twenty-gun frigate. Once there, he purchased "Greenwich House," a twenty-acre site on the Hudson River and the first acquisition of what grew to become a 300-acre estate now known as Greenwich Village. He later purchased 14,000 acres in the Mohawk Valley, an extensive tract managed by *William Johnson, his nephew and Britain's Indian agent in that region.

Beginning in 1745, Warren was assigned to active duty in the Anglo-French conflict. While Governor William Shirley of Massachusetts led an expedition against the French stronghold of Louisbourg on Cape Breton Island, Warren prevented an enemy supply ship from reaching the besieged fortress. In a dramatic address to the army just before Louisbourg's surrender, he said that he would rather die and be buried there than leave without capturing the city. For his efforts he was named rear admiral of the Blue Fleet and governor of Cape Breton Island. His popularity was such that a street in New York City was named for him and a tavern called the Admiral Warren was opened on Wall Street.

Warren's greatest naval victory, however, occurred when he defeated a French fleet off Cape Finisterre in 1747. This personal triumph led to knighthood, election to Parliament, and promotion to vice admiral of the White Fleet. He later led three other naval expeditions and retired with £200,000 of prize money. Following his death in Dublin, he was buried near Warrenstown and was honored with a monument in Westminster Abbey.

ℐ Greenwood Cemetery, 5th Avenue at 25th Street, Lower Manhattan.

Opened in 1840, this beautifully landscaped cemetery is noted for its Victorian statuary, some of which includes monuments in the form of mangled railroad cars, sinking steamboats, and fire hydrants. The 500,000 graves here include those of Irish-born Marcus Daly and Lola Montez and Irish-Americans DeWitt Clinton, Horace Greeley, and William Kingsley.

• Marcus Daly, the "Copper King" who developed the Anaconda

Mines in Montana. Born in Ballyjamesduff, County Cavan, Daly by 1876 was part owner of the Alice Mine in Butte, Montana. Four years later he bought the Anaconda Silver Mine and converted it to copper.

• Born Marie Dolores Eliza Rosanna Gilbert in Limerick, Ireland, Lola Montez was notorious for her multiple marriages and numerous love affairs. She counted among her lovers the musician Franz Liszt, the novelist Alexandre Dumas, and Bavaria's King Ludwig, the last of whom she infected with syphilis and generally so dominated that his government was mocked as the *Lolaministerium*. Montez was known not only for her paramours but also for her erotic Spider Dance, a feature of her famous dance tours. But the main attraction was Montez herself, known for carrying a pistol, smoking cigars, and humiliating and assaulting men. During the last years of her life, as syphilis ravaged her body, she preached to prostitutes about the dangers of the disease. At the end she suffered from incontinence, seizures, and loss of speech.

• The memorial to DeWitt Clinton consists of a heroic-size statue atop a pedestal with bas-reliefs depicting scenes from the construction of the Erie Canal. Clinton was a major proponent of such an engineering feat, which employed thousands of Irish workers along its course.

• The monument to William Kingsley – one of the major advocates of building a bridge across the East River – was erected by the board of trustees of the East River (Brooklyn) Bridge and is formed of a stone from that structure.

• [See entries about Horace Greeley elsewhere.]

§ Open daily 8-4. Phone: 718-768-7300.

¶ **Hall of Fame for Great Americans,** Bronx Community College of the City University of New York, on the heights overlooking the Harlem and Hudson rivers.

A 630-foot open-air colonnade dedicated in 1901 enshrines the bronze busts of 98 of the 102 Americans inducted into the Hall of Fame. The following honorees were of Irish descent: President Grover Cleveland; Stephen Collins Foster, composer of minstrel songs and popular ballads; Robert Fulton, inventor and steamship promoter; President Ulysses S. Grant; President Andrew Jackson; Thomas "Stonewall" Jackson, Civil War general; Sidney Lanier, musician, poet, and literary critic; Edward Alexander MacDowell, pianist, composer, and music teacher; Matthew Fontaine Maury, oceanographer and naval officer; President Theodore Roosevelt; Augustus Saint-Gaudens, sculptor; James McNeill Whistler, artist and portrait painter; and President Woodrow Wilson.

In addition, the busts of Abraham Lincoln and General William Sherman on display here are replicas of works by *Augustus Saint-Gaudens, while the likenesses of John Quincy Adams, Oliver Wendell

Holmes, and James Kent were sculpted by *Edmond Quinn.

¶ **Hercules Mulligan House Site,** 218 Pearl Street, Lower Manhattan.

Hercules Mulligan was born in Coleraine, County Antrim, Ireland, in 1740 and came to America with his parents at the age of six. He was descended from an O'Mulligan of County Cavan, one of the hereditary bards of the O'Reilly family. He probably worked for the haberdashery firm of Kortright and Company in New York City before opening a clothing and tailoring business of his own in the same city. A measure of his wealth is evident in the fact that he purchased a house on this site for £1,500.

As relations between the British and their American cousins continued to deteriorate, Mulligan was extremely active in the anti-British agitation in New York City. In January 1770, three months before the Boston Massacre, he reputedly was one of the "Liberty Boys" who fought with British troops in New York. In July 1776 he and Captain Isaac Sears led the mob that destroyed the famous bronze statue of King George III on Bowling Green.

Mulligan's most famous role during the revolutionary struggle, however, was as a "confidential agent" (spy) for General George Washington. In 1779 Mulligan informed the American commander-in-chief that the British general Sir Henry Clinton intended to send 300 infantry to intercept Washington as he led his men through Connecticut on their way to Newport, Rhode Island. Mulligan later helped frustrate another attempt to seize Washington when he overheard a British officer in his shop boast that Washington would be a captive "before another day." Mulligan immediately ran to the wharf and dispatched an African American with a warning to the American general. In addition, sometime before April 1781 Mulligan warned Washington that he and the governors of New Jersey and New York were the targets of an assassination plot. In acknowledging the warning, the commander-in-chief wrote that "I shall take precautions on the occasion, as appear to me necessary." Mulligan's activities prompted the suspicion of the turncoat Benedict Arnold, who believed that the Irishman was a spy for Washington. Arnold arrested and court-martialed Mulligan but failed to secure a conviction.

¶ **High Bridge (Aqueduct Bridge),** across the Harlem River at 174th Street, Midtown Manhattan.

Erected in 1842, this bridge was designed by Father Thomas Levins, a scientist, architect, and engineer from Drogheda, Ireland.

Levins had studied at Stonyhurst College in England before joining the Society of Jesus and coming to the United States in 1822. After teaching mathematics and natural philosophy at Georgetown College in the District of Columbia for three years, he left the Jesuits but not the priesthood. In the meantime, he had earned a reputation as a theologian, a mineralogist, and a lapidary and was twice appointed to the board of examiners of cadets at the U.S. Military Academy at West Point. By 1825 he was serving in the New York City diocese, but nine years later he was suspended during a controversy with Bishop DuBois. It was probably after this unpleasantness that Levins was employed as an engineer on the Croton Aqueduct and designed High Bridge.

Sometime during his career Levins served as editor and writer for *The Green Banner*. The purpose of this early Irish newspaper was "to recreate, to instruct, and to enlighten," and its motto was "Let all the ends thou aimst at be Thy Country's, thy God's, and Truth's." Levins used the pen name "Fergus McAlpin" and took the lead in attacking the Calvinist ministers who had played a part in writing the hoax *The Awful Disclosures of Maria Monk*. Eventually reinstated to the active ministry by *Bishop John Hughes, he served as pastor of old St. Patrick's Cathedral between Mott and Mulberry streets.

❡ Holy Cross Cemetery, 3620 Tilden Avenue, Brooklyn.

Among the cemetery's "permanent inhabitants" are Irish Americans James "Diamond Jim" Brady and James Fitzsimmons and Irish native William R. Grace.

• To prepare for his new job as a railroad equipment salesman, the young James Brady bought three hand-tailored black suits and a diamond ring, the first of many "sparklers" that earned him his nickname. (In time even his garter clasps and underwear buttons were gems.) His hospitality and gregariousness brought him increasing sales commissions, which, with investments in the railroads and other speculative ventures, were the basis of his formidable fortune. (In 1896 he won $180,000 after betting that McKinley would be elected president.)

Although he never drank anything stronger than orangeade, Brady's gastronomical feats were legendary (e.g., consuming six dozen oysters for a snack). Warned by his doctor to diet and exercise, Brady went through the motions on a gold-plated, diamond-studded bicycle. After a successful kidney stone operation, he donated $220,000 to establish a urological clinic named for himself at Johns Hopkins University in Baltimore. The operation also yielded rumors: one that he had paid a widow $200,000 for her husband's stomach, and another that he could now eat only grass because of his newly implanted cow's stomach.

Whatever the case, by 1916 Brady's gastric ulcers, diabetes, heart disease, and kidney problems were so severe that he moved to Atlantic City to await death – but in a $1,000-a-week suite which reflected the grand style that was his trademark. Not long before he died, he bought a $6,400 "diamondized" pair of glasses for his dog, and in his will he remembered his friends with thirty sets of "sparklers" valued at $1 million.

   • [See entries for Fitzsimmons and Grace elsewhere.]

ꝯ Horace Greeley Statue, Greeley Square, between West 32nd and West 33rd streets, Midtown Manhattan.

   This bronze statue of *Horace Greeley, the editor of the *New York Tribune* in the mid nineteenth century, was sculpted by *Alexander Doyle.

   In 1848, at a mass meeting of the Friends of Ireland in New York City, Greeley claimed that the immigration of thousands of Irish into America each year gave the United States the right to comment on Britain's policy toward its island colony. He particularly refuted the British charge that defects in the Irish character were responsible for the appalling state of the island by stressing the hard work which the Irish immigrants had contributed to America. He even questioned the very basis of Britain's claim upon Ireland: "In confessing that they know not how to make the Irish people contented, peaceful, prosperous and happy, [English] statesmen admit that they have not the ability to govern Ireland, and therefore have no moral right to persist in this attempt."

   Fifteen years later an editorial in the *Tribune* commented on the upcoming gubernatorial race: "The nomination of Fernando Wood and [John] Hoffman, neither of whom has a drop of Irish blood in his veins, for Mayor of a city, three-fourths of whose Democratic voters are Irish, is an insult to the honor of the Old Sod . . . . The Irish vote in New York is enough to elect two Mayors. . . . Nominate an Irishman, elect an Irishman, and then, when you call upon him in City Hall, you've got an Irish Mayor as sure as there's never a snake nor a toad in Ireland."

ꝯ Hugh O'Neil Store Site, Avenue of the Americas, between 21st and 22nd streets.

   In 1876, when *Hugh O'Neil opened his department store formerly on this site, New York's working class customers were treated to a relatively new phenomenon – a flashy public relations-oriented salesman who was out to top all competitors' prices. Known as "The Fighting Irishman of Sixth Avenue," O'Neil lassoed his customers with loss-leaders and beat the competition by undercutting their prices and providing delivery service. (He was particularly proud of his fleet of delivery wagons.) Despite his keen mercantile sense, he was a religiously devout man beloved by his employees. He took special care that they observed their religious faith, and he let them take time off from work to attend to those duties.

¶ **Hunter College,** 68th Street and Park Avenue, Midtown Manhattan.

Formerly a teacher training institution, this city college was founded in 1869, largely through the influence of Thomas Hunter, a native of Ardglass, County Down, Ireland, who served as president of the school until 1902.

While still in his native land, Hunter became a teacher at age eighteen but was quickly labeled *persona non grata* because of his political views and his involvement with the "Young Ireland" movement. After writing newspaper articles supporting Irish independence and expressing his views about the Established Church and the Anglo-Irish tie, he found it prudent to leave the country. After arriving in New York City in 1850, he began a career that made his name a byword in educational circles. Not yet nineteen and possessed of little money and only a box of books, he accepted employment as a drawing teacher.

Within seven years, however, Hunter had risen to the principalship of Public School 35 and proceeded to establish the school's reputation for scholarship and discipline. He later used his influence to support adult education, teacher training programs, tenure for teachers, and an end to corporal punishment. In 1866 he created the first evening high school in New York City and eventually campaigned for the creation of secondary schools for girls in the city.

¶ **Ireland House,** 1A Fifth Avenue, Greenwich Village.

This renovated townhouse serves as the focal point of New York University's Irish and Irish-American Studies curriculum. Future programs at the new center will include lectures, seminars, films, and performances.

Ireland House was made possible through the generosity of Lewis Glucksman, an N.Y.U. alumnus and trustee, and his wife, Loretta Brennan Glucksman, a member of the arts and science board of overseers at the university.

At the dedication ceremonies in April 1993, an honorary degree was conferred on Irish Prime Minister Albert Reynolds, while presidential medals were granted to a number of Irish personalities: actor Cyril Cusack, theatrical producer Noel Pearson, actress Geraldine Fitzgerald, author Seamus Heaney, actress Maureen O'Hara, flutist James Galway, and Sister Stanislaus Kennedy (founder of a service organization for Dublin's homeless).

§ Phone: 212-757-3318.

¶ **James Walker House,** 6 St. Luke's Place. Private.

This was once the home of James "Jimmy" Walker, the *bon vivant* mayor of New York City and the son of an Irish immigrant carpenter from County Kilkenny.

Before entering politics, Walker had achieved minor success as a Tin Pan Alley songwriter, known for his lyrics to sentimental numbers like "Kiss All the Girls for Me" and "Will You Love Me in December as You Do in May?" Even after his election to the state legislature and the mayor's office, he continued to frequent the world of vaudeville, gambling casinos, and night clubs. While in the New York Assembly, he sponsored legislation for a forty-hour work week for women and children and for the legalization of Sunday baseball. He also attacked the Ku Klux Klan, Prohibition, and the censorship that accompanied the Red Scare after World War I.

His tenure as mayor (1926-1932) was generally unexceptional, except for its corruption and his affair with an English actress. An official investigation of his administration revealed at least two embarrassing facts: the existence of a safe deposit box taken out in his name and containing at one time $750,000 in cash, and his reception of $300,000 in stock profits from men who did business with the city. After being divorced by the woman for whom he had left his first wife, Walker experienced a moral and religious transformation that brought him back to Catholicism. "The glamor of other days I have found to be worthless tinsel, and all the allure of the world just so much seduction and deception," he confessed. "I now have found in religion and repentance the happiness and joy that I sought elsewhere in vain."

⚓ John Finley Walk, near 81st Street, over East River Drive, Midtown Manhattan.

This promenade is appropriately named for *John Houston Finley, a pedestrian *extraordinaire* whose perambulations throughout New York were legendary.

A former president of the City College of New York, state commissioner of education, and editor-in-chief of the *New York Times*, Finley believed that "a good walk clears the mind and stimulates thinking." He regularly walked to work until past seventy years of age, and every year on his birthday he walked the thirty-two-mile circuit around Manhattan Island. Once when he had missed the last train from Princeton, New Jersey, he walked from there to New York City. On another occasion he covered seventy-two miles by shanks' mare in a single day.

⚓ John Street Methodist Church, 44 John Street, between William and Nassau streets, Lower Manhattan.

The present structure is located on the site of the first Methodist church in America, erected in 1768 by Irish Methodists under the leadership of Philip Embury.

Although descended from Palatine Protestants who had fled the persecution of Louis XIV, Embury was probably born in Ballingrane, County Limerick, Ireland, about 1728. As a youngster he was educated by both German and English schoolmasters and was apprenticed to a carpenter. When Methodist preachers appeared in Limerick in 1749, he was attracted by their message and three years later underwent a religious experience: "the Lord shone into my soul a glimpse of his redeeming love, being an earnest of my redemption in Christ Jesus."

In 1760 Embury joined a group of emigrants who sailed for New York. There he found work as a carpenter and as a teacher in a school on Little Queen Street. His earlier religious enthusiasm seems to have waned, however, until a friend's indignation over cardplaying by her fellow Palatines caused him to attempt their moral reformation. "Philip," said the friend, "you must preach to us, or we shall go to Hell, and God will require our blood at your hands." Embury soon took up preaching, initially in his own home and then in Wesley Chapel, the first church on this site.

§ Open Monday-Friday 11:30-3. Phone: 212-269-0014.

¶ **Judson Memorial Church,** 55 Washington Square and Thompson Street.

A marble relief on the south wall follows a design by *Augustus Saint-Gaudens, although it was executed by Herbert Adams.

¶ **Margaret Corbin Commemorative Plaque,** Margaret Corbin Plaza and Drive, 183rd Street and Fort Washington Avenue, Upper Manhattan.

The daughter of a Scotch-Irish pioneer in western Pennsylvania, Margaret Cochran Corbin was the "first woman to take a soldier's part" in the American Revolution. When her husband, John Corbin, enlisted in the Pennsylvania Artillery, she accompanied him into battle, serving, most likely, as cook, nurse, and laundress for the men. At the battle of Fort Washington on Manhattan Island in 1776, Margaret took her husband's place after he was struck down by attacking Hessians. She fought with "distinguished bravery" until she in turn was hit by grapeshot that tore away one of her arms.

Following her release from the army, she was awarded a sergeant's half pension as well as a ration per day and became the only woman in the Invalid Regiment, then stationed at West Point. A monument marks her grave in the West Point Cemetery near the Old Cadet Chapel.

¶ **Mathew Brady Studio Site,** Broadway and Fulton Street.

A plaque marks the site of the photographic studio which *Mathew Brady established near here in 1842. He and his assistants later seared the nation's conscience with photographs of the Civil War that belied earlier romantic notions about war.

❡ Matthew C. Perry House, Quarters A, U.S. Naval Facility, Brooklyn.

This frame clapboard building was the residence of *Matthew C. Perry while he served as commander of the New York Navy Yard from 1841 to 1843. Perry was famous for opening up Japan to American trade in the mid 1840s.

❡ McSorley's Old Ale House, 15 East 7th Street.

Founded by *John McSorley in 1854, this famous New York watering hole has been immortalized in art (*A Mug of Ale at McSorley's* by John Sloan, 1913) and literature (*McSorley's Wonderful Saloon* by Joseph Mitchell).

❡ Metropolitan Museum of Art, 5th Avenue and 82nd Street.

The museum's vast collection includes *The Last Moments of John Brown* and *Jerusalem the Golden,* among the best-known works of the Irish-born painter Thomas Hovenden. The former painting is an accurate depiction of the famous abolitionist's death, as described in the second stanza of "Brown of Ossawatomie" by John Greenleaf Whittier:

John Brown of Ossawatomie, they led him out to die;
And lo! a poor slave-mother with her little child press nigh.
Then the bold, blue eye grew tender, and the old harsh face
grew mild,
As he stooped between the jeering ranks and kissed the
negro's child.

Hovenden was born in County Cork in 1840 but was orphaned at the age of six. As a teenager he served an apprenticeship to a carver and gilder, who expressed his confidence in the boy's talent by sending him to the Cork School of Design. He later studied at the National Academy of Design in New York and then at the Ecole des Beaux-Arts in Paris.

Hovenden's first painting of note was a scene from the French Revolution, depicting the efforts of a family to protect itself during the Reign of Terror by casting bullets and sharpening its swords. Known as *Breton Interior of 1793,* this work established Hovenden's reputation with a European audience. Meanwhile, his numerous depictions of African-American life betrayed an interest in that suffering race. He met an untimely death at the age of fifty-five, however, when he was killed while unsuccessfully trying to save a young girl from an oncoming railroad.

§ Open Sunday and Tuesday-Thursday 9:30-5:15, Friday-Saturday 9:30-8:45. Closed January 1, Thanksgiving, and December 25. Fee.

Phone: 212-535-7710.

¶ Michael Corcoran Burial Site, Calvary Cemetery, Laurel Hill Boulevard, Woodside.

A new headstone erected in 1989 by the Sligo Mens' Association marks the grave of Michael Corcoran, the commander of the "Fighting 69th" New York State Militia, one of the three units which initially formed the famed Irish Brigade.

The headstone is inscribed as follows: "In Memory of Brigadier General Michael Corcoran, Irish Patriot, American Soldier, Catholic Citizen. Born at Carrowkeel, Sligo, Ireland, Sept. 21, 1827. Col. 69th N.Y. State Militia 1859-1861. Commanding the Regiment in Volunteer Service of U.S. Organizer of Corcoran's Legion N.Y. Volunteers. Died in the Service of the U.S. Dec. 22, 1863." Corcoran's wife, Elizabeth, is also buried here.

¶ Michael Hogan Tablet, Grace Church, 10th Street and Broadway, Lower Manhattan.

A memorial plaque inside the church honors Michael Hogan, an Irish sea captain, merchant, and philanthropist: "Sacred to the Memory of Michael Hogan. During many years a resident of this City. Born at Stone-Hall in the County of Clare, Ireland, September 29, A.D. 1766. In early manhood a bold and successful navigator and discoverer, in seas then almost unknown; In mature age, a prosperous merchant; The decline of life was not unmarked by vicissitudes of fortune; But prosperity did not elate, nor could adversity subdue his firm and constant spirit. Each quarter of the Globe, bore witness to his enterprise, and its success. Regretted by his friends, respected by his enemies, a life of stainless integrity closed at the City of Washington, March 26, A.D. 1833, Aetatis 67." Claremont Avenue in Upper Manhattan is named for his mansion house.

¶ Michael J. Quill Corner, on the southeast corner of Broadway and West 240th Street, the Bronx.

Dedicated in 1992, this memorial honors the longtime president of the Transport Workers Union.

Born in County Kerry, Ireland, in 1905, Quill came from a family that actively supported the Irish Republican Army during the 1916 Irish Rebellion and the civil war that followed. As a youngster he was a member of *Fianna Eireann*, the Republican Boy Scout movement, and by age fifteen had joined the I.R.A.

In 1933 Quill immigrated to New York City, where he was one of a number of former I.R.A. members interested in organizing the transit workers there. Quill was a founder of the Transport Workers Union and served as its president for more than thirty years. By 1945 the union numbered 45,000 members in New York, Philadelphia, Chicago, and Brooklyn. Twenty years later it counted 135,000 among its ranks.

Quill usually supported the position of the Communist Party on political and labor-related issues and was a leader in some Communist-led organizations. In 1948, however, he broke with the party and thereafter purged the T.W.U.'s leadership of Communists. The longtime labor leader died in 1966, soon after calling a general strike against the New York City transit system, a move which paralyzed the city.

¶ Moylan Place, 125th Street, between Broadway and Amsterdam Avenue, Upper Manhattan.

This square was named for Stephen Moylan, a native of Cork, Ireland, and aide-de-camp to General George Washington during the American Revolution.

¶ Old St. Patrick's Cathedral, 268 Mulberry Street, Lower Manhattan.

Consecrated in 1815, this church was the second in the United States to be dedicated to the patron saint of Ireland. Originally the largest church in the city, it remained the cathedral of the New York archdiocese until 1879, when the new cathedral on Fifth Avenue was completed.

The most historic event which occurred in Old St. Patrick's Cathedral was the final ceremony connected with the conferring of the cardinalate on *Archbishop John McCloskey, the first American Roman Catholic prelate to be so honored. The *New York Times* on April 28, 1875, described the pageantry of the installation ceremony in surprisingly sympathetic detail: "The imposition of the biretta on his Eminence, the newly-made Cardinal, was surrounded with all the elaborate pageantry which the Church of Rome mingles so frequently with its religious ceremonies. Everything that could give to the occasion, pomp, and lustre was rigidly carried out, and the ceremony was the most gorgeous ever connected with the ministrations of the Roman Catholic Church in this country. . . . The gold and scarlet decorations flashed, thurifers swung their censers, and sent up clouds of incense before the Altar, the jeweled mitres and rich vestments of the Bishops and Archbishops gave an additional lustre to the sanctuary, and the grand organ pealed through the cathedral the measures of a jubilant religion."

Earlier during his episcopacy in New York City, McCloskey had taken at least two controversial positions. Although a strong supporter of Irish nationhood, in 1866 he expressed his opposition to the violent tactics of the Fenians and warned New York Catholics against joining or supporting the revolutionary group. Later, while attending the First Vatican Council in Rome, he opposed the council's intention to promulgate the doctrine of papal infallibility. While he intellectually accepted such a doctrine, he believed that its formal definition would be ill-advised, causing a backlash of anti-Catholic sentiment throughout the world. Nevertheless, he voted for the definition in July 1870.

So highly regarded was McCloskey that following his death in 1885 the *New York Sun* editorialized: "His learning, his piety, his humility, his truly Christian zeal, earned for him universal respect which will be to-day manifested as his body is carried to the tomb. The first American cardinal has died at a time when all Christians are ready to honor his memory as that of a man who has done measureless service in the cause of religion, good morals, and humanity . . . . Protestants and Catholics will join in sincerely mourning the first American cardinal as a Christian hero lost."

¶ **Peter Cooper Statue,** Cooper Union Institute, 4th Avenue and 7th Street, Lower Manhattan.

Erected in 1897, this bronze statue by *Augustus Saint-Gaudens honors the famous inventor, manufacturer, and philanthropist who in 1859 opened an institute to provide the working people of the city with free instruction in the practical arts and sciences.

¶ **Police Academy Museum,** 235 East 20th Street, Lower Manhattan.

This museum is of interest to Hibernophiles because of its exhibits about "New York's finest." Many members of the force were Irish born, especially prior to 1859, when American citizenship became a prerequisite for the job.

As early as 1815 the city had a police marshal named *John McManus, while as late as 1888 the Irish constituted 28 percent of the city's police force even though that ethnic group comprised only 16 percent of the population. Even in 1933, 36 percent of the force was either native Irish or Irish American. Thomas Byrnes, one native-Irish officer, became nationally known for his successful investigations and for his work *Professional Criminals of America*. In 1918 Irish-born Ellen O'Grady became the country's first female deputy commissioner of police.

§ Open Monday-Friday 9-2. Closed holidays. Advisable to call ahead. ID required. Fee. Phone: 212-477-9753.

¶ **Prospect Park,** between Prospect Park West & Prospect Park Southwest and Parkside & Flatbush avenues, Brooklyn.

Three notable monuments associated with Irish Americans are located in the Grand Army Plaza:

• Erected in 1965, the John F. Kennedy Memorial consists of a bronze bust of the slain president on a white marble stele.

• The bronze equestrian statue of William T. Sherman was designed by *Augustus Saint-Gaudens. A figure of Victory waving an olive branch walks before the Union general, who cut a swath of destruction through Georgia during the Civil War. At its unveiling the statue was covered with gold leaf. Saint-Gaudens exhibited a full-size plaster model of this work at the 1900 Paris Exposition and at the Buffalo Pan-American Exposition.

• The life-size equestrian reliefs of Abraham Lincoln and *Ulysses S. Grant on the Soldiers' and Sailors' Memorial Arch are the work of *William O'Donovan. To ensure the historical accuracy of his reliefs, the artist spent weeks searching for a model horse as similar to Grant's stead as possible.

¶ **Provincetown Playhouse,** 133 MacDougal Street, Greenwich Village.

This former stable is where *Eugene O'Neill began his New York stage career, when in 1917 he and others established this theater and presented many of his plays during the following decade.

¶ **Richmondtown Restoration,** east of I-278 via Richmond Road/Clove Road exit to 441 Clarke Avenue, Staten Island.

Richmondtown Restoration is a 100-acre village that recreates 300 years of Staten Island history. On the property is the Kruser-Finlay House, purchased in 1875 by *Patrick Finlay and his wife, Catherine. Succeeding members of the family lived here until Mary Finlay donated it to the city of New York.

§ Museum open July and August, Wednesday-Friday 10-5, Saturday and Sunday 1-5; September-December 31, Wednesday-Sunday 1-5; April-June 30, Wednesday-Friday and Sunday 1-5; rest of the year, Wednesday-Friday 1-5. Closed January 1, Thanksgiving, and December 25. Fee. Phone: 718-351-1611.

¶ **Robert F. Kennedy Bust,** in a park to the west of Cadman Plaza, Brooklyn.

¶ **St. James Church,** 23 Oliver Street, Lower Manhattan.

Built in the 1820s to serve the Irish in the slums of the Five Points area, this church was the scene of the gathering which created the Ancient Order of Hibernians in America.

The A.O.H. was founded in 1836 to protect the Irish and their churches from anti-immigrant violence in New York City. Later during its history the organization strove to uphold the reputation of Irishmen from the "nefarious custom of criminals, pugilists, and the abandoned and submerged tenth of society adopting Irish names."

The A.O.H. also successfully fought the stereotype of the Irishman almost universally found in the American theater at the time. That image was described by Maurice Bourgeois in 1913: "The stage Irishman habitually bears the general name of Pat, Paddy, or Teague. He has an atrocious Irish brogue, perpetual jokes, blunder and bulls in speaking, and never fails to utter, by way of Hibernian seasoning, some wild screech, or oath of Gaelic origin, at every third word. . . . His hair is of a fiery red, he is rosy-cheeked, massive, and whiskey-loving. His face is one of simian bestiality, with an expression of diabolical archness written all over it. He wears a tall hat, with a clay pipe stuck in his face, an open collar shirt, a three-caped coat, kneebreeches, worsted stockings, and cockaded shoes. In his right hand he brandishes a stout blackthorn or sprig of shillelagh, and threatens to belabor therewith the daring person who will tread on the tail of his coat. For his main characteristics . . . are his swagger, his boisterousness, and his pugnacity. He is always ready with a challenge, always anxious to back a quarrel, and peerless for cracking skulls at Donnybrook Fair."

¶ The attendance of *Alfred E. Smith at St. James Elementary School across the street is commemorated by a plaque on the school door.

Smith was generally an indifferent student and preferred to perform in timely comedies and melodramas in the St. James parish hall. He was also known for his victories in speech contests and won a medal for elocution. (One of his favorite poems to recite was "Cohen on the Telephone.")

¶ **St. Malachy's,** 239 West 49th Street. Midtown Manhattan.

Located in the city's theater district, this famous chapel caters to actors and theatergoers alike. The chapel was named for a twelfth-century Irish monk who served as primate of Armagh in County Down. While on a papal mission to France, Malachy died at Clairvaux, with St. Bernard at his side.

§ Phone: 212-489-1340.

¶ **St. Patrick's Cathedral,** 5th Avenue and 50th Street.

Now in the heart of Manhattan, St. Patrick's was originally dismissed as "Hughes' Folly" when it was begun by *Archbishop John Hughes on a site which critics said was too far out in the country. In 1858, when Hughes kicked off a fund-raising campaign by asking for

100 contributions of $1,000 each, he received 103 such gifts. This response allowed him to lay the cornerstone of a church which he hoped would be "worthy of God, worthy of the Catholic religion, and an honor to this great city." Dedicated in 1879, the new marble Gothic Revival cathedral took up a full city block, could seat 2,500 worshippers, and had cost $1.9 million. The church's spires and the Lady Chapel inside were added by *Archbishop Michael Corrigan.

The window over the entrance to the south transept of the church depicts eighteen scenes from the life of St. Patrick. Another window celebrating Ireland's principal patron saint is on the west wall.

Hughes and Corrigan are buried in the church, as are fellow Irish-American archbishops John Farley, Patrick Hayes, John McCloskey, Francis Spellman, and Terence Cooke.

§ Open daily 6:30 a.m.-8:45 p.m. Phone: 212-753-2261.

¶ **St. Paul's Episcopal Chapel,** Broadway and Fulton Street, Lower Manhattan.

Within the precincts of Manhattan's oldest house of worship are the graves of native-born Irishmen Richard Montgomery and Thomas Addis Emmet. An obelisk in the churchyard marks the latter's grave, while a second monument honors William MacNeven, a fellow Irishman and, like Emmet, a political exile.

• Richard Montgomery was born in County Donegal in 1737, the son of an Anglo-Irish father who represented Lifford in the Irish Parliament. After enlisting in the British army, the younger Montgomery served under Wolfe at the capture of Quebec in 1759. Although he sailed home after the French and Indian War, he returned to America in 1772, purchased a small estate along the Hudson River, and married into the family of Robert Livingston.

At the outbreak of the Revolution, Montgomery sided with the patriots and was appointed brigadier general, accepting *Vox Populi* as *Vox Dei*: "The will of an oppressed people, compelled to choose between liberty and slavery, must be obeyed." Subsequently named America's first Irish general, he headed the American expeditionary force into Canada, taking Montreal on November 12, 1775, but failing in an attempted assault on Quebec on December 31. Montgomery died during the unsuccessful attempt and was denied "the poor courtesy of a coffin" by the British commander.

At the beginning of the new year, the Continental Congress ordered that a monument – the first in America to an Irishman – be erected in St. Paul's Church in memory of the fallen officer. In 1818 Montgomery's wife succeeded in obtaining possession of his remains, which were accordingly exhumed at Quebec and reburied within St. Paul's.

• Thomas Addis Emmet was born in Cork in 1764 and followed

careers in both medicine and the law. After graduating from Trinity College in Dublin, he earned a doctoral degree in medicine from the University of Edinburgh and returned to the Irish capital to practice. When his brother Robert, a member of the Irish bar, was executed by the British for his part in an abortive uprising in Dublin, however, the young doctor took up the study of law.

After achieving considerable renown as a lawyer, Emmet increasingly became involved with political issues. His legal defense of a member of the United Irishmen on a charge of treason became a *cause célèbre*, all the more so when Emmet took the society's oath at the end of an impassioned speech before the court. A government informer described Emmet as "the most dangerous man in Ireland, from the standpoint of zeal, bearing, power of speech, and ability." After becoming a member of the United Irishmen's executive committee, Emmet was arrested as a conspirator in 1798 and was subsequently jailed in a number of prisons. Finally released on condition that he leave the Empire, he and his family progressed through Europe before landing in New York City in 1804.

Once in New York, Emmet was granted the right to practice law, despite strong opposition from Federalist judges and lawyers, who considered him and other refugees as "wild Irishmen come to stir up sedition." His first appearance at the New York bar was as counsel for a society that sought the freedom of African-American slaves. In 1812 he was appointed attorney general of New York, and three years later he argued the first of several cases before the U.S. Supreme Court. The most famous – *Gibbons v. Ogden* – found him matched against Daniel Webster, who later graciously remarked that his opponent had brought to America the erudition and eloquence of the Irish bar. The political *émigré* suffered a stroke while engaged in the trial of a case involving Snug Harbor, a home for retired sailors. Emmet's admirers were quick to point out that his first speech at the American bar had been in defense of a slave and that his last effort in a court of law had been on behalf of a charitable institution.

In 1832 Emmet's "sympathizing countrymen" erected the monument which stands in St. Paul's churchyard. One side of the thirty-foot obelisk is inscribed with a short tribute in Gaelic. The English translation reads: "He contemplated invaluable benefits for the land of his birth; he gave *eclat* to the land of his death; and received in return her love and admiration." On the side of the monument facing Broadway is a bas-relief medallion of Emmet, below which is an inscription in English, partially quoted here: "In memory of THOMAS ADDIS EMMET who exemplified in his conduct, and adorned by his integrity, the policy and principles of the United Irishmen – 'To forward a brotherhood of affection, a community of rights, an identity of interests, and a union of power among Irishmen of every religious persuasion, as the only means of Ireland's chief good, an impartial and adequate representation in an Irish Parliament.' For this, (Mysterious fate of virtue!), exiled from his native land. In America, the land of freedom, he found a second country, which paid his love by reverencing his genius. . . ." Below this inscription is an American eagle supported by two hands – one Irish and the other American – clasped and crossing over an unstrung Irish harp. The lengthy inscription is repeated in Latin on a third side of the obelisk.

• A contemporary of Emmet's, William MacNeven was born in County Galway of a family whose ancestors had been expelled by Cromwell from their landed estates in Ulster and had been forced to settle in Connaught. Because Catholics in Ireland still suffered under educational disabilities which had not applied to the Protestant Emmet, for example, the young MacNeven moved to the Continent to study medicine at the universities of Prague and Vienna.

After returning to Dublin to begin a career in medicine, MacNeven became involved in dangerous political activities. His work as a member of the United Irishmen led to imprisonment before his release in 1802 under sentence of banishment. While in France, the Irish exile still fostered unrealistic hopes of support from Napoleon in a projected invasion of Ireland. He served in the Irish Brigade of the French army for two years before embarking for New York City, where he arrived on July 4, 1805.

From the first, MacNeven threw himself into his medical practice. After giving a series of clinical lectures at the New York Hospital, he was elected professor of obstetrics in the College of Physicians and Surgeons. During his academic tenure he published a number of scientific studies, one of them on the atomic theory of chemistry. For a time he was coeditor of the *New York Medical and Philosophical Journal and Review* and was elected to the American Philosophical Society in 1823. He subsequently established the forerunner of Rutgers Medical School.

Despite his success in America, MacNeven never wavered in his concern for Ireland and her people. To help newly arrived immigrants, he wrote and published a pamphlet with pertinent advice and joined with Thomas Emmet in establishing a free employment agency. He also created an organization called the Friends of Ireland, with which he sought American support for Catholic Emancipation in his homeland.

As Emmet had supported efforts to get Congress to sell public lands in Illinois to Irish immigrants, so MacNeven promoted Texas as a place where his "poor Irish countrymen . . . would at once possess a quantum of ground, power, and wealth, that would give them a real home, consideration, and happiness."

§ Open daily 8-4. Phone: 212-602-0800.

¶ **St. Peter's Church,** Barclay and Church Streets, Lower Manhattan.

Although the present church dates from 1836, it replaced an earlier structure built in 1786, the year after the first Roman Catholic congregation in New York City was incorporated.

One of the earliest members and benefactors of St. Peter's parish was Dominick Lynch, a successful business entrepreneur who had immigrated to America from Galway, Ireland, in 1785. He contributed generously to the construction of the church and even sough financial support for the project from his relatives in Galway. He was also one of the five signers of the famous address to George Washington in 1790 in which he congratulated the newly inaugurated president on behalf of the Catholics of the nation. Lynch and his wife – whom he had married in Dublin before coming to New York – had thirteen children. He died in 1825 and is buried in the family vault at St. Peter's.

• One of the memorials in St. Peter's Church is a tablet commemorating the life and career of *Governor Thomas Dongan. (See Albany, New York.)

• In 1988 a plaque in honor of *Father John Drumgoole was placed on the rectory of St. Peter's Church. Born in Abbeylara, County Longford, Ireland, in 1816, the immigrant priest was known as the "Shepherd of the Homeless Newsboys." The memorial tablet is inscribed with a summary of the priest's career: "In 1871 Father Drumgoole became the resident chaplain of the Saint Vincent de Paul Newsboys' Home at 53 Warren Street near Printing House Square, the location of New York City's great newspapers. In 1881 the Mission of the Immaculate Virgin was established for homeless children on Lafayette Street. He founded Mount Loretto on Staten Island in 1852 and it became the largest child caring institution in the United States. It stands today as a monument to Father Drumgoole."

¶ **St. Raymond's Cemetery,** Tremont Avenue, between Waterbury Street and Bruckner Expressway, the Bronx. Make inquiries at Lafayette Street and Randall Road.

Two famous Irish Americans are buried here: "Typhoid Mary" Mallon and Father Francis Duffy, the chaplain of the "Fighting 69th" Regiment.

• Mary Mallon was the first known carrier of typhoid fever in the United States. Born in Ireland about 1868, she worked as a cook after coming to New York and was linked to at least six outbreaks of typhoid fever in the state. The first episode occurred in 1904, when the fever was traced to a house in Oyster Bay in which she had been a cook. Fleeing from the authorities, she was not traced until three years later, when she was found in the kitchen of a Park Avenue home. When it was proved that she was a typhoid carrier – "a human culture tube," according to one physician – she was committed to a hospital on North Brother Island.

Although Mallon was released in 1910 on condition that she never accept a job handling food again, four years later she was found working at a sanitarium in New Jersey when an epidemic broke out there. Eluding authorities once again, she was employed at a maternity hospital when twenty-five of its employees were stricken with typhoid. In 1915 she was permanently committed to a hospital, where she remained until her death in 1938. In all, she infected fifty-three people, three of whom died.

• [See Father Duffey Statue and Square in New York City.]

℥ Shrine of Mother Elizabeth Ann Seton, 7 State Street, Lower Manhattan.

Originally designed in the early nineteenth century as a private residence, this Federal-style mansion was later purchased by Charlotte Grace O'Brien, an Irish immigrant, who operated it as a settlement house for Irish immigrant girls in the 1880s. Known then as the Mission of Our Lady of the Rosary, it today serves as a shrine to Mother Seton, the first American-born canonized saint of the Catholic Church. (Mother Seton, regrettably, was not Irish.)

℥ Songwriters' Hall of Fame, 1 Times Square.

In addition to the well-known Irish-American songwriters George M. Cohan and Stephen Collins Foster, the Songwriters' Hall of Fame includes such lesser known men of Irish heritage as Patrick Gilmore and Chauncey Olcott.

• Born in County Galway, Ireland, Patrick Sarsfield Gilmore immigrated to Canada in 1848 with a military band but soon moved to Boston. There he opened a music store and organized Gilmore's Boston Band. At the outbreak of the Civil War, he and his musicians joined the Union army. While in New Orleans in 1864, he orchestrated a music festival of several massed bands and introduced the use of cannon fire to the musical score. During the war he composed several songs reflecting the fratricidal conflict: "Freedom on the Old Plantation," "Good News from Home," "The Spirit of the North," and "When Johnny

Comes Marching Home."

In 1869 Gilmore presented the first of his gargantuan concert-festivals. To accommodate a chorus of 10,000 people, an orchestra of 1,000, six bands, and an audience commensurately large, the organizers of the five-day National Peace Jubilee in Boston constructed a 50,000-seat auditorium. This triumph was followed three years later by his World Peace Jubilee, also in Boston, to which he attracted international musicians (including Johann Strauss), an orchestra of 2,000, and a chorus ten times as large. During a performance of Verdi's "Anvil Chorus," 100 Boston firemen provided accompaniment on actual anvils. After this second *tour de force*, Gilmore and his band toured the United States, Canada, and Europe. He also composed *Columbia*, a choral work which he hoped would become a new national anthem.

• Chauncey Olcott was born of Irish parents in Buffalo, New York, in 1860 and early became associated with traveling companies of entertainers and minstrel shows. While in London, he obtained an Irish romantic role in a light opera, a break that inspired him to specialize in that kind of role. Once returned to America, he began a career in a succession of sentimental Irish comedies, including *The Irish Artist* (for which he wrote both the words and the music), *Edmund Burke*, and *The Minstrel of Clare*. He introduced American audiences to "Mother Machree" and "When Irish Eyes Are Smiling" (both of which he coauthored) and "My Wild Irish Rose," a composition of his own which appeared in *Romance of Athlone*. Two of his lesser-known airs are "Sweet Iniscara" and "Kate O'Donohue."

§ Open Monday-Saturday 11-3. Phone: 212-221-1252.

¶ **Sullivan Street,** Greenwich Village.

This street was named for *General John Sullivan, one of George Washington's most famous officers during the Revolutionary War.

¶ **Theodore Roosevelt Birthplace National Historic Site,** 28 East 20th Street, Lower Manhattan.

Built in 1922, this four-story building is a replica of the house in which Theodore Roosevelt was born in 1858 and lived until age fifteen. Five rooms in the house have been refurnished with their original contents, while Roosevelt memorabilia are on display in the museum rooms. The most impressive piece of art work in the house is an equestrian statue of Roosevelt as a Rough Rider.

Assertions of Roosevelt's Irish ancestry rest partially upon his descent from John Barnwell, who came to America from County Meath, Ireland, in 1701. On his maternal side Roosevelt was descended from John Dunwoody, who emigrated from Londonderry, northern Ireland, in 1730 and settled in Chester County, Pennsylvania, before moving with his family to Georgia.

During Roosevelt's first term in the New York Assembly, he recorded his unflattering estimation of his Irish colleagues on a legislative committee: "The Chairman is an Irishman named Murphy, . . . a Fenian; he is a tall, stout man with a swollen, red face, a black moustache . . . and has had a long experience in politics – so that to undoubted pluck and a certain knowledge of parliamentary forms he adds a great deal of stupidity and a decided looseness of ideas as regards the 8th Commandment. Next comes John Shanley of Brooklyn, an Irishman, but born in America; much shrewder than Murphy and easier to get along with, being more Americanized, but fully as dishonest; . . . a Tammany Hall gentleman named McManus, a huge, fleshy, unutterably course and low brute who was formerly a prize fighter, at present keeps a low, drinking and dancing saloon, and is more than suspected of having begun life as a pickpocket."

Following his election to the presidency in 1904, however, Roosevelt was much more flattering in his estimation of the Irish electorate: "One of the things I am most pleased with in the recent election is that while I got, I think, a greater proportion of the Americans of Irish birth or parentage and of the Catholic religion than any previous Republican candidate, I got this proportion purely because they knew I felt in sympathy with them and in touch with them, and they and I had the same ideals and principles, and not by any demagogic appeals about creed or race, or by any demagogic attack upon England."

§ Open Wednesday-Sunday 9-5. Closed major holidays. Fee. Phone: 212-260-1616.

¶ **Theodore Roosevelt Memorial,** American Museum of Natural History, Central Park West, Midtown Manhattan.

This sixteen-foot bronze group of *Theodore Roosevelt with an Indian is one of the largest equestrian statues in the world. The figures on either side of the horse represent Africa and America. This Native American was probably the model for the profile on the Indian-head nickel.

¶ **Trinity Church,** Broadway at Wall Street, Lower Manhattan.

Although the congregation at this church has always been of the Anglican or Episcopal denomination, during the colonial period it was attended by many Irish Catholics because no Catholic church existed in the city until 1786. One such Irish Catholic parishioner was John Leary, who both during and after the Revolution kept a livery stable on Leary (now Cortland) Street. Known as "the jockey of the day," he wrote an article on horse breeding which appeared in the *New York Mercury* under the byline "a lover of the turf." Although Leary seems to have attended Trinity Church regularly, once a year he journeyed to Philadelphia to attend mass at a Catholic church there.

Trinity churchyard contains the graves of many Irish and Irish Americans, both the famous and the less well known. Among them are the following five:

• The first Irish person to be buried here was Catherine O'Brien, the wife of the dissolute New York governor Edward Hyde, Viscount Cornbury. O'Brien, who was born in County Clare in 1673, married Cornbury at age fifteen and accompanied him to New York when he was appointed governor of that colony in 1701. When she attended an Indian council in Albany with her husband, one of the River Indians presented her with an otter skin as a token of the tribe's high regard for her. In 1839, 133 years after her death, her coffin was discovered in the foundations of the church.

• Christopher Colles, an engineer and a gunnery instructor in the American army during the Revolution, first proposed the idea of building a canal to join the Hudson River to the Great Lakes. (The notion was taken up and successfully promoted as the Erie Canal by *DeWitt Clinton.) Colles had earlier suggested that New York City abandon its dependence on springs and wells by building a system of reservoirs and piping throughout the city. He also conceived and developed the first semaphoric telegraph system for the United States and was the author of numerous scientific essays and pamphlets.

• Robert Fulton, the famous inventor and advocate of steam navigation, is honored with an indoor memorial erected in 1901 by the American Society of Mechanical Engineers. Fulton's American ancestor probably came from Kilkenny, Ireland, and by 1735 had settled in Lancaster, Pennsylvania. As a youngster Fulton displayed an inventive turn of mind, devising a rocket and a hand-powered paddle wheel. He later developed a "plunging boat" or submarine, which he actually demonstrated to the French government as a way to destroy British warships. With Fulton himself aboard, the underwater device reached a depth of twenty-five feet and remained submerged for four and a half hours.

Fulton is more renowned for his efforts to promote the steamboat, however. After building and successfully operating a prototype in France in 1802, he launched the *Clermont* in New York City five years later. The ship, 133 feet long and 18 wide, was powered by a steam engine that turned 15-foot side paddle wheels. The vessel's 150-mile cruise up the Hudson River in thirty-three hours prompted Fulton to say that "The power of propelling boats by steam is now fully proved." In partnership with Robert Livingston, Fulton subsequently demonstrated the economic viability of steam navigation.

• Hercules Mulligan, the famous spy for General George Washington, was a vestryman of Trinity Church from 1784 to 1787. After his death in 1825, he was buried here in the family vault of his wife, Elizabeth Sanders.

• The inscription on one of the tombstones in the churchyard memorializes one of the city's lesser known Irish: "James Woods / a native of Ireland / who died June 3d 1801 aged 46 years / Unseen to Mankind's view / An exile of Old Erin's true / His principles was [sic] just and good / And for his country's freedom stood."

§ Open Monday-Friday 8-6, Saturday and Sunday 8-4. Phone: 212-602-0800. Check times for museum.

⌘ Union Square, Broadway and 14th Street, Lower Manhattan.

In 1865 the Fenians held a convention in Philadelphia to draft a constitution creating an Irish Republic and providing for a congress and a president. The newly elected president established an Irish government in exile at the Fenians' headquarters in Union Square. Both the American flag and the Fenian flag – the latter emblazoned with a harp and a sunburst – flew from the building.

At the center of Union Square is the Independence Flagstaff, erected in 1926 as a memorial to Tammany Hall boss *Charles Murphy. The cost of the flagpole was defrayed from the $80,000 which the Tammany machine collected during the sesquicentennial of the signing of the Declaration of Independence. Although Tammany Hall dominated the political life of the city in the nineteenth century, it reached the height of its influence under Murphy in the next. The son of Irish immigrants, Murphy was the machine's absolute boss from 1902 to 1924 and was "responsible" for electing three mayors of the city and two governors of the state. Although he welcomed to Tammany Hall anyone who sought his help, he remained publicly aloof and generally unknown to all but his associates, for he never made speeches or gave interviews and, except for an early minor appointment, never held or sought political office.

⌘ The Roundabout Theater, northeast of Union Square, at 100 East 17th Street, was formerly the headquarters of the Tammany Society.

⌘ United Nations Plaza, 1st Avenue, between 42nd and 48th streets.

Three structures along 44th Street were designed between 1976 and 1987 by the architectural firm of *Kevin Roche, John Dinkeloo & Associates: One United Nations Plaza, a thirty-nine-story building which houses offices and hotel accommodations for U.N. personnel and delegates; Two United Nations Plaza, a companion glass and metal structure; and the UNICEF Building.

Other projects in New York City by Roche, Dinkeloo & Associates are the Ford Foundation Building, the Trans World Airlines Terminal at Kennedy International Airport, the CBS Headquarters Building, one of the theaters at the Lincoln Center for the Performing Arts, four wings on the Metropolitan Museum of Art, and the redesigned Central Park Zoo.

¶ **U.S. Customs House,** opposite Bowling Green.
Completed in 1907 at a cost of $7 million, this massive structure is decorated with numerous pieces of statuary. The largest are four groups representing Africa, America, Asia, and Europe. The façade is adorned with a series of statues that stand for the major commercial centers of world history: England, France, Germany, Denmark, Holland, Portugal, Venice, Spain, Genoa, Phoenicia, Greece, and Rome. The art work representing Holland and Portugal was done by *Augustus Saint-Gaudens.

¶ **Wave Hill,** 675 West 252nd Street, Upper Manhattan.
Now a public garden and a cultural center overlooking the Hudson River, Wave Hill was the summer home of young *Theodore Roosevelt, whose family rented the Georgian house when he was twelve and thirteen years old. Mark Twain, Arturo Toscanini, and Queen Mother Elizabeth were among the other famous residents or guests who stayed at the estate.
§ Open Tuesday-Sunday 9-4:30. Fee. Phone: 718-549-2055.

¶ **Woodlawn Cemetery,** Webster Avenue at East 233rd Street, the Bronx.
Established in 1863, this cemetery contains the graves of more than 250,000 people, including the following Irish or Irish Americans:
• Nellie Bly, the famous journalist who traversed the world in fewer than eighty days. Born Elizabeth Cochrane in 1865, she staked out a journalistic career dedicated to exposing evils in society. (She probably used the byline "Nellie Bly" because of the reference to cleaning out a kitchen in the Stephen Foster song of the same name.) She subsequently wrote stories for the *Pittsburgh Dispatch* about working girls and the conditions they endured in the slums and the sweatshops. Her later exposé of poverty and political corruption in Mexico resulted in her expulsion from that country.
After persuading Joseph Pulitzer of the *New York World* to let her write a story based on personal experience in the city's mental asylum, she prepared herself for living among the insane by perfecting self-induced trances. So convincing were her vegetative states that she was committed to the asylum on Blackwell's Island, where four doctors agreed that she suffered from hysteria. While there, she recorded the brutal treatment and the terrible food which the patients had to en-

dure. She herself was denied water until her throat was so parched that she could hardly talk. As the result of a grand jury investigation into her charges, the city earmarked $13 million to improve the Blackwell facility. On another occasion she committed theft in order to be arrested and jailed, the better to expose the verbal abuse and filthy conditions which women suffered in prison. The city subsequently began to provide matrons for the female prisoners.

Nellie Bly's most famous exploit was her successful attempt to best the record of Jules Verne's fictional Phileas Fogg. She set out from Jersey City in mid November 1889, provisioned with what became her trademark wardrobe: an ulster with shoulder cape, a hunting cap, a plaid cloth dress, a knapsack, and a crocodile skin traveling bag. Within a week her ship arrived in Southampton, England, and she was soon on her way to France, where she enjoyed an interview with Jules Verne himself before proceeding to Italy. At Brindisi she boarded an Indian mail steamer and sailed across the Mediterranean and through the Suez Canal to Ismailia. (In Port Said she rode a donkey through the streets of the city and described the Arab encampments there.) From Ismailia she sailed through the Red Sea to Aden before arriving in Colombo, Ceylon, on December 8. Her arrival in India was delayed, however, because the steamship from Calcutta was late. From India she sailed 2,000 miles to Singapore and then to Hong Kong, where she finally abandoned her flannel underwear for tropical muslin. After leaving Hong Kong, she visited Canton (where she picked up a monkey that was her constant companion at all subsequent press conferences) and touched at Yokohama (where her ship was hit by the monsoon). After disembarking in San Francisco on January 21, she proceeded to cross the United States by train – via Kansas City and Chicago – and arrived in New York on January 25. She had traveled a total of 24,899 miles in seventy-two days, six hours, and eleven minutes and had become a world celebrity.

Toys, clothing, games, a race horse, and a Broadway song ("Globe Trotting Nellie Bly") were named in her honor. A popular poster showed her on a tightrope, balancing a parasol, with the world at her feet. Her grave was unmarked until 1978, when the New York Press Club recognized her with an appropriate tombstone.

• Finley Peter Dunne, the Chicago journalist who filled 300 weekly columns with the observations of Martin Dooley, the fictional barkeep who chronicled the Irish neighborhood in which the author grew up. Dunne received national attention with the publication of *Mr. Dooley in Peace and War* and *Mr. Dooley in the Hearts of His Countrymen*.

• Charles Evans Hughes, New York governor, chief justice of the U.S. Supreme Court, presidential candidate, and secretary of state.

• John McCullaugh, the "First Chief of Police of Greater New York." A native of Ireland, he was first assigned as a rookie cop to a district few police would enter – Five Points, an Irish slum notorious for its bars, whorehouses, and gangs. He battled gambling, vice, and the Whyo Gang, leading the effort that finally resulted in the trial and execution of the gang's leader for killing his girlfriend.

• Edward McGlynn, a Catholic priest who was excommunicated for advocating the single-tax theories of Henry George, a social reformer who ran for mayor of New York in 1886 and 1897. One of twelve children born to Irish immigrants from Donegal, McGlynn had actively supported George, even though the reformer's major ideas had been condemned by some of the Catholic clergy as anti-Christian and destructive of the right to private property. After McGlynn openly disagreed on the issue with *Archbishop Michael Corrigan, the priest was stripped of his pastoral duties and ordered to Rome to recant. As a sign of solidarity with McGlynn, 25,000 Irish workers marched in protest, while McGlynn's refusal to travel to Rome resulted in his excommunication. As the situation simmered for the next five years, the recalcitrant priest received support from the *Freeman's Journal*, the *Catholic Herald*, the *Irish World*, and even *Cardinal James Gibbons, who defended McGlynn's right to advocate social reform. Despite McGlynn's eulogy at George's funeral, the rebel priest was reinstated in 1900.

• George McManus, the comic strip artist who struck it rich with "Bringing Up Father." Born in St. Louis, where his father, a native of County Meath, managed the Grand Opera House, McManus as a youngster showed a talent for drawing. One day when he was reprimanded by his teacher for drawing during class time, his father declined to join in the censure and instead showed his son's work to the editor of the *St. Louis Republic*. Immediately hired as a $5-a-week errand boy, McManus was soon employed to draw scenes at "hangings, murders and suicides."

While working for the *New York World* some years later, McManus tried his hand at producing comic strips, all of which, however, were short-lived, although the title of one – "Let George Do It" – entered the language. After being enticed to the *New York American*, McManus developed the husband and wife team that starred in "Bringing Up Father," a strip which became a regular feature of the Hearst paper in 1913. The storyline's appeal centered on the conflict between its antagonists as they dealt with their new circumstances after winning the Irish Sweepstakes. While Maggie, a former washerwoman, followed the allure of high society, her ex-bricklayer husband, Jiggs, continued to prefer the company of his drinking buddies at the local saloon. At its peak the strip was enjoyed by eighty million readers in forty-six countries, appeared in sixteen languages, and earned its creator $100,000 a year in royalties.

• Virginia Fair Vanderbilt, the daughter of *James Fair, one of the "Big Four" Comstock magnates who made their fortune in the Nevada gold and silver mines. She lies buried near her sister, Theresa Fair.

• George M. Cohan, Victor Herbert, and Chauncey Olcott. [See individual entries elsewhere.]

¶ **W. R. Grace Building,** 41 West 42nd Street, Midtown Manhattan.

W. R. Grace & Company was founded in 1865 by William R. Grace, a native of Queenstown, Ireland, who had come to America at the age of fourteen. Much of the Irishman's original fortune was made as the result of commercial agreements with Peru. As an advisor to Peruvian officials, Grace armed and equipped the country's army during the late 1870s and supplied it with munitions during its war with Chile. When the war left Peru $250 million in debt, Grace assumed that debt obligation in exchange for numerous concessions. Among the most lucrative were railroad leases and full ownership of silver mines, guano deposits, and five million acres of land containing oil and mineral deposits. For his exploitation of the country, he was dubbed the "Pirate of Peru."

After obtaining control of a large share of the trade between the United States and South America, Grace opened branches in almost every Latin American country. In Chile he developed power companies, nitrate properties, and cotton and sugar mills. In 1892 he formed the New York-Pacific Steamship Company, the original direct steamship service between New York and the west coast of South America. He also served as president, trustee, or director of numerous financial or commercial enterprises.

Prior to his entry into New York politics, Grace earned recognition for two humanitarian gestures to his native land. In 1880, in response to a campaign by the *New York Herald*, he contributed one quarter of the cargo shipped as famine relief to Ireland. This and a related gesture cost him about $50,000. That same year Grace was elected mayor of New York City, a position to which he was reelected until 1887. During his administration he opposed the Tammany machine and attacked organized vice and patronage. In 1897 he established the Grace Foundation to provide women with skills in dressmaking, stenography, and other practical domestic arts.

OYSTER BAY

℩ Sagamore Hill National Historic Site, 3 miles east, at 20 Sagamore Hill Road.

*Theodore Roosevelt helped design this twenty-three-room Victorian mansion, which became his permanent home from 1885 until his death in 1919. He had planned to name the estate "Leeholm" for his wife (Alice Hathaway Lee), but she died before construction got under way. The property was named for the Indian chief Sagamore Mohannis. While Roosevelt was president, the eighty-three-acre estate served as the summer White House. "At Sagamore," he wrote, " we love a great many things – birds and trees, and books . . . and horses and rifles, and children and hard work and the joy of life."

On exhibit are Roosevelt's hunting trophies, gun collection, art treasures, and various mementos, including a bust of the president by *William Clark Noble.

§ Open daily 9:30-5. Closed January 1, Thanksgiving, and December 25. Fee. Phone: 516-922-4447.

℩ Theodore Roosevelt Bird Sanctuary, 2 miles east on East Main Street, at Cove Neck Road.

The grounds include a museum exhibiting plant and animal life found on Long Island as well as a memorial to *President Theodore Roosevelt, known for his early conservation efforts.

§ Open Monday-Thursday 9-4:30, Friday 9-2, Saturday and Sunday hours vary. Closed January 1, Thanksgiving, and December 25. Phone: 516-922-3200.

℩ President Roosevelt's grave is located in Young Memorial Cemetery, adjacent to the bird sanctuary.

PLATTSBURGH

℩ Thomas Macdonough Memorial, South River Street.

This 135-foot obelisk honors *Thomas Macdonough, the victor of the battle of Plattsburgh in 1814. The monument is decorated with reliefs and the names of four of his ships: *Eagle, Preble, Saratoga,* and *Ticonderoga.*

Tradition maintains that a rooster aboard Macdonough's flagship crowed during most of the battle. The cock's alleged good luck popularized the use of the bird's image on local weather vanes.

Macdonough's victory over the British fleet frustrated Britain's attempt to control the Great Lakes and forced the enemy's army to retreat into Canada. As a result, Great Britain could press no claim upon

American territory at the peace negotiations ending the war.

POUGHKEEPSIE

⚓ Governor Dongan Statue, Dongan Square.
  This monument honors Thomas Dongan, the Irish Catholic propri-
etary governor of New York during the late seventeenth century. (See
Albany, New York.)

PURCHASE

⚓ General Thomas Monument, Purchase College, Andersonhill
Road.
  This granite obelisk in honor of the Revolutionary War general Tho-
mas Thomas was designed by *Andrew O'Connor.

ROCHESTER

⚓ Holy Sepulchre Cemetery, 2461 Lake Avenue.
  Very different monuments mark the graves of two Irish natives
whose obscurity in American history belies their significance:
  • Catherine De Valera Burial Site, Section 12 South, the second row
from the end. The predominant name on the tombstone on this site is
"Wheelwright," the surname of the Englishman whom Catherine
De Valera married sometime after the birth of her son Edward (or
Eamon), the first president of the Irish provisional government.
  Born Catherine Coll in County Limerick in 1879, the future
president's mother came to America at the age of twenty-three. While
employed by a French family in New York, she met a Spaniard by the
name of Vivion De Valera. Although Eamon De Valera later claimed
that his parents were married in New Jersey in 1881, at least one biog-
rapher denies that any marriage took place. According to this thesis,
Vivion De Valera abandoned his wife soon before their son was born in
the Child's Hospital in New York City in 1882. Whatever the case,
Catherine sent the youngster to Ireland when he was almost three years
old. She subsequently married Charles Wheelwright, a livery driver.
  Although Catherine saw her son only occasionally thereafter, she
came to his defense after the British sentenced him to death for his role
in the 1916 Easter Rising. Armed with his birth and baptismal certifi-
cates, she reminded the British that her son was an American citizen.
The British, hoping to persuade the United States to enter the Great
War on its side, prudently refrained from alienating Americans by executing De Valera. The son later visited his mother on his fund-raising
visits to the United States.

• Patrick O'Rorke Burial Site, under a Celtic cross on a small hill. O'Rourke arrived in America in 1837, brought here as a one-year-old infant by his parents, both natives of County Cavan. Although the youngster later won a scholarship to Rochester University, the school's association with a Protestant sect drew his mother's disapproval and caused him to decline the stipend. The young man was subsequently appointed to the U.S. Military Academy and was graduated at the top of his class – almost literally at the outbreak of the Civil War. After seeing action in several early battles, O'Rorke was named colonel of the 140th New York, although he was only twenty-six years of age. During the battle of Gettysburg, the Irishman initially led his command up Little Round Top, but almost immediately he was shot in the neck and died. Despite his death, his men repulsed the enemy charge and captured the summit.

¶ **Patrick O'Rourke Portrait Bust,** in the High Falls development in the Brown's Race Historic District, between State and Platt streets.
    This bust of *Colonel Patrick O'Rourke was unveiled in 1992. It is flanked by two large panels summarizing events in his life.
    § Phone: 716-325-2030.

ROME

Originally known as Lynchville, this area was settled by Dominick Lynch, whom George Washington called "the handsome Irishman." By 1786 Lynch had purchased almost 2,400 acres at Fort Stanwix, subdivided the property into village lots, and founded a settlement to which he gave his family name. The town's Dominick Street and Lynch Street were named for its founder, whose children are remembered in Depeyster, James, Jane, Jasper, and Louisa streets.

¶ **Erie Canal Village,** 3 miles west on State 49.
    This restored 1840 community offers insights into the way of life which many Irish workers on the Erie Canal experienced. The village includes a train station, a blacksmith shop, a hotel, and a settler's cabin. The visitor center presents an audiovisual program, and a thirty-minute mule-drawn packet ride along the canal is available.
    § Open mid May-October 31, daily 10-5. Fee. Phone: 315-337-3999.

SARATOGA NATIONAL HISTORIC PARK

This park commemorates the American victory over British general John Burgoyne in two battles fought in this area in September and October 1777.

❡ The Fraser Monument marks the spot where British general Simon Fraser fell wounded on October 7, 1777, a victim of Irish-American sharpshooter Timothy Murphy. Murphy's direct hit and Fraser's death the following morning contributed to the American victory.

❡ The Hibernian Monument in the Bemis Heights area honors the heroism of the soldiers of Irish descent who fought and died here for the American cause. The monument, which was erected in 1913 by the Ancient Order of Hibernians of Saratoga County, reads: "To the memory of Timothy Murphy, celebrated marksman of Col. Morgan's Rifle Corps whose unerring aim turned the tide of battle by the death of the British general Frazer on October 7, 1777, thereby adding to the world's history one of its decisive battles. In this monument is commemorated the heroic deeds of hundreds of other soldiers of Irish blood who laid down their lives on this bloody field that the union of states might be triumphant."

Born in 1751 to Irish immigrant parents living in New Jersey, Murphy had grown to manhood on the frontier of Pennsylvania's Wyoming Valley. Although unable to read and write, he was a legendary marksman during the Revolutionary War and earned the nicknamed "Sure-shot Tim." In July 1777 he joined Colonel Daniel Morgan's elite Rifle Corps. During the fighting at Saratoga the following October, Morgan entrusted Murphy and a few other sharpshooters with a spe-

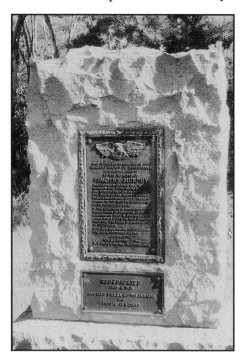

The Timothy Murphy Hibernian Monument.

cial mission: "That gallant officer is General Fraser[.] I admire and honor him but it is necessary he should die[;] victory for the enemy depends on him. Take your station in that clump of bushes and do your duty." After setting his rifle in the fork of a tree, Murphy took aim at his target. Although two bullets missed their mark (hitting Fraser's horse instead), the third struck the general, who was removed from the field and died the next morning. Murphy is also said to have been responsible for mortally shooting Sir Francis Carr Clerke, General Burgoyne's aide-de-camp.

Murphy's marksmanship and its geopolitical repercussions are commemorated in a poem which its author, Joseph Clarke, read at the battle site on July 26, 1913:

> 'Twas the brave Morgan lowered his glass,
> And pointing where Fraser stood,
> Cried, "Woodsmen say when a man must pass,
> 'He's the log that jams the flood.'
> . . . .
> One man holds back the flood of the fates
> That sweeps us on to be free;
> Let heaven open for him its gates."
> And Tim Murphy climbed a tree.
> Then Fraser fell, and the battle tide
> Flowed madly on for our cause,
> And John Burgoyne in his dandy pride
> Surrendered his king's applause;
> . . . .
> Then came the French and the war was done.
> And freedom's glory grew.
> So when we bless George Washington,
> Let us bless Tim Murphy, too

¶ The statue of General Philip Schuyler was sculpted by *Alexander Doyle.

§ Open July and August, daily 9-5:30; rest of the year, daily 9-5. Closed January 1, Thanksgiving, and December 25. Fee. Phone: 518-664-9821.

SARATOGA SPRINGS

¶ **The Casino,** Congress Park, on Broadway (U.S. 9) between Circular and Spring streets.

The Casino was originally known as the Saratoga Club when it was built by John Morrissey, the founder of three earlier gambling houses in New York City. He also built the first thoroughbred race track at

Saratoga.

Brought to the United States from Ireland at three years of age, Morrissey had spent many of his early years as a "runner," engaged to allure newly arrived immigrants to his employer's boarding house in New York City. He eventually joined a gang and before he was eighteen had compiled a rap sheet for burglary, assault, and battery. His pugilistic talents were soon enlisted by the local Tammany Hall politicians, who made him the head of the Dead Rabbits, their dependable gang of toughs. Before long, he parlayed his talent into a professional boxing career. In 1858 he won the American bare-knuckle heavyweight championship in an eleven-round bout with *J. C. Heenan. Morrissey was subsequently elected to Congress and the New York state senate.

¶ The National Museum of Racing and Hall of Fame, Union Avenue and Ludlow Street.

The museum features exhibits, sculpture, paintings, and videos on the history of thoroughbred racing in America. The Hall of Fame honors race horses, trainers, and jockeys.

One of the famous horsemen honored in the Hall of Fame is James "Sunny Jim" Fitzsimmons. Born in an area of New York that later became the race track of the Coney Island Jockey Club, Fitzsimmons almost literally had racing in his blood. By age eleven he had his first job around the track – mucking out stalls – but he soon took off on his own as a free-lance rider weighing eighty-four pounds. (Some years later, he spent all night shoveling clay, thereby losing eleven pounds in order to reach a qualifying weight.) By 1904 he was the leading trainer at Pimlico, and in 1906 he opened a public stable at Aqueduct, charging a mere $4 per day.

As Fitzsimmons' clientele grew – at times he was training more than fifty horses at once – so did the number of his winners. From 1906 to his retirement sixty years later, he saddled 2,275 winners, whose combined purses exceeded $13 million. He trained two winners of the Triple Crown, and Bold Ruler and Nashua were among his famous charges.

Fitzsimmons was dubbed "Sunny Jim" by George Dailey, the sports editor of the *New York World*, after an amiable and carefree comic strip character. During his eighty years in racing, Sunny Jim's only complaint was that he was never able to sleep late in the mornings. "I came into this game with nothing to give it . . . ," said the grand old man of American racing. "Racing gave me the happiest life you could want. Racing doesn't owe me a thing, but I owe the game a hell of a lot."

§ Open August, daily 9-5; May-July 31, Monday-Saturday 10-4:30, Sunday 12-4:30; January, February, September, and December, Tuesday-Saturday 10-4:30. Fee. Phone: 518-584-0400.

SCHOHARIE

¶ **Old Stone Fort Museum,** 1 mile north on North Main Street; 2 miles south on State 30 from I-88 Schoharie/Central Bridge exit.

The museum is housed in the Old Stone Fort, originally built in 1772 as a Dutch Reformed church. Six years later it was fortified and enclosed by a log palisade.

In October 1780 a force of Tories and Native Americans under the command of Sir John Johnson entered the Schoharie Valley, plundering and killing as they advanced. (Johnson was the son of *Sir William Johnson, Britain's superintendent of Indian affairs in New York) At the time, the fort was garrisoned by Americans, one of them *Timothy Murphy, the famous frontiersman, Indian killer, and marksman.

Realizing that Johnson's forces surrounded the fort, the American commander was willing to surrender and ordered one of his militiamen to exit the fort carrying a flag of truce. Murphy, however, shot the flag from the militiaman's hand rather than see the fort surrendered. When the commander ordered the other men to subdue Murphy, they refused. Encouraged in his defiance, Murphy threatened to kill anyone who tried to surrender.

The British commander had meanwhile withdrawn, believing that his artillery was incapable of breaching the walls of the fort. Murphy was only mildly reprimanded for his disobedience. He is buried in Middleburg Cemetery in Middleburg, about ten miles from Schoharie.

• A reenactment of Johnson's raid takes place here during the first weekend in October.

§ Open June-August 31, daily 10-5; May, September, and October, Tuesday-Saturday 10-5; Sunday 12-5. Fee. Phone: 518-295-7192.

SCHUYLERVILLE

¶ **Saratoga Battlefield Monument,** Burgoyne Street off State 32.

This 155-foot granite obelisk commemorates the American victory over the British in two battles fought near here in September and October 1777. The exterior niches contain statues of General Philip Schuyler, General Horatio Gates, and Colonel Daniel Morgan. The latter work was designed by *William O'Donovan.

STONY POINT

¶ **Stony Point Battlefield State Historic Site,** 2.5 miles northeast off U.S. 9 on Park Road.

The Patriot Soldiers Monument honors the American troops under *Brigadier General Anthony Wayne who in July 1779 captured a British garrison of 600 men posted here on the west bank of the Hudson River. "Our officers and men behaved like men who are determined to be free," said Wayne, who received a head wound during the surprise midnight assault, the last major northern battle of the Revolution.

§ Open late April-late October, Wednesday-Sunday; park open 8:30-5; museum open 9-4:30. Phone: 914-786-2521.

TAPPAN

¶ Dutch Reformed Church, Main Street at Old Tappan Road.

On September 29, 1780, Major John André, the captured British spy, was tried here by a tribunal of fourteen American generals (including *James Clinton, *Henry Knox, Arthur St. Clair, and the Marquis de Lafayette).

TARRYTOWN

¶ Captor's Monument, Patriots' Park, on U.S. 9.

Atop this monument is a bronze statue of John Paulding, one of the American soldiers who captured Major John André, the famous British spy, in September 1780. The statue is the work of *William O'Donovan.

§ Park open 24 hours. Phone: 914-631-1705.

TROY

¶ James Connolly Memorial, Riverside Park, River Street, just north of the city hall.

Erected in 1986 by the members of local trade unions, this memorial bust by the Irish sculptor Paula O'Sullivan commemorates the two years during which James Connolly lived in Troy.

Born in Scotland to Irish immigrants, Connolly moved to Dublin in 1896 to accept a post as secretary of the Socialist Club there. Although he proceeded to found the Irish Socialist Republican party, disagreements within its ranks caused him to sail to America and eventually settle in Troy. (He was soon followed by his wife and the four of their five children who survived the crossing.) During his eight years in the United States, he established the Irish Socialist Federation and was editor of its journal. In 1910, however, he returned to Dublin, where he helped orchestrate the massive – but unsuccessful – transport workers strike of 1913.

Although Connolly's socialist internationalism aroused the distrust of Irish nationalists, he was made commander of the Irish Citizen Army and helped prepare its members for the uprising that finally occurred in April 1916. During the fighting that erupted after Connolly and his 1,000 troops seized the General Post Office in Dublin, the commander was wounded in the ankle. When the rebels surrendered at the end of the week, Connolly was court-martialed and sentenced to death – all while he lay in a hospital bed. On May 12 he was driven to Kilmainham Jail, where he was propped up in a chair and shot.

¶ **Soldiers' and Sailors' Monument,** Monument Square, 2nd and River streets.

This impressive monument in front of City Hall is crowned by a seventeen-foot figure of Columbia, the work of *James Edward Kelly.

U.S. MILITARY ACADEMY

The visitor center (outside Thayer Gate) is open daily 9-4:45. Closed January 1, Thanksgiving, and December 25. Phone: 914-938-2638.

¶ **Cadet Library**
The library contains memorial plaques in honor of two famous Irish Americans whose careers at West Point were eclipsed by their later achievements in less bellicose pursuits.

• Edgar Allan Poe is commemorated with a plaque by *Augustus Saint-Gaudens and with a white marble doorway in the east hallway. Poe's name is engraved across the top of the doorway, as is an appropriate aphorism by Sir Francis Bacon: "There is no exquisite beauty without some strangeness in proportion."

Poe's career at West Point was marked by frequent absences, usually at a nearby tavern. These infractions soon led to his court-martial and dismissal in March 1831, after only eights months at the academy. Before he left, however, he sought subscriptions from the cadets to publish a book of verse. In the expectation that the poems in the volume would satirize the academy's superintendent, many of the cadets eagerly paid the seventy-five-cent subscription fee. When they saw the finished product, though, they felt that they had been deceived because it was filled with what one commentator called "sentimental rubbish."

• Near the Poe doorway is a white marble tablet by *Augustus Saint-Gaudens in honor of the famous painter James McNeill Whistler. The tablet is inscribed with an unusual quotation: "The Story of the Beautiful is Already Complete[,] Hewn in the Marble of the Parthenon and Broidered with the Birds upon the Fan of Hokusai." Below the words is the butterfly symbol with which Whistler usually signed his works. Although Whistler excelled in drawing while at West Point, he was dismissed in his third year for failing chemistry. "Had silicon been a gas," he reportedly said, "I would have been a major general."

¶ Cullum Hall

Among the portrait paintings of West Point graduates on display here are those of Irish Americans George Gordon Meade ('35), Irwin McDowell ('38), John Reynolds ('41), Ulysses S. Grant ('43), Alexander McDowell Cook ('52), and Philip Sheridan ('53) as well as a portrait of William T. Sherman by *George Healy.

¶ General John Sedgwick Statue

This statue of the Civil War officer is the work of sculptor *Launt Thompson.

¶ Grant Hall and Grant Barracks

Named for *Ulysses S. Grant, Grant Hall displays a portrait of the Civil War commander as well as portraits of generals George Washington, Winfield Scott, *Philip Sheridan, and William T. Sherman.

¶ Major Sylvanus Thayer Statue

This memorial to the "Father of the U.S. Military Academy" is the work of *Martin Milmore. Thayer was the academy's superintendent from 1817 to 1833.

¶ Mahan Hall

Opened in 1972, this is the newest academic building on campus and was named in honor of Dennis Mahan, a professor of engineering at the academy from 1832 to 1871.

Born in New York City soon after the arrival of his parents from Ireland, Mahan sought and obtained an appointment to the U.S. Military Academy primarily because of his interest in studying drawing there. Following his graduation from West Point in 1824, he pursued further study at the School of Application for Engineers and Artillery in Metz, France. Upon his return to the academy four years later, he was appointed professor of civil and military engineering. Because he was hampered by the unavailability of textbooks for his courses, he developed his own, some of which his students used as manuals when they commanded troops during the Mexican War and the Civil War.

At the height of his career, Mahan was a member of many scientific associations, including the National Academy of Sciences and the Geographical Society of Paris. Depressed, however, by the recommendation that he retire from the faculty at West Point, he sailed to New York to visit his doctor, but on the way he stepped over the side of the vessel and drowned.

¶ Margaret Corbin Burial Site, West Point Cemetery, near the Old Cadet Chapel.

A stone monument adorned with a bronze bas-relief marks the grave of *Margaret Cochran Corbin, the "first woman to take a soldier's part" in the American Revolution. The bas-relief depicts Corbin manning a cannon at the battle of Fort Washington, where she took her husband's place after he was struck down by attacking Hessians. (See Margaret Corbin Commemorative Plaque, New York City.)

Following her release from the army at the end of the Revolutionary War, Corbin was awarded a sergeant's half pension as well as a ration per day and became the only woman in the Invalid Regiment, stationed at that time at West Point. Described as a "stout, red-haired, freckled-face young Irish girl, with handsome, piercing eyes," she cut a colorful figure in camp. Because she usually wore a cocked hat and an artilleryman's coat over her dress, she was nicknamed "Captain Molly," although she was also dubbed "Dirty Kate" for her slovenly attire and unwashed appearance. Following her second marriage to a man whose name is unknown, she was described as being "far advanced in her pregnancy."

In September 1782 "Captain Molly" presented a requisition for 257 gills of whiskey, which she claimed was part of her rations. An aide to *General Henry Knox wrote to General Washington expressing his belief that army regulations prohibited the issuance of whiskey to women. Washington's aide, however, authorized Knox to grant her request, although he warned about the imprudence of giving her too much of the drink. He also asked Knox how it could be "that a woman with an old, decrepit husband should be far advanced in pregnancy."

⚓ Shea Stadium

This track and field stadium was named in 1958 for *1st Lieutenant Richard Shea Jr., a 1952 West Point graduate who was posthumously awarded the Medal of Honor for his heroic actions during the Korean War. Although seriously wounded in the torso and the neck while defending "Pork Chop" Hill, Shea refused five times to abandon his position but instead reorganized and led the remaining units on the hill. He and fifty other men died there, on July 8, 1953.

WESTFIELD

⚓ Old McClurg Mansion, at the junction of U.S. 20 and State 17.

This is the restored 1820 residence of James McClurg, a Scotch-Irish merchant and trader who hired bricklayers from Pittsburgh to build this structure in the style of an Irish manor house. Because of its ornamentation, the house was dubbed "McClurg's Folly." Today the building contains period furniture, farm implements, and a military exhibit.

McClurg's father had fled Ireland with his young family in 1798,

soon after the collapse of an uprising that year. (Because he was suspected of being a leader in the revolt, the elder McClurg was spirited
out of the country in an empty water barrel aboard ship. Although the
family's terrier showed unusual interest in the keg while authorities
searched the ship, the stowaway was not detected.) McClurg and his
family first lived in Philadelphia, but they later moved to Pittsburgh,
where they established that city's first iron foundry.

In 1808, however, James McClurg headed off on his own, travers-
ing the virgin lands as far as present-day Cleveland before settling in
Westfield. Here he built his brick mansion and a hotel that was considered the best west of Albany at the time. About 1831 he and two partners built a flour and grist mill in Westfield to supply the increasing
numbers of settlers coming into the region. McClurg later purchased
land in Chicago, Rock Island, and Racine, Illinois, and joined the Republican Party soon after its formation.

§ Open mid April-November 30, Monday 1-8, Tuesday, Thursday,
Friday, and Saturday 1-5. Fee. Phone: 716-326-2977.

WILTON

¶ **Grant Cottage State Historic Site,** southbound I-87 exit 17, 4
miles west to the junction of State 9 and Ballard Road, to Mount
McGregor Correctional Facility.

Impoverished because of bad business investments and suffering
from throat cancer, former president *Ulysses S. Grant came here in
June 1885 to finish his memoirs. After working feverishly on the volume so his family would have an income, he completed the book just
four days before his death on July 23, 1885. The publication of Grant's
memoirs later earned almost $500,000 for his family. The cottage con-
tains original furnishings and some of Grant's clothing.

§ Open Memorial Day-Labor Day, Wednesday-Saturday 10-4 and
on holidays during the season. Fee. Phone: 518-587-8277.

YOUNGSTOWN

¶ **Old Fort Niagara,** Fort Niagara State Park, north on State 18.

Located on the site of earlier French forts dating from 1678, the fort
was captured for the British by *Sir William Johnson in 1759. Today the
fort includes a moat, a drawbridge, ramparts, blockhouses, and the only
fortified French castle in the United States.

§ Open July-Labor Day, daily 9-7:30; November-March 31, daily 9-
4:30. Closed January 1, Thanksgiving, and December 25. Fee. Phone:
716-745-7611.

OHIO

CANTON

¶ **McKinley Museum of History, Science and Industry,** 800 McKinley Monument Drive, N.W., off I-77 exit 106.

Named for *William McKinley, the twenty-fifth president of the United States, this museum features displays in Historical Hall and Industrial Hall, presidential memorabilia in McKinley Hall, and nineteenth-century structures in the Street of Shops.

§ Open Monday-Saturday 9-5 (7 in summer), Sunday 12-5 (7 in summer). Closed Easter, Memorial Day, Labor Day, and December 25. Fee. Phone: 216-455-7043.

¶ **McKinley National Memorial,** 800 McKinley Monument Drive, N.W., off I-77 exit 106.

This circular stone monument – resembling both the Taj Mahal in India and Hadrian's Tomb in Rome – honors *President William McKinley. A nine-foot-high bronze statue depicts a standing McKinley – one hand holding some papers and the other in his pants pocket – delivering his last speech in Buffalo, New York. He is buried here with his wife and their daughters.

After coming to Canton in 1867 to begin practicing law, McKinley entered politics, serving in Congress for fourteen years and as governor of Ohio for four. Elected president in 1896 and again in 1900, he was assassinated by an anarchist in Buffalo on September 6, 1901. His last words were, "Goodbye all. It is God's will. His will, not ours, be done."

§ Open Memorial Day-Labor Day, Monday-Saturday 9-7, Sunday 12-7; mid March to day before Memorial Day, and day after Labor Day to December 1, Monday-Saturday 9-5, Sunday 12-5. Phone: 216-455-7043.

CARROLLTON

¶ **McCook House,** in the public square.

This brick Federal-style house was the home of *Major Daniel McCook Sr., whose ten sons were dubbed the "Tribe of Dan." Both he and nine of his sons served in the Union army during the Civil War. Four of them made the supreme sacrifice, including Daniel McCook Sr., who was mortally wounded in July 1863, while trying to intercept Confederate raiders near Buffington Island, Ohio. Because McCook's five nephews also fought for the Union, the family clan was known as the "Fighting McCooks."

The McCooks' first American ancestor was an Irishman of Scottish descent who had fled Ireland in 1780 when the United Irishmen movement collapsed. He eventually settled in Canonsburg, Pennsylvania.

§ Open June-mid October, Friday-Saturday 9-12 and 1-5, Sunday 1-5. Fee. Phone: 216-627-3345.

CINCINNATI

¶ **Stephen Foster Statue,** Alms Memorial Park, Mt. Lookout district, Tusculum and Columbia avenues.

This bronze memorial to Stephen Collins Foster depicts the famous Irish-American songwriter sitting on a knoll as he gazes toward the Kentucky hills. The statue of Foster, who spent several years in Cincinnati, was a gift of Eli Lily, the founder of the pharmaceutical company that bears his name.

CLEVELAND

¶ **President Garfield Statue,** Lakeview Cemetery, 12316 Euclid Avenue.

This marble statue by *Alexander Doyle is located inside the chapel in the base of the James A. Garfield Monument. The memorial, which was erected in 1890, is a circular tower fifty feet in diameter and 180 feet high and is located above the grave of the slain president.

The graves of John D. Rockefeller, *Senator Mark Hanna, and Secretary of State John Hay are also located in this cemetery.

§ Open April to late November, daily 9-4. Phone: 216-421-2665.

¶ **John Carroll University,** University Heights, Warrensville Center and Fairmount Boulevard.

This Jesuit institution was founded in 1886 and was named for *John Carroll, the first Catholic bishop of the United States.

¶ **Mark Hanna Statue,** University Circle, spreading north, east, and south from Euclid Avenue, east of East 107th Street.

Sculpted by *Augustus Saint-Gaudens, this seated bronze statue was placed here in 1907 to honor the Cleveland native who maneuvered the nomination of *William McKinley as the Republican candidate for president in 1896. Hanna was of mixed Irish and Scotch-Irish ancestry.

¶ **Oliver H. Perry Statue,** at the northern boundary of Gordon Park.

This bronze statue of *Oliver Hazard Perry commemorates the twenty-seven-year-old naval commander who defeated the British fleet on Lake Erie during the War of 1812.

COLUMBUS

¶ **O'Shaughnessy Reservoir,** 16 miles north on Riverside Drive. Fishing, water-skiing, boating, picnicking, and zoo.

Completed in 1925, the dam is 1,750 feet long and was named for *Jerry O'Shaughnessy, the former waterworks superintendent of Columbus, Ohio.

¶ **State Capitol,** Broad and High streets.

• The capitol rotunda is decorated with plaques honoring the eight U.S. presidents who were born in Ohio, among them three of Irish ancestry: Ulysses S. Grant, Benjamin Harrison, and William McKinley,

• Outside the west entrance to the capitol is a bronze statue of *President William McKinley reading an address at the Pan-American Exposition in Buffalo, New York, in 1901. This was his last speech before he was assassinated by an anarchist.

• On the capitol grounds is a memorial to seven Ohio statesmen and Civil War soldiers, including *Ulysses S. Grant and *Philip Sheridan. Known as the "My Jewels Monument," it includes bronze statues of the seven Ohioans around a shaft topped by the Roman aristocrat Cornelia, who said that her sons were her greatest jewels.

§ Open Monday-Friday 7 a.m.-9 p.m.; Saturday, Sunday, and holidays 9-5. Phone: 614-466-2125.

DAYTON

¶ **McKinley Monument,** Cooper Park, East 3rd and St. Clair streets.

This eighteen-foot bronze statue behind the Dayton Public Library depicts *President William McKinley in a speaking pose.

DEFIANCE

¶ **Fort Defiance Site,** Defiance City Park.

Stones, earthworks, and plaques mark the site of Fort Defiance, constructed in 1794 while *Major General Anthony Wayne campaigned against the Indians in the area.

When Wayne and his troops first arrived at this site in August 1794, he referred to it contemptuously as "the grand emporium of the hostile Indians of the West." The fort received its name from Wayne's challenge: "I defy the English, the Indians and all the devils in hell to take it."

DETROIT

₡ Ulysses S. Grant House, Michigan State Fair Grounds, State Fair and Woodward avenues.

The house can be viewed from the outside during the Fair (the last week before Labor Day).

After returning from the Mexican War, *Ulysses S. Grant lived in this house (originally located on East Fort Street) while he was company commander and quartermaster of the Detroit Barracks. Grant once described the two-story cottage as "a neat little house [with] a double parlor, a dining room, one small bedroom and kitchen in the lower level. There is a nice upstairs and a garden filled with the best kind of fruit."

FORT RECOVERY

₡ Fort Recovery State Memorial, on State 49 at State 119.

The centerpiece of this nine-acre site is a replica of the fort and stockade built here in 1793 by *General Anthony Wayne. The fort's museum has exhibits on the Indian Wars of the 1790s.

The construction of Fort Recovery was part of Wayne's effort to "recover" this area from control of the Indians, who had decisively defeated an American army under General Arthur St. Clair in 1791. It was not until three years later that Wayne avenged this defeat with his victory at Fallen Timbers, after which the Native Americans signed the Treaty of Greenville.

§ Museum open June-August 31, Tuesday-Saturday 1-5, Sunday 12-5; May and September, Saturday 1-5, Sunday 12-5. Fee. Phone: 419-375-4649.

FREMONT

₡ Memorial Monument, Birchard Library Park, 423 Croghan Street.

Besides honoring the soldiers and sailors of Sandusky County who gave their lives in America's wars, this monument marks the grave of *Major George Croghan. (See Lafayette, Indiana.)

In 1813 the twenty-one-year-old Croghan was in command of 150 American soldiers at Fort Stephenson (now Fremont) when they fought off an attack by 400 British soldiers and 300 of their Indian allies. Near the monument is the single cannon which the Americans used against their foes in that engagement.

§ Park open daily dawn-dusk.

GEORGETOWN

¶ **Ulysses S. Grant Boyhood Home,** 219 East Grant Avenue.

When *Ulysses S. Grant was a year old, his family moved to Georgetown, where his father built this white brick Federal-style house. His father's tannery is located across the street, while the two-room schoolhouse which the young boy attended is on South Water Street. Among the Grant memorabilia on display in the schoolhouse is a picture of West Point which Grant drew in 1840 and which he signed "H. U. Grant" – "H" for "Hiram." (He adopted the name "U. S. Grant" after a bureaucrat's error on his army commission.)

§ Open Tuesday-Saturday 9-1 and 2-5. Closed January 1, Thanksgiving, and December 25. Phone: 513-381-0800.

GIBRALTAR ISLAND

¶ **Perry's Lookout**

Located on an eminence at the eastern end of this island in Put-in-Bay, this lookout is reputedly where *Commodore Oliver H. Perry kept watch as a British naval squadron moved into the bay in 1813. Perry's subsequent victory at Put-in-Bay is commemorated by a nearby monument built in 1866.

JAMESTOWN

¶ **Dean Family Farm,** 5 miles northwest off U.S. 35 on Ballard Road. Private.

This farm, home to eight generations of the Dean family, was first tilled about 1812 by Daniel Dean, an Irish immigrant and pioneer settler in this area.

LISBON

¶ **McCook House,** Market Street.

Now a tavern, the McCook House was formerly the home of *Robert McCook, whose two sons and fifteen grandsons were known as the "Fighting McCooks" because of their service in the U.S. armed forces. All but one of the clan saw action in the Civil War, thirteen as officers: two generals, four major generals, one major, two colonels, two lieutenants, and two naval commanders. McCook's son John also lived here with his sons, in later life known as the "Tribe of John

• The member of the tribe who had perhaps the most varied career was Edward McCook. While only sixteen, the young adventurer followed the lure of the gold rush as far as Colorado, where he later practiced law and became a leader in the organization of that territory. Although he saw action on several fronts during the Civil War, he was best known for preventing the reinforcement of troops in Atlanta by destroying Confederate transport trains and cutting the rail lines to the south of the Georgia capital.

After the war McCook acted at various times as military governor of Florida, U.S. minister to Hawaii, and territorial governor of Colorado. As governor he encouraged railroad construction, organized a school system, and was instrumental in building Denver's water system. He also paved the way for the development of mineral resources and agricultural lands in the state by removing the Ute Indians to Utah. By the end of his life he was the largest real estate owner and taxpayer in Colorado. His first wife was Mary Thomson, the granddaughter of Charles Thomson, the Irish-born secretary of the Continental Congress during the 1770s.

MANSFIELD

¶ **Kingwood Center,** 900 Park Avenue, 1.5 miles west on State 430, then north on Trimble Road.

Kingwood Center occupies the forty-seven-acre former estate of industrialist **Charles Kelley King. The property features greenhouses, trails, and landscaped gardens. Kingwood Hall, King's twenty-seven-room Provincial-style mansion, has a horticultural reference library.

King was born in Calais, Maine, in 1867 and went on to become president, general manager, and chairman of the board of Ohio Brass Company before his death in 1952.

§ Gardens open daily 8 -dusk. Mansion open Easter-October 31, Tuesday-Saturday 9-5, Sunday 1:30-4:30; rest of the year, Tuesday-Saturday 9-5. Closed holidays. Phone: 419-522-0211.

MOUNT VERNON

¶ **Daniel Emmett Birthplace,** Senior Citizens' Center, at the juncture of Martinsburg, Newark, and Granville roads (State 583, 13, and 661).

It was here that Daniel Emmett, the composer of "Dixie," was born in 1815. His immensely popular tune was premiered in New Orleans in 1861 and was soon adopted as the war anthem of the Confederacy.

Before finally settling in Ohio, Emmett's Irish pioneer ancestors had crossed the Blue Ridge and the Allegheny mountains. As a youngster he was introduced to music by his mother, and it was probably while working in his father's blacksmith shop that he composed the song "Old Dan Tucker." After learning how to read and write, however, he was apprenticed to a printer and for a time worked for the *Western Aurora* newspaper in Mount Vernon.

At seventeen Emmett joined the army as a fifer but was soon discharged when he was found to be underage. Evidently intent upon making a mark in the musical field, he organized in 1842 the Virginia Minstrels, whose striped calico shirts, white trousers, and blue calico coats were of his own design. For a dozen years this group enjoyed phenomenal success popularizing African-American music. In 1857, however, Emmett joined the Bryant Minstrels, for whom he composed "Dixie." Some of his other Civil War songs were "The Road to Richmond," "Walk Along, John," and "Here We Are, or Cross Ober Jordan."

❡ Emmett is buried in Mound View Cemetery, off Wooster Road (State 3).

NEW LEXINGTON

❡ **J. A. MacGahan Burial Site,** Maplewood Cemetery, Swigart Street.

This is the final resting place of Januarius Aloysius MacGahan, a war correspondent and the master of nine languages, who was born near here of Irish parents in 1844. The monument over his grave is inscribed with his name and the honorific "Liberator of Bulgaria."

After studying law and foreign languages in St. Louis, MacGahan traveled to Europe, where he improved his linguistic skills while living in Paris, Brussels, and Germany. At the outbreak of the Franco-Prussian War in 1870, he sent back vivid descriptions of the conflict for the *New York Herald,* including reports about the Paris Commune and his own capture and release. After spending some time in the Crimea, he became a favored figure with the Czar's court. Probably because of that popularity, he risked defying the Russian prohibition against newspaper coverage of a military expedition against the Khanate of Khiva. For twenty-nine days he and two companions eluded the Czar's Cossacks in a pursuit of almost a thousand miles. Although finally captured, he was allowed to stay with the campaign.

MacGahan was later instrumental in achieving Bulgarian independence. His reports to the *London Daily News* verifying rumors about Turkish massacres of Bulgarians indirectly led to Russia's declaration of war against Turkey in 1876. A year later, with the Turks defeated and Bulgaria independent, MacGahan was proclaimed that country's liberator. Following his death in 1878, he was buried in Bulgaria until his body was brought to the United States and reinterred in Maplewood Cemetery in 1884.

At the unveiling of the monument over MacGahan's grave in 1911, Svetozar Tonjoroff, his Bulgarian eulogist, referred to him as the "patron saint of Bulgaria." The speaker also described one of the massacres which MacGahan had reported in the press: After about 4,000 Bulgarian villagers had sought refuge in a church, the Turkish commander besieging the village offered amnesty to any of the men who laid down their weapons. When the Bulgarian men in the village surrendered themselves and their arms, the Turks reneged on their promise and proceeded to torch the church and the women and children still inside. "[T]he most enduring monument to MacGahan . . . is to be seen on every map of Europe . . . ," Tonjoroff said, "[and] is builded of indestructible materials in the heart and soul of every Bulgarian, for all time. That monument is Bulgaria itself – free, with its face toward the light, marching steadily to the fulfillment of its destiny . . . ."

NEWARK

¶ **Ohio and Erie Canal Monument,** 3 miles south on State 79.

This monument commemorates the canal's ground-breaking ceremonies, which occurred here on July 4, 1825, with *DeWitt Clinton, the governor of New York and the "Father of the Erie Canal," officiating.

Many of the thousands of spectators who attended the ceremony barely heard the speeches because they were distracted by the flies and the tramping of cavalry horses near the rostrum. One wag commented that "it was all right to have the horses in front of the speaker's stand, for they cannot read and we can."

NILES

¶ **William McKinley Birthplace Site,** 36 South Main Street.

Although the building at this address is now a bank, a marker in the entranceway notes that *President William McKinley was born on this site in 1843. None of his personal residences survives today.

¶ **National McKinley Birthplace Memorial,** 40 North Main Street.

This huge neoclassical memorial to *William McKinley is located close to the spot where the twenty-fifth president was born in 1843. The monument consists of a colonnaded porch called the Court of Honor, at the center of which is a statue of McKinley surrounded by figures of his political associates. The attached museum displays items connected with McKinley's life and career.

McKinley's third-great-grandfather, a weaver named David McKinley, was born in northern Ireland about 1705 and immigrated to York County, Pennsylvania, about 1743.

§ Open Monday-Thursday 8-8, Friday and Saturday 8:30-5:30, Sunday (during the school year) 1-5. Closed on holidays. Phone: 216-652-1704.

The neo-classical National McKinley Birthplace Memorial.
(Photo by Justine Hill and courtesy of the National McKinley Birthplace Memorial.)

OXFORD

⚁ William McGuffey Monument, Miami University, Campus Avenue.

Located in the courtyard of McGuffey Hall, this monument includes a bust of McGuffey and a group of young children reading a book.

McGuffey, a Presbyterian minister of Scotch-Irish background, was famous for his *Eclectic Readers*, the first of which he wrote and saw published while he was a professor of philology and foreign language at Miami University. Over a period of seventy years, eight publishers issued 160 editions of his works, whose sales reached a phenomenal 122,000 copies.

⚁ William McGuffey Memorial Museum, Miami University, Spring and Oak streets.

From 1833 to 1836 this two-story brick house was the home of *William McGuffey. Today the museum contains a variety of McGuffey memorabilia, including a large collection of *McGuffey's Readers* and *Spellers* as well as his octagon desk with swivel top.

McGuffey became a champion of public education and an educational reformer whose *Readers* were second only to the Bible in their influence upon nineteenth-century America. Possessed of a prodigious memory, he could recite entire books of the Scriptures by heart. When preaching, he always spoke without text, and he claimed that he had

306   Ohio

given 3,000 srmons without ever writing a single one. His educational career included the presidency of three Ohio institutions of higher learning – Miami, Cincinnati, and Ohio universities – and a professorship at the University of Virginia.

Through the use of maxims, anecdotes, essays, and stories, McGuffey's *Readers* reflected an unambiguous moral code. Besides biblical excerpts the textbooks contained selections by Beecher, Rousseau, Webster, Jefferson, Irving, Grimké, Phillips, Channing, Longfellow, Lord Bacon, Addison, Bryant, Byron, Milton, and Shakespeare. Whatever the vehicle, these nineteenth-century "Books of Virtues" tried to inculcate in their young readers the virtues of piety, charity, patriotism, kindness, honesty, and gratitude. One story, for instance, put forward John Jones for emulation because "he did not love to play so much that he could not work." Another described Truthful George, whose offer to pay for a window he had broken brought him a partnership with a grateful merchant. And while laziness, drunkenness, and gambling were inevitably condemned in the readers, thrift, perseverance, and industry were praised: "If we strive, 'tis no disgrace, / Though we may not win the race; / What should you do in that case? / Try, Try Again."

§ Open Saturday and Sunday 2-4. Phone: 513-529-1809.

PIQUA

¶ **Piqua Historical Area State Memorial,** 1.25 miles north off State 66, at 9845 North Hardin Road.

Besides an Indian museum and a canal boat ride, one of the attractions of the park is the Johnston farm and Indian agency. The farm property was originally staked out in 1811 by John Johnston, a native of Ballyshannon, Ireland, whose parents had immigrated to Pennsylvania in 1786. The three-story brick Georgian residence in which Johnston lived until sometime in the 1840s has been restored, and the original outbuildings on the property have been reconstructed.

In the early 1790s Johnston served as supplymaster for *General Anthony Wayne during the campaign against the Native Americans of northwest Ohio. Beginning in 1802, he served as an Indian agent for the U.S. government and then from 1812 to 1829 for Ohio. He acted as paymaster and quartermaster during the War of 1812 and was influential in weaning significant Indian support away from Chief Tecumseh. (Johnston was also known for hosting on his property as many as 6,000 Indians at a time.) In the early 1840s he negotiated the removal of the Native Americans from the state and was the author of *An Account of the Indian Tribes of Ohio*. He was a founder of Kenyon College and Miami University.

§ Open Memorial Day-Labor Day, Wednesday-Saturday 9:30-5, Sunday and holidays 12-5; day after Labor Day-October 31, Saturday 9:30-5, Sunday 12-5. Fee. Phone: 513-773-2522.

The Ohio farmhouse of John Johnston, a native of Ballyshannon, Ireland.
(Photo courtesy of James O'Donnell.)

POINT PLEASANT

ℐ Ulysses S. Grant Birthplace, State 52 and 232.

Ulysses S. Grant, the famous Civil War general and eighteenth president of the United States, was born in this white frame cottage in 1822. The house contains memorabilia connected with the Grant family, among them the general's cradle, Bible, and West Point trunk.

Grant's great-great-grandfather was William Simpson, born in northern Ireland about 1710. Simpson's son, James, emigrated from Derigna, near Ballygawley, County Tyrone, in 1738. The president's paternal grandmother was Rachel Kelley.

§ Open April-October 31, Wednesday-Saturday 9:30-12 and 1-5, Sunday 12-5. Closed January 1, Thanksgiving, and December 25. Phone: 513-753-7211.

ℐ Ulysses S. Grant Memorial Bridge, on U.S. 52.

Built in 1925-26, the bridge is marked by stone pillars mounted with Civil War guns. A bas-relief of *President Grant is on one of the pillars.

POLAND

℘ McKinley House, 6 miles south on State 170 at 210 Main Street.

This was the residence of *William McKinley while he was a student in town here. In 1861 he enlisted in the Union army at a local stagecoach inn called the Sparrow Tavern.

POMEROY

℘ Buffington Island State Monument, 20 miles southeast on State 24.

This four-acre park is on the site of one of the few Civil War battles that took place in Ohio. In the park is a monument to *General Daniel McCook Sr. – one of the famous "Fighting McCooks" – who was killed during that engagement in July 1863.

PUT-IN-BAY

℘ Perry's Cave, Catawba Avenue.

Before the battle of Lake Erie, *Commodore Oliver H. Perry is said to have stored supplies in this cave, fifty-two feet below the surface.

§ Open June-Labor Day, Monday-Sunday; spring and fall, Saturday and Sunday. Fee. Phone: 419-285-2112/3045.

℘ Perry's Victory and International Peace Memorial, South Bass Island in Lake Erie.

The victory of *Commodore Oliver H. Perry at the battle of Lake Erie in September 1813 is commemorated by a 352-foot-high Doric column of granite topped by a bronze urn. The actual battle site ten miles to the northwest can be seen from the observation deck.

When his flagship, the *Lawrence*, was destroyed at the beginning of the naval engagement with the British, Perry transferred to the *Niagara*. His new flagship broke through the British line after a fifteen-minute barrage forced six British vessels to surrender. The twenty-seven-year-old victorious American sent his famous message to General William Henry Harrison: "We have met the enemy, and they are ours. Two ships, two brigs, one schooner, and one sloop." Perry's achievement won control of Lake Erie for the Americans and made possible Harrison's invasion of Canada. Harrison's victory at the battle of the Thames effectively ended the War of 1812 in the Northwest.

§ Accessible by passenger/auto ferry from Catawba and Port Clinton (April-November); by plane from Port Clinton (year-round). Open mid June-Labor Day, daily 10-7; rest of the year, daily 10-5. Closed November to late April. Fee for elevator. Phone: 419-285-2184.

SIDNEY

¶ *Titanic* **Memorial Museum,** I-75 exit 92, west to Vandemark Road, 1 mile north to Russell Road, and then 3 miles west to 10741 Russell Road.

This museum displays artifacts from the *Titanic*, the luxury passenger ship which was launched from Belfast, Ireland, in April 1912. Only five days later it struck an iceberg and sank in less than an hour. Of its 2,227 passengers and crew, only 705 survived. One of the survivors was *Margaret Tobin Brown ("Unsinkable Molly").

§ Open Monday-Wednesday 10-4:30, Saturday 9-4:30, Sunday 1-5. Closed major holidays. Fee. Phone: 513-492-7762.

SOMERSET

The Somerset Historic District contains three sites associated with *General Philip Sheridan, the famous Civil War cavalry officer whose victory over General Robert E. Lee at Five Forks led to the latter's surrender at Appomattox.

¶ **Philip Sheridan Boyhood Home,** 114 Sheridan Avenue (State 13).

As a youngster in Somerset, Philip Sheridan had two teachers, one of them the itinerant Irishman Patrick McNaly. Sheridan recalled that McNaly resorted to whipping every student in the class if he could not discover the "guilty mischief-maker." The famous officer later acknowledged the importance of his early education by saying that it was "the little white schoolhouse of the North [that] made us superior to the South."

It was from Somerset that the young Sheridan set out for West Point in 1848. Although he found that his Catholicism and Famine-Irish background were distinct handicaps, it was his Irish temper that almost ended his plans to pursue a military career. The unfortunate incident occurred at the beginning of his senior year, when a cadet sergeant began to berate Sheridan during a parade march. Provoked by the verbal harassment, Sheridan cursed the sergeant ("God damn you, sir, I'll run you through") and lunged at him with his bayonet. Perhaps because he missed his intended target, Sheridan was suspended from the academy for only a year. During that time he returned to Somerset.

¶ **Sheridan House,** 417 South Columbus Street. Private.
This house was built by Philip Sheridan for his parents.

¶ **Sheridan Statue,** in the town square (U.S. 22 and State 13).

SPRINGFIELD

This city had its origins in a sawmill and gristmill erected soon after 1800 by *Simon Kenton, a scout and spy who participated in the major campaigns against the Indian tribes in the Old Northwest. Here in 1807 Kenton and other settlers in Springfield met with the Indian chiefs Tecumseh, MacPherson, and Roundhead to reaffirm their mutual desire for peace in the area.

STEUBENVILLE

¶ Edwin Stanton Statue, in front of the courthouse, 301 Market Street.

This eighteen-foot monument to President Lincoln's secretary of war was sculpted by *Alexander Doyle. The statue, which depicts Stanton making a speech at the courthouse, was a gift of the artist to Steubenville, where both he and Stanton were born.

¶ "Fighting McCooks" Monument, town center.

This memorial honors *Daniel McCook and *John McCook and their fifteen sons, known as the "Fighting McCooks" because of their service in the U.S. armed forces. All but one of the clan saw action in the Civil War, thirteen as officers.

¶ Union Cemetery, 1720 West Market Street.

Among those interred here are the *Reverend Joseph Ruggles Wilson (the father of Woodrow Wilson) and three of the *"Fighting McCooks" (Anson, George, and Francis McCook).

TOLEDO

¶ General Steedman Statue, Riverside Park, Summit and Galena streets.

This statue of the Union commander James Steedman was sculpted by *Alexander Doyle.

¶ Wildwood Manor House, 5 miles northwest, at 5100 West Central Avenue, in the Wildwood Preserve Metropark.

Constructed in the 1930s, this Georgian mansion was the home of Robert Stranahan Sr., the cofounder of Champion Spark Plug Company. Stranahan was a cousin of Frank Stranahan, reputedly the first white settler in Fort Lauderdale, Florida, and the grandson of an immigrant from County Antrim, Ireland.

The manor house features seventeen baths, sixteen fireplaces, more than fifty rooms, and a solarium that overlooks the formal gardens.

§ Open Wednesday-Sunday and holidays 12-4:30. Closed January 1, Thanksgiving, late November and early December, and December 25. Phone: 419-535-3050.

URBANA

℘ **Simon Kenton Burial Site,** Oakdale Cemetery, south on U.S. 36.

This is the grave of Simon Kenton, the scout and famous Indian fighter who once saved Daniel Boone's life. The grave is marked by a monument erected in 1884 and adorned by the heads of an Indian chief, a panther, a fox, and a bear.

Born in Virginia in 1755 to an Irish father and a Scotch mother, Kenton at age fifteen fled across the Alleghenies after mistakenly thinking that he had killed the suitor of a young girl whose affections he had sought. For a time, as the unofficial guardian of white settlers coming into Kentucky via the Ohio River, he protected them against Indian attacks. During subsequent campaigns against the Native Americans, he was the friend and companion of Daniel Boone, whose life he saved during an Indian attack on Boonesborough. On several other occasions Kenton was in the service of General George Rogers Clark, at least once as captain of a retaliatory force that burned Indian huts, forts, and crops.

℘ **Simon Kenton House Site,** 10 miles south on U.S. 68.

The log manor house which *Simon Kenton built on this site in 1803 was located near a spring where, twenty-two years earlier as an Indian captive, he had stopped to take a drink.

WARREN

According to local boosters, two of the most famous musical compositions of *Stephen Collins Foster may have had their genesis in Warren. Foster is said to have begun writing "Jeanie with the Light Brown Hair" while staying at the Austin House, a local stagecoach inn, while a stroll along the Mahoning River supposedly provided the inspiration for "My Old Kentucky Home."

ZANESFIELD

℘ **Zane-Kenton Monument,** Sandusky Street.

This sixty-ton boulder was dedicated in 1914 to frontiersmen Isaac Zane and *Simon Kenton.

During his lifetime Kenton was a frequent captive of the Shawnee, who forced him to suffer the gauntlet eight times and condemned him to death three times (although he was invariably rescued). On one occasion he was tied to the stake for twenty-four hours, only to be released to run a mile-long gauntlet between two rows of 600 savages. During that particular trial he was knocked down, severely beaten, and again imprisoned.

In 1778 Kenton was brought captive to Wapatomica, a Shawnee village near present-day Zanesfield. There he was forced to run the gauntlet and was painted black in preparation for his expected immolation at the stake. While he awaited death, he was recognized by Simon Girty, a white man with whom he had scouted on Lord Dunmore's expedition but who had turned renegade and was then living with the Indians. Girty interceded on behalf of his former comrade, obtained his release, and took him home, where he washed his wounds and gave him new clothes.

¶ Kenton's farm, cabin site, and original grave are located off State 33. In 1865 his remains were removed to Urbana, Ohio.

PENNSYLVANIA

ALLENTOWN

¶ **George Taylor House and Park,** 4 miles north off U.S. 22 at Lehigh and Poplar streets, Catasauqua.

Constructed in 1768, this house was the home of George Taylor, one of the three Irish-born signers of the Declaration of Independence. The restored house features a museum and a walled garden.

Taylor, who was born in northern Ireland about 1716, came to Pennsylvania twenty years later and first worked for an ironmaker named Savage at his mill near Easton, Pennsylvania. Because the young Irishman was not physically strong enough to continue his first job of shoveling coal, he was soon put in charge of the enterprise's bookkeeping. After Savage's death Taylor came into possession of the mill by marrying his former master's widow.

With his election to the Pennsylvania legislature in 1764, Taylor began a political career that brought him much influence. He bitterly opposed the colony's royal government and became an outspoken critic of the Stamp Act and the closure of Boston harbor by the British. In 1775 he called for the creation of an intercolonial congress and a declaration of independence from Britain as soon as possible. Although he was not a member of the Continental Congress when it voted for independence, he was appointed to that body two weeks later to replace one of the five Pennsylvania delegates who had opposed independence. Taylor signed the Declaration of Independence the following August.

§ Open June-October 31, Saturday and Sunday afternoon; other times by appointment. Phone: 215-435-4664.

BELLEFONTE

¶ **Governor Curtin Statue,** in front of the courthouse, Allegheny and High streets.

This statue by *William Clark Noble honors Andrew Curtin, the popular Civil War governor of Pennsylvania, who was born here in 1815. The house in which Curtin was born no longer exists, and his home during his adult life is now the Elks Club on High Street.

Curtin's father, an immigrant of Scotch-Irish stock, came to this area in 1800 from County Clare, Ireland, and engaged in the manufacture of iron in nearby Milesburg.

BETHEL

¶ **Miller House,** Manse Drive.

This stone and masonry house was erected by James Miller on the site of a log structure built about 1763 by his Irish ancestor, immigrant Oliver Miller. The first shot fired in the Whiskey Rebellion of 1792 occurred here.

BRYN MAWR

¶ **Harriton House,** 1 mile north of U.S. 30 on Morris Avenue, 0.5 mile west on Old Guelph Road, then north on Harriton Road.

Originally called "Bryn Mawr," the 700-acre Harriton estate was bought by Richard Harrison in 1719, although the two-story stone house on the property had been built fifteen years earlier. Title eventually passed to Harrison's daughter, Hannah, who in 1774 married Charles Thomson, the secretary of the Continental Congress. With the creation of the new federal government in 1789, Thompson retired to Harriton.

Thomson had been born in County Derry, Ireland, in 1729. Ten years later his widowed father left Ireland with his six children but died on shipboard and was buried at sea off the Delaware Capes. After stripping the orphans of their valuables, the captain of the ship put the children ashore at New Castle, Delaware. Before long the young Thomson had taken the first steps in an academic career. He attended the academy of *Dr. Francis Alison in New London, Pennsylvania, and then conducted a private school for several years. He was so intent upon studying Greek that he walked sixty miles from Philadelphia to Amboy, New Jersey, to meet a British officer who was regarded as the foremost Greek scholar in America at that time. Through his acquaintance with Benjamin Franklin, he became a teacher at the Philadelphia Academy and later at the William Penn Charter School.

During his lifetime Thomson acquired a reputation for accuracy and fairness. On one occasion a group of Quakers asked him to record in short hand the events surrounding the signing of the Treaty of Easton in 1756. His unofficial record was accepted by the head of the Delaware tribe when the chief disputed the accuracy of the official minutes taken by the governor's representative. A year later the Indians adopted Thomson into their tribe and gave him a name meaning "man who tells the truth." His subsequent reputation for accuracy while secretary of the newly assembled Continental Congress earned him immortality in the saying, "Here comes the truth; here is Charles Thomson!"

Although at first his appointment as secretary to Congress was considered temporary, Thomson served for fifteen years. Predictably, he left a record of how he was asked to accept the undertaking while on his honeymoon in Philadelphia in 1774: "I . . . followed the messenger myself to the Carpenters' Hall, and entered Congress. Here was indeed an august assembly, and deep thought and solemn anxiety were observable on their countenances. I walked up the aisle, and standing opposite to the President, I bowed, and told him I waited his pleasure. He replied, 'Congress desire the favor of you, sir, to take their minutes.' I bowed in acquiescence, and took my seat at the desk." (History does not record his wife's opinion about the interrupted honeymoon.) During his tenure with Congress, he recorded the birth of a new nation and enjoyed the honor – with *John Hancock – of signing the first copy of the Declaration of Independence transmitted to the world. (The original document was in Thomson's hand.) Following his resignation in 1789, Thomson retired to Harriton. For the next twenty years he devoted himself to translating the Septuagint and the New Testament, publishing in 1815 a synopsis of the four Gospels. He died in 1824 at the age of ninety-five and was buried at Harriton.

§ Open Wednesday-Saturday 10-4. Closed holidays. Fee. Phone: 610-525-0201.

❡ In 1838 the promoters of nearby Laurel Hill Cemetery conceived the idea of obtaining the remains of distinguished individuals like Charles Thomson and his wife as a method of attracting patronage. Although Thomson's heirs objected to the scheme, one of his nephews gave his approval. When a farmhand unexpectedly came upon the exhumers at their ghoulish work, they quickly threw the supposed bodies of Thomson and his wife into a wagon and headed posthaste for the new cemetery. Although some doubt remains about the identity of the reburied corpses, a sixteen-foot obelisk in honor of Thomson marks the new grave site.

CANONSBURG

❡ **Log Academy,** East College and Central streets, in front of the Canon-McMillan Middle School.

Erected in 1780 by the Reverend *John McMillan, this log cabin college is the oldest school building west of the Allegheny Mountains. The school was the forerunner of Jefferson College, which subsequently merged with Washington College, now located in Washington, Pennsylvania.

The son of Irish immigrant parents who had settled in Chester County, Pennsylvania, McMillan was a graduate of the College of New Jersey (now Princeton) and had been ordained in 1776. Because of the onset of the war with Britain, however, it was not until two years later that his wife joined him in this part of the state.

Although he later described the generosity of his parishioners in helping him build and furnish the cabin in which he and his bride lived, he confessed that "Sometimes indeed we had no bread for weeks together, but we had plenty of pumpkins and potatoes and all the necessaries of life; as for luxuries, we were not concerned in them." Despite the cabin's privations, it was here that McMillan gave instruction in Greek, Latin, and theology from 1782 to 1791. Although in that latter year he turned over his students to the newly created Canonsburg Academy, he continued to teach theology to its graduates. In later years he served as professor of divinity and vice president of Jefferson College. During his long career he reputedly trained at least 100 students for the ministry. Until his death in 1833, he continued to wear the knee breeches, buckled shoes, and cocked hat of an earlier generation.

CARLISLE

¶ **Carlisle Barracks,** 1 mile north on U.S. 11.

The barracks once housed the Carlisle Indian School, established in 1879. Jim Thorpe, the winner of the pentathlon and decathlon in the 1912 Olympics, was one of the 6,000 Indians who attended the school. Thorpe was of mixed Irish, French, and Indian ancestry.

§ Open Monday-Friday 8-4. Closed federal holidays. Phone: 717-245-3152.

¶ **Jim Thorpe Monument,** county courthouse (High and Hanover streets).

CHAMBERSBURG

This town of 17,000 people was named for Benjamin Chambers, one of four brothers who had come to Pennsylvania from County Antrim, Ireland, between 1726 and 1730. Soon after their arrival, they settled in what is now Dauphin County, where they set up a mill. Benjamin and his brother Joseph later founded what became Chambersburg.

CONCORDVILLE

¶ **Newlin Mill Park,** 1.5 miles east on U.S. 1.

This 150-acre park preserves the home and mill operation of Nathaniel Newlin, an Irish immigrant who was a leader in local commercial and political affairs. The property includes Newlin's restored gristmill, brick house, blacksmith shop, springhouse, and original log cabin.

Newlin had emigrated with his father, Nicholas, from County Tyrone in 1683 when the latter feared further persecution because of his Quakerism ("of suffering there for the testing of Jesus"). After settling in Concordville and building a sawmill, Nicholas Newlin was elected to the Provincial Council and later served as a justice of the local court. By the time of his death in 1699, he had acquired almost 750 acres in Concord and Birmingham townships.

Nathaniel Newlin, meanwhile, gradually came to own almost 9,000 acres in Concordville and elsewhere. During his fourteen terms as a representative of Chester County in the Pennsylvania Assembly, he worked with the governor to obtain passage of a law that granted Pennsylvania Quakers the same legal rights enjoyed by their coreligionists in England. He also drew up legislation prohibiting the sale of rum to the Indians and threw his support behind the creation of a government loan office authorized to issue £15,000 of paper money in an effort to overcome a widespread recession. During his political career he also served as a justice of the peace, an assessor, and a tax commissioner. His contribution of £8 toward the construction of the Quaker meetinghouse in Concordville was the congregation's largest subscription. He was placed in an embarrassing position with his fellow Quakers, however, when he was required to pay a £10 fine because of his daughter's fornication.

§ Open March-September 30, daily 9-dusk; other months, daily 8-5. Nature trails and tennis courts. Fee. Phone: 610-459-2359.

COUDERSPORT

This small town of 3,000 people was founded by John Keating, an Irish mercenary who had served as a captain of the Irish Brigade in the French army. After coming to America in 1792, Keating became involved with land speculators and their colonization efforts along the Susquehanna River. It was during this time that he managed the Ceres Land Company, which owned 300,000 acres in this part of the state. Keating granted fifty acres to each of the first fifty settlers in the Coudersport area.

EASTON

¶ **Parsons-Taylor House,** on the northeast corner of 4th and Ferry streets. Private.

This two-story stone house was occupied by *George Taylor, who after 1763 began to live here much of the time in order to be closer to his ironworks. Taylor and his wife had two children, although he had five illegitimate children by his housekeeper. He died in this house in 1781.

§ Open by appointment. Phone: 215-253-1222.

ERIE

❡ **Oliver H. Perry Monument,** Presque Isle State Park, 5 miles north on Peninsula Drive (State 832). Accessible by ferry.

This monument marks the area where *Oliver Hazard Perry built the fleet that successfully engaged the British in the Anglo-American contest for control of Lake Erie in September 1813. After his victory, Perry declared, "We have met the enemy and they are ours."

§ Open daily Memorial Day weekend-Labor Day, 5 a.m.-dusk (11 p.m. to those in vehicles). Phone: 814-871-4251.

❡ **U.S. Brig *Niagara*,** 164 East Front Street.

The U.S. Brig *Niagara* was the small wooden vessel to which *Oliver H. Perry moved when his flagship was rendered indefensible during the battle of Lake Erie. The only original part of the reconstructed ship is a long section of the keel, recovered when the ship was raised from Misery Bay in 1875.

§ Open Memorial Day weekend-Labor Day, Monday-Saturday 9-5, Sunday 12-5; April 1 to day before Memorial Day weekend, and day after Labor Day to October 31, Saturday 9-5, Sunday 12-5. Fee. Phone: 814-452-2744.

❡ **Wayne Memorial Blockhouse,** State Soldiers' and Sailors' Home, 560 East 3rd Street.

This replica of the blockhouse in which *Anthony Wayne died in 1796 was erected as a memorial to the Revolutionary War general. Although his body was originally buried at the foot of the flagpole here, it was reinterred in Radnor, Pennsylvania, in 1809.

§ Open daily Memorial Day-Labor Day. Phone: 814-871-4531.

FORT WASHINGTON

❡ **Hope Lodge,** 1 mile south at 553 Bethlehem Pike.

After the battle of Germantown in 1777, this mansion was the headquarters of *John Cochran, the surgeon-general of the Continental Army.

§ Open Tuesday-Sunday. Closed most holidays. Phone: 215-646-1595.

GETTYSBURG

❡ **Dobbin House Tavern,** 89 Steinwehr Avenue.

Although the Dobbin House is now a restaurant, it was originally built in 1776 as the home of the Reverend Alexander Dobbin, a native of Londonderry, northern Ireland. Dobbin had come to this area to assume the pastorate of the Rock Creek Presbyterian Church. The house, built on a 300-acre tract which he had bought, served as the dwelling for his increasingly large family – ten children born to his first wife (Isabella Gamble, a native of County Down, Ireland) and nine children already born to his second wife.

To supplement his salary as a minister, Dobbin opened a "Classical Academy" in his home. This school was both a seminary and a liberal arts college, the only one of its kind west of the Susquehanna River. Among his students Dobbins was known not only for his scholarship in Latin, Greek, and Hebrew but also for his skill in biblical interpretation and criticism. He had a personal library of 300 volumes.

§ Phone: 717-334-2100.

¶ **Father Corby Memorial,** St. Francis Xavier Catholic Church, 22 West High Street.

A tablet in front of the church portrays *Father William Corby granting absolution to the Irish Brigade on July 2, 1863, the second day of the battle of Gettysburg.

GETTYSBURG NATIONAL MILITARY PARK

¶ **Father Corby Statue,** South Hancock Avenue.

Dedicated in 1910, this statue depicts *Father William Corby in the act of granting general absolution to the members of the Irish Brigade just before they set out to help occupy Little Round Top on July 2, 1863. The statue was designed by the sculptor *Samuel Aloysius Murray. A replica of the statue stands on the campus of Notre Dame University in South Bend, Indiana.

With the outbreak of the Civil War, Father Corby had been commissioned chaplain of the 88th New York Infantry, one of the many Celtic units in the Irish Brigade. In that capacity he participated in all the campaigns of the Army of the Potomac, seeing service most notably at the battles of Antietam, Fredericksburg, Chancellorsville, Gettysburg, Spotsylvania, and Petersburg. He is best remembered for granting general absolution to the members of the Irish Brigade at Gettysburg.

The scene was later described by St. Clair Mulholland, himself a native of County Antrim, Ireland, and at the time a colonel in the brigade: "As a large majority of the brigade were Catholics, the Chaplain of the brigade, Rev. William Corby, proposed to give a general absolution to all the men before going into the fight. While this is customary in the armies of Catholic countries in Europe, it was perhaps the first time it was ever witnessed on this continent. . . . Father Corby stood on a large rock in front of the brigade. Addressing the men, he explained what he was about to do, saying that each one could receive the benefit of the absolution by a making a sincere act of contrition and firmly

Statue of Father William Corby
as he granted absolution
to the Irish Brigade.

resolving to embrace the first opportunity to confess his sins, urging them to do their duty, and reminding them of the high and sacred nature of their trust as soldiers and the noble object for which they fought. . . . The brigade was standing at 'Order arms!' As he closed his address, every man, Catholic and non-Catholic, fell on his knees with his head bowed down. Then stretching his right hand toward the brigade, Father Corby pronounced the words of absolution . . . ."

Father Corby is remembered in these excerpts from "A Miracle of War" by Smith Johnson:

> With spirits ardent, undismayed,
> With flags uplifted toward the sky,
> There stands brave Meagher's old brigade
> Those noble laurels ne'er will fade
> Upon the page of history.
>
> "All forward, men!" No, pause a while –
> Dead silence follows like parade
> At "order arms," for 'long the file
> There moves a priest with holy smile –

The priest of Meagher's old brigade.

All eyes were toward him reverent turned,
For he was known and loved by all,
And every face with fervor burned,
And with a glance his mission learned –
A mission of high Heaven's call.

Then spake the priest: "My comrades, friends,
Ere long the battle fierce will surge,
Ere long the curse of war descends –
At such a moment God commends
You from the soul all sin to purge.
"Kneel, soldiers; lift your hearts to God,
In sweet contrition crush the pride
Of human minds; kneel on the sod
That soon will welter in your blood –
Look up to Christ, who for you died."

And every man, whate'er his creed,
Kneels down, and whispers pass along
The ranks, and murmuring voices plead
To be from sin's contagion freed
And turned from path of mortal wrong.

Across the vale the gray lines view
The priest and those who, kneeling now,
For absolution humbly sue
And joining hearts, the gray and blue,
Together make the holy vow.

¶ **General Meade Headquarters,** Taneytown Road.

This one-and-a-half-story farmhouse was the headquarters of *General George Gordon Meade, who had been given command of the Army of the Potomac only five days before the battle. Although he was driven from the house by artillery fire on the afternoon of July 3, 1863, the Union troops under his command successfully repulsed the Confederate drive.

After evacuating his headquarters, Meade was confronted by an angry civilian who complained that his house was being used as a hospital and that his property was littered with amputated limbs. When the citizen expressed his intention to seek reimbursement from the government, Meade rebuked him: "Why, you craven fool, until this battle is decided, you do not know, neither do I, if you will have a government to apply to. . . . If I hear any more from you, I will give you a gun and send you to the front to defend your rights." After the battle Meade was named brigadier general in the regular army and received recognition from Congress "for the skill and heroic valor which, at Gettysburg, repelled, defeated and drove back, broken and dispirited, beyond the Rappahannock, the veteran army of the Rebellion."

¶ **General Meade Equestrian Statue,** Hancock Avenue.

¶ **General Reynolds Monuments**
    Three memorials at Gettysburg honor General John Fulton Reynolds: a granite shaft on Reynolds Avenue, about 400 yards west of the road; a statue in the National Cemetery; and an equestrian statue on the Chambersburg road.
    The grandson of an Irish immigrant who had come to America in 1762, Reynolds was a graduate of the U.S. Military Academy and had been breveted for gallantry at Monterey and Buena Vista during the Mexican War. Between that conflict and the Civil War, his tours of garrison duty were interrupted by an overland expedition to Salt Lake City and participation in the campaigns against the Rogue River Indians in Oregon and the Mormons in Utah. On the eve of the Civil War, he was named commandant of cadets at West Point, where he was also a tactics instructor. During the war Reynolds was placed in command of the I Army Corps of the Army of the Potomac. If his plan to attack the enemy's left flank at Chancellorsville had been adopted, the victory might have gone to the Union. In the face of General Lee's expected incursion into the North, Reynolds was ordered to occupy Gettysburg. There, on the first of the three-day struggle that followed, he was killed by a sharpshooter as he led the Second Wisconsin Regiment near the Chambersburg road.

¶ **Irish Brigade Monument,** Sickles Avenue, the Loop.
    Designed by *William O'Donovan, this memorial was dedicated on July 2, 1888, the twenty-fifth anniversary of the Irish Brigade's participation in the battle of Gettysburg. The memorial, in the shape of a Celtic cross, specifically honors the 63rd, 69th, and 88th New York regiments, which initially formed the Irish Brigade. The five medallions on the cross represent the three regiments, New York State, and Ireland. (The Irish Brigade later included the 28th Massachusetts and the 116th Pennsylvania infantries.) During the fighting at Gettysburg, three Irish companies helped capture Little Round Top.
    At the dedication of the monument, William Collins read his poem "In Memory of the Fallen Dead of the Irish Brigade." Stanza VI is reprinted here:
    Here, on the field of Gettysburg, where treason's banner flew:
    Where rushed in wrath the Southern gray to smite the Northern

blue;
Where'er that blue, by valor nerved, in seried ranks was seen
There flashed between it and the foe the daring Irish Green!
And never yet, on any land, rushed forth to Freedom's aid
A braver or more dauntless band than Ireland's brave Brigade.
Pause on their graves! 'Tis holy dust ye tread upon to-day –
The dust of Freedom's martyred dead, whose souls have passed
      away!
   • The Irish Brigade was organized and first commanded by
Thomas Francis Meagher, a native of Waterford, Ireland, who had es-
caped to America from a British penal colony in Tasmania in 1852. He
had been banished to that remote part of the British empire for his in-
volvement in the failed Irish rebellion of 1848. After his arrival in New
York City, he studied and practiced law and was made editor of the
Irish News, a position from which he became the spokesman for the
"Young Ireland" movement in America.
   At the onset of the Civil War, Meagher organized a company of
Zouaves, which was later incorporated into the Irish 69th Volunteers.
In the winter of 1861-62, he organized and commanded the Irish Bri-
gade, whose banner boasted an Irish harp, a wreath of shamrocks, and
the Gaelic motto "They shall never retreat from the charge of lances."
The brigade fought at Bull Run, Fair Oaks, the Seven Days, Antietam,
Fredericksburg, Chancellorsville, and the siege of Yorktown.

¶ O'Rorke Memorial, on Little Round Top.
   This memorial statue of *Colonel Patrick O'Rorke was dedicated in
1889 by veterans of the 140th New York, the regiment which he commanded during its initial ascent of Little Round Top. O'Rorke was shot
in the neck, however, just as he prepared his men to fire on the advancing Confederates ("Here they are, men. Commence firing!"). Despite
his death, his troops repulsed the enemy charge and captured the summit.

¶ Pennsylvania Memorial, at Pleasonton and Sedgwick avenues.
   This huge granite structure was erected in 1910 to honor the 34,530
Pennsylvanians who participated in the battle of Gettysburg. One of
the bronze statues on the sides of the monument is a representation of
Andrew Curtin, the wartime governor of Pennsylvania and the son of
an immigrant from County Clare, Ireland.
   In his first inaugural address, Curtin proclaimed his state's loyalty
to the Union and subsequently aroused such a level of patriotism that
28,000 Pennsylvanians – more than twice the state's quota – responded
to Lincoln's call for troops. (The governor obtained funds from the state
legislature to maintain the extra forces.) Curtin's subsequent solicitude

for his state's soldiers – including caring for them in hospital, retrieving their bodies for burial, and obtaining funds for the support of their orphans – earned him the sobriquet the "Soldier's Friend."

¶ Soldiers' National Cemetery, Baltimore Road to Taneytown Road.
This seventeen-acre cemetery, which contains the graves of 3,604 soldiers, was established through the efforts of *Governor Andrew Curtin. While visiting the field soon after the battle, he was outraged to find that the bodies of some of the fallen men protruded from the ground because they had been buried in such shallow graves. He ordered that these bodies be reinterred decently.

¶ 6th New York Cavalry Memorial.
This commemorative monument was designed by *James Edward Kelly.

¶ 9th Massachusetts Volunteers Monument, on the north slope of Big Round Top.
Dedicated in 1885 by the Society of the Ninth Regiment, this memorial marks the center of the position which the Irish regiment held during the battle of Gettysburg.

¶ 28th Massachusetts Infantry Monument, Sickles Avenue, the Loop.
This memorial was dedicated in 1886 to honor the largest unit in the Irish Brigade. The monument incorporates an Irish harp and the Gaelic phrase *"Faugh A Ballaugh"* ("Clear the Way").

¶ 66th New York Infantry Monument, Sickles Avenue, east of the Loop.
Because this New York regiment contained a large number of Irish soldiers, this memorial features a shamrock in the representation of Union and Confederate soldiers shaking hands.

¶ 69th Pennsylvania Infantry Monument, at the Angle.
Located where the climax of the three-day battle occurred, this obelisk memorial is adorned with an Irish harp and honors the men in *Colonel Dennis O'Kane's infantry unit. Although he was killed in the fighting, his men pushed back a Confederate charge that hoped to break the Union line.

¶ 116th Pennsylvania Infantry Monument, Sickles Avenue, the Loop.
Dedicated in 1889, this unusual memorial depicts a dead soldier

lying near a shattered fence. This image recalls the fact that the 116th went into battle at Gettysburg with 142 men – far below a regiment's normal complement of a thousand soldiers – and emerged with only 100.

*Major St. Clair Mulholland, the 116th's commanding officer, later expressed the feelings which Gettysburg would ultimately arouse in Americans: "The field is fast becoming the National Mecca, and year after year the number of visitors to the ground increases until tens of thousands of Americans annually make a pilgrimage to the holy ground and worship at the shrine where so many noble men laid down their lives in defence of the State and cause. . . . No kings, princes or potentates lie here, but five thousand gallant men, greater than kings, more splendid in their deeds and in their death than any of the princes or great ones who slumber within the fretted walls of Europe's grand old cathedrals – fathers, brothers and kinsmen, men who came from eighteen states to shed their blood on Pennsylvania's soil in defence of the Union and human liberty. No wonder, then, that year by year thousands of Americans visit the field, linger on the long line of battle, dwell on the memories of the fight and meditate upon the heroism displayed in the battle."

HARMONY

⚑ **Legionville,** between Vuss Avenue and State 65. Private.

This was the site of the first training camp for American soldiers during the Revolutionary War. Founded in 1792 by *General Anthony Wayne, the camp was created to teach the troops discipline and combat techniques.

HARRISBURG

⚑ **William Maclay House,** 401 North Front Street. Private.

The oldest portion of this structure was built in 1791 by William Maclay, the son of a farmer from northern Ireland who had come to America in 1734. After settling in this area, the younger Maclay was asked by John Harris to survey and lay out what became known as Harrisburg.

Although Maclay was one of Pennsylvania's senators in the first Congress, his role in the new government did not become widely known until 1880 with the publication of the private journal which he had kept during those crucial years. His diary shows him to have been a determined defender of the small farming class against Alexander Hamilton's mercantile and commercial program. The journal vividly portrays the conflict between the Federalists and their opponents over such issues as protective tariffs, excise taxes, a national bank, the interpretation of the Constitution, and the location of the future national capital. He particularly lamented that so many members of Congress were lawyers ("wrangling is their business") and that Hamilton exercised such undue influence over the President ("[W]ould to God this same General Washington were in heaven! We could not then have him brought forward as the constant cover to every unconstitutional and irrepublican act.").

¶ **Paxton Presbyterian Church,** Paxtang Avenue and Sharon Street.

Organized in 1732, the congregation of this church erected its first house of worship eight years later, a date that makes this the oldest Presbyterian church in continuous use in the state. *William Maclay is buried in the cemetery adjacent to the church.

In 1763 the minister here at the time – the Reverend John Elder of County Antrim, Ireland – organized the "Paxton Boys," a ranger troop composed predominantly of Scotch-Irish settlers and created to defend against the Indians. In their zeal, however, the "Paxton Boys" murdered several Indians in the area and threatened the authorities in Philadelphia because of their failure to protect the settlers on the frontier. Elder and his rangers laid down their arms only because of the influence of Benjamin Franklin.

¶ **Bishop Shanahan Memorial,** St. Patrick's Cathedral, 212 State Street.

This memorial tablet by *Samuel Aloysius Murray honors *John Shanahan, the third bishop of Harrisburg, who served the diocese for seventeen years before his death in 1916. Prior to his installation, Shanahan had been the superintendent of Philadelphia's Catholic school system.

HAZELTON

¶ **Eckley Miners' Village,** 9 miles east off State 940.

This anthracite mining village is representative of the hundreds of such company-owned communities in Pennsylvania during the nineteenth century. Today the village encompasses fifty restored buildings, including a miner's house and two churches, one built in 1862 primarily to serve the Irish. The visitor center features exhibits and slide shows about the mining experience, which was the source of livelihood for thousands of Irish workers and their families. In 1970 Paramount Studios used the village as the setting for its film *The Molly Maguires*, starring Richard Harris and Sean Connery. The "Mollies" were members of a secret organization allegedly responsible for much of the violence against the mine owners.

§ Open Monday-Saturday 9-5, Sunday 12-5. Closed holidays (except Memorial Day, July 4, and Labor Day). Fee. Phone: 717-636-2070.

HERSHEY

¶ Derry Presbyterian Church, 248 East Derry Road.

The oldest part of the present church dates from 1884 and was built to serve a congregation that was first formed by Scotch-Irish settlers in 1724. From 1746 to 1791 its pastor was the *Reverend John Elder. The modern addition to the church is known as the John Elder Memorial Chapel.

For his courageous deeds during the French and Indian War and the Revolution, Elder was nicknamed the "Fighting Parson." In 1777, when the Continental Congress met in nearby York, Elder offered this prayer: "O Lord God of the universe, if Thou art unwilling by divine grace to assist us, then stand aside and let us fight it out for ourselves."

• Near the church is the Pastor's Study and Academy (also known as the First Session House), built of logs in 1732 and revered as the first school on this part of the frontier. The structure contains glass windows, the old pulpit, and a pew door from the original church and a wooden beam from Reverend Elder's barn. The entire structure is now enclosed in glass.

HUNTERSTOWN

¶ Great Conewago Presbyterian Church, Church Road.

Built in 1787, this Georgian fieldstone structure was one of the area's first churches organized by Scotch-Irish settlers.

JIM THORPE

This area of Pennsylvania was a center of activity by a secret society of Irish and Irish-American miners known as the Molly Maguires. Named for an organization that had used violence against the agents of absentee landlords in Ireland, the Molly Maguires were accused of committing fifty murders in this part of the state. The town of Jim Thorpe was created in the mid 1950s when two small communities merged and adopted the name of the famous Olympic athlete. The new town later erected a memorial in honor of Thorpe, who was of mixed Irish, French, and Indian ancestry.

¶ Carbon County Jail, 128 West Broadway.

In 1876 five alleged Molly Maguires were tried in Carbon County on the charge of conspiring to murder a mining company superintendent. Although only one may have been guilty of murder, all five Irishmen were convicted and were hanged in June 1877.

One of those executed was Alexander Campbell, a forty-three-year-old emigrant from Donegal, Ireland. Before leaving Cell 17 in Carbon County Jail, however, he swore his innocence as he placed his hand on the wall of his cell. After his execution his jailers were never able to remove the hand print, despite repeated painting and plastering. Even in modern times the hand print remains visible on the wall. In an unusual "retrial" of his case in December 1993, Campbell's conviction was overturned by a jury in Carbon County. The reenactment of the original 1876 trial took place in Jim Thorpe and was part of the sesquicentennial celebration of the county's court system.

By 1994 the Carbon County Jail had become outdated and after 123 years of use was slated to be razed and replaced by a modern facility. To save the historic jail, Tom McBride, the proprietor of an Irish shop in Jim Thorpe, purchased the structure for $160,000. He plans to open the jail and its fabled Cell 17 to the public.

¶ Jim Thorpe Memorial, 0.5 mile east on State 903.

This monumental mausoleum stands in honor of *Jim Thorpe, the winner of the pentathlon and decathlon in the 1912 Olympics. He was later stripped of his medals when he was accused of previous participation in professional sports. In 1982, however, he was reinstated in the Olympic records and his medals were presented to his family.

KANE

¶ Kane Manor Inn, 230 Clay Street.

This Victorian structure was built in 1870 as the home of General Thomas Kane, whose great-grandfather had emigrated from Ireland about 1750. The inn displays letters to members of the Kane family from five U.S. presidents; Arctic paintings by Elisha Kent Kane, Thomas Kane's brother; and personal belongings of Dr. Evan O'Neill Kane, the first surgeon to perform a self-operation.

• During his lifetime Thomas Kane was noted for his work on behalf of black slaves and the Mormons. By 1848 he had become an outspoken abolitionist, even going so far as to resign as a U.S. commissioner when he believed that his duty to enforce the Fugitive Slave Law of 1850 conflicted with his moral outrage over slavery. In time he became involved in the effort to spirit African Americans to freedom through the Underground Railroad. His concern for the underdog extended also to the Mormons, for whose westward migration he obtained the help of the U.S. government and whom he accompanied across the continent. He won the confidence of Brigham Young to such a degree that, when the Mormon leader urged his people to prevent the arrival of U.S. troops in Utah, Kane convinced him of the futility of such a course of action.

At the beginning of the Civil War, Kane recruited a regiment of hunters and woodsmen called the "Bucktails." Just before the battle of Gettysburg, he successfully delivered to the Union commander the message that the Confederates had obtained the U.S. military code. He was brevetted major general for "gallant and meritorious services at Gettysburg."

• A graduate of the University of Pennsylvania medical school, Elisha Kent Kane served as physician on various maritime expeditions, among them the unsuccessful search in 1850 for survivors of Sir John Franklin's disastrous attempt to find the Northwest Passage five years before.

In 1853 Kane accompanied a second expedition to the Arctic in search of an open polar sea that many scientists believed existed. After passing into unknown waters now known as Kane Basin, the members of the crew were stricken with scurvy but continued in their search, discovering an ice-free channel which they named for John Pendleton Kennedy, the Scotch-Irish secretary of the navy. (Fifty-four years later Kennedy Channel was used by Robert E. Peary on his trek to the Arctic Circle.) After spending a disastrous second winter in the Arctic, Kane and his crew managed to escape, reaching Upernivik, Greenland, in eighty-eight days. The expedition's astronomical, meteorological, geological, and anthropological investigations provided the foundation for future study of the Arctic.

When Kane died in 1857, he received national acclaim, and his body lay in state in New Orleans, Louisville, Columbus, Baltimore, and Independence Hall in Philadelphia.

• In the 1930s, while in his sixties, Dr. Evan O'Neill Kane performed hernia and gall bladder operations on himself, thereby proving the effectiveness of local anesthesia.

¶ **Kane Memorial Chapel,** 30 Chestnut Street.

This chapel was built in 1878 under the direction of *General Thomas Kane for the townspeople of the community which he had established here in 1859.

§ Open Tuesday-Sunday. Phone: 814-837-9729.

LANCASTER

¶ **Fulton Opera House,** 12-14 North Prince Street.

Restored to its nineteenth-century appearance, this 1852 theater was named for *Robert Fulton, a native of nearby Quarryville who proved the commercial viability of steamboat transportation. More than one ghost is said to haunt the interior of the opera house, which is home to local drama and symphony organizations.

¶ James Buchanan Burial Site, Woodward Hill Cemetery, south on State 272 to South Queen Street and then to 538 East Strawberry Street.

A simple monument near the brick chapel marks the grave of *James Buchanan, the fifteenth president of the United States.

§ Open daily sunrise to sunset.

¶ Rock Ford, 3 miles south on Rock Ford Road, off South Duke Street, at Williamson Park.

This was the home of General Edward Hand, a physician by profession and a highly regarded officer during the Revolutionary War.

A native of King's County, Ireland, Hand had studied medicine at Trinity College in Dublin before immigrating to Philadelphia as surgeon's mate with the 18th Royal Irish Regiment. He resigned from the British military in 1774, however, to practice medicine in Lancaster.

With the onset of the Revolution, Hand played a major military role. From heading a battalion of riflemen at the siege of Boston, he went on to serve bravely in the battles of Long Island, White Plains, Trenton, and Princeton. After his promotion to brigadier general, he was sent to mobilize the militia of western Pennsylvania against the Tories and their Indian allies. He also assisted *General John Sullivan in his campaigns against the same threats in central New York. After the war Hand served in the Confederation Congress and the Pennsylvania Assembly and in 1789 urged the new government to select Lancaster as the national capital. An ardent Federalist, he adamantly opposed the election of Thomas Jefferson in 1800. The general died from an apoplectic stroke at his home two years later.

¶ General Hand is buried in Carlisle, Pennsylvania (in the cemetery on East South Street, behind the Army War College).

¶ Wheatland National Historic Landmark, 1.5 miles west on Route 23 at 1120 Marietta Avenue.

Wheatland, a two-and-a-half-story brick mansion, was the permanent home of *James Buchanan from 1848 until his death twenty years later. Prior to becoming the only Pennsylvanian to be elected president of the United States, Buchanan had served in both the U.S. House and Senate and had been secretary of state and American minister to Russia and Great Britain.

In speaking of his beloved home, the former president praised "the

comforts and tranquility of home as contrasted with the troubles, per-
plexities, and difficulties" of political life. Here he wrote *Mr. Buchanan's
Administration on the Eve of the Rebellion* in defense of his policies toward the seceded Southern states. The mansion's seventeen rooms are
restored to their appearance when Buchanan lived here and contain
much of the President's furniture, silverware, and china.

§ Open April-November 30, daily 10-4:15. Closed Thanksgiving.
Fee. Phone: 717-392-8721.

LAUREL

¶ Guinston United Presbyterian Church.

This stone and brick church was erected by Scotch-Irish settlers in
1733.

McCONNELLSBURG

¶ Daniel McConnell House, 114 Lincoln Way. Private.

This late eighteenth-century dressed log house was the residence
of **Daniel McConnell, who founded this community and operated a
tavern here.

MERCERSBURG

¶ James Buchanan Birthplace State Park, 1 mile northwest off
State 16 (Main Street).

A stone pyramid in this eighteen-acre park marks the site of the
log cabin in which *President James Buchanan was born in 1791.
Buchanan's father and grandfather were born in County Donegal, Ireland, while his maternal grandparents had immigrated to Pennsylvania from northern Ireland. Buchanan's father conducted a profitable
trade business with Indians and frontiersmen in this area.

¶ The log cabin in which Buchanan was born is on exhibit on the
campus of Mercersburg Academy, one mile east on Route 16 (Main
Street). The interior of the cabin can be viewed from the outside from
May through November.

¶ James Buchanan Hotel, 17 North Main Street.

This red brick hotel was originally the home and store of *James
Buchanan Sr., whose son, the future president, spent his boyhood here
from 1796 to 1807, when he entered Dickinson College in Carlisle. The
younger Buchanan was expelled from the college, however, for "every
sort of extravagance and mischief," although he later returned and was
graduated *cum laude*. He later said that he had gone into politics "as a

distraction from a great grief," presumably the death of the young woman to whom he had been engaged.

MERION

¶ General Wayne Inn, 625 Montgomery Avenue.
In September 1777 this inn was host to the Marquis de Lafayette and American generals George Washington and *Anthony Wayne. The establishment was named for Wayne after he was the honored guest at celebrations here in 1795.

MILESBURG

¶ Curtin Village, 3 miles northeast of I-80 exit 23 on State 150.
Curtin Village includes the Federal-style mansion and ironworks operation of Roland Curtin, a native of Dysart, County Clare, Ireland. While attending the Irish College in Paris, he barely escaped the guillotine when the Reign of Terror ravaged the city and prompted him to flee to America. From 1807 until his death in 1850, he was engaged in the manufacture of iron at this site. His son Andrew Curtin was the popular governor of Pennsylvania during the Civil War.
§ Open Memorial Day weekend-Labor Day, Wednesday-Saturday 10-4, Sunday 1-5; day after Labor Day-mid October, Saturday 10-4, Sunday 1-5. Fee. Phone: 814-355-1982.

MOUNT JOY

¶ Donegal Presbyterian Church, 1891 Donegal Springs Road.
This church was erected about 1740 for a congregation of Scotch-Irish settlers who had probably come directly from County Donegal, Ireland, twenty years before. The spring near which the church was built is still a source of water.
§ Phone: 717-653-1943.

NEW HOPE

¶ John Chapman House, south on State 232 to Eagle Road. Private.
Prior to the battle of Trenton in December 1776, this structure was the headquarters of *General Henry Knox and Alexander Hamilton, captain of artillery in Washington's army. The two-and-a-half-story stone house belonged to Dr. John Chapman.

¶ Washington Crossing Historic Park, 6 miles south on State 32.
This 500-acre park honors General George Washington and the 2,400

soldiers of the Continental Army who crossed the Delaware River on Christmas Eve in 1776 to capture Trenton, New Jersey, from its Hessian-held garrison.

• McKonkey Ferry Inn, originally owned by ferryman Samuel McKonkey, an Irish Presbyterian, is believed to have been where General Washington dined before crossing the river from Morrisville. Some of the American commander's men, meanwhile, crossed into New Jersey from Taylorville on boats provided by McKonkey, while other troops were transported across the river with the help of Patrick Colvin, a Catholic Irishman who owned and operated a ferry service on the New Jersey side.

• The Memorial Building houses a copy of the famous painting *Washington Crossing the Delaware* by Emanuel Leutz. During the crossing – says the traditional tale – General Washington noticed that *Henry Knox, whose girth was almost as wide as the boat in which he sat, was causing it to list to one side. The usually taciturn commander-in-chief reportedly said to Knox, "Shift your tail and trim [level off] the boat!" The original painting is in the Metropolitan Museum of Art in New York City.

• Every year a reenactment of the crossing is held at 1 p.m. on December 25.

§ Open daily 9-5. Closed Martin Luther King Jr.'s Birthday, Columbus Day, and Thanksgiving. Phone: 215-493-4076.

PAOLI

¶ **Waynesborough,** 1 mile south of U.S. 30 via State 252 at 2049 Waynesborough Road.

This two-and-a-half-story stone house was built in 1724 by the grandfather of *Anthony Wayne, the famous Revolutionary War general. The structure, which was built of stone quarried on the property, displays personal items that belonged to Wayne and other members of his family. The story of the Waynes and Waynesborough is told through a slide presentation.

The elder Wayne was an Englishman who had settled in County Wicklow, Ireland, after fighting for King William at the battle of the Boyne. In 1722 he immigrated to this part of Pennsylvania. Two years later he was followed to America by his son Isaac Wayne, who had been born in Ireland. Isaac's son Anthony was born in this house in 1745. Although the famous American general possessed no Irish blood, he regarded himself as Irish because his father had been born in Ireland and his grandfather had settled there. To prove his sentimental attachment to the land of his father's birth, he always celebrated St. Patrick's Day and in later years became a member of the Friendly Sons of St. Patrick.

§ Open mid March-late December, Tuesday and Thursday 10-4, Sunday 1-4. Fee. Phone: 610-647-1779.

¶ The nearby Paoli Memorial Ground was the site of a surprise attack by the British against General Wayne and his Continental soldiers, encamped there in September 1777.

PERKASIE

¶ Deep Run Presbyterian Church, 16 Irish Meeting House Road.

This congregation was organized in the early 1700s by Scotch-Irish settlers and was a mission station served by *William Tennent after he became pastor at the Neshaminy church in 1726. The original log church at Deep Run was built sometime before 1732. The present church structure on this site is the third, built in 1841 and restored in 1956.

In 1738 the congregation received its first pastor, the Reverend Francis McHenry, a descendant of an old Irish family from County Antrim, northern Ireland. He had immigrated to America only three years before and was ordained the year of his arrival at Deep Run. Since McHenry served here until his death in 1757, he is most likely buried in the cemetery.

§ Phone: 215-249-3689.

PHILADELPHIA

¶ Balch Institute for Ethnic Studies, 18 South 7th Street.

The institute's library contains research material on at least seventy ethnic groups, including the Irish, while the museum features photographs, clothing, and other exhibits about America's many immigrants.

§ Library open Monday-Saturday 9-5; museum open Monday-Saturday 10-4. Phone: 215-925-8090.

¶ Christ Church Burial Ground, 5th and Arch streets.

Among those interred in the churchyard are three prominent members of the Irish-American community in Philadelphia: Pierce Butler, John Dunlap, and Philip Syng Physick.

Butler was born in County Carlow, Ireland, and was one of the Irish-born signers of the Constitution. Dunlap, a native of Strabane, County Tyrone, was a well known printer and publisher in the city. In 1784 he began publishing *The Pennsylvania Packet*, the first daily newspaper in the United States. He had the distinction of being the first to print the Declaration of Independence (from Thomas Jefferson's manuscript) and the Constitution of the United States. Physick, meanwhile, is known as the "Father of American Surgery" and was the grandson of an Irish immigrant.

¶ **City Hall,** Penn Square, Broad and Market streets.
  • The Irish Founders Memorial, a bronze tablet inside City Hall, was erected in 1926 by the United Irish Societies of Philadelphia to honor men of Irish birth or lineage who risked their lives and fortunes during the American Revolution.
  The plaque lists the names of thirteen signers of the Declaration of Independence, including two who are sometimes mistaken for Irish – John Hart and William Whipple. The tablet also includes the names of the following military and naval leaders: John Barry, James Clinton, Arthur Dillon, Edward Hand, William Irvine, Henry Knox, Andrew Lewis, Richard Montgomery, Stephen Moylan, Jeremiah O'Brien, Walter Stewart, John Sullivan, and Anthony Wayne. At the bottom of the memorial plaque is a famous remark which the British statesman Lord Chatham made during the Revolution: "The whole Irish Nation favors America. Ireland is with them to the man."
  At the dedication of the memorial, Michael Donohoe, the national president of the Ancient Order of Hibernians, commented that the tablet contains only a very small number of those who sacrificed for the American revolutionary cause. He added that the memorial "could not enumerate the 695 Kellys who fought for America, nor the 494 Murphys, or the 322 Ryans who volunteered on the side of liberty. It has been shown conclusively that twelve of the more familiar Irish family names furnished 3841 enlisted on the rolls of the patriot forces, an average of 320 for each of those good old Celtic names."
  • A bronze equestrian statue of *General John Fulton Reynolds, a Civil War officer who was killed while leading his troops at Gettysburg, is on the north side of City Hall.

¶ **Civil War Library and Museum,** 1805 Pine Street.
  The museum's collection includes life masks of Abraham Lincoln and uniforms worn by Union generals *George Gordon Meade and *Ulysses S. Grant.
  § Open Monday-Saturday 10-4, Sunday 11-4. Closed holidays. Fee. Phone: 215-735-8196.

¶ **Declaration House,** on the southwest corner of 7th and Market streets.
  This is a reconstruction of the original house built here in 1775 by Jacob Graff and used by Thomas Jefferson when he drafted the Declaration of Independence. The house was later occupied by the Irishman

John Dunlap, in whose printing office the Declaration of Independence and the U.S. Constitution were first set in type and printed.

From 1778 until the capital of the new federal government was moved to New York, Dunlap served as official printer to Congress. About his work the contemporary publisher Isaiah Thomas wrote: "Dunlap executed his printing in a neat and correct manner. It is said that, whilst he conducted a newspaper, he never inserted a paragraph which would wound the feelings of an individual!" The extent of Dunlap's financial success as a publisher is evident in his subscription of £4,000 for the creation of the National Bank of the United States in 1780.

§ Open daily 9-5. Closed January 1 and December 25. Phone: 215-597-8974.

ℐ Edgar Allan Poe National Historic Site, 532 North 7th Street.

This small building, which *Edgar Allan Poe knew as "Spring Garden Cottage," was his home from 1842 to 1844. Poe did most of his writing in the small first-floor room and in a bedroom upstairs. During this time he wrote "The Gold-Bug," "The Black Cat," "The Tell-Tale Heart," "The Murders in the Rue Morgue," "The Fall of the House of Usher," and the first draft of "The Raven." Poe's mysterious words "Death to the" can still be seen carved in the parlor.

Poe, his dying wife, and his mother-in-law were in such an impoverished condition that his wife's mother sold most of their furnishings to pay the rent and to cover her daughter's medical expenses. When Poe moved from Philadelphia, he reputedly left with only his books and two cats.

§ Open daily 9-5. Closed January 1 and December 25. Phone: 215-597-8780.

ℐ Fairmount Park

Throughout the park are several sculptures with Irish or Irish-American associations:

• The Catholic Total Abstinence Fountain on Concourse Drive, east of George's Hill, was erected in 1876 and is surrounded by statues of *Bishop John Carroll, *Father Theobald Mathew, *Charles Carroll of Carrollton, and *Commodore John Barry.

• Erected in 1899, a statue of Union commander *Ulysses S. Grant stands at East River Drive and Fountain Green Drive.

• A bronze equestrian statue of *General George Gordon Meade, the commander of Union troops at Gettysburg, is on Lansdowne Drive in West Fairmount Park.

• The Soldiers' Memorial at the 41st Street entrance includes colossal statues of generals *George Gordon Meade, *John Fulton Reynolds,

Winfield Scott Hancock, and George McClellan. One of the eight bronze busts on the monument is that of *Andrew Curtin, the wartime governor of Pennsylvania.

• A bronze portrait bust of President James Garfield by *Augustus Saint-Gaudens is located on East River Drive below the Gerard Avenue Bridge. The monument was erected in 1896.

• *The Pilgrim* by *Augustus Saint-Gaudens is located along Kelly Drive. This statue is almost identical to Saint-Gaudens' *Puritan*, a likeness of Deacon Samuel Chapin in Springfield, Massachusetts.

• *The Stone Age* by *John Boyle depicts a Native American mother holding a stone hatchet with which she has just killed a bear cub. One of her children is at her feet, while another is clasped in her arms.

Kelly Drive is named for John ("Jack") Kelly and his son of the same name – both of them native sons renowned for their feats in Olympic rowing competition.

¶ Franklin Statue, College Hall, University of Pennsylvania.

This heroic seated bronze statue of Benjamin Franklin in front of College Hall is the work of sculptor *John Boyle. The statue was presented to the city of Philadelphia in 1900 by J. C. Strawbridge and originally stood in front of the U.S. Post Office. When that building was razed in 1938, the statuary was placed on permanent loan with the University of Pennsylvania and was rededicated the next year.

¶ Free Quaker Meetinghouse, 5th and Arch streets.

During the American Revolution, the congregation of this church numbered about 100 members, some of Irish birth. This rebuilt 1804 building is the largest Quaker meetinghouse in the world. The diorama inside depicts events from the life of William Penn: writing his "Frame of Government," negotiating a treaty with the Indians, and perusing a map of Philadelphia by his surveyor, Thomas Holme, a native of Ireland. Among those buried in the church cemetery are two other Irish Quakers who were influential in the colonial history of Philadelphia: James Logan and Lydia Darragh.

• Tradition has it that Thomas Holme was born in Waterford, Ireland. He was certainly among the soldiers in Cromwell's army who received a land grant in Ireland about 1655. Holme subsequently joined the Society of Friends and coauthored a pamphlet describing the persecution of fellow Quakers in Ireland.

In 1682 he was appointed surveyor-general of Pennsylvania by that colony's founder and was ordered to select the site of the future Philadelphia. That same year he surveyed and mapped the earliest part of the city, naming the streets for famous personages. When Penn arrived in the City of Brotherly Love later that year, however, he expressed his dislike for such a naming system, considering it "man-worship," and replaced it with numbers and the names of trees and flowers.

Holme was also a member of Pennsylvania's first assembly and its provincial council and was for a time its acting governor. He died on his plantation in Dublin township in Philadelphia County. A copper plate which Holme engraved with his map of the city is in the collection of the Historical Society of Pennsylvania.

• Born in 1674 in County Armagh, Ireland, James Logan began his career in the province as William Penn's secretary, arriving in Philadelphia with the proprietor in 1699. In subsequent years he variously served as member of the provincial council, chief executive of the province, alderman and mayor of Philadelphia, and chief justice of the Pennsylvania Supreme Court.

Although Logan was a member of the Society of Friends and identified with the political interests of the colony's Quaker elite, he was not a "strict professor" of the sect's beliefs. On more than one occasion he demonstrated a belief in aggressive self-defense that alienated his coreligionists. When the ship that first brought him to America was attacked by pirates, for example, Logan defended the vessel with appropriate physical force. Later in his career he suggested that Friends should not be candidates for the colony's legislature unless they could in good conscience bring themselves to vote for measures to defend the citizenry.

Despite Logan's busy public and private life, he was renowned for his scholarship. By age sixteen he had mastered Latin, Greek, Hebrew, Italian, French, and Spanish. In his more mature years he published essays on ethics, science, law, and anatomy and translated Cato's *Moral Distiches* and Cicero's *On Old Age*. He was especially interested in botany and developed a friendship with the Philadelphia botanist John Bartram. Logan's botanical experiments even attracted the attention of Linnaeus, the famous Swedish botanist, who named for Logan an order of thirty genera and over 300 species (*Loganiaceae*). The Philadelphian's most important scientific work was a series of experiments to prove the sexuality of plants. Logan's grave in the Friends' cemetery is unmarked.

• Lydia Barrington Darragh was a woman of unusual daring known for her courage on behalf of the Patriot cause. Born in Dublin in 1729, she married William Darragh, most likely a tutor in her father's household, in a ceremony at the Friends' Meeting House in the Irish capital. By at least 1766 she and her husband had immigrated to Philadelphia, where they joined the congregation of the Monthly Meeting of Friends. Once in America, Lydia became engaged in midwifery and nursing and even expressed a desire to open a mortuary establishment. In carrying out this intention, she placed an advertisement in the *Pennsylvania Ga-*

zette for December 4, 1766, announcing her intention to "make Grave-Clothes, and lay out the Dead, in the Neatest Manner." At her death she left an estate worth more than £1,600.

> During their occupation of Philadelphia, the British occasionally held their staff meetings at the Darraghs' house on South Second Street, perhaps because of its proximity to British headquarters. Following one such meeting on the night of December 2, Lydia was presented with an unusual opportunity to help the Patriot cause. Although the British had told the Darraghs to retire for the evening, Lydia eavesdropped on the discussion and learned that General William Howe planned to attack General Washington and his troops at Whitemarsh – just outside the city – two days later. In addition, she discovered that the British were leaving the next day with 5,000 troops, thirteen cannon, a baggage train, and eleven boats on wagon wheels. After overhearing the plans, Lydia returned to her room and pretended to have been asleep by answering a British officer's call at her door only after the third knock.

After the British left the house, Lydia made every effort to inform Washington's troops, among whom was her son, an officer in the Second Pennsylvania Militia Regiment. Using a pass which she had previously obtained, she set out for Whitemarsh on the morning of December 4. Once past the British lines, she headed toward the encamped Americans, thirteen miles away. Along the route she encountered Lieutenant Colonel Thomas Craig of the American Light Horse Cavalry and informed him of the British plans, which he immediately carried to Washington. (Another account tells how either Lydia or a female messenger sent by her also passed the message on to Elias Boudinot, Washington's director of intelligence, while he was dining at a tavern outside Philadelphia. Boudinot rode to Washington's headquarters with the message, concealed in a needlebook which the woman had given him.) As a result of the heroine's actions, the Americans were ready with troops and cannon when the British arrived at Whitemarsh, although several days of skirmishing ensued. On December 8 the British returned to Philadelphia, chastened if not outright defeated.

When a British officer later questioned Lydia to determine whether any of her family had been awake when the British discussed their plans against the Americans, Lydia equivocated. To her statement that they had retired at 8 p.m., the officer naively replied: "I know *you* were asleep, for I knocked at your chamber door three times before you heard me; – I am entirely at a loss to imagine who gave General Washington information of our intended attack, unless the walls of the house could speak. When we arrived near White Marsh, we found all their cannon mounted, and the troops prepared to receive us; and we have marched back like a parcel of fools."

§ Open Memorial Day-Labor Day, Tuesday-Saturday 10-4, Sunday 12-4.

❡ Hill-Physick-Keith House, 321 South 4th Street.

For a time beginning in 1815, this four-story brick house was the home of Dr. Philip Syng Physick, the "Father of American Surgery."

Named for his Irish immigrant grandfather (Philip Syng, one of Philadelphia's finest silversmiths), Physick studied medicine in London and was graduated from the University of Edinburgh in 1792. He was subsequently a staff member at the Pennsylvania Hospital and a lecturer in surgery at the University of Pennsylvania. Especially noted for his innovations, he invented needle forceps and the guillotine tonsillotomy, for example, and is reputed to have been the first American physician to use the stomach tube. He promoted the use of animal ligatures in surgery and became famous for his skill in operating for bladder stone. In one celebrated instance, he performed such a procedure on seventy-three-year-old Chief Justice John Marshall, extracting almost 1,000 calculi. Before his own death Physick directed that his grave be guarded to prevent the theft of his body and its subjection to an autopsy.

§ Open Tuesday-Saturday 10-4, Sunday 1-4. Fee. Phone: 215-925-7866.

❡ Historical Society of Pennsylvania, 1300 Locust Street.

Among the society's holdings are paintings by Irish-American artists and a copper plate engraved by *Thomas Holme with his map of Philadelphia.

§ Museum and library open Tuesday-Friday 9-5; library also open Monday 1-9. Phone: 215-732-6200.

❡ Independence Hall, Chestnut Street, between 5th and 6th streets, on Independence Square.

The Declaration of Independence was adopted here in July 1776, although most of the signatures on it were not affixed until the following August. Three signers of the Declaration were natives of Ireland (James Smith, George Taylor, and Matthew Thornton), while eight other signers were American-born of Irish or Scotch-Irish descent (Charles Carroll, John Hancock, Thomas Lynch Jr., Thomas McKean, Thomas Nelson Jr., Robert Treat Paine, George Read I, and Edward Rutledge).

For approximately a month after the adoption of the Declaration, the only two signatures on the document were those of Hancock and Charles Thomson, the Irish-born secretary of the Continental Congress. § Open daily 9-5. Phone: 215-597-8974.

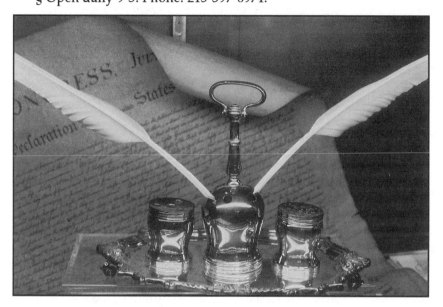

A copy of the Philip Syng inkstand, used in the signing of the Declaration of Independence.

• The inkstand which was used at the signing of the Declaration of Independence and the Constitution was made by Philip Syng, a native of Ireland and Philadelphia's famous silversmith. The inkstand, which is on exhibit in Independence Hall, was commissioned by the Pennsylvania Assembly in 1752 and cost £25. After being used by successive Speakers of the Assembly, it was given to the Continental Congress in 1775 and was used by each signer of the Declaration of Independence. When the state capital was transferred to Harrisburg, the inkstand made the move also and was used by the Pennsylvania legislature until 1849, when knowledge of its whereabouts became lost. After its recovery the historic silver piece was restored to Independence Hall on June 7, 1875, the centenary of the day on which a resolution calling for independence from Britain was first introduced in the Continental Congress.

• The Declaration of Independence was first read in public by Colonel John Nixon, the son of Richard Nixon of County Wexford, Ireland. The document was read at noon on July 8, 1776, from an observatory in the yard of Independence Hall.

❡ Today the yard of Independence Hall is dominated by a bronze statue of Irish-born John Barry, the "Father of the American Navy." Sculpted by *Samuel Aloysius Murray, the statue is nine and a half feet in height and stands atop a twelve-foot granite pedestal. With out-stretched arm as if in the act of giving a command, the admiral wears a great coat and carries a naval spy glass in one arm and a sheathed sword by his side. The front of the pedestal bears the name "Barry," while the rear is inscribed with the words: "Commodore John Barry, U.S.N., Fa-ther of the Navy, born in Wexford, Ireland, 1745, died in Philadelphia September 13, 1803. Presented to the City of Philadelphia by the Soci-ety of the Friendly Sons of St. Patrick, 1907."

❡ **John Keating Burial Site,** St. John the Baptist Catholic Church, 119 Rector Street, Manayunk district.

Born of Anglo-Norman descent in County Limerick, Ireland, in 1760, John Keating immigrated to France while still a child and was edu-cated at the College of the English Benedictines at Douay, Flanders. After joining the Irish Brigade in the French army, he commanded the Walsh Regiment when in 1792 it accompanied French troops to Santo Domingo to crush a native uprising there. Within a few days of his arrival, he realized the futility of the situation and determined to extri-cate himself from it. "The blacks were in full insurrection," he wrote. "The whole country was in their power. The plantations had all been burned, the whites and the troops were confined to the town. . . ." Keating left for America almost immediately, ironically with a letter of introduction to George Washington from General Rochambeau, the new governor of Santo Domingo and the son of Washington's revolution-ary comrade-in-arms.

Keating first lived in Wilmington, Delaware, where for a time he was a business associate of the Du Pont family. After moving to Phila-delphia, he became involved with land speculators and their coloniza-tion efforts along the Susquehanna River. It was during this time that he managed the Ceres Land Company, which owned 300,000 acres in this part of the state. He later became a trustee of the University of Pennsylvania and a manager of the Philadelphia Savings Fund Society.

In 1855, about a year before his death, the Irishman looked back over his career: "In 1783 Napoleon was a lieutenant of the 2nd battal-ion of the Régiment de la Frères Artillery, and I a captain of the 2nd battalion of the 92nd Regiment of Infantry. Two years afterwards I was captain, and I had the cross of St. Louis given me by Louis XVI. I am, perhaps, the only surviving chevalier created by that unhappy prince. Napoleon, for years master of Europe, but ending his astonishing ca-reer on a rock exiled from his country and family, dies immortalized by his triumphs and his misfortunes, and I live in the midst of my children without any ills, manager of a large land company." Keating died at the age of ninety-six.

§ Phone: 215-482-4600.

¶ John McCullough Burial Site, Mount Moriah Cemetery, Kingsessings Avenue.

An ornate monument erected in 1888 marks the grave site of John McCullough, an Irish-born actor who achieved a national reputation during a twenty-seven-year career. The bust of the actor was sculpted by *William Clark Noble.

Born to peasant parents near Londonderry, northern Ireland, McCullough came to America in 1847 and first worked as a chairmaker in Philadelphia. Although at age fifteen he was unable to read or write, a few years of study prepared him for the stage. His longest acting association was with Edwin Forrest, initially playing supporting roles but then taking the leads in Shakespeare's tragedies as well as in *Richelieu, Damon and Pythias,* and *Virginius.* Midway through his career, he spent two years at McGuire's Theater in San Francisco and then on a series of cross-country tours. His acting was cut prematurely short, however, because of illness.

Although McCullough returned to the stage in the last two years of his life, he suffered a breakdown during a performance in Chicago. The audience, unaware of the reason for his failure to remember his lines, responded to his embarrassment with laughter. His last words to an audience were delivered that night: "Ladies and gentlemen, you are the worst mannered audience I ever saw. If you had suffered tonight as I have, you would never have done this. Good night."

§ Phone: 215-729-1295.

¶ Kelly Memorial, in a small park along the Schuylkill River, near the intersection of Midvale Avenue and Kelly Drive.

This bronze statue depicting John ("Jack") Kelly in his Olympic rowing scull was erected in 1965 as a tribute to the Philadelphia native whose rowing victories were legendary. The statue is located near rowing grandstands along the river.

Kelly, the grandson of Irish immigrant parents, joined one of the city's rowing clubs at the age of twenty. During the next fifteen years, he scored 126 sculling victories, a record unmatched by an American rower. Following World War I, during which he served in the American Expeditionary Force in France, he established the construction company that eventually made him a millionaire many times over. After taking up rowing again, he promptly became the national single sculls champion for 1919 and 1920 and won the singles competition at the Olympics in that latter year. With his cousin Paul Costello, he won the doubles competition in both the 1920 and the 1924 Olympics. In 1945 Kelly established the John B. Kelly Award, to be given each year to the person who has done the most to promote athletics among young people. Kelly's daughter Grace became a film star and the princess of Monaco, while his namesake son participated in four Olympic rowing competitions.

¶ **Moylan Park,** 25th and Diamond streets.

This park is named in honor of Stephen Moylan, an officer during the Revolutionary War and the first president of the Friendly Sons of St. Patrick. A memorial in the park was dedicated to Moylan in 1922 by the Friendly Sons and is inscribed with the highlights of his military career.

Moylan was born in 1737 in Cork, Ireland, the son of a highly successful merchant and his wife, the Countess of Limerick. (His brother was the Catholic bishop of Cork, while his two sisters were Ursuline nuns. Later in America Stephen Moylan and his two half-brothers were called "the three polite Irishmen.") Because educational opportunities for Catholics were limited in Ireland, Moylan pursued his education in Paris and later spent several years in Lisbon associated with his father's shipping business. In 1771, three years after coming to Philadelphia, he was elected president of the Friendly Sons of St. Patrick even though this charitable society was composed almost entirely of Protestants.

With the outbreak of the Revolution, Moylan joined the Continental Army at Cambridge, Massachusetts. Because of his commercial experience, he was at first assigned to the commissariat department. He quickly became General Washington's secretary and then quartermaster general of the army, with the rank of colonel. After only four months, however, he resigned from the latter position, apparently because of his failure to reorganize the army. Now back in the field, he was easily recognized by his unusual uniform: red waistcoat, bright green coat, bearskin hat, and buckskin breeches. After serving with distinction in the battle of Princeton, he rhapsodized: "I know I never felt so much like one of Homer's Deities before. We trod on air – it was a glorious day!"

Moylan subsequently raised and led a cavalry unit known as the Fourth Pennsylvania Light Dragoon under the overall command of Casimir Pulaski. When Moylan and his Polish superior quarreled, the Irishman was court-martialed for insubordination but was later acquitted. (After the Polish officer resigned his command, Moylan was appointed in his place.) Toward the end of the war, Moylan and his dragoons assisted Lafayette in forcing Cornwallis's surrender at Yorktown.

¶ **Nathaniel Irish House,** 704 South Front Street. Private.

This three-and-a-half-story house with dormer windows was the home of Nathaniel Irish, a carpenter of most probably Irish descent who built it for himself about 1769. This Flemish bond brick house was one of several Georgian row houses built by Nathaniel Irish, a member of the Carpenters Company of Philadelphia.

¶ **Old St. Mary's Catholic Church**, 4th Street, above Spruce Street.

The graveyard of Philadelphia's second oldest Catholic church is the final resting place of several illustrious Irishmen: John Barry, Mathew Carey, Thomas FitzSimons, George Meade, and Stephen Moylan.

> In 1876 the tomb of John Barry was rededicated with the following inscription: "Sacred to the memory of Commodore John Barry, Father of the American Navy. Let the Christian, patriot and soldier who visits these mansions of the dead view this monument with respect and veneration. Beneath it rests the remains of John Barry, who was born in County Wexford, Ireland, in the year 1745. America was the object of his patriotism and the aim of his usefulness and ambition. At the beginning of the Revolutionary War he held the commission of captain in the then limited navy of the Colonies. His achievements in battle and his renowned naval tactics merited for him the position of Commodore, and to be justly regarded as the Father of the American Navy. He fought often, and bled in the cause of freedom. But his deeds of valor did not diminish in him the virtues which adorned his private life. He was eminently gentle, kind, just and charitable, and no less beloved by his family and friends than by his grateful country. Firm in the faith and practice of the Catholic Church, he departed this life on the 13th day of September, 1803, in the fifty-ninth year of his age. In grateful remembrance a few of his countrymen, members of St. Mary's Church, and others, have contributed toward this second monument. Erected July 1, 1876. *Requiescat in pace.*"

• Born in Dublin in 1760, Mathew Carey early determined on a career in printing and bookselling. When at age nineteen he published an anonymous pamphlet against British mistreatment of Irish Catholics, he wisely left Ireland for Paris. While in the French capital, he made the acquaintance of Benjamin Franklin and found employment for several months in the famous American's printing office in France.

By 1783 Carey had returned to Dublin and, with his father's patronage, assumed the ownership of the *Volunteer's Journal*. While carrying out the paper's purpose of defending the Irish against English oppression, Carey was arrested for a verbal attack on the Prime Minister and the House of Commons. Following his release, he prudently sailed for the United States, disguised as a woman.

Once in Philadelphia, Carey began his career as a publisher, thanks to a $400 gift from the Marquis de Lafayette. (Carey returned the gift forty years later, when the Frenchman revisited the United States.) As editor of the *Pennsylvaniaa Herald*, Carey introduced a novelty in American journalism by reporting almost verbatim the debates of the Pennsylvania Assembly, using a shorthand of his own invention. An unfortunate duel with a rival editor, however, left him permanently crippled.

In 1786, with five partners, Carey began publication of the *Columbian Magazine*, the first successful American production of that genre. In the magazine's first issue, the Irishman made a number of predictions about America sixty years into the future: the thirtieth state would have been admitted, 10,000 blacks would have been transported from Virginia to a settlement in Africa, "very few" African Americans would remain in the United States, and a canal across the Isthmus of Panama would have been completed. Before long, however, Carey left the partnership to found the rival *American Museum*, which published such articles as medical and educational essays, antislavery tracts, and serials like the *Federalist Papers*, Paine's *Common Sense* and *Crisis*, and Dickinson's *Letters from a Pennsylvania Farmer*. One selection – the reprint of a poem recounting the dialogue between a dead cat and a dog lying in the filth of Philadelphia's streets – led to the creation of the city's first street-sweeping brigade. In related civic activity, he founded the Hibernian Society for the relief of Irish immigrants and helped establish the first nonsectarian Sunday School in America.

Because of financial difficulties, Carey abandoned the *American Museum* and devoted himself to publishing and selling books. By 1824 he had published more works by American authors than any other publisher, and he was the first person in America to publish the works of Charles Dickens and Sir Walter Scott. He also published the first Catholic edition of the Bible in the United States. His trade eventually expanded to all parts of the country, and he had agents and exchange agreements with publishers in Europe and South America. One of

Carey's most regular customers was Thomas Jefferson, who, in a letter of 1820, acknowledged receipt of a chemistry book from Carey's bookselling business. At the height of his career, Carey did business amounting to $300,000 and frequently employed as many as 150 workers.

Carey himself was a prolific writer on many of the urgent issues of the day. He composed almost sixty pamphlets advocating a protective tariff and a series of pamphlets calling for reconciliation between the Federalists and the Democratic Republicans over sectional differences that threatened the Union. In the face of the 1832 tariff nullification crisis between the federal government and South Carolina, he wrote and issued *The Crisis; An Appeal to the good sense of the nation against the spirit of resistance and dissolution of the Union*. He ended the work with a monitory epitaph: "Here to the ineffable joy of the Despots, and Friends of Despotism, throughout the world, and the universal distress and mortification of the friends of human liberty, lie the shattered remains of the noblest fabric of Government ever devised by man, the Constitution of the United States."

• Thomas FitzSimons, George Meade, and Stephen Moylan were

One of several memorials in honor of John Barry at Old St. Mary's Church.

among the twenty-four founding members of the Friendly Sons of St. Patrick at its creation in Philadelphia on March 17, 1771. According to the rules of the society, each member had to provide for himself a gold medal inscribed accordingly: "On the right HIBERNIA. On the left AMERICA. In the center LIBERTY joining the Hands of HIBERNIA and AMERICA, to be represented by the usual figures of a Female supported by a Harp for HIBERNIA – an Indian with his quiver on his back and his bow slung for AMERICA. Underneath UNITE. On the reverse ST. PATRICK trampling on a snake, a Cross in his hand, dressed in his Pontifical robes."

§ Open daily 9-5. Phone: 215-923-7930.

¶ **Penn's Landing,** between Market and Lombard streets, along the Delaware River.

This thirty-seven-acre area marks the landing site of William Penn in 1682. Seventeen years later Penn returned to the city aboard the *Canterbury*, accompanied by his Irish secretary, James Logan, a native of County Armagh. Today the park features a sculpture garden, several historic ships, and concerts and festivals during the year.

Although Penn was of English ancestry, his father owned Macroom Castle in County Cork, and it was there that the younger Penn, while in his twenties, was converted to a new sect known as Quakers or Friends. Almost immediately, however, Penn and some of his Irish coreligionists were imprisoned for nonconformity.

¶ **Philadelphia Museum of Art,** Benjamin Franklin Parkway at 26th Street.

Besides its collection of Renaissance and contemporary American paintings, the museum has extensive holdings of Irish and Irish-American paintings, furniture, and silver. Its most treasured silver pieces are by the Irishman Philip Syng.

A native of Cork, Syng learned the silversmith trade from his father, who had brought his family to Philadelphia sometime before 1720. The younger Syng eventually became known as one of Philadelphia's finest craftsmen. His most famous work is the inkstand which he made for the Pennsylvania Assembly and which was used at the signing of the Declaration of Independence and the Constitution. His hallmark consisted of his initials in Roman capitals enclosed by a rectangle.

Probably through his acquaintance with Benjamin Franklin, Syng developed a machine which helped generate electricity. He was also the treasurer of the American Philosophical Society, a founder of the University of Pennsylvania, and a vestryman of Philadelphia's Christ Church. He and his wife had twenty-one children. One of his grandsons was Philip Syng Physick, the "Father of American Surgery."

§ Open Tuesday-Sunday 10-5, Wednesday 10-9. Closed holidays. Fee. Phone: 215-763-8100.

¶ **Presbyterian Historical Society,** Lombard and 3rd streets.

Three of the six stone statues outside the entrance to the society's headquarters are representations of Presbyterian ministers of Scotch-Irish descent: Francis Makemie, the founder of Presbyterianism in the United States; James Caldwell, the "Soldier Parson" known for his active military support for the American Revolution; and John McMillan, the "Father of Education in Western Pennsylvania."

Statue of Francis Makemie at the Presbyterian Historical Society.

¶ **South Front Street Historic District,** 700-712 South Front Street.

This is a continuous block of eighteenth-century Georgian row houses built before 1769 by such craftsmen as Daniel Harrison, Nathaniel Irish, and Samuel Smith, all of whom were most likely Irish.

¶ **Stenton,** 18th and Courtland streets, Germantown.

This Georgian colonial brick house was built in 1728 by *James Logan, William Penn's secretary, on what was originally a 500-acre estate. The mansion's second-floor library once housed Logan's collection of more than 3,000 books, at one time the finest private collection in America and now part of the holdings of the Library Company of

"Stenton," the home of Irish-born James Logan.

Philadelphia (on Broad Street between Christian and Carpenter Streets).

Despite his busy public life, Logan was able to acquire a fortune through land speculation and trade with the Indians. His relation with the Native Americans was so good that they were often his guests at Stenton. As many as 400 at a time visited for several weeks, some sleeping on the mansion's interior staircase. In 1742 the chief of the Onondagas saluted Logan as "a wise man and a fast friend to the Indians." Stenton was visited twice by General Washington: once on his way to the battle of Brandywine in 1777 and again during the Constitutional Convention, when he witnessed some farm experiments on the estate. The mansion was used by the British general Sir William Howe as his headquarters during the battle of Germantown. (See Free Quaker Meetinghouse, Philadelphia.)

§ Open April-December 31, Tuesday-Saturday 1-4. Fee. Phone: 215-329-7312.

ℐ Thomas FitzSimons Statue, Logan Circle.

This statue of one of the Irish signers of the Constitution was presented to the city of Philadelphia on Constitution Day, September 17, 1946, by the Society of the Friendly Sons of St. Patrick. The eight-foot bronze statue depicts FitzSimons in the act of stepping forward – with quill pen in hand – to sign the famous document. The inscription on the front pedestal reads: "Thomas FitzSimons. Born in Ireland 1741.

Died in Philadelphia in 1811. Member of the Continental Congress. Signer of the Constitution of the United States. Member of the 1st, 2nd & 3rd Congresses." He was the only Catholic signer of the Constitution.

While still a relative newcomer to Philadelphia, the Irish-born FitzSimons had formed a mercantile partnership with his brother-in-law, George Meade (whose father was an Irish refugee from County Limerick.) During the Revolution, FitzSimons contributed liberally in ships, supplies, and money to the Patriot cause. As a member of the first Congress under the new Constitution, he urged passage of a bill creating a protective tariff for America's developing industries.

In addition, FitzSimons was instrumental in creating the first bank in America, was a founder and director of the Insurance Company of North America, and served for many years as president of the Philadelphia Chamber of Commerce. He was also a trustee of the University of Pennsylvania, a member of the Hibernia Society in Philadelphia, and a benefactor of St. Augustine's Catholic Church. At the height of his commercial success, FitzSimons owned a fleet of fourteen ships. Because of imprudent loans and attacks upon American shipping during the Napoleonic era, however, he suffered financial failure.

¶ **Todd-Moylan House,** on the northeast corner of 4th and Walnut streets.

This house was the home of John Todd and his wife *Dolley Payne from 1791 to 1793, when both he and the couple's young son died during a fever epidemic. It was here that Aaron Burr introduced the young widow to James Madison, then a member of the House of Representatives and later president of the United States. The two were married in September 1794.

Between 1796 and 1807 this brick row house was the home of *Stephen Moylan, the Revolutionary War officer and aide-de-camp to General George Washington.

§ Open daily 9-5. Closed January 1 and December 25. Fee. Phone: 215-597-8974.

PITTSBURGH

¶ **Allegheny Cemetery,** 4734 Butler Street, Lawrenceville.

This is the final resting place of Pittsburgh pioneer *James O'Hara, renowned songwriter *Stephen Collins Foster, and financier and philanthropist *Andrew Mellon.

¶ **Croghan House,** Stanton Heights Golf Course, opposite 4424 Stanton Avenue.

This Classic Revival mansion was built about 1835 by William Croghan Jr., whose Irish-born father had distinguished himself as a soldier during the Revolutionary War.

The younger Croghan attended Litchfield Law School and Dickinson College and studied medicine at the University of Pennsylvania. His wife, Mary O'Hara, was the daughter of *James O'Hara, an Indian trader, a member of *General Anthony Wayne's campaign against the Indians, and one of the founders of Pittsburgh's first glassworks. (His home in Pittsburgh had some of the first carpets found west of the Alleghenies.) When the Croghans' daughter Mary was only fourteen years old, she ran away from the boarding school she was attending and married Captain Edward Schenley, a British soldier three times her age. Many years later, as a widow in England, Mary Croghan Schenley became a generous benefactor of the city of Pittsburgh.

¶ **Magee Memorial,** near the Carnegie entrance to Schenley Park.

This monument to Christopher Lyman Magee, the grandson of an immigrant from County Derry, Ireland, is adorned by a bronze cornucopia bas-relief by *Augustus Saint-Gaudens. Although Magee held various political positions in Pittsburgh, he was more renowned as a business entrepreneur who owned newspaper and real estate interests as well as stock in more than fifty enterprises. He once wished the children of Pittsburgh a Merry Christmas by donating $100,000 for a zoological garden. He left most of his $4 million estate for the foundation of the Elizabeth Steele Magee Hospital.

¶ **Mellon Institute,** 4400 5th Avenue. Phone: 412-268-4960.

Although now part of Carnegie Mellon University, this massive Greek Revival structure was dedicated in 1937 as a gift of *Andrew Mellon, longtime U.S. secretary of the treasury. The research center takes up a city block and consists of nine floors and 335 rooms. Under Mellon's guidance, Pittsburgh's aluminum and cokemaking industries were developed.

¶ **Schenley Park,** Oakland, east of the Triangle.

This 465-acre expanse grew from a 300-acre donation to the city made in 1889 by *Mary Croghan Schenley, the daughter and granddaughter, respectively, of two prominent names in the history of Pittsburgh – *William Croghan Jr. and *James O'Hara. At the time of her bequest, Mrs. Schenley had been living in London for forty years. In 1918 a statue in her honor was erected at the entrance to the park.

¶ **Stephen Foster Memorial Building,** on the northeast corner of Forbes Avenue and Bigelow Boulevard.

This Gothic memorial to Stephen Collins Foster, the famous song writer, was built in 1937 with $500,000 in donations from music clubs throughout the United States. Murals illustrate many of Foster's songs, while a museum on the main floor exhibits Foster memorabilia.

Foster was born in Pittsburgh in 1826 of Scotch-Irish parentage on both sides. The popularity of his early Negro ballads – "O Susanna," "Louisiana Belle," "Uncle Ned," and "Away Down South" – led him to consider musical composition as a full-time career and to determine to become "the best Ethiopian song writer." Beginning in 1852, some of his ballads became part of the repertory of the minstrel companies of the day, including the famous Christy's. His fame increased with the appearance of "The Old Folks at Home," "Massa's in the Cold Ground," "My Old Kentucky Home," and "Old Black Joe." Following an unhappy marriage and excessive drinking, however, he died in poverty in New York City in 1864.

§ Open Monday-Friday 9-4. Closed university holidays. Fee for guided tour. Phone: 412-624-4100.

¶ University of Pittsburgh, 5th Avenue and Bigelow Boulevard.

The university's forty-two-story Cathedral of Learning houses eighteen Nationality Rooms, each contributed by the host country and depicting its particular cultural and ethnic characteristics. The Irish Room resembles a sixth-century Irish oratory, while its vestibule entrance is copied from Killeshin Chapel in County Laois, Ireland.

§ Tours Monday-Saturday 9:30-3, Sunday 11-3. Closed January 1 and December 24, 25, 31. Fee for tour. Phone: 412-624-6000.

POTTSVILLE

Pottsville was a center of activity by a secret society of miners known as the Molly Maguires, modeled after an organization in Ireland that used violence against the agents of absentee landlords. Ironically, the Mollies' chief antagonists were both Irishmen. During a sensational trial of accused Mollies at Pottsville in June 1877, the prosecution's key witness was James McParlan, a redheaded, Irish-born Catholic who had worked as a lumberman, a policeman, a teamster, and a saloonkeeper before becoming a Pinkerton detective. He was subsequently hired to infiltrate the Mollies by Franklin Gowan, the son of Irish immigrant parents and the president of the Philadelphia and Reading Railroad Company, the largest mine operator in the anthracite region. As a result of the trial, ten Molly Maguires were hanged and fourteen were sentenced to prison.

QUARRYVILLE

❡ **Robert Fulton Birthplace National Historic Landmark,** 8 miles south on U.S. 222 to Swift Road.

This two-and-a-half-story structure was built from the ruins of the house in which Robert Fulton was born in 1765. Fulton, whose father had probably come from Kilkenny, Ireland, before settling in Lancaster, Pennsylvania, by 1735, proved the commercial viability of steamboat transportation.

§ Open Memorial Day-Labor Day, Saturday and Sunday. Phone: 717-548-2679.

SCRANTON

❡ **Terence Powderly House,** 614 North Main Street. Private.

This was the home of Terence Vincent Powderly, an early labor leader who was born in 1827 in Carbondale, Pennsylvania, to immigrant parents from County Meath, Ireland.

After working at various railroad jobs as a teenager, Powderly joined the Machinists' and Blacksmiths' Union and later became a labor organizer for the Industrial Brotherhood. Beginning in 1874 with his induction into the Knights of Labor, he held various leadership positions in that organization, including the post of Grand Master Workman from 1879 to 1893. Although he championed the Knights' call for abolition of child labor, government ownership of public utilities, and regulation of trusts and monopolies, he opposed the use of strikes. His ultimate goal was to abolish the wage system through creation of producers' cooperatives. Toward the end of his life he was appointed U.S. commissioner-general of immigration. The author of many works on labor issues, he is most remembered for *Thirty Years of Labor, 1859 to 1889*, a book that is not only an autobiography but also a history of the national labor struggle in which he played such a prominent role.

VALLEY FORGE

❡ **Freedoms Foundation at Valley Forge,** State 23.

Several points of interest are located on this 105-acre site:

• The Medal of Honor Grove honors the recipients of the nation's highest award for military valor.

• The Henry Knox Building – named for the famous Revolutionary War general – houses archives and photographs of many Medal of Honor recipients.

• The Obelisk of Honor commemorates the foreign-born recipients of the Medal of Honor, including the 202 Irish-born recipients (the largest group of immigrants to be so honored). These soldiers were recognized for valor in the Civil War, the Indian campaigns, the Korean campaign of 1871, the Spanish-American War, the Philippine Insurrection, the China Relief Expedition (during the Boxer Rebellion), World War I, and various interim periods. The obelisk is made of granite from Wicklow, Ireland, and was donated in 1985 by the Ancient Order of Hibernians in America.

§ Open Monday-Friday 9-5. Phone: 610-933-8825.

¶ Valley Forge National Historical Park.

From mid December 1777 to mid June of the following year, this 3,500-acre park was the site of the winter encampment of General George Washington and the 12,000 men of his Continental Army.

On St. Patrick's Day in 1778, wrangling broke out between Irish and German troops over the making of a "stuffed Paddy." The conflict arose, apparently, when the Germans – threadbare and suffering tremendously from the cold – resented what they regarded as the waste of clothing in the outfitting of an effigy of St. Patrick. When General Washington was informed of the row, he quieted things down with a Solomon-like decision. To placate the Irishmen, he said that "I too am a lover of St. Patrick and must settle the affair by making the whole army keep the day." And to satisfy the Germans, he ordered that all the men be given an extra allowance of grog that day.

• The National Memorial Arch, which is dedicated to the "incomparable patience and fidelity" of the American soldiers who were encamped here, is adorned with bronze tablets listing the names of the officers who served here under Washington, among them *General John Sullivan.

• West of the National Memorial Arch is a bronze equestrian statue of *General Anthony Wayne. The statue was dedicated in 1908 and is located in the area where his Pennsylvania troops were encamped. A plaque on the pedestal summarizes his career: He was born in Pennsylvania, was a member of various Pennsylvania legislative bodies (the provincial convention, the state assembly, and the convention called to ratify the U.S. Constitution), and served at the battles of Brandywine, Germantown, Monmouth, Stony Point, and Yorktown.

• In the headquarters area is the home of Samuel Brown, where *General Henry Knox and his wife lived during the army's encampment here. The troops and artillery pieces under Knox's command were located in what is now Artillery Park.

• The star-shaped redoubt overlooking the Schuylkill River is a reconstruction of the original built by army engineers under the supervision of *General John Sullivan. It was the largest of the fortifications at Valley Forge.

§ Open 9-5. Closed December 25. Phone: 610-783-1077.

WAYNE

¶ Anthony Wayne Burial Site, St. David's Episcopal Church, 763 Valley Forge Road.

A monument in the church cemetery marks the tomb of *Anthony Wayne, the famous Revolutionary War general.

WARMINSTER

¶ Log College Monument, York Road.

This granite memorial marks the location of "Log College," founded in 1737 by the Reverend William Tennent as the first educational institution of higher learning in America affiliated with the Presbyterian Church. The monument lists the names of the sixty-three schools which were founded by Log College graduates.

Tennent, a native of Ireland, was a graduate of the University of Edinburgh and was ordained a priest of the Church of Ireland in 1706. After coming to Philadelphia, however, he petitioned to be admitted to the Presbyterian ministry.

The famous revivalist preacher George Whitefield described Tennent's "college" as "a little log house about 20 feet long and nearly as many broad," resembling "the school of the old prophets." The college was closed when its successor, the College of New Jersey (now Princeton), was established in 1747.

¶ Neshaminy Warwick Presbyterian Church, 1401 Meetinghouse Road.

Erected in 1743, this stone structure was preceded by a log church built by the *Reverend William Tennent, its first pastor. Although his grave is located in the adjacent graveyard, his original tombstone is embedded in a wall of the church.

§ Phone: 215-343-6060.

YORK

¶ James Smith Burial Site, First Presbyterian Church, on the northeast corner of Market and Queen streets.

In the cemetery next to the church is the grave of James Smith, one of the Irish-born signers of the Declaration of Independence.

Smith was born in northern Ireland about 1719 and came to Pennsylvania when he was approximately ten years old. He studied Greek, Latin, and surveying at the school in Philadelphia conducted by the *Reverend Francis Alison and later read law in Lancaster.

Beginning in 1774, Smith took an active part in Pennsylvania's response to British policies. After raising the first company of volunteers for the defense of the colony, he was elected to various extralegal conventions held in Philadelphia. At one he read an essay surveying the constitutional relationship between Britain and America, called for a policy of nonimportation against the mother country, and urged the convening of a general congress of the colonies to deal with Britain from a common position.

In June 1776 Smith was a member of the committee which drafted a resolution asking the Continental Congress to declare independence. Although he was not a member of the Congress when it voted for such a step, he was among the delegates who signed the document the following August.

¶ **General Gates House,** 157 West Market Street.

Here in 1778 the Marquis de Lafayette toasted George Washington, thereby expressing his loyalty to his commander-in-chief and frustrating a plot to replace him with General Horatio Gates. Gates and others had been part of the "Conway Cabal," a conspiracy named after Thomas Conway, an Irish mercenary who had enjoyed rapid advancement in the Continental Army.

Because of his previous experience in the French army, Conway had been made a brigadier general immediately after his arrival in America in 1777. His animus against Washington may have been due to the latter's refusal to promote him to major general on the premise that to do so would have been unfair to veteran American officers. When Congress gave Conway the desired promotion, he proceeded to criticize Washington in letters to Gates, perhaps confident that congressional dissatisfaction with the commander-in-chief would result in Washington's dismissal. Conway was accordingly embarrassed when Washington confronted him over the issue and when Lafayette refused to accept him as his second in command for the proposed invasion of Canada. Even one of Conway's supporters in Congress wrote that his "conduct respecting General Washington is criminal and unpardonable, severely censured by all the foreign officers."

In a subsequent duel related to this unfortunate episode, Conway suffered a wound to the mouth. During his recuperation he penned an apology to Washington for all the harm his indiscretion had caused. After his return to France, he was appointed governor-general of the French possessions in India.

§ Open Monday-Saturday 10-4, Sunday 1-4. Closed major holidays. Fee. Phone: 717-848-1587.

RHODE ISLAND

CRANSTON

¶ **Cranston Print Works,** Cranston Street, west of Dyer Avenue. .

Originally founded in 1824 as the A. and W. Sprague Company, this early industrial enterprise printed finished textiles by machine. The operation was part of a company town known as Sprague's Village, whose "feudal lord" was Amasa Sprague (the "A" in the company's name).

One of the Irish immigrants who developed for Sprague a reciprocated hatred was Nicholas Gordon, who had emigrated from Ireland in the mid 1830s and had set himself up as the owner of a small store in Cranston. Gordon was described as "a man of much talk, a sportive, swearing little Irishman, beneath the size of an ordinary man," but "more genteel than the run of factory workers." Although his business flourished even more after he was issued a liquor license, his trade in *aqua vitae* apparently affected the productivity of some of the workers at the print shop. As a result, Sprague blocked renewal of the license in June 1843. Gordon's subsequent threat to take revenge on Sprague before the year was out seemed to have come true when the factory owner's bludgeoned body was found in a secluded spot outside the village. Gordon's brothers John and William were charged with murder, while Nicholas Gordon was indicted as an accessory before the fact, allegedly as the instigator of the crime.

As events unfolded, it became evident that a fair trial for the three brothers would be highly doubtful, given the prejudice against Catholics and the Irish at the time. According to a newspaper report, a red-stained shirt found in the Gordon house was covered with Sprague's blood. (The "blood" later proved to be dye from a factory in which John Gordon had worked.) Even the chief justice, in his charge to the jury, made a distinction between testimony by native-born witnesses and by "the countrymen of William Gordon."

Luckily, however, the testimony of a Yankee corroborated that of Irish witnesses who had claimed that William had been in Providence on the day of the murder. Although no direct testimony placed John at the scene of the crime, circumstantial testimony by a prostitute and the village idiot proved effective on the jury, which convicted John but acquitted William. Despite a petition for reprieve to the General Assembly, John was hanged in February 1845. Subsequent uncertainty about the fairness of his trial eventually led to the abolition of capital punishment in Rhode Island in 1852.

§ Open to visitors by arrangement.

MIDDLETON

¶ **Berkeley Memorial Chapel,** at the corner of Vauclause Avenue.

This English Gothic structure was consecrated in 1887 in honor of George Berkeley, the famous Irish philosopher, educator, and Anglican bishop of Cloyne, Ireland, who had lived in this area between 1729 and 1731. Stones from Cloyne Cathedral and the isle of Iona adorn the porch.

¶ **Whitehall Museum House,** 311 Berkeley Avenue, near Green End Avenue.

Following his arrival in Newport in 1729, George Berkeley erected this house and made it the centerpiece of his ninety-acre farm. He named the estate "Whitehall" after the royal palace in London.

Berkeley was a native of County Kilkenny, Ireland, where he was born in 1684. Following his appointment as dean of the cathedral in Londonderry in 1724, he became an advocate for the conversion of the Native American. After resigning his deanery, he left Britain in September 1728 to establish a college in Bermuda to provide pastors for colonial parishes and to train missionaries to the Indians. His ship lost its direction and landed instead in Newport, Rhode Island, in January 1729. For the next two years he resided at Whitehall, where he wrote the first chapter of *Alciphron*, a book in defense of Christianity against the criticism of freethinkers.

Whitehall House, the home of Irish-born missionary George Berkeley.

After realizing that his educational proposal would never receive the financial support he had expected from England, Berkeley returned to Ireland and bequeathed Whitehall to Yale College. The income from Berkeley's farm was subsequently a source of scholarship funds for Yale students, among them Eleazer Wheelock, founder and first president of Dartmouth College; Aaron Burr Sr., president of Princeton University; Timothy Dwight, president of Yale College; and Daniel Coit Gilman, president of the University of California and of Johns Hopkins University. In 1733 Berkeley donated 880 volumes to Yale, a gift that has been described as "the finest collection of books that ever came at one time into America."

1866 Frederick Billings, the chairman of the board of trustees of the University of California, suggested the name "Berkeley" for the proposed site of California's new university. He said that the city's location on the western perimeter of the country reminded him of George Berkeley's prophetic lines about a golden age in the New World:

> There shall be sung another golden Age,
> The rise of Empire and of Arts,
> The Good and Great inspiring epic Rage,
> The Wisest Heads and Noblest Hearts . . . .
> Westward the Course of Empire takes its Way;
> The four first Acts already past,
> A fifth shall close the Drama with the Day;
> Time's noblest Offering is the last."

§ Open July-Labor Day, daily 10-5; rest of the year by appointment. Fee. Phone: 401-846-3116 or 401-847-7951.

NARRAGANSETT PIER

¶ St. Peter-by-the-Sea Church, 72 Central Street.

The church has a stained-glass window in memory of Varina Anne (Winnie) Davis, the daughter of Confederate president *Jefferson Davis.

Born in the final year of the Civil War, Winnie spent her teenage years at a school in Germany and returned to America fluent in both French and German. During her father's last years, she was his constant companion, either at "Beauvoir" in Biloxi, Mississippi, or on his journeys through the South. At one of his appearances, she was dubbed "The Daughter of the Confederacy" by a Confederate veterans' group.

Her status as the symbol of the "Lost Cause" was compromised, however, when she became engaged to the grandson of a New York abolitionist. In the end, her mother blocked the marriage, probably because of the fiancé's less than promising financial prospects rather than because of his Northern connections. Winnie subsequently continued to support herself and her mother through her writing – magazine articles, two novels, and a biography of *Robert Emmet (*An Irish Knight of the Nineteenth Century*). She died in Narragansett Pier at the age of thirty-four.

§ Phone: 401-783-4623.

NEWPORT

℈ Belcourt Castle, 657 Bellevue Avenue.

Designed in 1891, this French Renaissance-style castle was the summer residence of *Oliver Hazard Perry Belmont and his wife. The house is noted for its antiques, stained glass collection, and coronation coach.

Belmont, whose maternal grandfather was the naval hero *Matthew C. Perry, served in the U.S. House of Representatives during the 1880s, notably as a member of the Foreign Relations Committee. His father was August Belmont, the New York banker and financier.

§ Open Memorial Day-mid October, daily 9-5; April 1 to the day before Memorial Day, and mid October-November 30, daily 10-5; rest of the year, 10-3. Closed Thanksgiving and December 25. Fee. 401-846-0669.

℈ Hammersmith Farm, Ocean Drive.

Following their marriage in Newport in 1953, *John F. Kennedy and his new wife, Jacqueline Bouvier, held their wedding reception here. During the next decade they were frequent guests at the twenty-eight-room shingled "cottage" on this 500-acre estate. The property was originally owned by John Auchincloss, whose son had married Jacqueline Bouvier's mother, Janet Lee Bouvier, after the latter's divorce from Jack Bouvier.

Despite the French blood which Jacqueline Bouvier inherited from her father, her mother was 100 percent Irish, the family's first American ancestor having come from Ireland to New York City in the 1840s. Jacqueline's grandfather – James Thomas Lee – was vice president of Chase Manhattan Bank and president and chairman of the board of New York Central Savings Bank. When he died at the age of ninety-five, he left a $12 million estate.

When J.F.K. and Jackie celebrated their tenth wedding anniversary in 1963 at Hammersmith Farm, the president gave his wife the inventory of a New York art dealer with permission to buy anything on the list. The First Lady, in turn, presented her husband with a leather scrapbook containing photographs of the newly landscaped White House Rose Garden. She also gave him a St. Christopher medal to replace the one which he had buried with their prematurely born son, Patrick Bouvier Kennedy, who had died the month before.

§ Guided tours daily April-November 30, 10-5. Fee. Phone: 401-846-0420

¶ **Irish Servant Memorial,** along Cliff Walk (at the bottom of the Forty Steps at the end of Narragansett Avenue).

This marker is located in the area where many Irish servants met to socialize at the end of their working day in the Newport mansions.

The early nineteenth-century prejudice against Irish-Catholic female servants was gradually dispelled as more and more prosperous American families sought domestic help and as the Irish "biddy" or "Bridie" (both diminutives of "Bridget") earned a reputation for honesty and ability.

Contemporaries could not have missed the irony in the fact that domestic service jobs in America were offered to young Irish girls totally unfamiliar with the "common duties of servants in respectable positions." To the visiting observer Dr. Daniel Cahill, "They can neither wash nor iron clothes. They don't understand the cleaning of glass or silver plate. They cannot make fires expeditiously, or dust the carpets, or polish the furniture." (An awareness of Irish naiveté was evident in the story of the Irish servant girl who always walked down the stairs backwards because in Ireland she had never climbed anything but a barn ladder.) Nor, of course, were young girls who had most likely never seen a leg of mutton boiled or roasted in their homeland ideal candidates for the chef's hat in an American kitchen.

Yet what they lacked in skill they made up for in willingness to learn and in their reputation for honesty. As early as 1829 a Boston placement office required that each applicant for a domestic service position exhibit "a Testimonial of moral conduct" from previous families or from a Catholic clergyman for "honesty, sobriety, and the practical observances of the Duties which the Holy, Catholic Religion enjoins and enforces." (Again self-deprecation was evident in the Irish girl who explained to her employer: "Sure I had a splendid character when I left the ould country, but I lost it on the ship coming over.") No matter how anti-papist in their views, many Protestant employers preferred young Irish girls precisely because of their moral upbringing. By 1860 such girls enjoyed a near monopoly in Yankee households in Boston and New England and in most hotels throughout the country.

¶ **Island Cemetery,** Farewell and Warner streets.

A monument here marks the graves of Newport heroes *Matthew C. Perry and *Oliver H. Perry. *The Standing Angel*, a statue by the Irish-born sculptor Augustus Saint-Gaudens, is in the Alfred Smith plot toward the back of the cemetery.

¶ **Matthew C. Perry Birthplace,** 31 Walnut Street. Private.

This small, gambrel-roofed house was the birthplace in 1794 of Matthew C. Perry, known chiefly for his successful efforts in opening Japan to American trade. He lived here until about 1810.

Perry was the son of Christopher Perry, who had seen service on both land and sea during the Revolutionary War and four times had been taken prisoner by the British. During his confinement in Ireland, he met Sarah Wallace Alexander, a blue-eyed Irish beauty whom he vowed to make his wife. In 1784 she accompanied him to America, where they were soon married. Matthew, the couple's fourth child, was given the middle name "Calbraith" for an Irish fellow passenger on his parents' voyage to America. Another of the couple's sons was Oliver H. Perry.

Prior to his mission to Japan, Matthew C. Perry enjoyed a varied career in the U.S. Navy. His brief service in the War of 1812 was followed by an assignment in 1820 as executive officer of a naval vessel that escorted the first group of African Americans to be settled in Liberia. In 1843 he commanded a squadron that helped suppress the slave trade and protect the African-American colonies on the west coast of Africa. During the Mexican War he rose to commander-in-chief of the squadron cruising the east coast of Mexico and commanded the naval forces that helped General Winfield Scott force the surrender of Vera Cruz.

Despite his reputation for gruffness and strict discipline, "Old Bruin" was at the forefront of reform efforts within the Navy. Early in his career he stressed the importance of proper hygiene among his men in order to prevent diseases. On one voyage he ordered that the men be required to wear flannel and be forbidden to sleep on deck, wear wet clothes, or be turned out at night unnecessarily. He also insisted that the deck be fumigated and whitewashed every day. Always interested in improving naval education, in 1824 he proposed and lobbied for a naval apprenticeship system until it was adopted by Congress thirteen years later. Upon his appointment as second in charge at the New York Navy Yard, he led the way to creation of the U.S. Naval Lyceum for the further education of naval officers. In addition, he helped prepare the first curriculum for the Naval Academy at Annapolis.

¶ **Naval War College Museum,** Founders Hall, Coasters Harbor Island.

Founders Hall is the original site of the U.S. Naval War College, created in 1884. The second president of the college was Captain Alfred Thayer Mahan, whose famous work *The Influence of Sea Power upon History, 1660-1783* influenced the thinking of Theodore Roosevelt when he was assistant secretary of the navy.

Mahan, whose grandparents had fled Ireland after the unsuccessful uprising in 1798, chose a naval career, even though his father was an instructor at the U.S. Military Academy at West Point. Following his graduation from the Naval Academy in 1859, Mahan began a career that alternated between sea and shore duty. Cruises to Japan, Rio de Janeiro, Capetown, Aden, and Bombay were interrupted by blockade duty during the Civil War. While sailing along the west coast of South America, he received an invitation to lecture on tactics and naval history at the War College.

After delivering his first lectures in 1886, Mahan was appointed president of the college, a position that required him to defend its role in the face of opposition from the secretary of the navy. In 1890 his lectures were published as the famous *Influence of Sea Power*, in which he surveyed the waxing and waning of the world's great maritime nations, examined the factors which contributed to a nation's sea power, and analyzed the relationship between naval and political history. Two years later Mahan published a companion work on the influence of sea power on the French Revolution and the French Empire. The two works made their debut at an opportune time, almost as if to justify the naval buildup that had been occurring in Britain, Germany, and the United States. *Theodore Roosevelt predicted that the first work would become a classic, while Kaiser Wilhelm II announced that he was "devouring" both books and had made them standard reading on all his ships. The British, meanwhile, lionized Mahan and his works, hosting him at a dinner attended by the Queen and awarding him honorary degrees from both Cambridge and Oxford.

Despite his retirement from the Navy in 1896, Mahan continued to write and to influence American policy. His ideas undoubtedly played a significant role in promoting and sanctioning American expansionism in the Caribbean and the Pacific. To an earlier biography about Admiral Farragut, he added one on Nelson and authored additional works on naval strategy and sea power in the American Revolution and the War of 1812. His autobiography, *From Sail to Steam*, appeared in 1907.

§ Open June-September 30, Monday-Friday 10-4, Saturday and Sunday 12-4; rest of the year, Monday-Friday 10-4. Phone: 401-841-4052.

¶ Newport Casino, 194 Bellevue Avenue.

One of the first country clubs in the nation, the Casino was founded by *James Gordon Bennett Jr. following his expulsion from the Newport Reading Room, the town's premiere social club.

Bennett, the publisher of the *New York Herald*, had already made a name for himself in the world of sports. In his youth he had become a well known yachtsman, boasting a crew of 100 on the largest steam yacht ever built on the River Clyde in Scotland. In the 1870s he introduced polo among the upper classes in Newport and later sponsored various international competitions involving airplanes, automobiles, and balloons.

¶ Oliver H. Perry Statue, Washington Square.

After joining the Navy in 1799 at the age of fourteen, *Oliver Hazard Perry first saw action in the West Indies during the naval war with France and then in the Mediterranean during the war with Tripoli. In the spring and summer of 1813, Perry supervised the building, equipping, and manning of the American fleet which defeated a British squadron on Lake Erie the following September. This unprecedented victory gave the United States control of the lake until the end of the War of 1812.

¶ Redwood Library and Athenaeum, 50 Bellevue Avenue.

The library, which dates from 1750, contains a fine collection of books and early American paintings, including seven by Gilbert Stuart. The library evolved from a suggestion by *George Berkeley that Newport establish a literary society.

§ Open Monday-Saturday 9:30-5:30. Closed holidays. Phone: 401-847-0292.

¶ Rosecliff, Bellevue Avenue.

Designed after Louis XIV's Grand Trianon palace at Versailles, Rosecliff was built by Hermann Oelrichs and his wife, Theresa Fair Oelrichs, at the turn of the century. The mansion, notable for its forty-by-eighty-foot ballroom, was featured in the 1974 film *The Great Gatsby*. Rosecliff's billiard room reflects Oelrichs' tastes: the wooden mantelpiece is carved with the heads of Irish kings and reputedly was saved from the wreck of a ship that was bringing it from Ireland. The garden ornamentation, including the *Court of Love*, is the work of *Augustus Saint-Gaudens.

Mrs. Oelrichs was the daughter of James Fair, an Irish immigrant who had struck it rich in the Nevada Comstock silver lode. Fair was one of a group of young Irishmen known as the "Silver Kings" because of their success in developing the Comstock Lode, which yielded more than $500 million of ore before it was exhausted in 1898. Fair served as a U.S. senator from Nevada from 1881 to 1887. In 1883, however, after twenty-one years of marriage, his wife divorced him on the grounds of habitual adultery. The ex-Mrs. Fair received a $5 million divorce settlement, the largest in American history until that time. After the divorce Theresa lived with her two daughters in the magnificent Fair Mansion in San Francisco. It was there that one of the girls – Theresa, or Tessie –

married Hermann Oelrichs, a German whose family was in the steamship business.

As mistress of Rosecliff, Tessie Oelrichs was known for her unconventionality and the magnificence of her fetes. Although distinguished by her white lace dresses and "towering picture hats," she was not above wielding a mop herself to make up for the deficiencies of her domestic staff. In addition, she regularly shocked and amused her acquaintances with her racy monologues and "up-to-the-minute profanity." In 1904 Tessie dazzled Newport society with her "Bal Blanc" and reflected the white motif of the dance with an elegant lace dress embroidered with silver. One of the fountains on the property was stocked with white swans that evening, and the guests were treated to the sight of a mock fleet of white ships in the surf below the house.

§ Open April-October 31, daily 10-5. Fee. Phone: 401-847-1000.

¶ St. Mary's Catholic Church, 250 Spring Street, at Memorial Boulevard.

This brownstone Gothic Revival church was designed by *Patrick Keely and was built between 1848 and 1852. A hundred years later – on September 12, 1953 – *John F. Kennedy and *Jacqueline Bouvier were married here. Almost 3,000 people broke through the police lines outside the church that morning, nearly crushing the bride.

When Jackie became engaged to J.F.K., her friend John White bet her that she wouldn't go through with the planned marriage. She promised to give him two dollars if she didn't marry Kennedy, and White in turn promised to give her one dollar if she did marry him. White arrived late at the wedding, but just in time to see the bride walk down the aisle. Realizing that he had lost the bet, he waved his dollar bill at his friend as people around him laughed. Jackie acknowledged his sportsmanship with a big smile.

¶ Soldiers' and Sailors' Monument, Niantonomi Park.

This memorial to the veterans and victims of World War I is the work of *William Clark Noble.

¶ Touro Park, Bellevue Avenue and Mill Street.
• The statue of Dr. William Ellery Channing is the work of *William Clark Noble.
• The pedestal on which the statue of *Matthew C. Perry stands is faced with bas-reliefs depicting episodes in his career and captioned with the words "Africa, 1843," "Mexico, 1846," and "Treaty with Japan, 1854."

In January 1852 Perry was chosen to lead a historic diplomatic mission to Japan. He was commissioned to negotiate with that isolated nation a treaty that would ensure the protection of American sailors and property in Japan and bring about the opening of Japanese ports to American trade. About his assignment Perry wrote: "We pray God that our present attempt to bring a singular and isolated people into the family of civilized nations may succeed without resort to bloodshed." After anchoring in Yedo Harbor in July 1853, Perry proceeded to insist that he be greeted by a Japanese emissary equal to his own rank. Perry's bluster finally won for him an elaborate welcome by representatives of the Emperor. Almost immediately Perry wrote his wife: "This achievement of mine I consider an important event in my life. The Pageant was magnificent and I am the only Christian that has ever before landed peacefully [in Japan] without submitting to the most humiliating degradation."

Although a full-scale commercial treaty was not negotiated until 1858, Perry and his men had given the Japanese their first introduction to Americans and western technology. The Japanese were amused and delighted by Perry's crew – by the African Americans who entertained their hosts with a minstrel show and by the other Americans' light hair,

*Statue of Commodore
Matthew C. Perry.*

fair complexions, and regrettable table manners. The Americans, in turn, examined an enormous sumo wrestling champion, demonstrated the telegraph wire, and presented the Japanese with clocks, a small-scale locomotive, a telescope, and a barrel of whiskey. From these first encounters Perry concluded that the Japanese "are in most respects a refined and rational people . . . . I have never met in any part of the world, even in Europe, with a people of more unaffected grace and dignity. . . ." The American commander was equally complimentary about Japanese resourcefulness: "Their curiosity to learn the results of the material progress of other people, and their readiness in adapting them to their own uses, would soon . . . raise them to a level with the most favored countries." The Japanese, he predicted correctly, "would enter as powerful competitors in the race for mechanical success in the future."

¶ **Trinity Church,** Queen Anne Square.

Constructed in 1726, the church boasts a wine glass (three-tiered) pulpit, the only one of its kind in New England and the only remaining pulpit used by George Berkeley, the eighteenth-century Irish-born philosopher. The central part of the organ in the church was presented by Berkeley in 1733. His gift had been refused by the town of Berkeley, Massachusetts, "as an instrument of the devil for the entrapping of men's souls." His daughter Lucia is buried in the churchyard.

Berkeley was impressed by the degree of religious toleration in Rhode Island and wrote to a Dublin friend: "Here are four sorts of Anabaptists, besides Presbyterians, Quakers, Independents and many of no profession at all. Notwithstanding so many differences here are fewer quarrels about religion than elsewhere, the people living peaceable with their neighbors of whatsoever permission."

§ Open May-October 31, daily 10-4; rest of the year, Monday-Friday 10-1. Phone: 402-846-0660.

NORTH KINGSTON

¶ **James MacSparran Burial Site and Monument,** Old St. Paul's churchyard, Scrabbletown Road.

Although Old St. Paul's (Old Narragansett) Church was removed to Wickford in 1800, the church's cemetery still remains and is the final resting place of the Reverend James MacSparran, the Anglican rector of the church for thirty-seven years. An obelisk marks his grave.

Born in 1693 in County Derry, Ireland, MacSparran was graduated from the University of Glasgow and took preparatory steps toward ordination in the Presbyterian ministry before sailing to America. While in Boston, however, he came into conflict with the Puritan minister Cotton Mather, who proceeded publicly to challenge the newcomer's credentials and otherwise to delay his ordination. After returning to Ireland, MacSparran carried out his intention to seek ordination, but to the Anglican priesthood instead. Within a year of his ordination he had returned to the American colonies, this time as a missionary of the Society for the Propagation of the Gospel in Foreign Parts.

One of MacSparran's most important published works was *America Dissected*, a 1753 account of the British colonies which he composed in the form of letters to friends in Ireland. In that work he expressed his opposition to any political union of Ireland and England: "You [Irish] are greater slaves already than our negroes, and an union of that kind would make you more underlings than you are now. The accounts of the open irreligion on the greater island inclines me to imagine, that Ireland is on the brink of obtaining . . . its ancient name of Insula Sanctorum [Isle of Saints]." While the rector at St. Paul's, he baptized Gilbert Stuart, the future artist, and entertained the philosopher George Berkeley, another native of Ireland and the future bishop of Cloyne, Ireland. (During their visits the two clergymen conversed in the Irish language.)

PROVIDENCE

¶ Ambrose Burnside Statue, City Hall Park.

This equestrian statue of the Civil War general Ambrose Burnside was sculpted by *Launt Thompson.

¶ Brown University, College Hill, College Street.

Originally founded as Rhode Island College in 1764, the school was renamed in 1804 when Nicholas Brown Jr. created a $5,000 endowment for a professorship in oratory and belles lettres. His subsequent benefactions to the university totaled $160,000.

Brown belonged to the city's most illustrious merchant family and was descended from Nicholas Power, a native of Ireland who had served in the Rhode Island General Assembly. In 1791 Nicholas Brown Jr. married Ann Carter, the granddaughter of an Irish naval officer who had died in the service of the Crown.

• The John Carter Brown Library on the campus was named for the son of *Nicholas Brown Jr. and *Ann Carter. The library contains one of the best collections of Americana printed before 1825. Brown's collection of about 7,500 volumes formed the nucleus of the library's holdings.

§ Library open during the academic year, Monday-Friday 8:30-5, Saturday 9-12; rest of the year, variable times. Closed holidays. Phone: 401-863-2725.

¶ John Brown House, 52 Power Street.

This large brick Georgian mansion was built in 1786 by John Brown, a China trade merchant and a member of the famous mercantile family that dominated the city's history. (Brown's maternal grandfather was Nicholas Power, a native of Ireland.) Abigail Adams once described the house as "one of the grandest I have seen in the country. Everything in and about it wore the marks of magnificence and taste." John Quincy Adams later spoke of the mansion in even more superlative terms, calling it "the most magnificent and elegant private mansion I have ever seen on this continent." Today the John Brown House is furnished with colonial antiques, decorative arts, and silver and pewter collections.

§ Open March-December 31, Tuesday-Saturday 11-4, Sunday 1-4; rest of the year, Saturday 11-4, Sunday 1-4. Closed holidays. Fee. Phone 401-331-8575

The John Brown House, the home of a wealthy China trade merchant.

¶ John Reynolds House, 88 Benefit Street. Private.

Between 1803 and 1878 this was the home of Sarah Helen Whitman, a woman with whom *Edgar Allan Poe fell in love and to whom he wrote his famous poem "To Helen." Miss Whitman had first attracted Poe's attention when he saw her standing in her garden on a moonlit evening in 1845. After corresponding with her for four years, the poet returned to Providence and proposed to her in the churchyard behind her house. Although she accepted his offer of marriage, she later broke the engagement. Poe died a month later.

¶ **Kennedy Plaza,** between Exchange and Dorrance streets.

This public square in the center of Providence was named for *President John F. Kennedy.

¶ **St. Joseph Catholic Church,** 86 Hope Street.

Constructed from 1851 to 1853 by architect *Patrick Keely, this is the oldest standing Catholic church in the state. It was erected to minister to the Irish immigrants who had come to work on the Providence and Worcester Railroad. The famous showman George M. Cohan was the son of Irish immigrants who lived in this area.

• Keely also designed the Cathedral of Saints Peter and Paul (1889) in Cathedral Square.

¶ **State Capitol,** Smith Street, between Gaspée and Francis streets.

A tablet at the entrance to the capitol commemorates *General John Sullivan, the American commander during the battle of Rhode Island, when the Americans besieging British-held Newport in 1778 were driven back.

§ Open Monday-Friday 8:30-4:30. Closed holidays.

WAKEFIELD

¶ **Oliver H. Perry Birthplace,** 2 miles south on U.S. 1, at 184 Post Road.

This two-story gambrel house is located on land owned by the Perry family since 1702. The residence has been called the "house that launched a fleet of ships." From here *Oliver Hazard Perry went to take command of the American inland fleet on Lake Erie. The house contains memorabilia associated with Perry as well as with his younger brother, *Commodore Matthew C. Perry.

WICKFORD

¶ **Old Narragansett Church,** Church Lane, off Main Street.

This church, one of the oldest Episcopal churches in the nation, was moved to this site in 1800 from North Kingston, Rhode Island, where it was built in 1707 and where the *Reverend James MacSparran had served as pastor.

§ Open mid June to mid September, Friday-Sunday 11-4. Phone: 401-294-4357.

VERMONT

FAIRFIELD

¶ Chester A. Arthur Historic Site, 6 miles north on State 36.

The site features a replica of the parsonage in which Chester A. Arthur, the twenty-first president of the United States, lived as an infant. Arthur's father, a Baptist minister, had moved to the parsonage a year after his son's birth in a cabin in North Fairfield in 1829. The parsonage contains an exhibit on President Arthur's life and political career.

A replica of the house in which Chester Arthur lived as an infant.
(Courtesy of the Vermont Division for Historic Preservation.)

The president's father, William Arthur, was a native of Ballymena, County Antrim, Ireland, and a graduate of Belfast College. (The thatched cottage which Arthur left behind in Ireland is still located on its original site in Cullybackey, near Ballymena.) After immigrating in 1816 to Durham, Quebec, where he taught school for a time, the elder man became a Baptist preacher, ministering to eleven parishes in New York and Vermont. He and his wife and their four daughters moved to Fairfield in 1828, a year before Chester's birth. After moving his family to New York State in 1835, William Arthur became an outspoken abolitionist and the cofounder of the New York Antislavery Society.

Eleven years later Chester Arthur was admitted to the New York bar and continued his father's commitment to securing civil rights for African Americans. In the "Lemmon Slave Case" he successfully argued that slaves brought into New York while in transit to a slave state were legally free. In another case he obtained a judgment that recognized equal rights for blacks and whites on public transportation within the state.

§ Open Memorial Day-Columbus Day, Wednesday-Sunday 10-4. Fee. Phone: 802-828-3226.

FAIR HAVEN

¶ Zenas Ellis House, South Main Street. Private.

This house is reputed by some authorities to have been the home of Matthew Lyon, a native of County Wicklow, Ireland, known for a variety of firsts.

Lyon arrived in New York in 1755, indentured to the Connecticut farmer who had paid the cost of his transatlantic passage. Following the outbreak of hostilities at the battle of Lexington, the Irishman enlisted in the Patriot army and was soon commissioned as a lieutenant in the "Green Mountain Boys." After the war Lyon built Fair Haven's first sawmill, first meetinghouse, and first gristmill, established its first printing press, and published its first newspaper. He also began several manufacturing enterprises in New England, among them iron casting and paper making. He combined the two processes by casting the type and manufacturing the paper for a thoroughly democratic newspaper which he published under the name *The Scourge of Aristocracy*.

> Following his election to Congress in 1797, Lyon immediately became the object of attack and ridicule by the Federalists and their allies in the press. After receiving repeated insults from a Connecticut congressman, Lyon spat in his antagonist's face – on the very floor of the House of Representatives. When that chamber failed to expel Lyon for "the first breach of decorum in Congress," the Connecticut Federalist physically attacked him on the floor of the House and beat him with a cane. The hot-tempered Lyon responded in kind. He later defended himself by saying that he had "not come here to have my ___ kicked by everybody."

In 1798 Congress passed the Sedition Act, a broadly worded piece of legislation intended to silence criticism of the new government by foreign-born journalists and the anti-Federalist press in general. The

Irish-born Mathew Carey, editor of the *Pennsylvania Herald*, declared that under "the execrable law, . . . to laugh at the cut of a congressman's coat . . . will be treason." John Daly Burk, the Irish editor of a journal in New York, escaped prosecution by promising to leave the country. Meanwhile, the libel action against the Irishman William Duane, the editor of the most prominent Republican newspaper in Philadelphia, failed to result in a conviction. The first conviction under the new law was obtained against Matthew Lyon, still a congressman from Vermont. The fiery Irishman was fined $1,000 and jailed for four months for making libelous remarks about President Adams. On one occasion the congressman had referred to Adams and his Puritan ancestors as "the bastards of Oliver Cromwell" and as the "witch-hunting Puritans of New England who persecuted the Quakers and despised all joy." At another opportunity to antagonize his opponents, Lyon had said that "the pomp of the White House better became the court of a king than the residence of the President of a Republic!" From prison Lyon had the last laugh: In 1799 he was easily reelected to Congress.

Lyon also enjoyed the distinction of being "the man who elected Jefferson" and the first person to be elected to Congress by the people of three different states. In 1801, when the House of Representatives had failed in thirty-five ballots to break the Electoral College tie between Jefferson and Aaron Burr, Lyon cast the deciding vote. That same year Lyon moved to Kentucky, which he represented in Congress from 1804 to 1812. After heading west to Arkansas, he was elected to Congress from that state, but he died before he was able to take his seat.

FRANKLIN

¶ Fenian Monument, near the border of Vermont and Quebec.

This memorial commemorates the Fenians' unsuccessful attempt in 1870 to invade Canada and hold it hostage to their demand for Irish independence from Britain.

*Colonel John O'Neill, a veteran of a failed incursion four years earlier, led a force of 200 men across the border, only to see them retreat in the face of stiff Canadian resistance near the village of Eccles Hill in Quebec. While riding to the rear for reinforcements, O'Neill was arrested by a U.S. marshal sent to enforce the neutrality laws.

Although sentenced to two years' imprisonment, O'Neill was released in three months after obtaining a pardon from *President Ulysses S. Grant. (During a visit to St. Louis, the President had received a ten-foot-long petition with two columns of signatures seeking O'Neill's release from prison.)

Following this second Fenian disaster, an editorial in the *New York Times* remarked that even if the Fenians had been successful "nobody believes it would produce the liberation of Ireland from British rule. It would be just as sensible to expect Russia to liberate Poland if she heard that our Polish fellow-citizens had overpowered the garrisons of Alaska."

Despite the folly of the Fenians' efforts, O'Neill attempted another invasion of Canada. In September 1871, without the support of the Fenian council, he and a few followers seized the Hudson's Bay post in what is now Manitoba before being arrested by American troops. He later became an agent for a group of land speculators who attempted to attract Irish settlers to Nebraska. The town of O'Neill in Holt County, Nebraska, is named for him.

NORTH BENNINGTON

❡ **Park-McCullough Mansion,** Park and West streets, 1 block west off State 67A.

Built in 1865, this thirty-five room Victorian house was the home of John McCullough, governor of Vermont from 1902 to 1904. Members of his family lived here until 1965.

McCullough, whose Scotch-Irish grandfather had immigrated to America in 1701, received a degree from the University of Pennsylvania law school in 1858. His early practice in Philadelphia was interrupted, however, by a pulmonary attack, which caused him to seek a change of climate in California. Following the outbreak of the Civil War soon after his arrival on the West Coast, the twenty-five-year-old lawyer made a name for himself with his speeches in defense of the Union. Beginning in 1862, he was elected successively to the state assembly, the state senate, and the post of attorney general. Between 1867 and 1872 he carried on a lucrative legal practice in San Francisco before settling in southern Vermont.

This second phase of McCullough's life revolved around his commercial, financial, and railroad interests. In 1873 he became vice president of the Panama Railway until assuming the presidency in 1882 at the urging of Ferdinand de Lesseps. At various times over the next decade, he served as president of the Bennington & Rutland Railroad and the Chicago & Erie Railroad before being elected governor of Vermont. During his tenure the state abandoned the prohibition of liquor for a policy of licensing and local option. Once out of political office, McCullough served either as president or director of numerous enterprises, including the Lackawanna Steel Company and the Atcheson, Topeka & Santa Fe Railroad Company.

§ Open late May-October 31, daily 10-4; December, daily 10-4. Admission. Phone: 802-442-5441.

ST. ALBANS

¶ The Common.

In June 1866 about a thousand Fenians were massed at St. Albans in preparation for an invasion of Canada, the first in a series of steps which they hoped would lead to the creation of an independent Irish republic. As many as 300 volunteers arrived on a single train, and many of them slept on the St. Albans Common.

Although the Fenians advanced six miles into Canada, they were forced to turn back, their only accomplishment being the capture of a British flag. Before long, U.S. troops under *General George Gordon Meade arrived in St. Albans to put an end to the Fenians' violation of American neutrality. During their two-week stay on the Common, the U.S. troops dispatched the demoralized Fenians south by train and entertained the residents of St. Albans with band concerts.

SHELDON JUNCTION

¶ **Fenian Marker,** on the bridge across the Black River along State 105 just west of State 78.

This marker takes note of the raids and other Fenian activity which took place in northern Vermont in 1866 and 1870. (See Franklin and St. Albans, Vermont.)

WISCONSIN

APPLETON

¶ Joseph McCarthy Bust, Outagamie County Courthouse, 410 South Walnut Street.

The courthouse foyer contains a bust of Joseph McCarthy, the controversial senator who during the 1950s launched a crusade against what he described as Communist influence in the U.S. government.

McCarthy was born in 1908 in a farming area known as the "Irish settlement" near Grand Chute, Wisconsin. His father was of German and Irish background, while his mother – Bridget Tierney – was a native of Ireland. At age twenty he enrolled in a local high school and completed the four-year curriculum in a year. In 1935 he was graduated from Marquette University with a law degree. After his admission to the Wisconsin bar, he won election as a state circuit court judge. During his tenure he was reprimanded by the state supreme court for destroying court records before they could be used in an appeals case. (Other critics castigated him for turning his court into a divorce mill.) At the beginning of World War II, he took a leave of absence from the bench to accept a commission as a first lieutenant in the Marines. Although he served in the Pacific as an intelligence officer, he later claimed that he had been a tail gunner and that he had been wounded in action.

In 1946 McCarthy easily won election to the U.S. Senate as a Republican. During the campaign he had stressed his opposition to the New Deal in general and to farm price controls and national health care in particular and attacked his opponent as "communistically inclined." As a senator he generally opposed price controls and social welfare programs and was dubbed the "Pepsi Cola Kid" because of his lobbying efforts for the soft drink industry.

But it was McCarthy's anti-Communist fervor which brought him nationwide attention. His charge in 1950 that American foreign policy was being shaped by 205 members of the Communist Party who worked for the State Department came soon after the Communist victory in China and the conviction of Alger Hiss as a Soviet spy. Although a congressional investigation found no evidence to substantiate the senator's charges, he continued his attacks on the Truman administration. In 1954, as chairman of a Senate investigating committee of his own, McCarthy sought to ferret out alleged Communists in the U.S. Army. During the nationally televised hearings, he continued to attack the army and even began to assail the Eisenhower administration, a move which ultimately alienated most of the Republican leadership and increasing numbers of the public. Toward the end of that year the Senate censured McCarthy for behavior that was "contemptuous, contumacious, and denunciatory." Calling the 67-22 vote a farce, McCarthy issued his own challenge: "I'm happy to have this circus ended so I can get back to the real work of digging out communism, crime and corruption. That job will start officially Monday morning after ten months of inaction."

CEDARSBURG

By the middle of the nineteenth century, local limestone and water power from Cedar Creek had turned this community into a milling and quarrying center. The original downtown area was called New Dublin. Now known as Hamilton, this historic district southeast of the present downtown section includes several nineteenth-century stone buildings, including the Concordia Mill.
   § Information: 414-377-9620 or 414-375-1426.

CUDAHY

This town of 20,000 population dates from 1893, when Patrick Cudahy relocated his meat-packing plant from Milwaukee to a 700-acre tract he had acquired here. In laying out the city, he named the first streets after well known Midwestern meat packers – Armour, Layton, Plankinton, and Swift.
   Born in County Kilkenny, Ireland, Cudahy and his brothers Michael and John came to America in 1849 with their parents, who eventually settled in Milwaukee. At one time or another each of the sons worked for the meat-packing houses in the city as those firms combined and recombined under various names. Of the three brothers, Michael seems to have made the most rapid advance in the industry. After advancing to the position of meat inspector on the Milwaukee Board of Trade, in 1875 he accepted a partnership with Armour & Company of Chicago. His most important contribution to the industry was the curing of meats under refrigeration, a process which permitted the consumption of meat during the entire year. He was also instrumental in applying refrigeration to the transportation phase of the business, an innovation that was perfected in the 1870s with the invention of the refrigerated railroad car. In 1887 he and his younger brother, Edward, joined with Philip D. Armour in acquiring a small packing plant in South Omaha, Nebraska, which they conducted under the name Armour-Cudahy Packing Company. Three years later Michael Cudahy bought out Armour's interests and changed the name of the company to the Cudahy Packing Company.
   In the meantime, Patrick Cudahy had entered into a partnership with his brother Edward to operate a meat-packing company in Mil-

waukee under the name the Cudahy Brothers. It was this business which he relocated to the newly established town of Cudahy in 1893. After serving as vice president of the company, Patrick's son John was the American ambassador to Poland and minister to Ireland and Belgium.

EAGLE

¶ **Old World Wisconsin,** 1 mile south on State 67.

This 576-acre outdoor "living museum" consists of fifty restored and furnished structures built by nineteenth-century immigrants. One of the buildings on display is a house erected in 1885 in Hubbleton, Wisconsin, for Mary Hafford, an Irish-born widow. The Ramsey Barn Visitor Center offers a slide presentation about early Wisconsin.

§ Open May, June, September, and October, Monday-Friday 10-4, Saturday and Sunday 10-5; July and August, daily 10-5. Fee for museum. Tram service available. Phone: 414-594-2116.

ERIN

Erin Township was largely settled by Irish immigrants, who first came here in 1841. The area may have attracted the Irish because its kettle moraine landscape is similar to the land formations in Ireland.

FOND DU LAC

¶ **Galloway House and Village,** 1 mile north on State 175 and then 1 mile east on Pioneer Road to 336 Old Pioneer Road.

Although the original portion of this structure was built in 1868, it was remodeled into a thirty-room Victorian-Italianate mansion by Edwin Galloway. The mansion is surrounded by gardens, a log cabin, and a carriage house. The nearby village includes the following structures: schoolhouse, general store, church, gristmill, pharmacy, doctor's office, law office, court room, blacksmith shop, and print shop. The village sponsors several special events during the year: a crafts day, an ice cream social, and Christmas at Galloway House.

Edwin Galloway was most likely descended from William Galloway, who had accompanied other Scotch-Irish families into southern Wisconsin in the early 1800s. Edwin Galloway arrived in the Fond du Lac area in 1848 and became active in banking, lumbering, and dairy farming. His grandson, Edwin P. Galloway, donated the family residence to the Fond du Lac County Historical Society in 1954.

§ Open Memorial Day weekend-Labor Day, daily 10-4; day after Labor Day-September 30, Saturday and Sunday 10-4. Fee. Phone: 414-922-6390.

The thirty-room Victorian-Italianate Galloway House.
(Photo courtesy of the Fond du Lac County Historical Society.)

GREENDALE

¶ **Jeremiah Curtin House,** 8685 West Grange Avenue.

Built in 1846-47, this residence was the birthplace of Jeremiah Curtin, linguist, author, and student of comparative mythology.

This son of Irish immigrants was early attracted to the study of foreign languages, beginning with those spoken by Norwegian, Polish, and German immigrants in nearby Milwaukee. Soon after graduating from Harvard, he accepted an invitation from the admiral of a visiting Russian fleet to come to St. Petersburg, where he served as a translator and then as an assistant secretary at the American Legation.

To acquaint himself with the Slavonic languages, he traveled through eastern Europe and Asia, even living for three months among the last Mongol tribe to practice the traditional horse sacrifice. After spending time in the British Isles collecting myths and legends, he began to study the customs and languages of the Iroquois, Shawnee, and other Native American tribes. Although he was renowned as a translator of many European works (including Sienkiewicz's *Quo Vadis*), he is chiefly remembered for his numerous ethnological works about Celtic, Slavonic, Mongolian, and American Indian peoples. He was reputed to have had either a working knowledge of or an acquaintance with seventy languages and dialects.

§ Open July and August, Sunday 1-5.

MADISON

¶ **Old Executive Mansion,** 130 East Gilman Street.

Now the home of the state's governors, this house was purchased in 1882 by Governor Jeremiah Rusk, the first chief executive to live here and popularly referred to as "Uncle Jerry."

Rusk was descended from Scotch-Irish grandfathers who fought in the Revolutionary War soon after coming to America from Ireland. After managing his widowed mother's farm and working as a stage driver and a railway construction foreman, he moved in 1853 with his wife and children – Charity and Lycurgus – to Viroqua, Wisconsin. With his earnings from the operation of a public house, he bought a farm, a stage line, and part ownership of a bank. His capture of a horse thief earned him the respect of the voters of Bad Axe County, who elected him sheriff in his first foray into politics. At the beginning of the Civil War, he resigned his seat in the state assembly to recruit and command the 25th Wisconsin Infantry, which participated in the sieges of Vicksburg and Atlanta. Beginning in 1871, he served three terms in the U.S. House of Representatives.

During his record seven years as governor, Rusk faced two major crises that could have sabotaged his political career. When a bankrupt railway company left 1,700 of its workers stranded in a remote area without food and pay, property owners asked the governor for military protection against expected violence and rioting. The governor responded by sending supplies to the workers, saying that "These men need bread, not bayonets." He also refused to allow the bankrupt company to liquidate its other debts until it had paid the workers in full. In the second crisis he acted in accord with public opinion when, after repeatedly warning that violence and the destruction of property by rioting strikers in Milwaukee would not be tolerated, he dispatched a militia unit to the city. He gained national recognition when the rioting ended, although with the death of five people killed by the militia. His comment after this latter episode – "I seen my duty and I done it" – reflected most people's expectations from the governor.

¶ **Studio of the Artist in Residence,** University of Wisconsin, 1645 Linden Drive, between Babcock Hall and Stock Pavilion.

The Studio of the Artist in Residence was built in 1937 for John Steuart Curry, the first such artist appointed by the university. Curry, who traced his lineage to an eighteenth-century ancestor from County Tyrone, Ireland, amused his students with the informality of his dress. While at the university, he initiated the Rural Arts Project to encourage local artistic talent.

Having studied at the Art Institute of Chicago, Curry received his first commissions from Wild West journals that expected him to capture the spirit of that most characteristic of American regions. After further study in Paris and Russia and at the New York Art Students' League, he was accepted as a serious artist with the exhibition of his *Baptism in Kansas* in Washington, D.C., in 1928. With *State Fair, Hogs Killing a Rattlesnake,* and *Tornado,* he became a leading exemplar of Regionalism and the darling of eastern critics eager for purely American representational art. His other major pieces are *Kansas Stockman, The Line Storm, Spring Shower, The Gospel Train,* and *Return of Private Davis.*

MARINETTE

¶ **Isaac Stephenson Monument,** along Riverside Drive.

This memorial honors Isaac Stephenson, a wealthy pioneer lumberman who represented Wisconsin in Congress for many years.

Of Scotch-Irish ancestry, Stephenson was born in New Brunswick, Canada, but moved to Milwaukee at the age of sixteen. After laboring at odd jobs in eastern Wisconsin, he began to acquire property in Michigan, hired himself out to move logs up Lake Michigan, and invested in steamships on the lake. By 1858 he had joined N. Ludington & Company and had settled in Marinette. He supplied Chicago and Milwaukee not only with logs and lumber but also with a variety of wood products from his factories at Peshtigo, the profits of which he invested in mining companies, railroads, and banks. Sadly, however, his factories were destroyed by forest fires that swept the northeastern section of the state in 1871, on the first day, ironically, of the Great Chicago Fire. Within only four hours the flames had killed 600 people and deforested a strip of land forty miles long and ten miles wide.

Like many other venture capitalists of his time, Stephenson tried his luck in the political arena. He was twice elected to the Wisconsin Assembly and three times to the House of Representatives during the 1880s. After falling victim to the state machine, he threw in his lot with Democratic Party rebels, helping to finance not only the successful gubernatorial candidacy of Robert M. LaFollette in 1900 but also the creation of the Milwaukee *Free Press.* In 1907 Stephenson was chosen to fill a resigned seat in the U.S. Senate but came under attack for disbursing $107,000 in his reelection primary campaign. A fellow politician pointed out the sinister influence of money upon the political process by complaining that "through the agency of the primary the state of Wisconsin offers its rich old men an opportunity to buy the senatorship as sort of a floral tribute to themselves." Stephenson was elected by the state legislature in 1909, but his right to remain in the Senate was challenged by members of the next legislature, although unsuccessfully.

MILWAUKEE

¶ **Milwaukee Art Museum,** War Memorial Building, 750 North Lincoln Memorial Drive.

The museum's 20,000 pieces include works of the Old Masters, German Expressionism, and nineteenth- and twentieth-century European and American art. *Georgia O'Keeffe, Picasso, and Warhol are among the modernists whose work is on display.

§ Open Tuesday, Wednesday, Friday, and Saturday 10-5, Thursday 12-9, Sunday 12-5. Closed January 1, Thanksgiving, and December 25. Fee. Free for Milwaukee County residents Wednesday and Saturday 10-12. Phone: 414-224-3200.

¶ **Milwaukee County Historical Society,** 910 North 3rd Street.

Among the society's holdings is a door from the *Lady Elgin,* an excursion steamer which collided with a lumber schooner and sank near Winnetka, Illinois, in 1860. Of its 400 passengers, 295 drowned, many – if not most – of them of Irish descent.

§ Open Monday-Friday 9:30-12, 1-4:30. Fee to view collection. Phone: 414-273-8288.

¶ **Haggerty Museum of Art,** Marquette University campus, east mall, 13th and Clybourn streets.

The museum was named for *Patrick Haggerty and his wife, Beatrice Menne Haggerty, who in 1980 donated to the museum their collection of 105 hand-colored biblical etchings by Marc Chagall. Among the museum's more than 6,000 *objets d'art* are Renaissance, Baroque, and modern paintings; Asian decorative arts; and sculpture and photography.

Patrick Haggerty was a 1936 graduate of Marquette University and a cofounder of Texas Instruments, Inc. Between 1945 and 1976 he held a variety of positions with that enterprise, including those of chief executive officer and chairman. Under his direction Texas Instruments moved into the manufacture of transistors, a development which made possible the first pocket radio and the application of semiconductor technology to military and space electronic systems. These advances were followed in 1958 with the invention of the integrated circuit. During his tenure as president, Texas Instrument's annual sales grew from $92 million to $1.3 billion.

Before his death in 1980, Haggerty had been a trustee of the University of Dallas, a member of the President's Science Advisory Committee, and the recipient of the 1970 Brotherhood Award of the National Conference of Christians and Jews. He had also received honorary degrees from eight universities, including Brooklyn Polytechnic and Rensselaer Polytechnic institutes, as well as the papal decoration of the Equestrian Order of the Holy Sepulchre.

§ Open Monday-Saturday 10-4:30, Thursday 10-8, Sunday 12-5. Closed January 1, Easter, Thanksgiving, and December 25. Phone: 414-288-7290.

Works Consulted

Ahern, Patrick Henry. *The Catholic University of America 1887-1896: The Rectorship of John J. Keane*. Washington, D.C.: The Catholic University of America Press, 1948.

Alden, Carroll Storrs. *Lawrence Kearny: Sailor Diplomat*. Princeton: Princeton University Press, 1936.

Allen, Gay Wilson. *William James: A Biography*. New York: The Viking Press, 1967.

Allen, Hervey. *Israfel: The Life and Times of Edgar Allan Poe*. New York: Farrar & Rinehart, Inc., 1934.

Alper, M. Victor. *America's Freedom Trail: A Tour Guide to Historical Sites of the Colonial and Revolutionary War Period*. New York: Macmillan Publishing Company, Inc., 1976.

Alsberg, Henry G., ed. *Delaware: A Guide to the First State*. American Guide Series. New rev. ed. New York: Hastings House, 1955.

American Automobile Association Tour Books.

"The American Cardinal." *New York Times* 28 April 1875: 10.

"Andrew O'Connor, Noted Sculptor, 67." *New York Times* 11 June 1941: 21.

Andrews, Matthew Page. *The Founding of Maryland*. Baltimore: The Williams & Wilkins Company, 1933.

Architect of the Capitol. *Compilation of Works of Art and Other Objects in the United States Capitol*. Washington, D.C.: Joint Committee on the Library, 1965.

Arnebeck, Bob. *Through a Fiery Trial: Building Washington 1790-1800*. New York: Madison Books, 1991.

Avery, Elroy McKendree. *A History of Cleveland and its Environs*. Chicago: The Lewis Publishing Company, 1918.

Avrich, Paul. *The Haymarket Tragedy*. Princeton: University Press, 1984.

Bailyn, Bernard, et al., eds. *The Great Republic: A History of the American People*. 3rd ed. Lexington, Mass.: D.C. Heath and Company, 1985.

Bakeless, John E. and Katherine L. *Signers of the Declaration*. Boston: Houghton Mifflin, 1969.

Banning, Kendall. *West Point Today*. New York: Funk & Wagnalls Company, 1937. Reprint 1943.

Barbour, Hugh, and J. William Frost. *The Quakers*. New York: Greenwood Press, 1988.

Barnes, Jack A. *Irish-American Landmarks: A Traveler's Guide*. Detroit: Visible Ink Press, 1995.

Barton, George. *Angels of the Battlefield: A History of the Labors of the Catholic

Sisterhoods in the Late Civil War. 2nd rev. ed. Philadelphia: The Catholic Art Publishing Company, 1898.

Bateman, Newton, et al. *Historical Encyclopedia of Illinois.* Vol. 1. Chicago: Munsell Publishing Company, 1925. 3 vols.

Bearse, Ray, ed. *Maine: A Guide to the Vacation State.* The New American Guide Series. Boston: Houghton Mifflin Company, 1969.

———, ed. *Massachusetts: A Guide to the Pilgrim State.* The New American Guide Series. 2nd ed. rev. Boston: Houghton Mifflin Company, 1971.

———, ed. *Vermont: A Guide to the Green Mountain State.* The New American Guide Series. Boston: Houghton Mifflin Company, 1968.

Bennett, William Harper. *Catholic Footsteps in Old New York: A Chronicle of Catholicity in the City of New York from 1524 to 1808.* New York: Schwartz, Kirwin and Fauss, 1909.

Bergman, Edward R. *Woodlawn Remembers: Cemetery of American History.* Utica, N. Y.: North County Books, Inc., 1988.

Bicknell, Thomas Williams. "Major General Anthony Wayne." *The Journal of the American Irish Historical Society* 10 (1910-11): 277-300.

Bigelow, Francis Hill. *Historic Silver of the Colonies and its Makers.* New York: The Macmillan Company, 1917.

Bigelow, E. Victor. *A Narrative History of the Town of Cohasset, Massachusetts.* Cohasset: The Committee on Town History, 1898.

Biographical Dictionary of the American Congress 1774-1927. Washington, D.C.: U.S. Government Printing Office, 1928.

Biographical Sketches of American Artists. 5th ed. rev. Lansing: Michigan State Library, 1924.

Birmingham, Stephen. *Real Lace: America's Irish Rich.* New York: Harper & Row, 1973.

Bishop, Joseph Bucklin. *Theodore Roosevelt and His Times.* Vol. 1. New York: Charles Scribner's Sons, 1920. 2 vols.

Blade, Robert E. "Pioneer Presbyterian Congregations." *American Presbyterians, Journal of Presbyterian History* 67 (1989).

Blanco, Richard, ed. *The American Revolution 1775-1783: An Encyclopedia.* 2 vols. New York: Garland Publishing, Inc., 1993.

Boatner, Mark Mayo III. *The Civil War Dictionary.* New York: David McKay Company, Inc., 1959.

———. *Encyclopedia of the American Revolution.* New York: David McKay Company, Inc., 1974.

Boisgilbert, Edmund. [pseud. for Ignatius Donnelly]. *Caesar's Column: A Story of the Twentieth Century.* Chicago: The Garden Vity Book Company, 1890.

Bolino, August C. *The Ellis Island Source Book.* 2nd ed. Washington, D.C.: Kensington Historical Press, 1990.

Bothwell, Margaret Pearson. "The Astonishing Croghans." *The Western Pennsylvania Historical Magazine* 48 (April 1965): 119-144.

Bottigheimer, Karl S. *Ireland and the Irish: A Short History*. New York: Columbia University Press, 1982.

Boylan, Henry. *A Dictionary of Irish Biography*. New York: Barnes & Nobles Books, 1978.

Brasher, Earl L. *Mathew Carey: Editor, Author and Publisher*. New York: The Columbia University Press, 1912.

Brown, John Howard, ed. *Lamb's Biographical Dictionary of the United States*. 7 vols. Boston: James H. Lamb Company, 1900-1903.

Bryan, Wilhelmus Bogart. *A History of the National Capitol*. Vol. 1. New York: The Macmillan Company, 1914. 2 vols.

Bryan, William Jennings, and Mary Baird Bryan. *The Memoirs of William Jennings Bryan*. Philadelphia: The United Publishers of America, 1925.

Callahan, North. *Henry Knox: General Washington's General*. New York: Rienhart & Company, Inc., 1958.

Campbell, John H. *History of the Friendly Sons of St. Patrick and of the Hibernian Society for the Relief of Emigrants from Ireland*. Philadelphia: Hibernian Society, 1892.

Carey, Mathew. *Autobiography of Mathew Carey*. Brooklyn: Eugene L. Schwaab, 1942.

Carr, William H. A. *The du Ponts of Delaware*. New York: Dodd, Mead & Company, 1964.

Castle, Henry A. "General James Shields, Soldier, Orator, Statesman." *Collections of the Minnesota Historical Society* 15 (1915):

Catholic University of America. *New Catholic Encyclopedia*. 17 vols. New York: McGraw-Hill, 1967-79.

Champlin, John Denison. *Cyclopedia of Painters and Painting*. New York: C. Scribner's Sons, 1886-87.

Chidsey, Donald Barr. *The Siege of Boston*. New York: Crown Publishers, Inc., 1966.

Churchyards of Trinity Parish 1697-1947. New York: Corporation of Trinity Church, 1948.

Claghorn, Charles Eugene. *Biographical Dictionary of American Music*. West Nyack, N.Y.: Parker Publishing Company, Inc., 1973.

——. *Woman Patriots of the American Revolution*. Metuchen, N.J.: The Scarecrow Press, Inc., 1991.

Clarke, Joseph I. C. "Unveiling the Sullivan Monument." *The Journal of the American Irish Historical Society* 12 (1913): 217-237.

Clarke, William J. "John Barry – Poem." *The Journal of the American Irish Historical Society* 13 (1914): 307-308.

Cleaves, Freeman. *Meade of Gettysburg*. Norman: University of Oklahoma Press, 1960.

Clement, J., ed. *Noble Deeds of American Women*. Buffalo: George H. Derby and Company, 1852.

Cohalan, Florence D. *Popular History of the Archdiocese of New York*. Yonkers: U.S. Catholic Historical Society, 1983.

Collar, Helen. "Irish Immigrants to Beaver Island." *The Journal of Beaver Island History* 1 (1976): 27-49.

Condon, Edward O'Meagher. *The Irish Race in America*. Glasgow: Cameron & Ferguson, n.d.

Condon, William H. *Life of Major-General James Shields*. Chicago: Press of the Blakely Printing Company, 1900.

Conley, Patrick T. *The Irish in Rhode Island: A Historical Appreciation*. Providence: The Rhode Island Heritage Commission and The Rhode Island Publications Society, 1986.

Conyngham, D. P. *The Irish Brigade and Its Campaigns*. Boston: William McSorley & Company, 1867.

Cooper, Brian, ed. *The Irish-American Almanac and Green Pages*. Rev. ed. New York: Harper & Row, 1990.

Cooper, J. Fenimore. *History of the Navy of the United States of America*. New York: G. P. Putnam & Company, 1854.

Corby, William, C.S.C. *Memoirs of Chaplain Life: Three Years with the Irish Brigade in the Army of the Potomac*. Chicago: La Monte, O'Donnell & Company, 1893.

Cottman, George S. *Centennial History and Handbook of Indiana*. Indianapolis: Max R. Hyman, 1915.

Couper, Colonel William. *One Hundred Years at V.M.I.* Vol. 4. Richmond: Garrett and Massie, Incorporated, 1939. 4 vols.

Craven, Bvt. Lieut.-Col. John J., M.D. *Prison Life of Jefferson Davis*. New York: Carleton, 1866.

Crimmins, John D. *Irish-American Miscellany*. New York: Published by the author, 1905.

Crofut, Florence S. Marcy. *Guide to the History and the Historic Sites of Connecticut*. Vol. 1. New Haven: Yale University Press, 1937. 2 vols.

Cromie, Alice Hamilton. *Restored America: A Tour Guide*. New York: American Legacy Press, 1979.

————. *A Tour Guide to the Civil War*. Chicago: Quadrangle Books, 1965.

Culbertson, Judi, and Tom Randall. *Permanent New Yorkers: A Biographical Guide to the Cemeteries of New York*. Chelsea, Vt.: Chelsea Green Publishing Company, 1987.

Cullen, Virginia. *History of Lewes, Delaware*. N.p.: Lewes and Rehoboth Hundred, Colonel David Hall Chapter, National Society, Daughters of the American Revolution, 1956.

Cushman, Clare, ed. *The Supreme Court Justices: Illustrated Biographies, 1789-1993*. Washington, D.C.: Congressional Quarterly, 1993.

Crew, H. W. *Centennial History of the City of Washington, D. C.* Dayton, Ohio: United Brethren Publishing House, 1892.

Cullen, James Bernard, ed. *The Story of the Irish in Boston*. Boston: James B. Cullen & Company, 1889.

D'Arcy, Mary Ryan. *The Saints of Ireland*. St. Paul, Minn.: The Irish American Cultural Institute, 1974.

David, Henry. *The History of the Haymarket Affair*. New York: Russell & Russell, 1958.

Davie, Michael. *Titanic: The Death and Life of a Legend*. New York: Alfred A. Knopf, 1986.

Davis, John H. *The Kennedys: Dynasty and Disaster, 1848-1983*. New York: McGraw-Hill, 1984.

Davis, W. W. H. *The History of Bucks County, Pennsylvania*. Doylestown, Pa.: Democrat Book and Job Office Prints, 1876.

DeGregorio, William. *The Complete Book of U.S. Presidents*. 4th ed. New York: Barricade Books, Inc., 1993.

Delaney, John J. *Dictionary of American Catholic Biography*. Garden City, N.Y.: Doubleday & Company, Inc., 1984.

de Mare, Marie. *G. P. A. Healy: An American Artist*. New York: David McKay Company, Inc., 1954.

Descriptive Catalogue of Painting and Sculpture in the National Museum of American Art. Boston: G. K. Hall & Company, 1983.

Dickie, Anna Adams. "Scotch-Irish Presbyterian Settlers in Southern Wisconsin." *Wisconsin Magazine of History* 31 (March 1948): 291-304.

Dijon, Harold. "Goody Glover, an Irish Victim of the Witch Craze, Boston, Mass., 1688." *The Journal of the American Irish Historical Society* 5 (1905): 16-22.

Dinen, Joseph. *The Purple Shamrock: The Hon. James Michael Curley of Boston*. New York: W. W. Norton & Company, Inc., 1949.

Documentary History of the Construction and Development of the United States Capitol Building and Grounds. Washington, D.C.: Government Printing Office, 1904.

Dolin, Mary C. "American Irish Women 'Firsts.'" *The Journal of the American Irish Historical Society* 24 (1925): 215-221.

Donovan, Herbert D. A. "William C. Kinsella." *The Journal of the American Irish Historical Society* 21 (1922): 146-153.

Dougherty, Daniel J. *History of the Society of the Friendly Sons of St. Patrick*. Philadelphia: Friendly Sons of St. Patrick, 1952.

Downs, Robert, et al. *Memorable Americans 1750-1950*. Littleton, Colo.: Libraries Unlimited Inc., 1983.

Drury, Clifford Merrill. *The History of the Chaplain Corps, United States Navy*. Vol 1 (1778-1939). Washington, D.C.: U.S. Government Printing Office, 1948-1950. 6 vols.

Durham, Michael S. *The Smithsonian Guide to Historic America: The Mid-Atlantic States*. New York: Stewart, Tabori & Chang, 1989.

Durkin, Joseph T., S.J. *William Matthews: Priest and Citizen*. New York: Benziger Brothers, Inc., 1963.

Eastman, John. *Who Lived Where: A Biographical Guide to Homes and Muse-*

ums. New York: Facts on File Publications, 1983.

Eberlein, Harold Donaldson, and Cortlandt Van Dyke Hubbard. *Portrait of a Colonial City: Philadelphia 1670-1838*. Philadelphia: J. B. Lippincott and Company, 1939.

Egle, William H., ed. *Andrew Gregg Curtin: His Life and Services*. Philadelphia: Avil Printing Company, 1895.

Eleuterio-Connor, Susan K. *Irish American Material Culture*. New York: Greenwood Press, 1988.

Eliot, Alexander. *Three Hundred Years of American Painting*. New York: Time Incorporated, 1957.

Ellis, Nancy, and Parker Hayden. *Here Lies America: A Collection of Notable Graves*. New York: Hawthorne Books, Inc., 1978.

Emmet, Thomas Addis. *Memoir of Thomas Addis and Robert Emmet with Their Ancestors and Immediate Family*. Vol. 1. New York: The Emmet Press, 1915. 2 vols.

Estes, J. Worth. "Honest Dr. Thornton: The Path to Rebellion." *Physician Signers of the Declaration of Independence*. New York: Science History Publications, 1976.

Fairman, Charles. Art and Artists of the Capitol of the United States. Washington, D.C.: U.S. Government Printing Office, 1927.

Falk, Peter Hastings, ed. *Who Was Who in American Art*. Madison, Conn.: Sound View Press, 1985.

Fetherling, Dale. *Mother Jones: The Miners' Angel*. Carbondale, Ill.: Southern Illinois University Press, 1974.

Federal Writers' Project of the Work Projects Administration. *Connecticut: A Guide to its Roads, Lore, and People*. American Guide Series. Boston: Houghton Mifflin Company, 1938.

———. *Kansas: A Guide to the Sunflower State*. American Guide Series. New York: The Viking Press, 1939. 141-142.

———. *Maryland: A Guide to the Old Line State*. American Guide Series. New York: Oxford University Press, 1940.

———. *Massachusetts: A Guide to its Places and People*. American Guide Series. Boston: Houghton Mifflin Company, 1937.

———. *New Hampshire: A Guide to the Granite State*. American Guide Series. Boston: Houghton Mifflin Company, 1938.

———. *New Jersey: A Guide to its Present and Past*. American Guide Series. New York: Viking Press, 1939.

———. *The Ohio Guide*. American Guide Series. New York: Oxford University Press, 1940.

———. *Philadelphia: A Guide to the Nation's Birthplace*. American Guide Series. Philadelphia: William Penn Association of Philadelphia, Inc., 1937.

———. *Rhode Island: A Guide to the Smallest State*. American Guide Series. Boston: Houghton Mifflin Company, 1937.

———. *Washington: City and Capital*. American Guide Series. Washington,

D.C.: Government Printing Office, 1937.

Fell, Thomas, ed. *Some Historical Accounts of the Founding of King William's School and its Subsequent Establishment as St. John's College*. Annapolis: Friendenwald Company, 1894.

Ferrier, William Warren. *The Story of the Naming of Berkeley*. Berkeley: n.p., 1929.

Ferris, Robert G., ed. *Signers of the Constitution*. Washington, D.C.: U.S. Department of the Interior, 1976.

Fielding, Mantle. *Dictionary of American Painters, Sculptors and Engravers*. New York: James F. Carr, 1965.

Fink, Gary M., ed. *Biographical Dictionary of American Labor Leaders*. Westport, Conn.: Greenwood Press, 1974.

Finley, Pepper Rae. "The Molly Maguires Are Still Polarizing Historians!" *Irish American Celebration*. Fall 1994: 6.

Fitzgerald, Margaret E., and Joseph A. King. *The Uncounted Irish in Canada and the United States*. Toronto: P. D. Meany Publishers, 1990.

"Five Iowa Brothers Lost in Pacific Battles." *New York Times* 13 January 1943: 10.

"5 Sullivans Died, Survivor Writes." *New York Times* 15 January 1943: 7.

Foley, Dylan. "Destination: Ellis Island." *Irish Echo* 14-20 July, 1993: 27.

"Foley in Politics for the Love of it." *New York Times* 16 January 1925: 2.

Formisano, Ronald P., and Constance K. Burns, eds. *Boston 1700-1980: The Evolution of Urban Politics*. Westport, Conn.: Greenwood Press, 1984.

Foner, Philip S., ed. *Mother Jones Speaks: Collected Writings and Speeches*. New York: Monad Press, 1983.

Forbes, Allan. *Towns of New England and Old England, Ireland and Scotland*. Vol. 1. Boston: State Street Trust Company, 1920. 2 vols.

Ford, Worthington Chauncey, ed. *The Writings of George Washington*. Vol. 9. New York: G. P. Putnam's Sons, 1891. 14 vols.

Foster, Morrison. *Biography, Songs and Musical Compositions of Stephen C. Foster*. Pittsburgh: Morrison Foster, 1896.

Foster, R. F. *Modern Ireland 1600-1972*. London: Allen Lane, The Penguin Press, 1988.

Freely, John. *Blue Guide: Boston and Cambridge*. New York: W. W. Norton & Company, Inc., 1984.

Fried, Frederick. *New York Civic Sculpture: A Pictorial Guide*. New York: Dover Publications, Inc., 1976.

Froncek, Thomas, ed. *The City of Washington*. New York: Alfred A. Knopf, 1979.

Gallagher, H. S. "An Irish Island Colony." *The Journal of the American Irish Historical Society* 28 (1929-30): 198-203.

Gannon, Robert J., S.J. *The Cardinal Spellman Story*. New York: Doubleday & Company, 1962.

Gardner, Martin, ed. *The Annotated Casey at the Bat: A Collection of Ballads*

About the Mighty Casey. New York: Clarkson N. Potter, 1967.

Germain, Aidan Henry. *Catholic Military and Naval Chaplains 1776-1917*. Dissertation, Catholic University of America, 1929. Washington, D.C.: Catholic University of America, 1929.

Gibson, Florence E. *The Attitudes of the New York Irish Toward State and National Affairs 1848-1892*. New York: Columbia University Press, 1951.

Gilchrist, Agnes Addison. "John McComb, Sr. and Jr. in New York City, 1784-1799." *Society of Architectural Historians Journal* 31 (March 1972): 10-21.

Glaspell, Susan. *The Road to the Temple*. New York: Stokes, 1927.

Gleeson, John. *The Book of Irish Lists and Trivia*. Dublin: Gill and Macmillan Ltd., 1989.

Goldman, John J. "Rose Kennedy, 104, Dies; Matriarch of a Dynasty." *Los Angeles Times* 23 January 1995: A1+.

Goode, James M. *The Outdoor Sculpture of Washington, D.C.* Washington, D.C.: Smithsonian Institution Press, 1974.

Goodwin, Doris Kearns. *The Fitzgeralds and the Kennedys*. New York: Simon and Schuster, 1987.

"Governor Shaken by Friend's Death." *New York Times* 16 January 1925: 2.

Grant, Gay. "W. Clark Noble: Maine Sculptor." *The Kennebec Proprietor* 6 (Summer 1989): 20-25.

Greenberg, Ronald M, ed. *The National Register of Historic Places 1976*. 2 vols. Washington D.C.: U.S. Department of the Interior, 1976.

Greenbie, Sydney, and Marjorie Barstow Greenbie. *Anna Ella Carroll and Abraham Lincoln*. Tampa, Fla.: University of Florida Press, 1952.

Greenhow, Rose O'Neal. *My Imprisonment and the First Year of Abolition Rule at Washington*. London: Richard Bentley, 1863.

Griffin, Martin J. "Capt. Jeremiah O'Brien of Machias, Me." *American Catholic Historical Researches* 20 (1903): 80-81.

———. *Commodore John Barry, "The Father of the American Navy": The Record of His Services for Our Country*. Philadelphia: Published by the author, 1903.

———. "The First American Catholic Bible." *American Catholic Historical Researches* 4 (April 1887): 64-68.

———. *The History of Commodore John Barry*. Philadelphia: The American Catholic Historical Society, 1897.

———. "James Hoban, the Architect and Builder of the White House and the Superintendent of the Building of the Capitol." *American Catholic Historical Researches* 24 (1907): 35-52.

———. "James Reed Dermott, the Planner of the City of Washington." *American Catholic Historical Researches* 27 (1910): 356-357.

Griffin, William D. *The Book of Irish Americans*. New York: Times Books, 1990.

A Guidebook to Newport Mansions. Newport, R.I.: The Preservation Society of Newport County, 1984.

Guelcher, Leslie A. *The History of Nininger . . . More than Just a Dream.* Stillwater, Minn.: The Croixside Press, 1982.

Gurn, Joseph. *Commodore John Barry: Father of the American Navy.* New York: P. J. Kenedy & Sons, 1933.

Hall, David D., ed. *Witch-hunting in Seventeenth-Century New England: A Documentary History, 1638-1692.* Boston: Northwestern University Press, 1991.

Haltigan, Patrick J. *The Irish in the American Revolution and their Early Influence in the Colonies.* Washington, D.C.: Patrick J. Haltigan, 1908.

Hammond, John Martin. *Colonial Mansions of Maryland and Delaware.* Philadelphia: J. B. Lippincott Company, 1914.

Hanchett, William. *Lincoln Murder Conspiracies.* Chicago: University of Illinois Press, 1983.

The Handbook of Private Schools. 75th ed. Boston: Porter Sargent Publishers, Inc., 1994.

Hanna, Charles A. *The Scotch-Irish or The Scot in North Britain, North Ireland, and North America.* Vol. 1. New York: G. P. Putnam's Sons, 1902. 2 vols.

Hansen, Harry, ed. *Illinois: A Descriptive and Historical Guide.* American Guide Series. New rev. ed. New York: Hastings House, 1974.

Harris, John. *Historic Walks in Old Boston.* Chester, Conn.: The Globe Pequot Press, 1982.

Harting, Emilie C. *A Literary Tour of the United States: Northeast.* New York: William Morrow and Company, Inc., 1978.

Hatfield, Edwin F. *History of Elizabeth, New Jersey.* New York: Carlton & Lanahan, 1868.

Healy, George P. A. *Reminiscences of a Portrait Painter.* Chicago: A. C. McClurg and Company, 1894.

Hearst, William Randolph Jr. *The Hearsts, Father and Son.* Niwot, Colo.: Roberts Rinehart Publishers, 1991.

Hedlund, Nancy M. "The Buckley Homestead." Crown Point, Ind.: Lake County Parks and Recreation Department, n.d.

Heise, Kenan, and Mark Frazel. *Hands on Chicago.* Chicago: Bonus Books, 1987.

Herbermann, Charles George, et al. *Catholic Encyclopedia.* 15 vols. New York: Appleton, 1907-12.

Hergesheimer, Joseph. *Sheridan: A Military Narrative.* Boston: Houghton Mifflin Company, 1931.

Heymann, C. David. *A Woman Named Jackie.* New York: A Lyle Stuart Book, 1989.

Highsmith, Carol M., and Ted Landphair. *Embassies of Washington.* Washington, D.C.: The Preservation Press, 1992.

The History of Peoria County, Illinois. Chicago: Johnson & Company, 1880.

Hogarth Paul. *Walking Tours of Old Philadelphia*. Barre, Mass.: Barre Publishing, 1976.

Holli, Melvin G. and Peter d'A. Jones, eds. *Biographical Dictionary of American Mayors, 1820-1980*. Westport, Conn.: Greenwood Press, 1981.

Holt, Glen E., and Dominic A. Pacyga. *Chicago: A Historical Guide to the Neighborhoods: The Loop and South Side*. Chicago: Chicago Historical Society, 1979.

Horan, James D. *Mathew Brady: Historian with a Camera*. New York: Bonanza Books, 1955.

Horle, Craig W., et al. *Lawmaking and Legislators in Pennsylvania: A Biographical Dictionary*. Vol. 1. Philadelphia: University of Pennsylvania Press, 1991.

Hughes, Rupert. *George Washington, The Savior of the States 1777-1781*. New York: William Morrow & Company, 1930.

Hunter, W. H. "The Pathfinders of Jefferson County." *Ohio Archaeological and Historical Publications* 6 (1898): 95-313.

Illustrated Guide to the Treasures of America. Pleasantville, N.Y.: The Readers' Digest Association, Inc., 1974.

Irwin, Robert, ed. *Baltimore: 200th Anniversary 1729-1929*. Baltimore: Baltimore Municipal Journal, 1929.

Jackson, Joseph. *Encyclopedia of Philadelphia*. Harrisburg: The National Historical Association, 1933.

"Jeremiah Sullivan House." Madison, Ind.: Historic Madison, Inc., n.d.

"John Gibbons and the Gibbons House." Wilmington, Del.: Hagley Museum and Library, 1970.

Johnson, Allen, et als., eds. *Dictionary of American Biography*. 28 vols. New York: C. Scribner's Sons, 1928-88.

Johnson, James E. *The Scots and Scotch-Irish in America*. Minneapolis: Lerner Publications Company, 1966.

Johnson, Robert Underwood. *Saint-Gaudens: An Ode and Other Verse*. New York: The Century Company, 1910.

Jolly, Ellen Ryan. *Nuns of the Battlefield*. Providence: The Providence Visitor Press, 1927.

Jones, Louis C. *Cooperstown*. Cooperstown, N.Y.: New York State Historical Association, 1982.

Jones, Maldwyn Allen. *American Immigration*. 2nd ed. Chicago: The University of Chicago Press, 1992.

Jones, Thomas C., ed. *The Halls of Fame*. Chicago: J. G. Ferguson Publishing Company, 1977.

Jordan, John W. "Bishop J. C. F. Carmmeroff's Narrative of a Journey to Shamokin, Pennsylvania, in the Winter of 1748." *The Pennsylvania Magazine of History and Biography* 19 (April 1905): 160-179.

Karlsen, Carol F. *The Devil in the Shape of a Woman: Witchcraft in Colonial New England*. New York: W. W. Norton & Company, 1987.

Karpel, Bernard, ed. *Arts in America: A Bibliography*. Vol. 1. Washington, D.C.: Smithsonian Institution Press, 1979. 4 vols.

Keany, Harry. "Molly Maguire' Found Not Guilty." *Irish Echo* 22-28 December 1992.

———. "Sainthood Beckons for Ordinary Irish American." *Irish Echo* 23-29 August 1995.

Keating, Percy. "John Keating and His Forebears." *Records of the American Catholic Historical Society* 29 (December 1918): 289-335.

Kenneally, James J. *The History of American Catholic Women*. New York: Crowrood, 1990.

Kennedy, J. H. "Governor Dongan and Religious Liberty in New York 1683-1688." *The Journal of the American Irish Historical Society* 28 (1929-30): 100-106.

Kobles, John J. *F. Scott Fitzgerald's Minnesota: His Homes and Haunts*. St. Paul, Minn.: Minnesota Historical Society Press, 1978.

Koenig, Louis W. *Bryan: A Political Biography of William Jennings Bryan*. New York: G. P. Putnam's Sons, 1971.

Kohl, Lawrence Frederick, ed. *Memoirs of Chaplain Life: Three Years with the Irish Brigade in the Army of the Potomac by William Corby, C.S.C.* New York: Fordham University Press, 1992.

Kruh, David, and Louis Kruh. *Presidential Landmarks*. New York: Hippocrene Books Inc., 1992.

Kussart, Mrs. S. "One Hundredth Anniversary of the Birth of Mrs. Mary E. Schenley." *Western Pennsylvania Historical Magazine* 9 (October 1926): 209-220.

Lake, Benjamin J. *The Story of the Presbyterian Church in the United States of America*. Philadelphia: Westminster Press, 1956.

Lee, Thomas Z. "American Irish Historical Notes." *The Journal of the American Irish Historical Society* 25 (1926): 218-222.

Levingston, Steven E. *Historic Ships of San Francisco*. San Francisco: Chronicle Books, 1984.

LeVot, Andre. *F. Scott Fitzgerald: A Biography*. Garden City: Doubleday & Company, Inc., 1983.

"Lewis and Loretta Glucksman Honor the Irish." *New York Times* 17 May 1991: B6.

Livermore, Mary A. *My Story of the War: A Woman's Narrative of Four Years Personal Experience*. Hartford: A. D. Worthington and Company, 1888.

Lockwood, George B. *The New Harmony Movement*. New York: D. Appleton and Company, 1905.

Logan, Rayford W., and Michael R. Winston, eds. *Dictionary of American Negro Biography*. New York: W. W. Norton & Company, Inc., 1982.

Lonn, Ella. *Foreigners in the Union Army and Navy*. New York: Greenwood Press, 1951.

"The MacGahan Monument." *Ohio Archaeological and Historical Quarterly*

21 (April-July 1912): 215-244.

MacNutt, Francis Augustus. *Six Decades of My Life*. Vol. 1. Brixen, Italy: Weigers Press, 1927. 2 vols.

Madden, R. R., M. D. *The United Irishmen: Their Lives and Times*. Vol. 2 (2nd series). London: J. Madden & Company, 1843. 7 vols. in 3 series.

Madison, James. *Notes of Debates in the Federal Convention of 1787*. Edited by Adrienne Koch. Athens, Ohio: Ohio University Press, 1984.

Maier, Eugene F. J. "Mathew Carey, Publicist and Politician." *Records of the American Catholic Historical Society* 39 (June 1928): 71-154.

Makers of History in Washington 1800-1950. Washington, D.C.: National Gallery of Art, 1950.

Malone, Russ. *Hippocrene U.S.A. Guide to Irish America*. New York: Hippocrene Books, 1994.

Mather, Cotton. *Memorable Providences, Relating to Witchcraft and Possessions*. Reprinted in *Narratives of the Witchcraft Cases, 1648-1706*. Edited by George L. Burr. New York: C. Scribner's Sons, 1914.

McCaffrey, Lawrence J., et al. *The Irish in Chicago*. Urbana, Ill.: University of Illinois Press, 1987.

McCann, James H. "Towers of Silence Speak." *The Journal of the American Irish Historical Society* 30 (1932): 134-163.

McGee, Thomas D'Arcy. *A History of the Irish Settlers in North America from the Earliest Period to the Census of 1850*. 2nd ed. Boston: P. Donahue, 1852.

A Memorial of Crispus Attucks, Samuel Maverick, Jonas Caldwell, Samuel Gray, and Patrick Carr. Boston: City of Boston, 1889.

A Memorial of John Boyle O'Reilly from the City of Boston. Boston: The Board of Aldermen, 1891.

"Memorial to Jeffrey Roche." *The Journal of the American Irish Historical Society* 9 (1910): 441.

Meyers, Albert Cook. *Immigration of the Irish Quakers into Pennsylvania 1682-1750*. Swarthmore, Pa.: Published by the author, 1902.

Mintz, Max M. *The Generals of Saratoga*. New Haven: Yale University Press, 1990.

Mitchell, Brian C. *The Paddy Camp: The Irish of Lowell 1821-61*. Urbana, Ill.: University of Illinois Press, 1988.

Mitchell, Broadus. *Alexander Hamilton: Youth to Maturity 1755-1788*. New York: The Macmillan Company, 1957.

Mizener, Arthur. *Scott Fitzgerald and His World*. New York: G. P. Putnam's Sons, 1972.

Mobile Travel Guide: Great Lakes. New York: Prentice Hall General Reference and Travel, 1993.

Mobile Travel Guide: Middle Atlantic. New York: Prentice Hall General Reference and Travel, 1994.

Morison, Samuel Eliot. *Admiral of the Ocean Sea: A Life of Christopher Co-*

lumbus. Boston: Little, Brown and Company, 1942.

———. *The European Discovery of America: The Northern Voyages A.D. 500-1600*. New York: Oxford University Press, 1971.

———. *"Old Bruin": Commodore Matthew C. Perry 1794-1858*. Boston: Little, Brown and Company, 1967.

Mosier, Richard D. *Making the American Mind: Social and Moral Influences in the McGuffey Readers*. New York: King's Crown Press, 1947.

"A 'Most Magnificent' Mansion." Providence: The Rhode Island Historical Society, 1985.

"Mother's Tears for Her Five Heroic Sons Christen New Destroyer 'The Sullivans.'" *New York Times* 5 April 1943: 11.

Mott, Frank Luther. *A History of American Magazines 1741-1850*. New York: D. Appleton and Company, 1930.

Mulholland, St. Clair A. *The Story of the 116th Regiment Pennsylvania Volunteers in the War of the Rebellion*. Philadelphia: F. McManus, Jr., & Company, 1903.

Mulligan, Hercules. "Narrative of Hercules Mulligan." In *Hercules Mulligan: Confidential Correspondent of General Washington.*, by Michael J. O'Brien. New York: P. J. Kenedy & Sons, 1937.

Murdock, Myrtle Cheney. *National Statuary Hall in the Nation's Capitol*. Washington, D.C.: Monumental Press, Inc., 1955.

Murphy, Robert T. "Keely, Patrick Charles." Vol. 2. *Macmillan Encyclopedia of Architects*. Edited by Adolf K. Placzek. New York: The Free Press, 1982. 4 vols.

Murray, Thomas Hamilton. "Rev. James MacSparran, Irishman, Scholar, Preacher and Philosopher, 1680-1757." *The Journal of the American Irish Historical Society* 3 (1900): 52-61.

Muse, Vance. *The Smithsonian Guide to Historic America: Northern New England*. New York: Stewart, Tabori & Chang, 1989.

Naden, Corinne J. *The Haymaket Affair, Chicago, 1886*. New York: Franklin Watts, Inc., 1968.

"Name 'The Sullivans' Set for Destroyer." *New York Times* 10 February 1943: 16.

National Cyclopaedia of American Biography. 81 vols. New York: J. T. White Company, 1893-1978.

National Gallery of Art. *Makers of History in Washington 1800-1950*. Washington, D.C.: National Gallery of Art, 1950.

National Portrait Gallery, Smithsonian Institution, Permanent Collection Illustrated Checklist. Washington, D.C.: National Portrait Gallery, 1987.

Nelson, Paul David. *Anthony Wayne: Soldier of the Early Republic*. Bloomington, Ill.: Illinois University Press, 1985.

Nevins, Allan. *Grover Cleveland: A Study in Courage*. New York: Dodd, Mead & Company, 1933.

Nevins, Allan, and Frank Ernest Hill. *Ford: Expansion and Challenge 1915-*

1933. New York: Charles Scribner's Sons, 1957.

Newberry, Linda, ed. *New Jersey: A Guide to its Present and Past*. American Guide Series. New York: Hastings House, 1977.

Norris, Walter B. *Annapolis: Its Colonial and Naval Story*. New York: Thomas Y. Crowell Company, 1925.

North, S. W. D. "The Story of a Monument." *Magazine of American History* 12 (July-December 1884): 97-112.

O'Brien, Michael J. *George Washington's Associations with the Irish*. New York: P. J. Kenedy & Sons, 1937.

———. "Hercules Mulligan." *The Journal of the American Irish Historical Society* 26 (1927): 96-104.

———. *Hercules Mulligan: Confidential Correspondent of General Washington*. New York: P. J. Kenedy & Sons, 1937.

———. *In Old New York: The Irish Dead in Trinity and St. Paul's Churchyards*. New York: The American Irish Historical Society, 1928.

———. "The Irish Ancestors of Theodore Roosevelt." *The Journal of the American Irish Historical Society* 17 (1918): 144-145.

———. *The Irish at Bunker Hill*. Shannon, Ireland: Irish University Press, 1968.

———. *Irish Settlers in America*. A Consolidation of Articles from *The Journal of the American Irish Historical Society*. 2 vols. Baltimore: Genealogical Publishing Company, Inc., 1979.

———. "Washington's Irish Friends." *The Journal of the American Irish Historical Society* 25 (1926): 344-369.

O'Conor, Charles. *"Negro Slavery Not Unjust": Speech of Charles O'Conor, Esq., at the Union Meeting at the Academy of Music, New York City, December 19th, 1859*.

O'Hanlon, Ray. "Antietam Irish to Get Memorial." *Irish Echo* 12-18 July 1995: 4.

Olcott, Charles S. *The Life of William McKinley*. Vol. 1. Boston: Houghton Mifflin Company, 1916. 2 vols.

O'Neill, Eugene. *Long Day's Journey into Night*. New Haven: Yale University Press, 1955.

O'Neill, James L. "Rev. James Caldwell, a Patriot of the American Revolution." *The Journal of the American Irish Historical Society* 3 (1900): 89-94.

O'Reilly, John Boyle. *Selected Poems*. New York: P. J. Kenedy & Sons, 1913.

O'Sheel, Shaemus. "Breakfast with Hercules Mulligan." In *Hercules Mulligan: Confidential Correspondent of General Washington.*, by Michael J. O'Brien. New York: P. J. Kenedy & Sons, 1937.

Parmet, Herbert S., and Marie B. Hecht. *Aaron Burr: Portrait of an Ambitious Man*. New York: The Macmillan Company, 1967.

Phelan, Thomas P. "Thomas Dongan, Colonial Governor of New York." *The Journal of the American Irish Historical Society* 16 (1917): 22-36.

Piggott, Michael. "Irish Pioneers of the Upper Mississippi Valley." *The Jour-*

nal of the American Irish Historical Society 9 (1910): 301-330.

Plummer, Mary H., and Gerald W. Gillette, eds. *On Holy Ground: American Presbyterian/Reformed Historical Sites*. Philadelphia: Presbyterian Historical Society, 1982.

The Poetical Works of T. Buchanan Read. New rev. ed. Philadelphia: J. B. Lippincott & Company, 1883.

Pollack, Queena. "An Irish Innkeeper and His Internationally Known 'Innkeeper's Daughter.'" *The Journal of the American Irish Historical Society* 28 (1929-30): 94.

The Postal Service Guide to U.S. Stamps. 19th ed. Washington, D.C.: U.S. Postal Service, 1993.

Potter, George. *To the Golden Door: The Story of the Irish in Ireland and America*. Boston: Little, Brown and Company, 1960.

Powell, Walter Louis. *The Alexander Dobbin House: A Short History*. N.p.: Published by the author, 1986.

"President Wilson's Speech." *The Journal of the American Irish Historical Society* 13 (1913-14): 300-302.

Purcell, L. Edward. *Who Was Who in the American Revolution*. New York: Facts on File, Inc., 1993.

Pusey, Merlo J. *Charles Evans Hughes*. Vol. 1. New York: The Macmillan Company, 1951. 2 vols.

Putnam, Carleton. *Theodore Roosevelt*. Vol. 1. New York: Charles Scribner's Sons, 1858. 2 vols.

Quinn, C. Edward, F.S.C. *The Signers of the Constitution of the United States*. The Bronx: The Bronx County Historical Society, 1987.

Quinon, Stephen. "Careers of the Croghans." *Western Pennsylvania Historical Magazine* 5 (July 1922): 215-219.

Reagan, Ronald. *An American Life*. New York: Simon and Schuster, 1990.

Ridge, Martin. *Ignatius Donnelly: The Portrait of a Politician*. St. Paul, Minn.: Minnesota Historical Society Press, 1991.

Roche, James Jeffrey. *Life of John Boyle O'Reilly*. Chicago: J. S. Hyland & Company, 1891.

Rose, William Ganson. *Cleveland: The Making of a City*. Cleveland: The World Publishing Company, 1950.

Ross, Betty. *A Museum Guide to Washington, D.C.* Washington, D.C.: Americana Press, 1986.

Ross, Ishbel. *Charmers and Cranks*. New York: Harper & Row, 1965.

A Rush County Retrospect. Vol. 1. Rushville, Ind.: Rush County Historical Society, 1984.

Ryan, Leo Raymond. *The Mother Church of Catholic New York (1785-1935)*. New York: The United States Catholic Historical Society, 1935.

Salwen, Peter. *Upper West Side Story*. New York: Abbeville Press, 1989.

Scharf, J. Thomas. *History of Delaware 1609-1888*. Vol. 1. Philadelphia: L. J. Richards & Company, 1888. 2 vols.

Schlesinger, Arthur M. Jr., ed. *The Almanac of American History*. New York: Bramhall House, 1986.

Seale, William. *The President's House*. Vol. 1. Washington, D.C.: White House Historical Association, 1986. 2 vols.

Semmes, Rafael. *Captains and Mariners of Early Maryland*. Baltimore: The Johns Hopkins Press, 1937.

Shannon, William V. *The American Irish*. Rev. ed. New York: The Macmillan Company, 1966.

Shapiro, Mary J. *Ellis Island: An Illustrated History of the Immigrant Experience*. New York: Macmillan Publishing Company, 1991.

Shea, John Gilmary. *"History of Georgetown University": Memorial of the First Centenary of Georgetown College, D.C.* Washington, D.C.: Published by the College, 1891.

———. *History of the Catholic Church in the United States 1808-15 to 1843*. New York: Published by the author, 1890.

———. *The Life and Times of the Most Rev. John Carroll*. New York: Published by the author, 1888.

Sheaffer, Louis. *O'Neill: Son and Playwright*. Boston: Little, Brown and Company, 1968.

Sheahan, James W., and George P. Upton. *Chicago: Its Past, Present and Future*. Chicago: Union Publishing Company, 1871.

Shenkman, Richard, and Kurt Reiger. *One-Night Stands with American History*. New York: William Morrow & Company, Inc., 1980.

Shipman, David. *Judy Garland: The Secret Life of an American Legend*. New York: Hyperion, 1992.

Siegel, Beatrice. *Sam Ellis's Island*. New York: Four Winds Press, 1985.

Sifakis, Stewart. *Who Was Who in the Civil War*. New York: Facts on File Publications, 1988.

"Sister of 5 Sullivans in Waves." *New York Times* 7 April 1943: 22.

Smith, George. *History of Delaware County, Pennsylvania*. Philadelphia: Henry B. Asgmead, 1862.

Smith, Page. *The Nation Comes of Age: A People's History of the Ante-Bellum Years*. New York: McGraw-Hill Book Company, 1981.

———. *A New Age Now Begins. A People's History of the American Revolution*. New York: McGraw-Hill Book Company, 1976.

———. *The Rise of Industrial America*. New York: McGraw-Hill Book Company, 1984.

———. *The Shaping of America: A People's History of the Young Republic*. New York: McGraw-Hill Book Company, 1980.

Smylie, James H. *American Presbyterianism: A Pictorial History*. Philadelphia: Presbyterian Historical Society, 1985.

Sobel, Robert, and John Raimo, eds. *Biographical Dictionary of the Governors of the United States 1789-1978*. 4 vols. Westport, Conn.: Meckler Books, 1978.

Soderberg, Paul, et al. *The Big Book of Halls of Fames in the United States and Canada*. New York: R. R. Bowker Company, 1977.

Sorensen, Theodore C. *Kennedy*. New York: Harper & Row, 1965.

Stanley, Sadie, ed. *The New Grove Dictionary of Music and Musicians*. London: Macmillan Publishers Limited, 1980.

Steinberg, Sheila, and Cathleen McGuigan. *Rhode Island: An Historical Guide*. Providence: Rhode Island Bicentennial Foundation, 1976.

Stewart, James. *The DuPont Company and Irish Immigration 1800-1857: A Study of the Company's Efforts to Arrange Passages for the Families of its Workmen*. Unpublished work, 1976.

Stewart, William Rhinelander. *Grace Church and Old New York*. New York: E. P. Dutton & Company, 1924.

"Sullivans Typify War Spirit of U.S." *New York Times* 8 February 1943: 21.

"Sunny Jim." *The Blood Horse* 83 (July 13, 1963): 108-111; 85 (July 20, 1963): 220-225; 91 (March 19, 1966): 714-715.

Sylvester, Lorna Lutes. "Conner Prairie Pioneer Settlement and Museum." *Indiana Magazine of History* 65 (March 1969): 1-24.

Taylor, Robert M. et al. *Indiana: A New Historical Guide*. Indianapolis: Indiana Historical Society, 1989.

Thatcher, John Boyd. *Christopher Columbus: His Life, His Work, His Remains*. Vol. 1. New York: G. P. Putnam's Sons, 1903. 3 vols.

Thavis, John. "U.S. Capuchin Solanus Casey Declared Venerable by Vatican." Tidings 14 July 1995.

Thayer, Theodore. *As We Were: The Story of Old Elizabethport*. Elizabeth, N.J.: The Grassman Publishing Company, Inc., 1964.

Thomas, Samuel W. "William Croghan, Jr. (1794-1850): A Prominent Pittsburgh Lawyer from Kentucky." *Western Pennsylvania Historical Magazine* 51 (July 1868): 213-227.

Thompson, Charles N. "Sons of the Wilderness: John and William Conner." *Indiana Historical Society Publications* 12 (1937).

Thompson, Ray. *Washington at Whitemarsh: Prelude to Valley Forge*. Fort Washington, Pa.: The Bicentennial Press, 1974.

Thoreau, Henry David. *Cape Cod*. New York: Literary Classics of the United States, 1985.

Thornton, Francis Beauchesne. *Our American Princes: The Story of the Seventeen American Cardinals*. New York: G. P. Putnam's Sons, 1963.

Tolchin, Martin. "Thomas P. O'Neill Jr., a Democratic Power in the House for Decades, Dies at 81." *New York Times* 7 January 1994: A21.

Truett, Randall Bond, ed. *Washington, D.C.: A Guide to the Nation's Capital*. American Guide Series. New rev. ed. New York: Hastings House, 1968.

Tucker, Glenn. *Dawn Like Thunder: The Barbary Wars and the Birth of the U.S. Navy*. Indianapolis: The Bobbs-Merrill Company, Inc., 1963.

Turnbull, Andrew. *Scott Fitzgerald*. London: The Bodley Head, 1962.

Tyler, Samuel. *Memoir of Roger Brooke Taney*. Baltimore: John Murphy &

Company, 1876.

"Typhoid Mary' Dies of a Stroke." *New York Times* 13 November 1938: 30.

"Uncle to Sail on The Sullivan." *New York Times* 22 April 1943: 5.

Van Doren, Carl. *Mutiny in January*. New York: The Viking Press, 1943.

Varble, Rachel M. *Jane Clemens: The Story of Mark Twain's Mother*. Garden City, N.Y.: Doubleday & Company, 1964.

Villard, Oswald Garrison. *John Brown 1800-1859: A Biography Fifty Years After*. New York: Alfred A. Knopf, 1943.

Volwiler, Albert T. *George Croghan and the Westward Movement*. Cleveland: The Arthur H. Clarke Company, 1926.

von Pressentin Wright, Carl. *Blue Guide: New York*. 2nd ed. New York: W. W. Norton & Company Inc., 1991.

Waggoner, Hyatt H., ed. *The Poetical Works of Whittier*. Boston: Houghton Mifflin Company, 1975.

Wakin, Edward. *Enter the Irish-American*. New York: Thomas Y. Crowell Company, 1976.

Walke, Mrs. Edwin S. "Soldiers of the American Revolution Buried in Illinois." *Journal of the Illinois State Historical Society* 8 (April 1915): 46-54.

Waller, George. *Saratoga: Saga of an Impious Era*. Englewood Cliffs, N.J.: Prentice-Hall, Inc., 1966.

Waln, Robert Jr. *The Biographies of the Signers of the Declaration of Independence*. 9 vols. Philadelphia: R. W. Pomeroy, 1824.

Walsh, J. C. "Charles O'Conor." *The Journal of the American Irish Historical Society* 27 (1928): 285-313.

Walworth, Arthur. *Woodrow Wilson: World Prophet*. Vol. 2. New York: Longmans, Green and Company, 1958. 2 vols.

Ward, Geoffrey C. *Baseball: An Illustrated History*. New York: Alfred A. Knopf, 1994.

"A Warm Welcome for N.Y.U.'s Irish Center." *New York Times* 27 April 1993: C12.

Warsaw, Michael P. *The National Shrine of the Immaculate Conception: America's Church*. Washington, D.C.: The National Shrine of the Immaculate Conception, 1990.

Waters, Edward N. *Victor Herbert: A Life in Music*. New York: The Macmillan Company, 1955.

Watson, John F. *Annals of Philadelphia and Pennsylvania*. 3 vols. Philadelphia: Edwin S. Stuart, 1899.

Weber, Francis J. *America's Catholic Heritage*. N.p.: St. Paul Editions, 1976.

———. "These Immortal Chaplains." San Buenaventura, Calif.: Junipero Serra Press, 1976.

Webster, Daniel. "An Address delivered at the Laying of the Corner-Stone of the Bunker Hill Monument at Charlestown, Massachusetts, on the 17th of June 1825." *The Writings and Speeches of Daniel Webster*. Vol. 1. Boston: Little, Brown, & Company, 1903. 18 vols.

Webster's American Military Biographies. Springfield, Mass.: G. & C. Merriam Company, 1978.

Wecter, Dixon. *Sam Clemens of Hannibal.* Boston: Houghton Mifflin Company, 1952.

Weichmann, Louis J. *A True History of the Assassination of Abraham Lincoln and of the Conspiracy of 1865.* Edited by Floyd E. Risvold. New York: Alfred A. Knopf, 1975.

Westerhoff, John H. III. *McGuffey and His Readers: Piety, Morality, and Education in Nineteenth-Century America.* Nashville: Abingdon, 1978.

Whalen, Richard J. *The Founding Father: The Story of Joseph P. Kennedy.* New York: The New American Library, 1964.

Whitney, David C. *Founders of Freedom in America: Signers of the Declaration of Independence.* Chicago: J. G. Ferguson Publishing Company, 1964.

Who Was Who in American History: Arts and Letters. Chicago: Marquis Who's Who, Inc., 1975.

Wibberly, Leonard Patrick O'Connor. *The Coming of the Green.* New York: Henry Holt and Company, 1958.

Wiencek, Henry. *The Smithsonian Guide to Historic America: Southern New England.* New York: Stewart, Tabori & Chang, 1989.

———. *The Smithsonian Guide to Historic America: Virginia and the Capital Region.* New York: Stewart, Tabori & Chang, 1989.

Wildes, Harry Emerson. *Anthony Wayne: Troubler Shooter of the American Revolution.* New York: Harcourt, Brace and Company, 1941.

Wilkinson, Burke. *Uncommon Clay: The Life and Works of Augustus Saint-Gaudens.* New York: Harcourt Brace Jovanovich, 1985.

Willcox, Joseph. "Biography of Rev. Patrick Kenny." *Records of the American Catholic Historical Society of Philadelphia* 7 (1896): 27-79.

———, ed. "Extracts from the Diary of Rev. Patrick Kenny, from June 23, 1827, to February 6, 1829." *Records of the American Catholic Historical Society of Philadelphia* 9 (June 1898): 223-256.

Wilson, James Grant, and John Fiske, eds. *Appleton's Cyclopaedia of American Biography.* 8 vols. New York: D. Appleton and Company, 1887-1918.

Wilson, Mary Poe. "Dr. William Beattie Laughlin." *Rush County Sesquicentennial.* Shelbyville, Ind.: Tippecanoe Press, 1972.

Winckler, Suzanne. *The Smithsonian Guide to Historic America: The Great Lakes States.* New York: Stewart, Tabori & Chang, 1989.

Winson, Justin. *Narrative and Critical History of America.* Boston: n.p., 1890.

Wirt, William. *The Two Principal Arguments of William Wirt, Esquire, on the Trial of Aaron Burr, for High Treason, and on the Motion to Commit Aaron Burr and Others, for Trial in Kentucky.* Richmond: Samuel Pleasants, Jr., 1808.

Wittke, Carl. *The Irish in America.* Baton Rouge: Louisiana State University Press, 1956.

———. *We Who Built America: The Saga of the Immigrant.* Rev. ed. Cleveland:

The Press of Western Reserve University, 1964.

Wolfe, Gerard R. *New York: A Guide to the Metropolis*. New rev. ed. New York: McGraw-Hill Book Company, 1988.

"A Woman's Trip Around the Globe." *New York Times* 26 January 1890: 8.

Writers' Program of the Work Projects Administration. *Indiana: A Guide to the Hoosier State*. American Guide Series. New York: Oxford University Press, 1945.

————. *Michigan: A Guide to the Wolverine State*. American Guide Series. New York: Oxford University Press, 1941.

————. *Missouri: A Guide to the "Show Me" State*. American Guide Series. New York: Duell, Sloan and Pearce, 1041.

————. *New York: A Guide to the Empire State*. American Guide Series. New York: Oxford University Press, 1940.

————. *Pennsylvania: A Guide to the Keystone State*. American Guide Series. New York: Oxford University Press, 1940.

————. *Wisconsin: A Guide to the Badger State*. American Guide Series. New York: Duell, Sloan and Pearce, 1941.

Young, Agatha. *The Women and the Crisis: Women of the North in the Civil War*. New York: McDowell, Obolensky, 1959.

Zobel, Hiller B. *The Boston Massacre*. New York: W. W. Norton & Company, Inc., 1970.

Site Index

¶ Although some of the statues and monuments in this list do not honor Irish or Irish Americans, they are included because they were created by sculptors of Irish descent.

A

Abraham Lincoln Equestrian Relief 270
Abraham Lincoln Statue 35, 74, 76, 77, 86, 89
Abraham Pierson Statue 19, 22
Adams Monument 35
Alfred E. Smith Boyhood Home 241
Alfred E. Smith Monument 220
Alfred E. Smith Park 242
Alfred E. Smith Plaque 271
Alfred E. Smith Statue 242
Albright-Knox Art Gallery 227
Allegheny Cemetery 351
Ambrose Burnside Statue 369
American Immigrant Wall 251
American Irish Historical Society 242
American Labor Museum/Botto House National Landmark 211
Anderson House 36
Andrew Curtin Statue 313, 323, 336
Andrew F. Scott House 101
Andrew Jackson Bust 259
Andrew Jackson Equestrian Statue 36
Andrew Jackson Statue 64
Andrew Mellon Gravesite 351
Andrew Mellon Memorial Fountain 37
Anna Ella Carroll Gravesite 125
Ann Glover Memorial 137
Annie Moore Statue 251, 252
Anthony Wayne Equestrian Statue 355
Anthony Wayne Gravesite 356
Anthony Wayne Monument 95
Antietam National Battlefield 133
Antrim 135
Arsenal Monument 125
Art Institute of Chicago 71
Aspet 201, 202
Auditorium Building and Theater 72
Augustus Saint-Gaudens Bust 259
Augustus Saint-Gaudens Gravesite 202

B

Balch Institute for Ethnic Studies 334
Baltimore & Ohio Railroad Museum 118
Baltimore & Ohio Railroad Station Museum 125
Barbara Fritchie House 127
Barbara Fritchie Monument 128
Barnegat Lighthouse State Park 209
Basilica of the Assumption of the Blessed Virgin Mary 117
Basilica of the National Shrine of the Immaculate Conception 37
Battle Cove 116
Bayard-Condict Building 242
Belcourt Castle 361
Benjamin Franklin Statue 337
Benjamin Harrison Gravesite 96
Benjamin Harrison House 96
Benjamin Harrison Statue 299
Bennett Park 242
Berkeley College 22
Berkeley Memorial Chapel 359
"Big Jim" O'Leary's Saloon 73
Blaine House National Historic

Landmark 105
Blaine Mansion 39
Blair House 39
Boston Athenaeum 138
Boston College 164
Boston Massacre Location 138
Boston Massacre Monument 140
Boston Museum of Fine Arts 156
Boston Public Library 141
Brooklandwood 124
Brown University 369
Buckley Homestead 98
Bunker Hill Monument 141
Burke's Tavern 237
Burnham Tavern Museum 109

C

Caesar Rodney Monument 30
Caldwell Gravesites 210
Caldwell Parsonage Museum 223
Calhoun College 22
Cantigny 92
Carbon County Jail 327
Cardinal Cushing Memorial 142
Cardinal Gibbons Statue 40
Cardinal Hayes Place 244
Cardinal O'Connell Bust 167
Cardinal O'Connell Way 143
Cardinal Spellman Philatelic Museum 174
Carey Mission Site 182
Carlisle Barracks 316
Carroll-Barrister House 115
Carroll Park 118
Carroll Viaduct 119
Carson, Pirie, Scott & Company Building 73
The Casino 289
Castle Clinton National Monument 244
Catalpa Memorial 171
Cathedral of the Immaculate Conception 225
Cathedral of St. Paul 191
Catherine De Valera Gravesite 286
Catherine O'Brien Gravesite 279

Catholic Total Abstinence Fountain 336
Catholic University of America 40
Chapel of Our Lady, Queen of Ireland 38
Charles Carroll "Barrister" Gravesite 114
Charles Carroll Mansion 119
Charles Carroll Statue 64, 336
Charles Evans Hughes Birthplace 234
Charles Evans Hughes Gravesite 283
Charles O'Conor Birthplace Site 246
Charles O'Conor Bust 242, 246
Charles Thomson Gravesite 315
Charles Whelan Gravesite 135
Chauncey Olcott Gravesite 284
Chester A. Arthur Gravesite 240
Chester A. Arthur Historic Site 372
Chester A. Arthur House 247
Chester A. Arthur Statue 247
Chicago Fire Academy 73
Chicago Historical Society 74
Christ Church Burial Ground 334
Christopher Colles Gravesite 279
Christopher Colles Residence 248
Church of the Ascension 247
Church of the Immaculate Conception 144
Civil War Library and Museum 335
Claremont Avenue 248
Coffee Run Mission Site 30
Comisky Park 74
Conference House 249
Congressional Cemetery 42
Conner Prairie Pioneer Settlement 100
Connie Mack Birthplace 165
Constellation, U.S.S. 124
Constitution, U.S. Frigate 144
Convent of the Visitation 43
Copley Square 145
Copley Studio Site Plaque 146
Corby Hall 103
Corcoran Gallery of Art 43
Corpus Christi Church 74

Cranston Print Works 358
Croghan House 351
Crown Hill Cemetery 96
Curtin Village 332

D

Daniel Carroll Gravesite 134
Daniel Dulany Gravesite 120
Daniel Emmett Birthplace 302
Daniel Emmett Gravesite 302
Daniel McConnell House 331
Daniel McCook Sr. Monument 308
Daniel Morgan Statue 291
Darnall's Chance 135
David Farragut Statue 241
David Poe Gravesite 120
David Shanahan Statue 90
Dean Family Farm 301
Dean William McNulty Statue 216
Death and the Young Sculptor 172
Declaration House 335
Deep Run Presbyterian Church 334
Defenders' Monument 20
Derry Presbyterian Church 327
DeWitt Clinton Memorial 259
Diana of the Crossroads 156
Dinand Memorial Library 175
Dobbin House Tavern 318
Dominick Lynch House 249
Donegal Presbyterian Church 332
Dongan's Charter 225
Dorchester Heights National
    Historic Site 146
Doughoregan Manor 126
Dowling Urban Environmental
    Center 189
Drumm House 237
Duane Street 249
Dumbarton Oaks 44
DuPont Statue 31

E

Eamon De Valera Bust 242
East Durham Irish Cultural and
    Sports Centre 232

Eckley Miners' Village 326
Edgar Allan Poe Bust 250
Edgar Allan Poe Cottage 249
Edgar Allan Poe Gravesite 120
Edgar Allan Poe House 250
Edgar Allan Poe Monument 121
Edgar Allan Poe National Historic
    Landmark 121
Edgar Allan Poe National Historic
    Site 336
Edgar Allan Poe Plaque 293
Edmund Burke Statue 45
Edgar Allan Poe Street 250
Edsel and Eleanor Ford House 179
Edward Alexander MacDowell Bust
    259
Edward Alexander MacDowell
    Gravesite 208
Edward Hand Gravesite 330
Edward McGlynn Gravesite 283
Edwin Booth Statue 258
Edwin Stanton Statue 310
Ellis Island 251
Embassy of Indonesia (Walsh-
    McLean House) 45
Embassy of Ireland 46
Emigrant Savings Bank 253
Ephraim McDowell Statue 65
Erie Canal Village 287
Eugene O'Neill Collection 22
Eugene O'Neill House 171
Eugene O'Neill Memorial Theater
    Center 22
Evangelical Reformed Church 128
Essex County (N.J.) Courthouse
    215

F

Fairmount Park 336
Faneuil Hall 146
Father Francis Duffy Gravesite 276
Father Francis Duffy Statue and
    Square 253
Father Michael McGivney Statue
    24, 25
Father Patrick Kenny Gravesite 31

Father Solanus Casey Gravesite 179
Father Theobald Mathew Statue 336
Father William Corby Memorial 319
Father William Corby Statue 103, 319, 320
Fenian Monument 374
Ferry House 223
Fighting McCooks Monument 310
Finley Peter Dunne Gravesite 282
First Division Museum 92
First Grant House 88
First Presbyterian Church 232
Fisher-Martin House 26
Fisher's Paradise 26
Five Points 253
Flanagan Hotel 239
Foley Square 254
"For Humanity" Memorial 108
Ford Foundation Building 254
Fordham University 254
Ford's Theater 46
Forest Hills Cemetery 172
Fort Clinton 255
Fort Constitution 207
Fort Defiance Site 299
Fort Johnson 235
Fort Knox II 104
Fort Knox State Historic Park 112
Fort McClary 109
Fort McHenry National Monument and Historic Shrine 121
Fort O'Brien 110
Fort Ouiatenon Historical Park 97
Fort Recovery State Memorial 300
Fort Sheridan 85
Fort Stanwix 235
Fort Ticonderoga 236
Fort William Henry Museum 239
Francis Blair Jr. Statue 64
Francis Makemie Statue 349
Francis Scott Key Monument 128
Francis Spellman Gravesite 272
Frank Murphy Birthplace Museum 180
Frank Murphy Gravesite 181

Fraunces Tavern 255
Frawley Circle 256
Frazer Monument 287
Freedom 63
Freedoms Foundation at Valley Forge 354
Free Quaker Meetinghouse 337
Freer Gallery of Art 46
French and Irish Soldiers Monument 19
F. Scott Fitzgerald Birthplace 192
F. Scott Fitzgerald Gravesite 132
F. Scott Fitzgerald House 192, 237
Fulton Opera House 329

G

Galena Historical Society 83
Galloway House and Village 379
Gallows Hill 223
Garfield Park 74
Gates House 110
General Gates House 359
General Wayne Inn 332
George Clinton Gravesite 43, 238
George Clinton Statue 64, 240
George Croghan Gravesite 300
George Meade Equestrian Statue 322, 336
George Meade Gravesite 345
George Meade Headquarters 321
George Meade Memorial 46
George Meade Statue 336
George McManus Gravesite 283
George M. Cohan Gravesite 284
George M. Cohan Statue and Square 256
George Read I Gravesite 28
George Read II Gravesite 28
George Read II House and Garden 28
George Rogers Clark Statue 88
George Taylor House and Park 313
Georgetown Astronomical Observatory 49
Georgetown University 47
Getty Tomb 75

Gibbons House 32
Graceland Cemetery 75
Gramercy Park 257
Grant Cottage State Historic Site
    296
Grant Home State Historic Site 84
Grant Park 76
Great Conewago Presbyterian
    Church 329
Greenfield Village 178
Greenwich Village 258
Greenwood Cemetery 258
Grover Cleveland Birthplace 209
Grover Cleveland Bust 259
Grover Cleveland Gravesite 220
Grover Cleveland House 234
Guinston United Presbyterian
    Church 321
Guy Park Historic Site 226

H

Hackley Park 182
Haggerty Museum of Art 383
Hagley Museum and Library 31
Hall of Fame for Great Americans
    259
Hammersmith Farm 361
Hannah Milhous Plaque 93
Harriton House 314
Havre de Grace Lighthouse 130
Haymarket Monument 78, 79
Haymarket Square 76
Healy Building 175
Healy Hall 48
Helen Keller Gravesite 65
Henry Ford Birthplace 178
Henry Ford Estate-Fair Lane 177
Henry Ford Museum 177
Henry Knox Building 354
Henry Lawton Statue 96
Hercules Mulligan Gravesite 279
Hercules Mulligan House Site 260
Hibernian (Timothy Murphy) Mon-
    ument 288
High Bridge 260
Hill-Physick-Keith House 340

Historical Society of Pennsylvania
    340
Historic Fort Wayne 95
Historic Murphy's Landing 199
Holyhood Cemetery 161
Homewood 122
Holy Cross Cathedral 147
Holy Cross Cemetery 261
Holy Sepulchre Cemetery 286
Holy Trinity Church 125
Holy Trinity Orthodox Church 76
Home Statue 76
Hope Lodge 318
Hopewell Cemetery 93
Horace Greeley Birthplace 201
Horace Greeley Gravesite 258
Horace Greeley Statue 248, 262
Hugh O'Brien Bust 141
Hugh O'Neill Store Site 262
Hunter College 263

I

Ignatius Donnelly Gravesite 195
Ignatius Donnelly House Marker
    187
Immanuel Episcopal Church 28
Independence Flagstaff 280
Independence Hall 340
Indian Castle Church 237
International Harvester Company
    76
Ireland House 263
Irish American Heritage Museum
    232
Irish Brigade Monument 322
Irish Castle 76
Irish Founders Memorial 335
Irish Round Tower 171
Irish Servant Memorial 362
Isaac Stephenson Monument 382
Island Cemetery 362

J

James Brady Gravesite 261
James Buchanan Birthplace State

Park 331
James Buchanan Gravesite 330
James Buchanan Hotel 331
James Buchanan Statue 50
James Caldwell Statue 349
James Connolly Memorial 292
James Curley Memorial 153
James Curley Residence 154
James Family House 147
James Fitzsimmons Gravesite 261
James Garfield Bust 337
James Garfield Statue 298
James Hoban Gravesite 50
James G. Blaine Gravesite 56
James Gibbons Gravesite 117
James Jeffrey Roche Gravesite 161
James J. Hill House 195
James J. Hill Reference Library 196
James Kavanagh House 111
James Kent Bust 260
James Logan Gravesite 337
James MacSparran Gravesite and
     Monument 368
James McHenry Gravesite 120
James McNeill Whistler Bust 259
James McNeill Whistler Tablet 293
James O'Hara Gravesite 351
James Otis Statue 164
James Shields Monument 193
James Shields Statue 65
James Smith Gravesite 356
James Steedman Statue 310
James Sullivan Gravesite 157
James Walker House 263
James Woods Gravesite 280
Januarius A. MacGahan Gravesite
     303
Jefferson Davis Statue 64
Jeremiah Curtin House 380
Jeremiah O'Brien 110
Jeremiah Rusk House 381
Jeremiah Sullivan House 98, 99
Jim Thorpe Memorial 328
Jim Thorpe Monument 316
John Barry Bridge 209
John Barry Bust 145
John Barry Gravesite 345

John Barry Memorial 347
John Barry Statue 41, 336, 342
John Boyle O'Reilly Bust 41, 141
John Boyle O'Reilly Gravesite 161
John Boyle O'Reilly House 147
John Boyle O'Reilly Memorial 147,
     148, 166
John Brown House 370
John Calhoun Statue 64
John Carroll Bust 117
John Carroll Gravesite 117
John Carroll Statue 48, 336
John Carroll University 298
John Carter Brown Library 369
John Chapman House 332
John Conner Trading Post Site 93
John Drumgoole Plaque 275
John Dunlap Gravesite 334
John E. Lawe Memorial 232
John E. Lawe Memorial Sports
     Stadium 232
John Finerty Statue 75
John Finley Walk 264
John Fitzgerald Gravesite 158
John Fitzgerald House 150
John F. Kennedy Bust 209, 242
John F. Kennedy Center for the
     Performing Arts 50
John F. Kennedy Federal Building
     152
John F. Kennedy Houses 50
John F. Kennedy Memorial 166, 270
John F. Kennedy Museum 167
John F. Kennedy Museum and
     Library 155
John F. Kennedy School of Govern-
     ment 162
John F. Kennedy Statue 152
John Farley Gravesite 272
John Flanagan House 87
John Howard Payne Gravesite 57
John Hughes Cabin 126
John Hughes Gravesite 272
John Hughes Statue 254
John Hancock Gravesite 156
John Ireland Marker 185
John Ireland Memorial Window

197
John Ireland Statue 197
John J. Burns Library 164
John Johnston House 306, 307
John Keating Gravesite 342
John Kenna Statue 65
John Logan Equestrian Statue 76
John Logan Statue 70
John McCloskey Gravesite 272
John McCullaugh Gravesite 283
John McCullough Gravesite 343
John McKinly Gravesite 33
John McLaughlin Statue 65
John McMillan Statue 349
John O'Connor House 200
John Paulding Statue 292
John Quincy Adams Bust 259
John Rawlins House 84
John Reynolds Equestrian Statue 335
John Reynolds House 370
John Reynolds Monuments 322
John Reynolds Statue 47, 336
Johns Hopkins Hospital 122
Johns Hopkins University 122
John Sedgwick Statue 294
John Shanahan Memorial 326
John Street Methodist Church 264
John Sullivan House 206
John Sullivan Memorial Bridge 206
John Sullivan Tablet 371
Johnson Hall State Historic Site 238
John Wood Gravesite 88
John Wood Mansion 88
John Wood Statue 89, 90
Joseph Coveney Gravesite 176
Joseph P. Kennedy, U.S.S. 166
Joseph McCarthy Bust 377
Joseph Ruggles Wilson Gravesite 310
Josiah Porter Statue 256
J. R. Grant Leather Store Site 84
Judson Memorial Church 265
Judy Garland Childhood Home 186
Judy Garland Historical Center 187

K

Kane Manor Inn 328
Kane Memorial Chapel 329
Kearny Cottage Museum 218, 219
Kells 26
Kelly Memorial 343
Kelly's Livery Stable 101
Kemble Estate 213
Kennedy Compound National Historic Landmark 167
Kennedy Farmhouse 133
Kennedy National Historic Site 161
Kennedy Plaza 371
Kennedy Residence 162
Kingston Hall 130
Kingwood Center 302
Knights of Columbus Grand Council Museum 20
Knox Gun 236
Knox Monument 236
Knox's Headquarters State Historic Site 240
Kruser-Finlay House 270

L

Lady Wisdom 106
Lafayette Statue 123
Last Moments of John Brown 266
Lauinger Library 49
Lee and Jackson Statue 123
Lee-Jackson Memorial Windows 65
Legionville 325
Lew Wallace Statue 65, 94
Liberty and Union, Now and Forever 146
Library of Congress 50
Log Academy 316
Log College Monument 356
Lola Montez Gravesite 259
Lomasney Way 157
Long Branch Historical Museum 213
Longfellow National Historic Site 162
Louis Sullivan Gravesite 75
Lowell National Historical Park 168

Lydia Darragh Gravesite 337

M

Macdonough Hall 116
Macdonough House 26
MacDowell Colony National
    Historic Landmark 207
Magee Memorial 352
Magnolia Manor 70
Mahan Hall 116, 294
Marcus Daly Gravesite 258
Margaret Corbin Commemorative
    Plaque 265
Margaret Corbin Gravesite 294
Mark Hanna Gravesite 298
Mark Hanna Statue 298
Martin Milmore Gravesite 172
Mary Croghan Schenley Statue 352
Massachusetts Institute of Technol-
    ogy 163
Mathew Brady Gravesite 42
Mathew Brady Photo Studio 50
Mathew Brady Photo Studio Site
    265
Mathew Carey Gravesite 345
Matthew Cottrill House 108
Matthew C. Perry Birthplace 363
Matthew C. Perry Gravesite 362
Matthew C. Perry House 266
Matthew C. Perry Statue 366, 367
Matthew Fontaine Maury Bust 259
Matthew Thornton Home and
    Gravesite 206, 207
Matthew Thornton House 204
Maury Hall 116
McCone Sod House Exhibit 198
McCook House 297, 301
McCormack Building 155
McCormick Place Convention
    Complex 77
McCormick Theological Seminary
    78
McDowell Hall 115
McGuire Air Force Base 213
McKinley Museum of History,
    Science and Industry 297

McKinley National Memorial 297
McKonkey Ferry Inn 333
McLaughlin Library 221
McMahon Hall 41
McManus Collection 221
McSorley's Old Ale House 266
Mellon Institute 352
Metropolitan Museum of Art 266
Michael Corcoran Gravesite 267
Michael Corrigan Gravesite 272
Michael Hogan Tablet 267
Michael J. Quill Corner 267
Michael J. Quill Cultural Centre
    233
Michael Lawler Monument 83
Military Park 215
Miller House 313
Milwaukee Art Museum 383
Milwaukee County Historical
    Society 383
Minneapolis Historical Society 196
Minneapolis Institue of Arts 190
Monmouth Battle Monument 211
Monsignor George Doane Statue
    215
Monte Cristo Cottage 22, 23
Montpelier 113
Morristown National Historic Park
    213
Mother Jones Gravesite 86
Mount Auburn Cemetery 163
Mount Clare 118, 119
Mount Olivet Cemetery 128
Moylan Park 344
Moylan Place 268
Museum of the Presidents 85
Muskegon Museum of Art 182

N

Nathaniel Irish House 344
National Archives 51
National Baseball Hall of Fame and
    Museum 230
National Gallery of Art 53
National McKinley Birthplace
    Memorial 304, 305

National Memorial Arch 355
National Museum of Racing and
     Hall of Fame 290
National Portrait Gallery 53
National Presbyterian Church 233
National Shrine of the Immaculate
     Conception 37
National Shrine of Our Lady of
     Knock 233
National Statuary Hall 63
Naval and Servicemen's Park 228
Naval War College Museum 363
Navy Museum 54
Nellie Bly Gravesite 281
Neshaminy Warwick Presbyterian
     Church 356
New Bedford Whaling Museum
     172
Newberry Library 78
New Britain Museum of American
     Art 20
Newlin Mill Park 316
Newport Casino 364
New York Avenue Presbyterian
     Church 54
Niagara, U.S. Brig 318
9th Massachusetts Volunteers
     Monument 324
Northfield Historical Society Mu-
     seum 190
Norwest Bank 190
Nuns of the Battlefield Memorial
     54

O

Oak Hill Cemetery 56
Obelisk of Honor 354
O'Briens' Gravesite 169
Octagon House National Historic
     Landmark 57
O'Hare International Airport 78
Ohio and Erie Canal Monument
     304
Old Erie Canal State Park 229
Old Fort Niagara 296
Old Granary Burial Ground 256

Old McClurg Mansion 295
Old Mission Church 183
Old Narragansett Church 371
Old St. John the Evangelist Church
     134
Old St. Mary's Church 345
Old St. Patrick's Church (New York)
     268
Old Stone Fort Museum 291
Old Tennent Church 211
"Old No. 201" Engine 190
Old World Wisconsin 379
Oliver H. Kelley Farm 185
Oliver H. Perry Birthplace 371
Oliver H. Perry Gravesite 362
Oliver H. Perry Monument 318
Oliver H. Perry Statue 228, 298, 365
Oliver Wendell Holmes Statue 259
116th Pennsylvania Infantry Monu-
     ment 324
O'Neill Building 157
Oriskany Battle Monument 236
O'Shaughnessy Hall 104
O'Shaughnessy Plaza and Audito-
     rium 197
O'Shaughnessy Reservoir 299

P

Paoli Memorial Ground 334
Park-McCullough Mansion 375
Parsons-Taylor House 317
Paterson Museum 216
Patrick Carr Gravesite 156
Patrick Collins Gravesite 161
Patrick Collins Monument 152
Patrick Guiney Gravesite 161
Patrick Hayes Gravesite 272
Patrick H. Sullivan Foundation
     Museum 104
Patrick H. Sullivan Memorial 104
Patrick Kellegher Little League
     Baseball Field 232
Patrick McCarran Statue 65
Patrick O'Rorke Bust 287
Patrick O'Rorke Gravesite 287
Patrick O'Rorke Memorial 323

Patriot Soldiers Monument 291
Patterson Park 123
Paxton Presbyterian Church 326
Peace Monument 241
Peggy O'Neale Eaton Gravesite 56
Penn's Landing 348
Pennsylvania Memorial 323
Perry's Cave 308
Perry's Lookout 301
Perry's Victory and International
    Peace Memorial 308
Peter Cooper Statue 269
Peter J. O'Neill Library
Peter McGuire Gravesite 218
Philip Connelly Cabin 176
Philip Embury Gravesite 229
Philip Kearny Statue 65
Philip Schuyler Statue 289
Philip Sheridan Boyhood Home 309
Philip Sheridan Memorial 299
Philip Sheridan Statue 75, 182, 226,
    309
Philip Syng Physick Gravesite 334
Philadelphia Museum of Art 348
Phillips Brooks Statue 161, 243
Pierce Butler Gravesite 334
Pierre Menard Statue 90
The Pilgrim 337
Pinkerton Academy 205
Police Academy Museum 269
Presbyterian Historical Society 348
Progress of Civilization 63
Provincetown Playhouse (Mass.)
    172
Provincetown Playhouse (N.Y.) 270
The Puritan 173

R

Rainey Memorial Park 70
Redwood Library and Athenaeum
    365
Rehobeth Presbyterian Church 135
Richard Daley Center and Plaza 78
Richard Daley Statue 90
Richard Meade Bust 242
Richard Montgomery Gravesite 272

Robert Emmet Statue 57
Robert F. Kennedy Bust 270
Robert F. Kennedy Memorial 58
Robert Fulton Birthplace National
    Historic Landmark 354
Robert Fulton Bust 259
Robert Fulton Gravesite 279
Robert Fulton Statue 64
Robert R. McCormick Museum 92
Robert Treat Paine Gravesite 156
Robert Treat Paine Statue 173
Rochambeau Monument 24
Rock Ford 320
Roger Taney House 128
Roger Taney Gravesite 129
Roger Taney Law Office 129
Roger Taney Statue 114, 124, 129
Ronald Reagan Birthplace 90
Ronald Reagan Boyhood Home 82
Ronald Reagan Plaque 83
Ronald Reagan Statue 83
Rosecliff 365
Rose Fitzgerald Kennedy Garden
    152
Roundabout Theater 280
R. R. Donnelley and Sons Company
    94

S

St. Anne's Church 114
St. Denis Church 112
St. Francis Xavier Church and Old
    Bohemia Manor 135
Saint-Gaudens House and Studio
    203
Saint-Gaudens National Historic Site
    201
St. James Church 270
St. John's Church (Bangor, Me.) 107
St. John's College 115
St. John the Evangelist Church 129
St. John Memorial 164, 165
St. Joseph's Cemetery 158
St. Joseph's Church (Irish Hills,
    Mich.) 182
St. Joseph's Church (Providence,

R.I.) 371
St. Joseph's on the Brandywine
    Church 33
St. Malachy's Chapel 271
St. Mary's Church (Beaver Island,
    Mich.) 176
St. Mary's Church (Newport, R.I.)
    366
St. Mathew's Cathedral 58
St. Patrick's Cathedral 271
St. Patrick's Church (Chicago) 80
St. Patrick's Church (District of
    Columbia) 58
St. Patrick's Church (Lowell, Mass.)
    169
St. Patrick's Church (New Castle,
    Me.) 111, 112
St. Paul's Church 272
St. Paul Seminary 197
St. Peter-by-the-Sea Church 360
St. Peter's Episcopal Church 220
St. Peter's Catholic Church 275
St. Raymond's Cemetery 275
St. Stanislaus Church 80
St. Stephen's Church 158
St. Thomas Academy 197
Sagamore Hill National Historic Site
    285
Sam Houston Statue 64
Samuel Brown House 355
Samuel Clemens House 21
Saratoga National Historic Park 287
Schenley Park 352
Schuyler-Hamilton House 214
Seton Hall University 221
Settlers of the District of Columbia
    Memorial 58
Shaw Memorial 158, 159
Shea Stadium 295
Sheridan Circle 59
Shrine of the Little Flower 183
Sidney Lanier Bust 259
The Signing of the Declaration of
    Independence 63
Simon Kenton Gravesite 311
Simon Kenton House Site 311
6th New York Cavalry Memorial

324
66th New York Infantry Monument
    324
Society of the Cincinnati Tablet 241
Soldiers' Monument 172, 201
Soldiers' and Sailors' Monument 21,
    160, 366
Songwriters' Hall of Fame 276
South Front Street Historic District
    349
The Sphinx 164
The Standing Angel 362
Stenton 349
Stephen Foster Bust 259
Stephen Foster Gravesite 351
Stephen Foster Memorial Building
    352
Stephen Foster Statue 298
Stephen Moylan Gravesite 345
Stephen Moylan Memorial 344
The Stone Age 337
Stoneham 29
Studio of the Artist in Residence 381
Sullivan (Newtown Battlefield)
    Monument 233
Sullivan Street 277
The Sullivans 228
Supreme Court Building 59
The Surrender of Lord Cornwallis at
    Yorktown 22, 63
Sylvanus Thayer Statue 294

T

Taney Place 114
Terence Cooke Gravesite 272
Terence Powderly House 354
Theodore Roosevelt Bird Sanctuary
    285
Theodore Roosevelt Birthplace
    National Historic Site 277
Theodore Roosevelt Bust 242, 259
Theodore Roosevelt Gravesite 285
Theodore Roosevelt Inaugural
    National Historic Site 229
Theodore Roosevelt Memorial 62,
    85, 278

Thomas Addis Emmet Gravesite and Monument 272
Thomas Carlin Monument 71
Thomas Cass Gravesite 164
Thomas Cass Statue 145
Thomas Dongan Statue 286
Thomas Dongan Tablet 275
Thomas FitzSimons Gravesite 345
Thomas FitzSimons Statue 350
Thomas Hart Benton Statue 65
Thomas Lynch Gravesite 14
Thomas Macdonough Memorial 285
Thomas Moore Bust 244
Thomas Shahan Gravesite 39
Thomas "Stonewall" Jackson Bust 259
Thomas Thomas Monument 286
Timothy Murphy Monument 240
Timothy Murphy (Hibernian) Monument 288
Titanic Historical Society Museum 173
Titanic Memorial Museum 309
Todd-Moylan House 351
Touro Park 366
Trenton Battle Monument 222
Trinity Church (Boston) 160
Trinity Church (N.Y.) 278
Trinity Church (Newport, R.I.) 368
Trinity College 62
28th Massachusetts Infantry Monument 324
"Typhoid Mary" Mallon Gravesite 276

U

Ulysses S. Grant Birthplace 307
Ulysses S. Grant Boyhood Home 301
Ulysses S. Grant Bust 259
Ulysses S. Grant Equestrian Relief 270
Ulysses S. Grant House 300
Ulysses S. Grant Memorial 299
Ulysses S. Grant Memorial Bridge 307
Ulysses S. Grant National Memorial 256
Ulysses S. Grant Statue 84, 182, 298, 338
Union Square 280
United Nations Plaza 280
University of Delaware 27
University of Notre Dame 102
University of Pittsburgh 353
University of St. Thomas 197
U.S. Capitol Building 63
U.S. Naval Academy 116

V

Valley Forge National Historical Park 355
Victor Herbert Gravesite 284
Victor Herbert Statue 244
Vinegar Hill Lead Mine and Museum 84
Virginia Fair Vanderbilt Gravesite 284

W

Walden Pond Reservation 165
Walnut Hall 71
Walsh-McLean House (Embassy of Indonesia) 45
Walters Art Gallery 124
Washington Crossing Historic Park 332
Washington Crossing State Park 223
Washington National Cathedral 65
Washington's Headquarters State Historic Park 241
Wave Hill 287
Wayne Memorial Blockhouse 318
Waynesborough 333
Westland 220
Wheatland National Historic Landmark 330
Whistler House Museum of Art 170
Whitehall Museum House 359
White House 66
"Wild Bill" Hickok State Monument

91
Wildwood Manor House 310
William Ellery Channing Statue 366
William Clark Noble Gravesite 109
William Corcoran Gravesite 56
William Hughes Statue 217
William J. Bryan Birthplace 89
William J. Bryan Memorial Park 89
William J. Bryan Statue 64
William Johnson and King Hendrick Monument 239
William Johnson Gravesite 238
William Johnson Statue 238
William Kingsley Monument 259
William Laughlin Monument 102
William Maclay House 325
William MacNeven Bust 242
William MacNeven Monument 272
William McGuffey Birthplace 178
William McGuffey Memorial Museum 305
William McGuffey Monument 305
William McKinley Assassination Site 228
William McKinley Birthplace Site 304
William McKinley House 308
William McKinley Memorial 133
William McKinley Monument 137, 182
William McKinley Statue 297, 298, 299
William O'Donovan Bust 242
William Paterson Statue 218
William Pinkney Statue 57
William R. Grace Gravesite 261
William Tennent Gravesite 211
William T. Sherman Equestrian Statue 270
Will Rogers Statue 65
Wilmington and Brandywine Cemetery 33
Winfield Scott Statue 47
Woodlawn Cemetery 281
Woodrow Wilson Bust 259
Woodrow Wilson Gravesite 65
Woodrow Wilson House 220

Woodrow Wilson House National Historic Landmark 69
Woodrow Wilson School of Public and International Affairs 220
Workingmen's Institute 99
W. R. Grace Building 284

Y

Yale University 22

Z

Zane-Kenton Monument 311
Zenas Ellis House 373

Subject Index

¶ Only individuals of Irish descent are included in this index.

A

Alexander, Sarah Wallace 363
Alison, Francis 27, 29, 314, 356
Ancient Order of Hibernians 41, 271
Arthur, Chester A. 44, 53, 68, 213, 240, 247, 372, 373
Arthur, William 372
Ayres, William 16

B

Barnwell, John 277
Barrett, John 76
Barry, D. F. 51
Barry, John 41, 42, 54, 103, 145, 174, 209, 335, 336, 342, 345
Belmont, Oliver H. Perry Jr. 361
Bennett, James Gordon Jr. 242, 364
Bennett, James Gordon Sr. 242
Berkeley, George 22, 359, 360, 365, 368
Blaine, James G. 39, 56, 69, 75, 105
Blair, Francis Preston 40, 64
Bly, Nellie 281, 282
Bouvier, Jacqueline 50, 361, 366
Bouvier, Janet Lee 361
Boyle, John 41, 50, 77, 337
Brady, James 122, 261
Brady, Mathew 42, 46, 51, 54, 57, 265
Brendan the Navigator 15
Brennan, Patrick 251
Brennan, William 61
Bresnahan, Roger 230
Brown, Alexander 125
Brown, George 124

Brown, John 370
Brown, John Carter 369
Brown, Margaret Tobin 173, 309
Brown, Nicholas Jr. 369
Bryan, William Jennings 63, 89, 174, 180
Buchanan, James 44, 50, 53, 68, 174, 330, 331
Buchanan James Sr. 31
Buckley, Dennis 98
Burk, John Daly 374
Burke, Edmund 45
Butler, Pierce 52, 61, 334
Butler, Richard 36, 214
Byrnes, James 61
Byrnes, Thomas 269

C

Caffrey, Anthony 58
Cairnes, Elizabeth 120
Caldwell, James 210, 222-224, 255, 349
Calhoun, John C. 22, 45, 64
Callan, Nicholas 67
Campbell, Alexander 328
Campbell, John 60
Carey, Mathew 345-347, 374
Carr, Patrick 139, 140, 156
Carroll, Anna Ella 125, 130
Carroll, Charles ("Barrister") 114, 115, 118, 119
Carroll, Charles (of Bellevue) 67,
Carroll, Charles (of Carrollton) 63, 64, 118-120, 122, 124, 126, 135, 336, 340
Carroll, Charles (of Ireland) 115
Carroll, Charles Jr. 122
Carroll, Dr. Charles 118
Carroll, Daniel (of Annapolis) 58
Carroll, Daniel (of Duddington) 34,

419

52, 58, 59, 117, 134
Carroll, John 44, 47, 58, 108, 111,
   117, 123, 134, 135, 298, 336
Carroll, John Lee 122
Carroll, Philip 126
Carroll, Thomas King 130
Carter, Ann, 369
Casey, Bernard
   See Casey, Solanus.
Casey, Daniel Henry 231
Casey, Solanus 179
Cashman, Nellie 174
Cass, Thomas 145, 164
Chambers brothers 316
Clark, William 44
Clary, Andrew 109, 142
Clemens, Samuel 21
Cleveland, Grover 53, 96, 174, 209,
   210, 220, 234, 259
Clinton, DeWitt 229, 244, 248, 255,
   258, 279, 304
Clinton, George 43, 64, 238, 240
Clinton, James 63, 292, 335
Cochran, John 214, 318
Cochrane, Elizabeth 281
Cochrane, "Mickey" 230
Codd, Nicholas 108, 111
Cody, William "Buffalo Bill" 91,
   106, 174
Cohan, George M. 174, 256, 257,
   276, 284, 370
Cole, Mary 164
Colles, Christopher 229, 248, 279
Collins, James 165
Collins, Patrick 152, 161
Colvin, Patrick 223, 333
Comiskey, Charles 74, 230
Connelly, Philip 176
Conner, John 94
Conner, Richard 93
Conner, William 100
Connolly, James 293
Connor, Jerome 44, 47, 55, 57
Conway, Thomas 357
Cook, Alexander McDowell 294
Cooke, Terence 272
Copley, John Singleton 20, 145, 146,

190
Corbin, Margaret Cochran 265, 295
Corby, William 103, 319, 320
Corcoran, Michael 267
Corcoran, William 43, 54, 56, 69
Corrigan, Michael 272, 283
Cottrill, Matthew 108, 111
Coughlin, Charles 183, 184
Coveney, Joseph 176
Cranston, Richard 171
Crawford, Thomas 63, 156, 164
Crean, Henrietta Agnes 242
Crimmins, Daniel 243
Crockett, David 174
Croghan, George 97, 300
Croghan, William Jr. 352
Crosby, Bing 174
Crosby, Michael 179
Cudahy, Edward 378
Cudahy, John 378
Cudahy, Michael 378
Cudahy, Patrick 378
Cuddahy, Patrick 171
Cummisky, Hugh 168
Curley, Fr. James 49
Curley, James 151, 153, 154
Curry, John Steuart 182, 381, 382
Curtin, Andrew 107, 323, 324, 332,
   337
Curtin, Jeremiah 380
Curtin, Roland 332
Cusack, Cyril 263
Cushing, Richard 143, 158

D

Daley, Richard 79, 90
Daly, Marcus 258
Darragh, Lydia 337-339
Darragh, Thomas 171
Davis, Jefferson 64, 246, 360
Davis, Varina Anne (Winnie) 360
Davitt, Michael 212
De Valera, Catherine 286
De Valera, Eamon 44, 242, 286
Dean, Daniel 301
Degan, Mathias 76

Delahanty, Ed 230
Delahunty, John 63
Dermott, James Reed 34, 35
Diamond, James 63
Dillon, Arthur 19, 24, 335
Dobbin, Alexander 318, 319
Donahue, Betsy 67
Dongan, Thomas 225, 275, 286
Donnelley, Richard R. 94, 95
Donnelly, Ignatius 187, 188, 195, 196
Donoghue, John 141
Dougherty, Peter 183
Dowling, Michael 189
Doyle, Alexander 21, 57, 65, 97, 128, 262, 289, 298, 310
Drumgoole, John 275
Duane, James 249, 257
Duane, William 374
Duffy, Francis 253, 275
Duffy, Hugh 230
Dulany, Daniel 120
Dunlap, John 334, 336
Dunne, Dennis 80
Dunne, Finley Peter 80, 81, 282
Dunwoody, John 277

E

Eaton, Peggy O'Neale 56
Ege, Andrew 135
Elder, John 326, 327
Embury, Philip 229, 264
Emmet, Robert 44, 57, 212, 361
Emmet, Thomas Addis 272-274
Emmett, Daniel 302

F

Fair, James 284, 365
Fair, Theresa 284
Farley, James 230, 253
Farley, John 244, 272
Farrell, James 74
"Fighting McCooks" 297, 301, 310
Finerty, John 75
Finlay, Patrick 270

Finley, John Houston 264
Fisher, Henry 26
Fitz-Gerald, Margery May 33
Fitzgerald, Eva 186
Fitzgerald, F. Scott 132, 192, 237
Fitzgerald, Geraldine 263
Fitzgerald, John 150, 158
Fitzgerald, Rose 150, 151, 158
Fitzpatrick, John 147, 175
Fitzsimmons, James 261, 290
FitzSimons, Thomas 52, 345, 350, 351
Flanagan, Edward 174
Flanagan, John 87
Flannery, Lot 35, 43
Flavin, Timothy 76
Flynn, Elizabeth Gurley 211
Flynn, Raymond 147
Foley, Thomas 254
Ford, Edsel 179
Ford, Henry 177-179
Ford, John 178
Foster, Stephen Collins 174, 259, 276, 298, 311, 351, 353
Foster, William Z. 212
Frawley, James 256
Fulton, Robert 64, 174, 259, 279, 330, 354
Furlong, John 84

G

Galloway, Edwin 379
Gallows Hill
Galway, James 263
Gamble, Isabella 319
Gardner, Alexander 51
Garland, Judy 186, 187
Gibbons, James 25, 38, 40, 62, 117
Gibbons, John 31, 32
Gillespie, Mother Angela 55, 106
Gilmore, Patrick Sarsfield 276
Glover, Ann 137, 138
Gordon, John 358
Gordon, Nicholas 358
Gowan, Franklin 353
Grace, William R. 261, 284

Grady, Henry 21
Grant, Jesse 84
Grant, Ulysses S. 46, 47, 53, 59, 68,
    70, 76-78, 83, 84, 160, 174,
    182, 213, 226, 239, 248, 256, 259,
    294, 296, 299-301, 307, 335,
    336, 374
Greeley, Horace 22, 174, 201, 246,
    248, 258, 262
Guiney, Patrick 161

H

Hafford, Mary 379
Haggerty, Patrick 383
Hallahan, Cornelius 27
Hancock, John 63, 156, 340
Hand, Edward 36, 63, 330, 335
Hanna, Mark 298
Hannon, Mary "Josie" 158
Harrington, John 174
Harrington, Michael 171
Harris, Joel Chandler 174
Harrison, Benjamin 53, 96, 174, 213,
    299
Harrison, Daniel 349
Hasset, Thomas 171
Haughery, Margaret 22
Hayes, Patrick 244, 272
Healy, George 44, 48, 53, 68, 69, 78,
    146, 156, 162
Healy, James Augustine 175
Healy, Michael 175
Healy, Michael Morris 175
Healy, Patrick 48, 294
Heaney, Seamus 263
Hearst, William Randolph 254
Heenan, J. C. 290
Herbert, Victor 174, 244, 250, 284
Hickok, James "Wild Bill" 91
Hill, James J. 195-197
Hines, T. J. 51
Hoban, James 50, 66, 67, 174
Hogan, Martin 171
Hogan, Michael 248, 267
Holland, John 216
Holme, Thomas 337, 340

Horgan, Stephen 51
Houston, Sam 64, 174
Hovenden, Thomas 266
Hughes, Charles Evans 61, 174,
    237, 283
Hughes, John 126, 127, 222, 223,
    254, 261, 271
Hughes, Margaret Anna 222
Hughes, William 217
Hunter, Thomas 263

I

Ireland, John 185, 186, 191, 197, 198
Irish Brigade 133, 319, 322, 323
Irish, Nathaniel 345, 349
Irvine, William 36, 335
Irwin, Archibald 96

J

Jackson, Andrew 36, 44, 53, 64, 68,
    174, 259
Jackson, Samuel 123
Jackson, Thomas "Stonewall" 65,
    123, 127, 128, 174, 259
James, Frank 190
James, Henry Sr. 147
James, Jesse 190
James, William 147
Jaspar, William 21
Jemmy the Rover 214
Johnson, Andrew 53, 84, 174
Johnson, John 291
Johnson, William 97, 226, 235-239,
    244, 291, 296
Johnston, John 306, 307
Jones, Jonathan "Casey" 174, 191
Jones, Mary Harris "Mother" 86, 87

K

Kane, Elisha Kent 328, 329
Kane, Evan O'Neill 328, 329
Kane, Thomas 328, 329
Kavanagh, Edward 111
Kavanagh, James 108, 111

Kearny, Lawrence 218, 220
Kearny, Michael 212
Kearny, Philip 65, 212, 215, 220
Kearny, Stephen 174
Keating, John 317, 342
Keely, Patrick 107, 144, 147, 215,
    225, 366, 371
Kellegher, Patrick 232
Keller, Helen 65, 174
Kelley, Oliver 185
Kelley, Rachel 307
Kelly, Eugene 221
Kelly, Gene 187
Kelly, Grace 344
Kelly, Howard, 122
Kelly, James Edward 20, 24, 30, 128,
    211, 293, 324
Kelly, John ("Jack") 337, 343
Kelly, Michael "King" 230, 231
Kenna, John 65
Kennedy, Anthony 62
Kennedy, John F. 50, 53, 91, 143,
    150, 152, 155, 157, 158, 161, 166,
    174, 178, 209, 215, 242, 270, 361,
    366, 371
Kennedy, John Pendleton 121
Kennedy, Joseph 158, 162, 167
Kennedy, Joseph Jr. 166
Kennedy, Robert "Booth" 133
Kennedy, Robert F. 58, 155, 166,
    167, 174
Kennedy, Rose 152, 158, 162, 167
Kennedy, Sister Stanislaus 263
Kenny, Patrick 31
Kenton, Simon 310, 311
King, Charles Kelley 302
Kingan, Samuel 96
Kingan, Thomas 96
Kingsley, William 243, 259
Kinsella, William 243
Knox, Henry 36, 63, 104, 112, 113,
    138, 146, 174, 236, 240, 241, 292,
    295, 332, 333, 335, 354, 355

L

Lalor, Alice 43

Lanier, Sidney 259
Laughlin, William 102
Lawe, John E. 232
Lawler, Michael 83
Leary, John 278
Lee, James Thomas 361
Levins, Thomas 260
Lewis, Andrew 335
Logan, James 337, 338, 348, 349, 350
Lomasney, Martin 157
Lynch, Dominick 249, 275, 287
Lynch, Thomas 63, 114
Lynch, Thomas Jr. 340
Lyon, Matthew 373, 374

M

MacCarran, Patrick 65
Macdonough, Thomas 26, 116, 174,
    285
MacDowell, Edward Alexander
    174, 207, 208, 259
MacGahan, Januarius A. 243, 303
Mack, Connie 166, 230
Maclay, William 325, 326
MacNeven, William 242, 253, 272,
    274
MacNutt, Francis 101, 102
MacSparran, James 368, 369, 371
MacSwiney, Terence 80
Madison, Dolley 57, 67, 351
Magee, Christopher Lyman 352
Maginnis, Charles 38, 164
Maguires, Molly 41
Mahan, Alfred Thayer 116, 363, 364
Mahan, Dennis 294
Makemie, Francis 54, 136, 349
Mallon, John 233
Mallon, "Typhoid Mary" 275
Martin, James 26
Martin, John 142
Matthew, Theobald 169, 336
Matthews, William 58
Maury, Matthew Fontaine 116, 259
Maxwell, William 36
McCabe, Patrick 148
McCarthy, Joseph 377, 378

McCloskey, John 54, 69, 160, 225, 268, 272
McClurg, James 295
McCone, Stan 199
McConnell, Daniel 331
McCook, Daniel Jr. 297, 310, 310
McCook, Edward 301
McCook, John 310
McCook, Robert 301
McCormack, John 155, 157, 174
McCormick, Cyrus 77, 78, 174
McCormick, Robert 77, 92
McCoy, Isaac 182
McCullaugh, John 283
McCullough, John 106, 343, 375
McDowell, Ephraim 65, 174
McDowell, Irwin 294
McDowell, John 115
McDowell, William 96
McElroy, John 129, 144, 164
McGillycuddy, V. T. 51
McGinnity, Joseph 230
McGivney, Michael 21, 25
McGlynn, Edward 283
McGroarty, Sister Julia 62
McGuffey, William 178, 305
McGuire, Peter 218
McGuire, Thomas 213
McHenry, Francis 334
McHenry, James 52, 120, 121
McKean, Thomas 26, 30, 340
McKenna, Joseph 60
McKinley, David 304
McKinley, William 20, 53, 75, 78, 102, 133, 134, 137, 174, 182, 213, 228, 229, 297-299, 304, 308
McKinly, John 33
McKonkey, Samuel 333
McLaughlin, John 65, 174
McLean, John 60
McMahon, James 41
McManus, George 283
McManus, John 269
McMillan, John 315, 349
McNaly, Patrick 309
McNulty, William 216
McParlan, James 353

McQuaid, Bernard 41
McReynolds, James Clark 61
McShain, John 39
McSorley, John 266
Meade, George 345, 347
Meade, George Gordon 46, 47, 209, 239, 294, 321, 335, 336, 376
Meade, Richard 242
Meagher, Thomas Francis 103, 323
Mellon, Andrew 37, 53, 174, 351, 352
Milhous, Hannah 93
Miller, James 108, 314
Milmore, Joseph 164
Milmore, Martin 160, 164, 172, 201, 294
Mitchell, Margaret 174
"Molly Maguires" 326, 327, 353
Montez, Lola 258
Montgomery, Richard 335
Mooney, Edward 184
Moore, Annie 251
Moore, Thomas 44, 244
Moran, John 51
Morgan, James 210, 224
Morrissey, John 289
Moylan, Stephen 36, 268, 335, 344, 345, 347, 351
Mulholland, St. Clair 319, 325
Mulligan, Charles 74, 77, 78, 87, 95
Mulligan, Hercules 255, 260, 279
Murphy, Charles 280
Murphy, Edward 100
Murphy, Frank 61, 180, 181
Murphy, Richard 199
Murphy, Timothy 240, 288, 291
Murray, Samuel Aloysius 103, 319, 326, 342

N

Nation, Carrie 181
Neale, Leonard 43
Nelson, Samuel 60
Nelson, Thomas Jr. 63, 340, 174
Nelson, Thomas Sr. 174
Newlin, Nathaniel 316

Newlin, Nicholas 316
Nixon, John 41, 341
Nixon, Richard 53, 157, 341
Nixon, Richard Milhous 93
Noble, William Clark 106-109, 215, 243, 256, 285, 313, 343, 366
Nunan, Jeremiah 233

O

O'Brien, Catherine 279
O'Brien, Charlotte Grace 244, 276
"O'Brien Dynasty" 169
O'Brien, Hugh 141, 156
O'Brien, Jeremiah 109, 110, 335
O'Connell, Daniel 65
O'Connell, Margaret Middleton 252
O'Connell, Sister Anthony 56
O'Connell, William 143, 144, 149, 151, 167
O'Connor, Andrew 65, 85, 90, 94, 96, 123, 215, 286
O'Connor, Edwin 155
O'Connor, John 200
O'Conor, Charles 242, 246, 247
O'Daly, Bryan 131
O'Donnell, Charles 176
O'Donnell, Mary Madeleine 55
O'Donovan, William 222, 236, 241, 242, 254, 270, 291, 322
O'Dwyre, Edmund 131
Oelrichs, Theresa Fair 365
O'Grady, Ellen 269
O'Hara, Charles 22, 63
O'Hara, James 351, 352
O'Hara, Mary 352
O'Hara, Maureen 263
O'Hare, "Artful Eddie" 78
O'Hare, Edward "Butch" 78
O'Hern, Patrick 178
O'Kane, Dennis 324
O'Keeffe, Georgia 190, 383
Olcott, Chauncey 277, 284
O'Leary, Kate 73
O'Neil, Hugh 262
O'Neill, Eugene 22-24, 171, 172, 174, 250, 270

O'Neill, James 23
O'Neill, John 130, 227, 374, 375
O'Neill, Mary (Quinlan) 23
O'Neill, Peter 232
O'Neill, Sister de Sales 55
O'Neill, Thomas "Tip" 157
O'Reilly, John Boyle 41, 141, 147-150, 161, 166, 171, 172
O'Rorke, Patrick 287, 323
O'Rourke, Jim 230
O'Shaughnessy, Ignatius Aloysius 104, 197, 198
O'Shaughnessy, Jerry 299
O'Shaughnessy, Thomas 80
O'Sullivan, Paula 292
O'Sullivan, Philip 207
O'Sullivan, Timothy 51

P

Paine, Robert Treat 63, 156, 173
Parnell, Charles Stewart 203, 212
Paterson, William 52, 60, 218
Patterson, Elizabeth 123
Patterson, William 123
Patton, John 36
Patrick, St. 38, 39
Perry, Matthew C. 174, 266, 361, 362, 363, 366, 367, 371
Perry, Oliver H. 117, 174, 228, 298, 301, 308, 318, 362, 365, 371
Physick, Philip Syng 334, 340, 348
Pinkerton, James 205
Pinkerton, John 205
Poe, David 120
Poe, Edgar Allan 120, 121, 174, 251, 293, 336, 370
Polk, James K. 53, 68, 145, 174, 199
Powderly, Terence Vincent 354
Power, Nicholas 369, 370

Q

Quill, Michael J. 233, 267
Quinn, Edmond 250, 258, 260

R

Rainey, Henry 71
Rawlins, John 47, 84
Read, George I 28, 30, 52, 63, 340
Read, George II 28, 174
Read, George III 28
Reagan, Ronald 53, 83, 91, 157
Reaney, William Henry 144
Reddin, Thomas 76
Reynolds, Albert 263
Reynolds, John Fulton 294, 322,
  335, 336
Roberts, Owen 61
Roche, James Jeffrey 161
Roche, Kevin 254, 280
Roche, T. C. 51
Rochford, Dennis 29
Roe, Cornelius McDermot 63
Roe, Patrick McDermot 63
Rogers, Patrick Kerr 163
Rogers, Will 65
Rogers, William Barton 163
Rooney, Mickey 187
Roosevelt, Theodore 20, 35, 53, 62,
  65, 85, 87, 106, 144, 174, 217,
  229, 242, 259, 278, 281, 285
Rossa, O'Donovan 212
Rusk, Jeremiah 381
Rutherford, Griffin 36
Rutledge, Edward 174, 249, 340
Rutledge, John 52, 60

S

Saint-Gaudens, Augustus 35, 70,
  74, 76, 77, 141, 156, 158, 160,
  173, 174, 201-203, 227, 241, 242,
  247, 259, 265, 270, 281, 293, 298,
  337, 352, 362, 365
Saint-Gaudens, Louis 141, 203
Schenley, Mary Croghan 352
Shahan, Thomas 38, 39, 40
Shanahan, John 326
Shea, John Dawson 49
Shea, Richard Jr. 295
Shee, John 36
Sheehan, Michael 76
Sheridan, Philip 20, 59, 75, 78, 85,

  91, 95, 174, 182, 294, 299, 309
Shields, James 65, 193, 194, 195
Simpson, William 307
Smith, Alfred E. 220, 241, 242, 253,
  254, 271
Smith, James 340, 356, 357
Smith, Samuel 349
Spaight, Richard Dobbs 53
Spellman, Francis 174, 272
Stephenson, Isaac 382
Stewart, Walter 36, 214, 335
Stranahan, Frank 310
Stranahan, Robert Jr. 310
Sullivan, Annie 65, 174
Sullivan, Daniel 73
Sullivan, James 157
Sullivan, Jeremiah 98
Sullivan, John 162, 174, 206, 207,
  233, 237, 277, 330, 335, 355, 371
Sullivan, John L. 141
Sullivan, Louis 71-73, 75, 76, 190,
  242
Sullivan, Patrick Henry 104
Sullivan, Timothy 76
Sullivan brothers 228
Sweeny, Thomas 227
Syng, Philip 340, 341, 348

T

Talbot, George 131
Taney, Roger 60, 114, 124, 128, 129
Taylor, George 313, 317, 340
Tennent, John 211
Tennent, William 54, 211, 334, 356
Thompson, Launt 19, 22, 31, 47,
  294, 369
Thomson, Charles 63, 174, 302, 314,
  315
Thomson, William 36
Thornton, Matthew 204, 205, 207,
  340
Thornton, William 205
Thorpe, Jim 316, 327, 328
Tone, Wolfe 212
Tunney, James 253
Twain, Mark 21

V

Vanderbilt, Virginia Fair 284

W

Walker, James 263
Walsh, John 33
Walsh, Thomas 45
Walters, Henry 124
Warren, Peter 258
Wayne, Anthony 63, 95, 107, 211,
    213, 291, 299, 300, 306, 318, 325,
    332, 333, 335, 352, 355, 356
Wayne, Isaac 333
Whelan, Charles 135
Whistler, James McNeill 20, 46, 170,
    182, 259, 293
Whistler, John 95
White, Edward Douglass 60
Wilson, James 171
Wilson, Joseph Ruggles 310
Wilson, Woodrow 42, 53, 65, 69, 71,
    213, 220, 221, 259
Wood, John 90
Woods, James 280

DATE DUE
